Letts

Study Guide

Business Studies

AS & A2 Success

AS & A2 Success

Business Studies

David Floyd

Contents

Contents

Chapter 18: Ensuring operational efficiency

Specification lists

AQA AS

Module (Unit)	Specification topic	Chapter reference
1 (M1)	*Starting a business*	*1.1–1.4, 2.4, 5.3, 7.1, 7.2, 7.6, 8.1, 8.2, 9.1, 11.2, 16.1*
	Financial planning	*1.2, 1.3, 13.3, 14.1–14.3*
2 (M2)	*Finance*	*13.4, 14.1, 14.2*
	People in business	*10.2, 11.2, 12.1*
	Operations management	*9.1, 9.3, 17.1, 17.2, 18.1, 18.3, 18.4*
	Marketing and the competitive environment	*7.1, 7.3, 7.4, 7.6, 8.3, 9.1–9.4, 16.2*

Examination analysis

The specification comprises two unit tests at AS and two unit tests at A2.

Unit 1 *(BUSS1)* ***Planning and Financing a Business*** *(40% of AS, 20% of A-Level)*
Candidates sit a 1 hour 15 minutes examination (60 marks) and answer short-answer and extended response questions based on a mini case study.

Unit 2 *(BUSS2)* ***Managing a Business*** *(60% of AS, 30% of A-Level)*
Candidates sit a 1 hour 30 minutes examination (80 marks) and answer compulsory, multi-part data response questions.

AQA A2

Module (Unit)	Specification topic	Chapter reference
3 (M3)	*Functional objectives and strategies*	*3.1*
	Financial strategies and accounts	*13.1–13.4, 15.1, 15.2*
	Marketing strategies	*7.5, 8.2–8.4*
	Operational strategies	*1.2, 2.2, 2.3, 3.1, 4.1, 4.3, 16.1, 17.2, 17.3*
	Human resource strategies	*7.2, 7.3, 9.2, 10.1–10.3, 11.1, 12.2*
4 (M4)	*Corporate aims and objectives*	*1.5, 3.1, 3.2, 3.3*
	Assessing changes in the business environment	*2.3, 4.1, 4.2, 5.1–5.3, 6.1–6.4*
	Managing change	*3.1–3.5, 6.4*

Examination analysis

The specification comprises two unit tests at AS and two unit tests at A2.

Unit 3 *(BUSS3)* ***Strategies for Success*** *(25% of A-Level)*
Candidates sit a 1 hour 45 minutes examination (80 marks) and answer questions based on an unseen case study and requiring extended answers, drawing upon knowledge from AS units.

Unit 4 *(BUSS4)* ***The Business Environment and Managing Change*** *(25% of A-Level)*
Candidates sit a 1 hour 45 minutes examination (80 marks) divided into two sections.

The first section consists of pre-release research tasks. The second section consists of a choice of essays (synoptic style).

Edexcel AS

Module (Unit)	Specification topic	Chapter reference
1 (M1)	*Characteristics of successful entrepreneurs*	*1.2, 3.4, 12.1*
	Identifying a business opportunity	*7.1, 7.2*
	Evaluating a business opportunity	*1.1, 7.2, 7.6, 8.1, 8.2, 9.1*
	Economic considerations	*4.1, 5.3*
	Financing the new business idea	*1.3, 13.1*
	Measuring the potential success of a business idea	*9.2, 13.3, 14.3*
	Putting a business idea into practice	*1.1, 1.2*
2 (M2a)	*Marketing plan*	*7.3–7.5, 8.3, 9.1–9.4*
	Managing the provision process	*6.3, 11.2, 16.2, 17.1, 17.2, 18.1–18.4*
	How does a company budget efficiently?	*1.2, 8.4, 13.1, 13.4, 14.1, 14.2*
	Managing other people	*10.1–10.3, 11.1, 11.2, 12.1*

Examination analysis

The specification comprises two unit tests at AS and two unit tests at A2.

Unit 1 *(6BS01)* ***Developing New Business Ideas*** *(50% of AS, 25% of A-Level)*
Candidates sit a 1 hour 15 minutes examination (70 marks) in two sections.

Section A (32 marks) consists of multiple-choice questions.
Section B (38 marks) consists of questions based on data provided.

Unit 2a *(6BS02)* ***Managing the Business***
Candidates sit a 1 hour 15 minutes examination (70 marks) in two sections.

Section A (24 marks) consists of multiple-choice questions.
Section B (46 marks) consists of questions based on data provided.

Edexcel A2

Module (Unit)	Specification topic	Chapter reference
3 (M3)	*Why does a business seek international markets?*	*1.1, 4.1, 4.2, 16.1*
	Key players in the world economy	*4.1*
	How does a company decide which countries to target?	*1.1, 4.1, 5.2*
	Other considerations before trading internationally	*4.1, 5.1, 6.3*
	Globalisation	*4.1*
	Are multinationals a force for good or should they be controlled?	*4.3, 6.1–6.3*
4 (M4)	*Corporate objectives and strategy*	*1.2–1.5, 3.1–3.3, 5.1, 6.4*
	Making strategic decisions	*1.3, 3.5, 7.5, 13.3, 15.1, 15.3, 17.3*
	Assessing competitiveness	*11.2, 13.4*
	Company growth	*2.1–2.4*

Examination analysis

The specification comprises two unit tests at AS and two unit tests at A2.

Unit 3 *(6BS03)* ***International Business*** *(25% of A-Level)*
Candidates sit a 1 hour 30 minutes examination (80 marks) in two sections.

Section A (35 marks) consists of questions based on data provided.
Section B (45 marks) consists of a case study and questions.

Unit 4 *(6BS04)* ***Making Business Decisions***
Candidates sit a 1 hour 30 minutes examination (80 marks) in two sections.

Section A (30 marks) consists of questions based on data provided.
Section B (50 marks) consists of questions set on a pre-released decision-making report.

Specification lists

OCR AS

Module (Unit)	Specification topic	Chapter reference
1 (M1)	*The nature of business*	*1.1–1.3, 1.5, 3.1–3.3, 7.1, 7.2, 8.1, 8.2, 10.1, 10.2, 13.1, 13.2*
	Classification of business	*1.1–1.4, 2.1–2.4*
	Objectives	*1.2, 1.5, 3.1, 3.2*
	The market	*7.1, 7.2*
	Other influences	*5.1, 5.2, 6.4*
2 (M2)	*Marketing*	*7.1, 7.3–7.6, 9.1–9.4*
	Accounting and finance	*13.2, 13.3, 14.1–14.3, 15.1–15.3*
	People in organisations	*3.4, 10.1, 10.2, 11.1, 12.1*
	Operations management	*3.3, 17.2, 18.1–18.3*

Examination analysis

The specification comprises two unit tests at AS and two unit tests at A2.

***Unit 1** (F291) **An Introduction to Business** (40% of AS, 20% of A-Level)*
Candidates sit a 1 hour examination (60 marks) and answer five short-answer and data-response questions.

***Unit 2** (F292) **Business Functions** (60% of AS, 30% of A-Level)*
Candidates sit a 2 hour examination (90 marks) in two sections (five questions in total).

Candidates answer one 6-part question in Section A. Section B consists of four questions set on a pre-released case study.

OCR A2

Module (Unit)	Specification topic	Chapter reference
EITHER **3 (M3)**	*Marketing*	*4.1, 4.2, 6.3, 7.4, 7.6, 8.1–8.4, 9.1–9.4*
OR **4 (M4)**	*Accounting*	*13.1–13.4, 14.1–14.3, 15.1–15.3*
OR **5 (M5)**	*People in organisations*	*6.3, 10.1–10.3, 11.1, 11.2, 12.1, 12.2*
OR **6 (M6)**	*Business production*	*1.1, 1.2, 2.1–2.4, 3.1–3.3, 6.3, 9.1, 11.2, 14.3, 15.1, 15.2, 16.1, 16.2, 17.1–17.3, 18.1–18.4*
7 (M7)	*Business objectives and strategy*	*1.2, 1.5, 3.1, 3.2, 5.3, 6.2, 7.5*
	Business analysis	*3.3, 4.1, 4.2, 7.1, 7.5, 8.3, 8.4, 11.2, 13.4, 14.1*
	External influences	*1.2, 4.1–4.3, 5.1–5.3, 6.1, 6.3, 6.4, 11.2*
	Change	*3.5, 9.1, 11.2, 12.1, 12.2, 16.1*

Examination analysis

The specification comprises two unit tests at AS and two unit tests at A2.

Units 3–6
***Unit 3** (F293) **Marketing** OR*
***Unit 4** (F294) **Accounting** OR*
***Unit 5** (F295) **People in Organisations** OR*
Unit 6** (F296) **Business Production
Candidates sit a 2 hour examination (60 marks). They are required to answer six questions based on the case study material for the chosen Unit (20% of A-Level).

***Unit 7** (F297) **Strategic Management** (30% of A-Level)*
Candidates sit a 2 hour examination (90 marks) and answer four questions, one of which includes a numerical element, based on a pre-release case study.

WJEC AS

Module (Unit)	Specification topic	Chapter reference
1 (M1)	*What is business?*	*1.1–1.5, 3.1*
	Marketing	*1.1, 1.6, 2.1*
	Producing goods and services	*1.2, 1.3, 2.1–2.4, 4.1, 13.1, 16.1, 17.1*
	Types of business organisation	*1.2–1.4*
	External influences	*3.5, 5.1–5.3, 6.1–6.4, 7.1*
2 (M2)	*Marketing*	*4.1, 7.1, 7.4, 7.6, 8.1, 8.3, 9.1–9.4*
	Accounting and finance	*13.2, 13.3, 14.1–14.3*
	People in organisations	*3.4, 10.1, 10.2, 11.1, 11.2, 12.1*
	Operations management	*3.3, 9.1, 9.2, 11.2, 16.1, 17.2, 18.1–18.4*

Examination analysis

The specification comprises two unit tests at AS and two unit tests at A2.

Unit 1 *(BS1)* **The Business Framework** *(40% of AS, 20% of A-Level)*
Candidates sit a 1 hour 15 minutes examination (50 marks).

Unit 2 *(BS2)* **Business Functions** *(60% of AS, 30% of A-Level)*
Candidates sit a 1 hour 15 minutes examination (70 marks) containing compulsory data response and short-answer questions.

WJEC A2

Module (Unit)	Specification topic	Chapter reference
3 (M3)	*Business objectives and strategy*	*1.2, 1.5, 2.1–2.4, 3.1–3.4, 8.3*
	Change	*3.5*
	External influences	*4.1–4.3, 5.1–5.3, 6.1–6.4*
	Business analysis	*1.3, 13.3, 13.4*
4 (M4)	*Business objectives and strategy*	*3.2, 3.3, 10.3*
	Business analysis: Marketing	*7.1, 7.3, 7.5, 8.4, 9.1*
	Business analysis: Finance and accounting	*13.3, 14.1, 15.1–15.3*
	Business analysis: People in organisations	*10.1, 10.3, 12.2*
	Business analysis: Operations management	*3.3, 17.3, 18.1*

Examination analysis

The specification comprises two unit tests at AS and two unit tests at A2.

Unit 3 *(BS3)* **Business Decision-Making** *(25% of A-Level)*
Candidates sit a 2 hour examination (60 marks) consisting of compulsory questions based on a case study.

Unit 4 *(BS4)* **Business Strategy and Practice** *(25% of A-Level)*
Candidates sit a 2 hour examination (60 marks) in two sections.

Section A (40 marks) contains compulsory short-answer and problem-solving questions.
Section B (20 marks) contains a choice of three synoptic essay questions, one of which must be answered.

Specification lists

CCEA AS

Module (Unit)	Specification topic	Chapter reference
1 (M1)	*Central purpose of business activity*	*7.1, 9.1*
	Forms of business organisation	*1.2, 1.3, 1.4, 13.1*
	Markets and market forces; Spectrum of competition; Market research; Marketing mix; Product lifecycle; Market planning and strategy	*6.1, 6.3, 7.1–7.5, 7.6, 8.1, 8.2, 9.1–9.4, 16.2*
	Quality management	*3.3, 18.3*
	Investment and productivity	*2.1–2.4, 11.2, 17.1, 17.2, 18.1*
2 (M2)	*Organisational design; Communication*	*5.2, 10.1–10.3*
	Motivation; Non-monetary methods of motivation	*12.1*
	Principles of management and leadership	*3.4, 10.2, 12.1*
	Investing in people	*11.1, 11.2*
	Break-even analysis	*14.3*
	Budgeting, cash flow and variance analysis	*13.4, 14.1, 14.2*
	Final accounts; Depreciation	*13.2, 13.3*

Examination analysis

The specification comprises two unit tests at AS and two unit tests at A2.

***Unit 1** (AS 1) **The Competitive Business** (50% of AS, 25% of A-Level)*
Candidates sit a 1 hour 30 minutes examination (40 marks) containing two compulsory structured data response questions.

***Unit 2** (AS 2) **Managing Business Resources** (50% of AS, 25% of A-Level)*
Candidates sit a 1 hour 30 minutes examination (40 marks) containing two compulsory structured data response questions.

CCEA A2

Module (Unit)	Specification topic	Chapter reference
3 (M3)	*Business objectives; Stakeholder objectives*	*1.5, 3.1, 3.2*
	Business strategy and planning	*3.2, 7.5, 8.3, 9.1*
	Decision tree analysis	*3.3*
	Contingency planning	*3.3*
	Company accounts; ratio analysis	*13.4*
	Investment appraisal	*15.1*
4 (M4)	*Macroeconomic framework; Globalisation*	*1.1, 4.1–4.3, 5.3, 6.3, 16.1*
	Business ethics and corporate responsibility	*5.1, 6.4*
	Corporate culture	*1.2, 3.4*
	Change	*3.5, 5.1, 6.2, 6.3, 18.1, 18.2, 18.4*

Examination analysis

The specification comprises two unit tests at AS and two unit tests at A2.

***Unit 3** (A2 1) **Making Business Decisions** (25% of A-Level)*
Candidates sit a 2 hour examination (80 marks) containing one compulsory structured data response question.

***Unit 4** (A2 2) **The Changing Business Environment** (25% of A-Level)*
Candidates sit a 2 hour examination (40 marks). They are required to produce a report, based on an unseen case study with a problem-solving and decision-making focus. The report will analyse problems, evaluate evidence and propose and justify solutions.

Revision tips

Exam technique

Examiners use instructions to help you to decide the length and depth of your answer:

State, define, list, outline: These key words require short, concise answers, and recall of material that you have memorised.

Explain, describe, discuss: Some reasoning or some reference to theory is needed, depending on the context. Explaining and discussing require you to give a more detailed answer than when you are asked to 'describe' something.

Apply: With an 'apply' question, you must make sure that you relate your answer to the case study (this is always good practice in Business Studies exams).

Evaluate: You are required to provide full and detailed arguments, often 'for' and 'against', to show your depth of understanding.

Calculate: A numerical answer is required here.

Some dos and don'ts

- **Do** answer the question. No credit can be given for good Business Studies knowledge that is not relevant to the question.
- **Do** use the mark allocation to guide how much you write. Writing more than necessary will not result in extra marks.
- **Do** use real-life business-based examples in your answers. These often help illustrate your level of knowledge.
- **Do** write legibly. An examiner cannot give marks if the answer cannot be read.
- **Do** use correct 'business language'. Marks will be lost if you fail to use terms appropriately.

- **Don't** fill up blank spaces on the exam paper. If you write too much on one question, you may run out of time to answer some of the others.
- **Don't** contradict yourself. Present reasoned arguments for and against.
- **Don't** spend too much time on a part that you find difficult. Exam time is limited, and you can always return to the difficult part if you have enough time at the end of the exam.

What grade do you want?

Everyone would like to improve their grades, but you will only manage this with a lot of hard work and determination. Your final A-Level grade depends on the extent to which you meet the assessment objectives listed earlier. The hints below offer advice on how to improve your grade.

A* or A grade

To achieve a grade A* or A, you have to:

- show in-depth knowledge and critical understanding of a wide range of business theories and concepts
- apply your knowledge and understanding to familiar and unfamiliar situations, problems and issues, using appropriate numerical and non-numerical techniques
- evaluate evidence and arguments effectively
- make reasoned judgements in presenting appropriate conclusions.

You have to be a very good all-rounder to achieve a grade A* or A. The exams test all areas of the syllabus, and any weaknesses in your understanding of Business Studies will be found out.

C grade

To achieve a grade C, you have to have a good understanding of the aspects shown in the criteria to gain an A grade (shown above), but you will have weaknesses in some of these areas. To improve, you will need to work hard to overcome these weaknesses, and also make sure that you have an efficient and effective exam technique.

AS/A2 Business Studies courses

AS and A2

A-Level Business Studies courses are in two sections. Students first study the AS (Advanced Subsidiary) course. Some will then go on to study the second part of the A-Level course, called A2. There are two modules (units) at AS level and two at A2 level.

The AS and A2 courses are designed so that the level of difficulty increases from AS to A2:

- AS Business Studies builds on GCSE Business Studies.
- A2 Business Studies builds on AS Business Studies.

How will you be tested?

Assessment units

For AS Business Studies, you will be tested by two assessment units. For the full A-Level in Business Studies you will take a further two units. AS Business Studies forms 50 percent of the assessment weighting for the full A-Level.

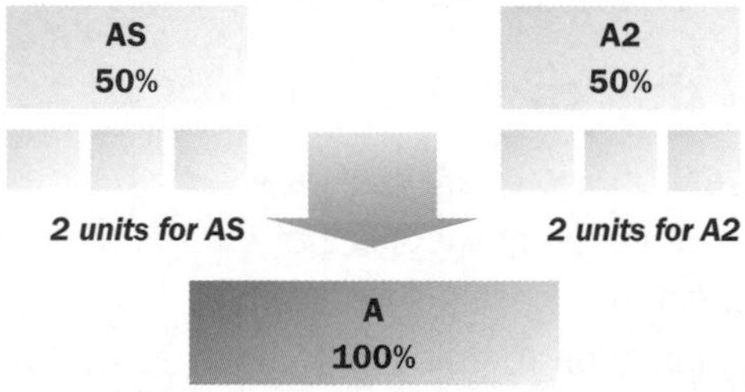

Depending on the exam board, a unit can be taken in January or June, or both. Alternatively, you may be able to study the whole course before taking any of the unit tests. There is some flexibility about when exams can be taken, and the diagram below shows just some of the ways that the assessment units may be taken for AS and A-Level Business Studies.

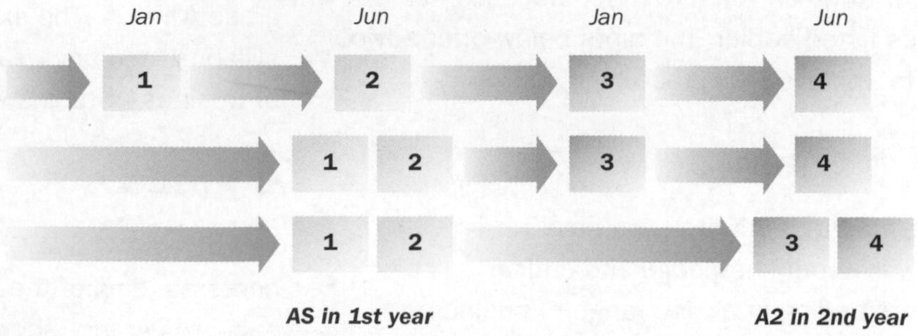

If you are disappointed with a module result, you can resit a module. The higher mark counts.

A2 and synoptic assessment

After having studied AS Business Studies, you may wish to continue studying Business Studies to A-Level. For this you will need to take two further Business Studies units at A2. The A2 units assess the course using a 'synoptic' approach to assessment. Synoptic assessment tests your ability to apply knowledge, understanding and skills you have learnt throughout the course, and to make business decisions and/or solve business problems. It takes place across the two A2 units and encourages candidates to:

- gain a holistic understanding of business
- develop the ability to deal with the interrelationships between external and internal factors affecting business in different contexts.

What skills will I need?

The Advanced Subsidiary GCE and Advanced GCE in Business Studies draw on the subject criteria for Business Studies, which are prescribed and are compulsory.

AS and A-Level Business Studies should encourage you to:

- develop enthusiasm to study business
- gain a holistic understanding of business
- develop a critical understanding of organisations and their ability to meet society's needs and wants
- understand that you can study business behaviour from different perspectives
- come up with enterprising solutions to business issues
- be aware of the ethical dilemmas and responsibilities relating to business
- acquire relevant business and generic skills, including decision making, problem solving, the challenging of assumptions and the quantification and management of information.

It is important that you develop your key skills throughout your AS and A2 courses. These are important skills that you need whatever you do beyond AS and A2 levels.

The main key skill areas relevant to Business Studies are:

- communication
- application of number
- information and communication technology
- working with others
- improving own learning and performance
- problem solving.

Each examination board will 'signpost' where key skill developments can best take place whilst studying A-Level Business Studies. You will have opportunities during your study of A-Level Business Studies to develop your key skills.

You will have to meet the following assessment objectives:

- Demonstrate knowledge and understanding of the specified content.
- Apply knowledge and understanding to problems and issues arising from both familiar and unfamiliar situations.
- Analyse problems, issues and situations.
- Evaluate, distinguish between and assess appropriateness of fact and opinion, and judge information from a variety of sources.

Types of exam questions

In Business Studies examinations, different types of question are used to assess your abilities and skills. Unit tests mainly use structured questions, requiring both short answers and more extended answers. These questions are often linked directly to a given case study, requiring you to read and study the stimulus material (a paragraph or short article about a real or imagined business situation).

Short-answer questions

Short-answer questions can be set at AS and A2 level. A short-answer question may test recall or it may test understanding. Short-answer questions may have space for the answers printed on the question paper.

Here is an example (a brief answer is shown below).

Outline how entering into a franchise reduces the benefits of being a sole trader. [6]

Benefits may be reduced: e.g. a loss of independence in decision making; reduced profits (royalties payable to franchisor); dependent on general success of franchisor rather than own ability/success.

Structured questions

Structured questions are in several parts. The parts usually have a common context and they often become progressively more difficult and more demanding as you work your way through the question. A structured question may start with simple recall, then test understanding of a familiar or an unfamiliar situation. Many of the questions in this guide are structured questions, as this is a popular type of question used in A-Level Business Studies exams.

Here is an example of a structured question that becomes progressively more demanding.

(a) Explain the benefits and drawbacks to the employer from having trade unions in the workplace. [8]

(b) 'A modern business must regard its human resource as its most valuable resource. As a result it will provide excellent conditions of work and reward employees with above-average wages.'

Given that such organisations exist, analyse whether trade unions are still necessary in today's business world. [12]

When answering structured questions, do not feel that you have to complete one question before starting the next. The further you are into a question, the more difficult the marks are to obtain. If you run out of ideas, go on to the next question.

You need to respond to as many parts of the questions on an exam paper as possible. You will not score well if you spend so long trying to perfect the first questions that you do not reach later questions at all.

Extended answers

In A-Level Business Studies, questions requiring more extended answers may form part of structured questions or they may form separate questions (e.g. linked to a case study). These questions are often used to assess your abilities to communicate ideas, relate your knowledge to the case study in the question, and put together a logical argument.

The 'correct' answers to extended questions are often less well-defined than those requiring shorter answers. Examiners may have a list of points for which credit is awarded up to the maximum for the question.

Marks for your answer may be allocated using a 'levels of response' mark scheme.

Such a scheme for a 12-mark question might be written as follows:

- **10–12 marks:** You have seen all the consequences and produced an evaluative answer.
- **7–9 marks:** You see all the consequences but do not consider all issues (e.g. you ignore quality or cost issues).
- **4–6 marks:** You limit your answer to basic points (e.g. you do apply some of your knowledge, but show gaps in understanding).
- **1–3 marks:** You show only a limited knowledge (e.g. of some theory points).

AS and A-Level specifications will assess your quality of written communication (QWC). Marks are likely to be allocated for legible text with accurate spelling, punctuation and grammar, and for a clear, well-organised answer in which you use specialist business terms effectively.

1 The business environment

The following topics are covered in this chapter:

- The economic environment
- Enterprise
- The UK's private sector
- The UK's public sector
- Stakeholders

1.1 The economic environment

LEARNING SUMMARY

After studying this section, you should be able to:

- describe and compare the industrial sectors found in the UK
- outline the differences between the market, planned and mixed economies

Industrial sectors in the UK

AQA	**M1**	WJEC	**M1**
Edexcel	**M3**	CCEA	**M1**
OCR	**M1**		

The UK consists of three traditional industrial (production) sectors:

- The **primary** sector consists of extractive industries such as fishing, forestry, farming, mining and quarrying.
- The **secondary** sector – often described as 'industry' – consists of firms involved with manufacturing and construction.
- The **tertiary** sector contains organisations supplying services – both commercial services such as banking, finance and retail, as well as direct service providers, e.g. health.

Many people suggest that a fourth sector now exists – some analysts identify a **quaternary** sector (an extension of the tertiary sector) containing information-based businesses, e.g. computing and ICT, and education.

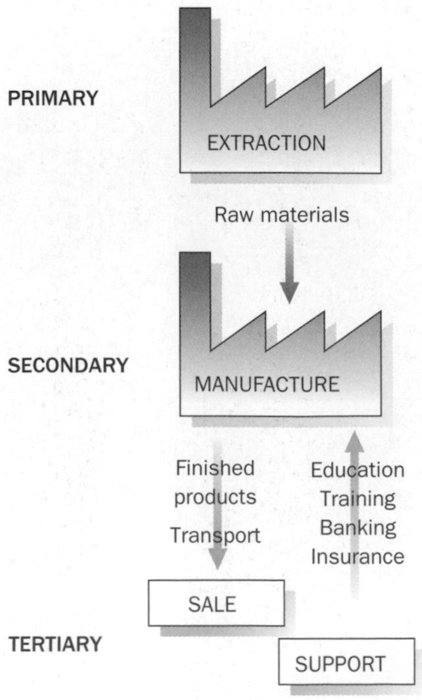

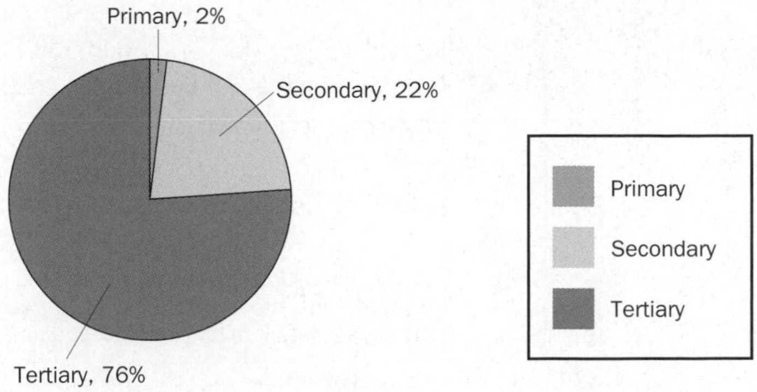

Figure 1.1 Percentages of economic activity in the UK by production sector, 2009

Figure 1.2 illustrates the change in the relative importance of the sectors.

	2009 (quarter 4)	1999 (quarter 4)	2009 as % of 1999
Agriculture and related	220	285	77.2
Manufacturing	2 592	4 018	64.5
Construction	1 198	1 152	104.0
Total services	22 095	19 819	111.5

Figure 1.2 Employee jobs by industry (thousands)

The statistics show that the manufacturing industry has declined in relative importance in the UK in recent years. This **de-industrialisation** reflects a long-term move towards tertiary production. In the first Industrial Revolution, many workers moved from the country to the towns, and changed from primary (agriculture) to secondary production. The trend away from agriculture and extraction continued, together with a further shift from secondary to tertiary. This is typical of other developed Western economies, whereas a number of developing economies are still experiencing a major shift from primary to secondary production.

Some estimates suggest that the BRIC economies could have 40 percent of world trade by 2025.

Reasons for de-industrialisation in the UK include:

- increasing substitution of capital for labour (due to technological developments in production) in both primary and secondary sectors
- the fall in the UK's competitiveness in secondary production, leading to more manufactured goods being imported
  - newly industrialised competitor economies, notably the **BRIC** countries (Brazil, Russia, India and China), have some of the world's fastest growing economies.

KEY POINT

Developments in the UK and other economies affect firms' organisational culture and strategy, and how they manage change.

PROGRESS CHECK

1. Give an example of a business in each of the three traditional industrial sectors.
2. What do the following terms mean, and how do they relate to classifying production?
   (a) de-industrialisation **(b)** extractive industry **(c)** tertiary

1 Farm (primary); builder (secondary); bank (tertiary) (**accept any other suitable answers**).
2 **(a)** De-industrialisation refers to the trend away from secondary to tertiary production
(b) Extractive industries remove value from the land (including the sea) **(c)** Tertiary refers to the UK's service sector.

Types of economy

AQA	**M1**	WJEC	**M1**
Edexcel	**M1, M3**	CCEA	**M4**
OCR	**M1, M6**		

Economies differ in the way that they **allocate scarce economic resources to competing uses**. As production takes place, the goods and services consume (use up) economic resources. These resources have costs associated with them. An accountant measures the financial cost of these resources, for example the cost of paying wages, or the cost of interest on borrowed money. An economist considers the **opportunity cost** of production – resources that are allocated to one use cannot be used for something else at the same time. For example, land being used for agriculture cannot also be built upon; labour employed in making cars cannot also work at the same time in the retail industry.

KEY POINT

All economies must find answers to these questions:
- What do we produce?
- How do we produce it?
- For whom do we produce?

The market economy

In a true market economy (free enterprise), resources are privately owned. Production decisions are made by entrepreneurs and private individuals, and not by the state on behalf of its people.

The **profit motive** is important, because it affects demand, supply and price. The **price mechanism** allocates scarce resources through changes in the price of these resources.

These are the main features of a market economy:
- A market economy is efficient in producing and allocating resources. However, few 'perfectly competitive' markets exist and so collusion between producers, incomplete price knowledge by consumers, restrictions on entry to new firms, and taxes/subsidies all limit economic efficiency in practice.
- A market economy has decentralised decision-making, which should reduce bureaucracy ('red tape') for firms, but centralisation and bureaucracy may still exist (e.g. to control cartels).
- Producers must satisfy their customers in order to make profits, and so the consumer influences what is produced – **consumer sovereignty** – but the price mechanism and profit motive may result in social judgements being ignored, and the state must still intervene to ensure that non-profitable services (e.g. universal health care, defence) are provided.

Changing prices give signals and act as an incentive to buyers and sellers, e.g. increased petrol prices signal lower car sales to vehicle manufacturers and act as an incentive to use public transport.

KEY POINT

Increasing concern over environmental issues – considering not only financial costs ('price') but also social ones – is a good example of how the price mechanism is distorted in practice.

The command (planned) economy

A centrally planned 'command' economy is the opposite of the market economy. Although largely discredited in the West, in theory a planned economy can allocate resources as efficiently as a market one. Real-life command economies, such as those once widely found in Eastern Europe, concentrate on the central control of what is produced, how it is distributed, and at what price.

In recent years, many countries with planned economies have switched towards greater use of the price mechanism; examples include China, Russia and East European ex-communist countries.

For firms based in planned economies:

- all costs are considered, the central planning authority taking into account social and other costs not easily measured in financial terms – as a result, market forces are less influential
- public goods are provided on the basis of need rather than profit – though the lack of a profit motive means a lack of incentive and therefore little encouragement to innovate and be efficient.

KEY POINT

Because prices are less influenced by demand/supply interaction, producers have fewer price signals. Production targets have to be met, with surpluses or shortages resulting from planning imperfections.

The mixed economy

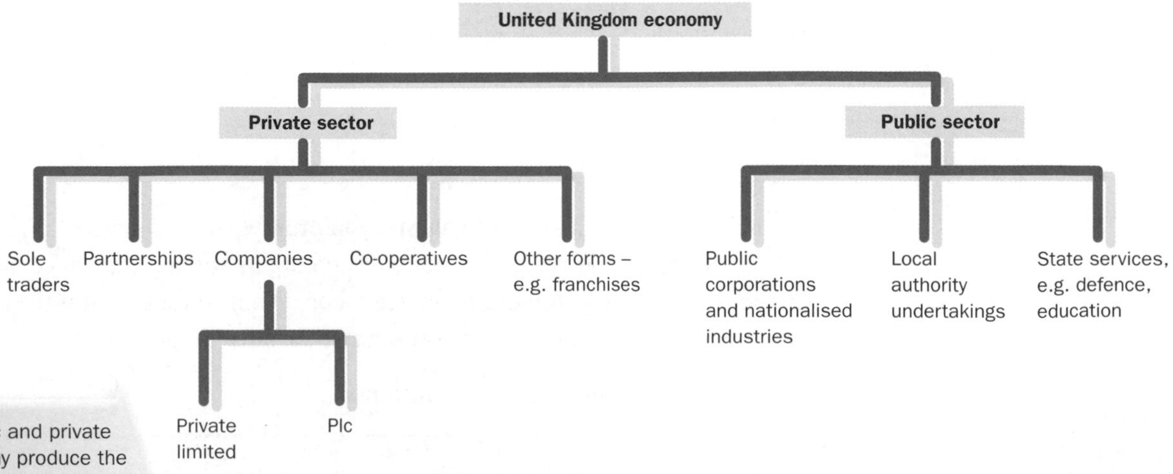

Figure 1.3 The UK economy's private and public sectors

Both public and private sectors may produce the same items/services. For instance, health services are provided by the public (National Health Service – NHS) and private (e.g. BUPA) sectors.

Two main sectors – public and private – exist in a mixed economy. The distinction between these sectors is based on **ownership**, as well as on how resources are allocated. In practice, a wider range of goods and services is likely to be found in mixed economies.

In recent years the UK's private sector has grown at the expense of the public sector, e.g. through privatising many public sector organisations.

Private sector firms are set up by individuals who seek to make profit from their business activities. Although many private sector firms are controlled by entrepreneurs, they may be owned by different people or organisations, for example companies owned by private or institutional (organisation-based) investors. This can lead to a conflict between ownership and control.

The **public sector** consists of organisations owned and/or financed by central and local government. This sector provides goods and services to the community through public corporations, local government and other statutory agencies (e.g. the NHS). The profit motive is not so prominent – the emphasis in the public sector is on providing for the community by the community, using funding supplied through taxes and government borrowing.

Sector of the economy	Ownership	Sources of finance	Reason for existence
Private sector	**Private individuals**	**Individuals and firms**	**Profit motive**
Sole traders	One person	Sole trader	Profit for owner
Partnerships	Two or more individuals	Partners	Profit for partners
Limited companies	One or more shareholders	Shareholders Other sources, e.g. commercial banks	Profit for shareholders
Public sector	**Central and local government**	**Public funds**	**Service motive**
Public corporations	Central government	Taxation and trading	To provide a service, and break even or make profit
Local authority undertakings	Local government	Local finance and trading	To provide a service, and break even or make profit

The UK also has a substantial **voluntary sector**, which consists of organisations such as charities and religious bodies. Such organisations may have some commercial aims and seek to generate income (e.g. through 'charity shops') – their main purpose is to carry out charitable or other activities.

Below is the Dogs Trust mission statement.

> Our mission is to bring about the day when all dogs can enjoy a happy life, free from the threat of unnecessary destruction.
>
> *Dogs Trust website, 2010*

KEY POINT

Exclusively market or planned economies do not exist in practice, and countries use a mixed economy to allocate their scarce resources.

PROGRESS CHECK

1 What do the following terms mean, and how do they relate to economic systems?
(a) free enterprise **(b)** bureaucracy **(c)** opportunity cost

1 **(a)** Free enterprise is where market economies operate through the interaction of supply and demand **(b)** Bureaucracy involves over-centralisation of control
(c) Opportunity cost is the cost of an opportunity forgone.

1.2 Enterprise

LEARNING SUMMARY

After studying this section, you should be able to:

- explain the role and importance of entrepreneurs to the UK economy
- comment on the roles of profit and risk in entrepreneurial activity
- outline why business plans are constructed
- describe the role of social enterprises

Entrepreneurs

AQA	**M1**
Edexcel	**M1, M2a**
OCR	**M1, M6, M7**
WJEC	**M1, M3**
CCEA	**M1, M4**

Individuals in the private sector try to make profit by acting as **entrepreneurs** in the marketplace.

The qualities of a good entrepreneur vary from person to person, but they often include:

- being willing to work hard and for long hours
- a high motivation level to succeed
- being well organised
- being creative and innovative
- a willingness to take business risks.

Business births and deaths

All economies are dynamic in that entrepreneurs set up new businesses and/or close existing ones.

Businesses fail due to reasons such as poor cashflow management and stock control, over-estimation of sales, and not responding effectively to changed market conditions.

In the UK in 2008, business administration and support services had the highest rate (16.2 percent) of business births. Professional, scientific and technical services had the highest number (54 000) of business births.

The highest rate of business deaths was in accommodation and food (13.1 percent), with construction showing the highest number of failures (33 000).

Birth rate — Death rate

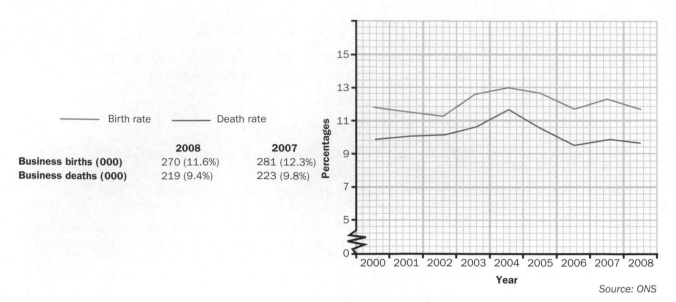

	2008	2007
Business births (000)	270 (11.6%)	281 (12.3%)
Business deaths (000)	219 (9.4%)	223 (9.8%)

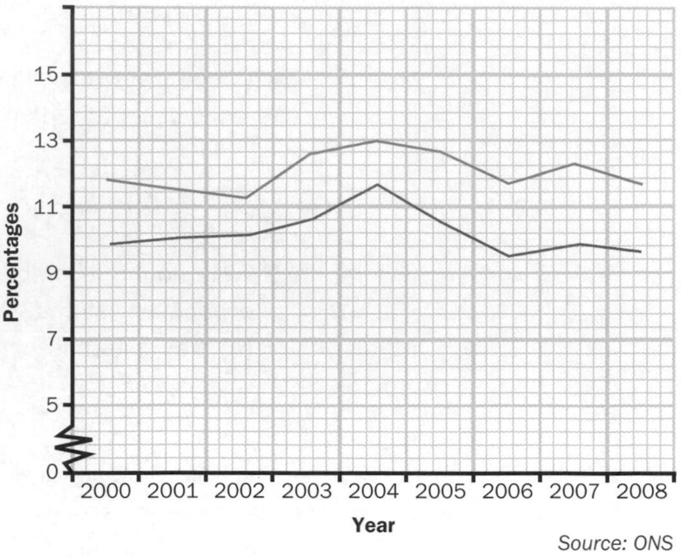

Figure 1.4 Business births and deaths from 2000–2008, with a focus on the decrease in births and deaths from 2007–2008

The UK government encourages enterprise for reasons such as increasing economic output and employment.

Government strategies to encourage enterprise may include:

- keeping taxation rates low for new businesses
- offering inexpensive loans or grants for business start-ups
- simplifying the 'red tape' necessary to start a business.

Entrepreneurs, profit and risk

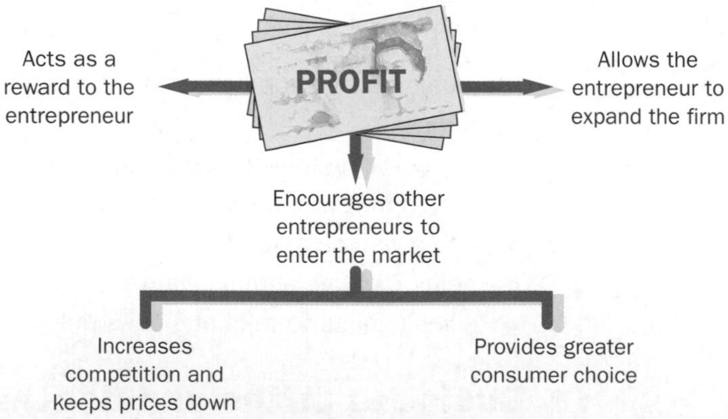

Figure 1.5 Profit

It is important for entrepreneurs to get a **competitive advantage**, i.e. a distinct advantage that a business has which helps it to do better than its competitors. By doing so the entrepreneur is taking a calculated risk in the hope of making a **profit**.

Economists view profit as the reward of one of the factors of production (enterprise).

Why is profit important to an entrepreneur? It provides a measure of success for the business, as well as acting as an indicator to others. Prospective lenders use the profit figure to decide whether to lend, and potential entrepreneurs look at present profit levels when deciding whether to enter an industry.

Profit, being the reward for taking **risk**, is not guaranteed – many firms make losses and close. Even when profit is made it may be small and regarded by the entrepreneur as a poor reward for risk-taking – the firm's **profitability** may be too low. This results in continual change in the structure of the private sector.

As well as having the desire to make profit, entrepreneurs start up in businesses for reasons such as personal satisfaction, and the wish to operate independently and make their own decisions.

The business idea and plan

An entrepreneur needs to decide on the type of business to set up. Where there is more than one option, the **opportunity cost** of setting up one business will be reviewed in terms of the 'trade-offs' from not setting up the alternative business.

Whatever the reason for starting the business, the entrepreneur will need to consider **sources of business ideas**. Examples include visits to trade or industry shows, the local Chamber of Commerce, the Internet, and printed sources such as magazines, Yellow Pages, the Thomson directory, or business sections of newspapers.

Innovation is a key business process that enables an entrepreneur to compete, although there is no guarantee the innovation will be commercially successful.

Innovation occurs when an entrepreneur turns an idea or an invention into a product that can be sold – it is when a new idea is successfully exploited. Some business ideas are developed by individual innovators who are able to recognise how to change or adapt an existing product, or who spot a gap in the range of products being sold.

Entrepreneurs need to protect their business ideas because they face the risk that someone will copy what they have created, market this copy and therefore compete with them. **Intellectual Property** (IP) protects their ideas – it is created when an idea takes some tangible (physical) form.

IP can be legally owned.

There are four main types of IP:

- **Copyright** protects many types of ideas and work, typically involving music, films and broadcasts, and other literary and artistic works. The copyright holder's permission is needed before someone else can use the work in question – otherwise the person using the copyrighted material without permission can be taken to court.
- **Patents** protect the features and processes that make things work – anyone who copies a business's patented idea can be taken to court. The creator of the patent is also able to sell or license the invention.
- **Designs** protect the appearance and appeal of products, so a business creating a product with a unique design can seek to register the design and stop anyone from copying it.
- **Trade marks** are like brand names and logos, distinctive to the goods and services being provided because they distinguish them from others. Registering a trade mark gives a business the exclusive right to use it, and stops others from using it without permission.

A business plan acts as a marketing document to attract potential investors.

Entrepreneurs create a **business plan** to:

- see if the business is viable – whether it is practicable to run the business
- review the effectiveness of the business
- help raise the finance the business needs.

A business plan must be updated regularly because of changes that occur internally (e.g. in how the factory floor is organised) and externally (e.g. changes in tax rates, consumer tastes or in the strength of the economy).

These are the typical sections in a business plan:

- An **executive summary** – an overview of the new business (some lenders and investors make judgements about the business based only on this).
- A **description of the business** – information on the business and its products, to whom the business will sell, and why it is a suitable idea.
- The **marketing strategy** – why customers are likely to buy the products, and how the products will be sold to them.
- The **management team** – information on the entrepreneur and the staff.
- The **operations** – information about the premises, production facilities and information systems.
- **Financial forecasts** – financial summaries based on the above information.

An entrepreneur will need to assess the strengths and weaknesses of the business plan.

KEY POINT

The exact content and structure of business plans varies from business to business and from industry to industry.

Social enterprises

In 2010 there were over 60 000 **social enterprises** in the UK, employing about 800 000 people.

Social enterprises operate in many industries in the UK, from health and social care to renewable energy, retail to recycling, sport to employment services. Although entrepreneurs run social enterprises and compete to deliver goods and services and to make profits, **they are driven by a social or environmental purpose** rather than by profit. Any profits made by a social enterprise are normally re-invested to help it achieve its aim.

Examples of social enterprises include *The Big Issue* magazine and social project, the Fairtrade chocolate company Divine Chocolate, and the Eden Project.

KEY POINT

The profit motive is the foundation of the private sector.

PROGRESS CHECK

1. Why is profit important to an entrepreneur?

1 It is a measure of success, the source of the entrepreneur's income and acts as evidence to others (e.g. when they are deciding whether to lend the entrepreneur money).

1.3 The UK's private sector

LEARNING SUMMARY

After studying this section, you should be able to:

- distinguish between the private and public sectors
- explain the difference between incorporated and unincorporated businesses
- explain the terms 'unlimited liability' and 'limited liability'
- describe the nature of the main private sector organisations
- explain the phrase 'divorce of ownership and control'

Legal liability and legal status

AQA	**M1**	WJEC	**M1**
Edexcel	**M1**	CCEA	**M1**
OCR	**M1**		

A limited company has the legal authority to own property, enter contracts in its own name, and sue or be sued in the courts.

'Limited' in the name warns those trading with a limited company that any trading debts may not be recoverable due to limited liability.

Sole traders remain the most popular form of business in the UK. Sole traders and **partnerships** do not possess a legal existence separate from that of their owners – they are **unincorporated** businesses. Private and public **limited companies** are incorporated bodies. **Incorporation** means the company has a **separate legal existence** from its owners (shareholders).

Sole traders and partnerships also have **unlimited liability** – if business debts cannot be met from the firm's own resources, the owner(s) can be forced to sell personal assets to cover these business debts. Limited companies offer the benefit of **limited liability** to investors – when a limited company cannot pay its debts from its own financial resources, its owners do not have to use their personal finances to meet these debts.

Most large commercial companies are limited by share and must include 'limited' or 'plc' as appropriate in their name. Other companies, for example some examination bodies and professional associations, are limited by guarantee – members of such a company guarantee its business debts up to a given maximum.

KEY POINT

Limited liability encourages people to risk starting – or investing in – companies, because they know their losses will be limited to the amount they have agreed to invest.

Sole traders and partnerships

Sole traders can employ as many people as they wish.

A sole trader (sole proprietor) business exists when there is **only one owner**. Sole trader businesses are often found where personal services are provided, little start-up capital is needed, and large-scale production is not needed.

Figure 1.6, on the next page, illustrates the main advantages and disadvantages of being a sole trader.

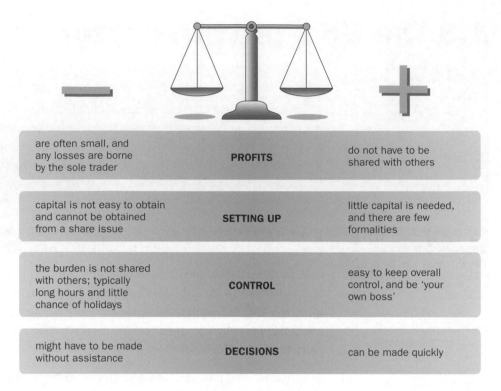

−		+
are often small, and any losses are borne by the sole trader	**PROFITS**	do not have to be shared with others
capital is not easy to obtain and cannot be obtained from a share issue	**SETTING UP**	little capital is needed, and there are few formalities
the burden is not shared with others; typically long hours and little chance of holidays	**CONTROL**	easy to keep overall control, and be 'your own boss'
might have to be made without assistance	**DECISIONS**	can be made quickly

Figure 1.6 Features of the sole trader

Partnerships are also unincorporated businesses with unlimited liability. They are traditionally associated with professions such as accountants and lawyers, where capital outlay is small.

The minimum number of partners is two. The partners often draw up a written **partnership agreement** expressing the rights and duties of individual partners with reference to:

- profit sharing
- the amounts of capital to be contributed
- the different business responsibilities of each partner
- regulations concerning the withdrawal of profits by individual partners, on introducing new partners, and the dissolution (ending) of the partnership.

The Partnership Act 1890 rules apply if there is no agreement – profits and losses are shared equally, partners' loans receive 5 percent interest, each partner has an equal say.

A partnership, like a sole trader business, is simple to establish. Other similarities are that the partnership can keep its financial affairs private, and the owners face the drawback of unlimited liability.

Partners are better able to **specialise** and therefore overcome the likely limitations of knowledge and skill levels associated with a one-person sole trader operation. A **sleeping partner** may join, who will invest in the business but take no part in its management.

If a sole trader is thinking of converting to a partnership, the key benefits and drawbacks to consider are as follows:

Benefits	*Drawbacks*
Specialisation can take place (each partner can specialise in a different business function)	**Decision making may take longer** (the new partner must be consulted)
Additional skills may also be introduced by the new partner	If/when the new partner dies or leaves, a **new partnership** must be created
More capital is available (an extra owner is an extra investor)	The **profit must be shared** between the partners
Expansion is therefore easier	**Control** of the business must also be shared

In 2000, the Limited Liability Partnerships Act allowed **limited liability partnerships** (LLPs) to be established.

This new form of business ownership is similar to a limited company, in that an LLP:

- is registered at Companies House
- becomes a legal person separate from its members
- offers limited liability to the partners
- must use an abbreviation (LLP) at the end of its name.

Many large, professional partnerships (e.g. accountants and lawyers) have become LLPs.

Differences between LLPs and limited companies include tax liability – an LLP's members pay income tax and LLP does not pay corporation tax.

Limited companies

Incorporation gives a limited company a separate legal existence from its owners (shareholders). There are over one million limited companies registered in the UK, varying in size from small family-owned businesses to large public limited companies (plcs).

A limited company is classed as private (Ltd) unless its memorandum of association states that it is a plc. The owners – **shareholders** – gain a share of the profits (**dividend**) from owning shares, and may also make a capital gain if the share price rises.

A private company can have one or more members (shareholders), but cannot advertise its shares for sale to the public or through the Stock Exchange. Plcs must have a minimum £50 000 share capital, and can sell their shares to the public and be quoted on the Stock Exchange. A Stock Exchange acts as the market for second-hand stocks and shares (securities), encouraging investment in business by offering investors a degree of protection through its strict rules for admitting firms.

The London Stock Exchange is one of the world's major stock exchanges.

KEY POINT

Plcs find it easier to raise finance, tend to be much larger than private companies, and find that ownership and control are more clearly separated.

In comparison with sole traders and partnerships:

- limited liability is offered to investors, encouraging greater investment
- greater investment = greater size = greater economies of scale
- through its separate legal existence from the owners, a limited company owns assets, takes legal action in its own name, and does not face problems of continuity when an owner dies, retires or otherwise leaves.

However:

- greater expense and more formalities are incurred in setting up the company
- its business affairs are less private
- greater size may result in diseconomies of scale
- owners of private companies may face difficulties in selling shares
- ownership of plcs can be transferred (via the Stock Exchange) against the wishes of the directors, and shareholders may seek to operate short-term policies to make short-term profits, leading to greater instability.

Starting a private sector business

AQA **M1** WJEC **M1**
Edexcel **M1**
OCR **M1**

	All self-employed	*Men*	*Women*
	(000)	(000)	(000)
January–March 2010	3 935	2 764	1 171
January–March 2009	3 829	2 765	1 064

Figure 1.7 Number of self-employed people in the UK

There are many practical difficulties when starting a new business:

1. Obtaining sufficient **finance** – the amount needs careful calculation, and it must be obtained at a cost (rate of interest) acceptable to the entrepreneur. **Security** will be required by the lender, which may be difficult to find. The most popular source of finance is the bank, offering loans and/or the facility to overdraw on a business current account.
2. Finding a suitable **location** – what is needed is an affordable site in a location suitable for employing staff (and to enable them to commute), and for transport and communications from both a supplier and a customer perspective.
3. Identifying a **gap in the market** – all firms depend on a satisfactory demand for their goods and services, so the entrepreneur of a new business must try to avoid duplicating a product that is already available at a competitive price and meeting demand in the market.
4. Ensuring adequate **cash flow** – bad cash flow management is the most common cause of business failure. **Liquidity** is more important than profitability in the short term, particularly in the early part of a firm's existence.

KEY POINT

Liquidity measures the ability of a firm to meet its debts as they fall due.

Registering a company

The Companies Acts (2006 and others) set out the legal requirements to create and run a limited company. All limited companies are registered at Companies House. They must submit annual returns summarising changes to their affairs, and annual financial statements.

The company's **Memorandum of Association** governs its relationship with the outside world. Its clauses include the following information.

Name	the proposed company name
Situation	the address of the registered office
Objects	the purposes for which it was formed (stated in general terms)
Liability	a statement that its members have limited liability
Capital	the amount of capital registered and the types of shares
Association	directors' names and addresses

The **Articles of Association** govern the internal workings of the company, including details of directors (number, rights and duties), the conduct and calling of meetings, and the division of profits.

'Divorce of ownership and control'

The phrase 'divorce of ownership and control' is closely associated with plcs – shareholders own the company but do not control it. Few shareholders have a direct say in the daily running of a plc, because – through the **Annual General Meeting** (AGM) – they appoint specialist directors to exercise day-to-day control on their behalf.

Once ownership and control is separated in this way, the decisions made by the directors – the controllers – may clash with the wishes of (some of) the shareholders – the owners. A common example is where the shareholders may wish to see a policy of profit maximisation, which may not be the wish of the directors, who see long-term growth as a more important strategy to pursue.

PROGRESS CHECK

1. Name three occupations where sole traders are commonly found.
2. State two reasons why a sole trader may convert the business into a limited company rather than a partnership.

1 Hairdresser; plumber; builder (**accept any other suitable answers**).
2 Easier to obtain more capital; limited liability.

Other private sector business types

AQA	M1	WJEC	M1
Edexcel	M1	CCEA	M1
OCR	M1		

Examples include Burger King, Cartridge World, Dyno-Rod and Prontaprint.

Franchises

Franchise businesses use the **name and logo of an existing company**. **Franchising** is a major growth area in the UK economy – by 2000 there were approximately 600 business format franchises, comprising about 30 000 franchisees, employing a quarter of a million people.

Types of franchise agreements include:

- manufacturer–retailer (some petrol stations and car dealers)
- wholesaler–retailer (Spar and other voluntary groups)
- trademark–retailer ('fast food' outlets).

We're with you from day one

Join us as a franchisee and you'll benefit from a first class training programme to help you take advantage of our proven system. You'll get ongoing support and advice to help progress you and your business throughout your twenty year term ... your training programme which typically takes nine months. This involves visiting and working in several restaurants as well as classroom-based tuition.

Extract from McDonald's website, 2010

The **franchisee** buys the franchise, entering into a contract with – and paying a fee to – the **franchisor** (the company).

Typically, the **franchisee**:

- agrees to follow set rules, e.g. layout of premises and product standards
- buys only from the franchisor or other named supplier.

The **franchisor**:

- supplies the decor and assists with layout
- allows the franchisee to use their product and logo.

> With a Card Connection franchise all you need is [a] reasonably sized storage facility, a van, telephone, computer and plenty of determination.
>
> *Extract from Card Connection franchise brochure (accessed via Card Connection website, 2010)*

The 'new business failure rate' for franchise businesses is much lower than for non-franchise ones.

A franchisee gains a recognised product or service backed by successful marketing and business methods, and receives expert business support – success is therefore more likely than for an 'independent' entrepreneur. The franchisor can expand without making a large capital investment, since the franchisee provides the capital. The company knows that its franchisees, who are not on a salary, will be highly motivated by the direct financial incentive to make their franchise a financial success.

The **British Franchise Association** is the voluntary self-regulating body for UK franchising, promoting ethical franchising through its member franchisor companies.

A **franchise agreement** typically covers:

- the length of the franchise and how it can be ended
- the territory covered by the franchise and whether the franchisee has exclusive selling rights
- the nature of support given by the franchisor
- fees – the initial fee (which can be £100 000 or more), the management fee and/or percentage of sales revenue payable to the franchisor
- restrictions set by the franchisor (e.g. on display, products sold).

Co-operatives

Although the larger UK co-operatives operate as limited companies, owning capital is not the dominating factor in the co-operative movement. Most co-operative societies exist to provide a service for their member-owners and for the public. Control is shared democratically, with each member having a single vote, and trading surpluses ('profits') are often distributed to the members in proportion to their trade with the society.

In 2010, the Co-op offered over 200 Fairtrade products, ranking it as arguably the UK's leading ethical supermarket.

Consumer co-operatives – where customers own the business collectively – are found in Europe and Japan. Types of consumer co-operatives in the UK include housing co-operatives and credit unions – formed to allow people to benefit from collective saving and borrowing. The Co-operative Group (the 'Co-op') has over 3000 food stores and supermarkets in the UK – it is the only major retailer to sell food grown on its own farms – and sells a wide range of products such as food, banking and insurance, travel and health care. It is owned by its members, who receive a share of the profits based on how much they spend, and emphasises its ethical business activities.

In 2008, the world's 300 largest co-operatives had a turnover of $1.1 trillion.

Producer (worker) **co-operatives** also exist. Co-operatives UK is the organisation that supports the development of co-operative, mutual and social enterprises in the UK and overseas. Leading worker co-operatives include John Lewis.

> The John Lewis Partnership's 70 000 Partners own the leading UK retail businesses – Waitrose, John Lewis and Greenbee. Our founder's vision of a successful business powered by its people and its principles defines our unique company today. The profits and benefits created by our success are shared by all our Partners.
>
> *John Lewis website, 2010*

Mutuality

Some building societies and life assurance firms are non-profit making organisations, existing for the benefit of their members (customers). In the 1990s, many changed status (e.g. the Halifax converted from a building society to a bank, becoming a limited company), producing cash 'windfalls' for the existing members, many of whom became shareholders.

KEY POINT

Some commentators argue that the new profit-focused companies now operate in the interests of their new owners (shareholders), having to meet new priorities – such as profitability and dividend payments – at the expense of old priorities, based on satisfying the old owners (customers).

PROGRESS CHECK

1. Identify two differences between a franchisee and a sole trader.
2. What forms of co-operative exist in the UK?

1 Sole trader is independent, franchisee operates according to franchisor's rules; sole trader keeps all profits, franchisee pays royalty or other fee.
2 Consumer; producer (worker).

1.4 The UK's public sector

LEARNING SUMMARY

After studying this section, you should be able to:

- distinguish between the main forms of public sector organisation
- comment on the nature and purpose of privatisation and nationalisation

Public sector organisations

AQA	**M1**	WJEC	**M1**
Edexcel	**M1**	CCEA	**M1**
OCR	**M1**		

Public corporations have a separate legal existence through the Act of Parliament creating them. Their assets are **owned by the state** on behalf of the community. Their objectives, whilst influenced by commercial considerations, often emphasise social aspects. They normally have financial targets to achieve, such as a target return on capital employed.

A public corporation is controlled by:

- its government minister and through a board appointed by the minister
- a consumer council protecting the consumer interest
- being audited by the Competition Commission.

In 2008 there were about 800 NDPBs, of which half had the role of advising ministers on specific policy areas.

Other forms of public sector organisation include:

- **local government bodies**, which run services for the local community
  - many local authorities make profits from operating businesses, such as leisure centres
- **NDPBs** – non-departmental public bodies that work with public sector organisations but are separate from them (e.g. UK Sport).

Nationalisation takes an industry into public ownership. Industries such as coal, gas and the railways were nationalised following the Second World War. By the end of the 1970s, however, many nationalised industries were regarded as inefficient and over-subsidised monopolies, lacking competition and being in a position to exploit their monopoly status. The government's response was to **privatise** – return to private ownership – most nationalised industries.

A criticism of recently privatised industries is that their monopoly power may still remain. These 'privatised monopolies' are therefore regulated by 'watchdogs', e.g. OFGEM (for gas and electricity), OFCOM (for telephones and communications) and OFWAT (for water and sewerage).

Other criticisms of privatising industries include the following:

- Privatising 'natural monopoly' industries may mean losing economies of scale.
- Private monopolies are likely to be less well regulated than public sector ones.
- Revenue from state-owned assets has been used for government current expenditure rather than for long-term investment.

Deregulation has also been used by the UK government (and the EU) to stimulate competition in areas such as transport and broadcasting.

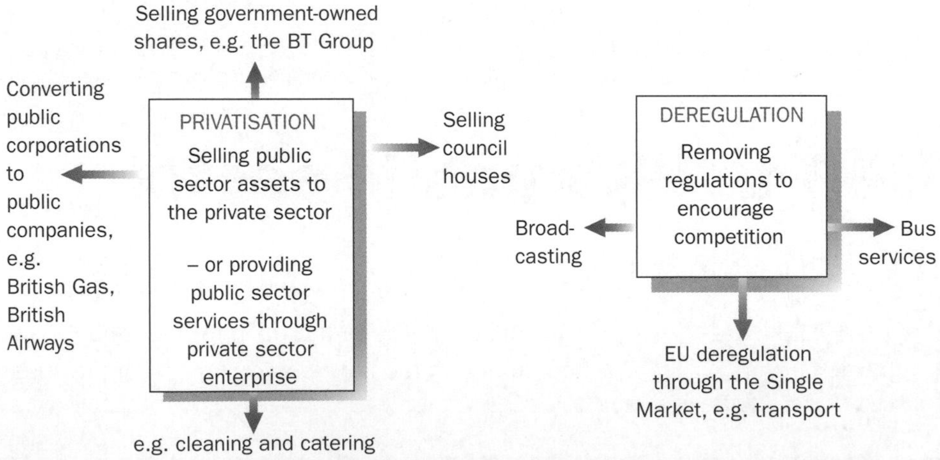

Figure 1.8 Privatisation and deregulation

PROGRESS CHECK

1. Identify three differences between a public corporation and a plc.

1 Ownership (corporations by the state, plcs by shareholders); control (corporations by a minister, plcs by directors); objectives (corporations focus on society, plcs on profit).

1.5 Stakeholders

LEARNING SUMMARY

After studying this section, you should be able to:

- explain the range, nature and influence of internal and external stakeholders on the work of a business

Types – and influence – of stakeholders

AQA	**M4**
Edexcel	**M1, M4a**
OCR	**M1, M7**
WJEC	**M1, M3**
CCEA	**M3**

Stakeholders are individuals or groups that have an influence on – or are influenced by – an organisation's decisions. Different stakeholder groups may be **accountable** for their actions or policies. For example, a clerk is accountable to the supervisor for their quality of work, and directors are accountable to shareholders for the effect of strategic business decisions.

> Stakeholder engagement is vital in ensuring our CSR [corporate social responsibility] programme remains relevant and effective. It enables us to identify issues and be responsive to changing needs by incorporating views and feedback... .
>
> *Morrisons Annual Report, 2009*

Figure 1.9 Internal and external stakeholders

The organisation's **internal stakeholders** – directors and managers – face a possible conflict between their duty to other stakeholders (such as employees, the other internal stakeholder group) and their duty to shareholders. Because shareholders appoint directors and (through the directors) employ managers to run the firm, directors and managers should undertake policies for the benefit of the shareholders. This shareholder concept implies that policies maximising share price and dividend should be followed at the expense of other policies.

The objectives of other stakeholder groups, whether internal or **external** (e.g. suppliers, customers, local community), may conflict with this, and there may also be conflict between the objectives of any two stakeholder groups. For example, improving employee morale and efficiency by training will increase costs and affect profit (in the short term); by establishing closer links with a supplier, a company may start using new manufacturing processes that will affect its relationships with the local community. In the longer run there may not be a conflict – improvements for employees, and better links with suppliers and customers improve quality, efficiency and profitability, and therefore bring higher profits.

Stakeholder and policy/action	***Benefit***
Close involvement with **local community**	Good publicity for the firm; support from local community when needed
Improving working conditions for **employees**	Improved morale and motivation; higher profits; reduced labour turnover
Better links with **suppliers** and **lenders**	Good long-term relationships; better communications; better quality

PROGRESS CHECK

1 Name two internal and two external private sector stakeholders.

1 Internal: directors, employees; external: suppliers, customers.

Sample question and model answer

1. Arthur and Brian were school friends, and after finishing their education they became equal partners in a printing firm. They discussed the type of business they wanted, considering structure and ownership issues such as liability and continuity.

Today, the business is successful, and Arthur and Brian are now discussing whether to take on another partner, take on a sleeping partner, or change the business to a LLP.

(a) Describe what is meant by the following:

(i) liability **(2)**

(ii) continuity **(2)**

(iii) sleeping partner **(2)**

(iv) LLP **(2)**

(a) (i) *If Arthur and Brian's business fails, they will have to find money from their own wealth to pay the business debts.*

(ii) *When there is a change in the people who own the business (e.g. if Arthur or Brian decided to leave), a business such as a limited company continues automatically, but there is no continuity for a partnership or sole trader.*

(iii) *This partner gives finance to the partnership, but takes no part in daily decision making.*

(iv) *LLP means Limited Liability Partnership, a form of partnership that gives the partners limited liability.*

These are acceptable definitions for both marks, but for part (i) explain that the partners only pay business debts if the partnership's net assets are not sufficient.

(b) What are the benefits and drawbacks to Arthur and Brian of taking on another partner rather than just a sleeping partner? **(8)**

(b) *If Arthur and Brian decide to admit a full third partner, they can specialise further in business functions and will gain more capital. However, if they take on a sleeping partner, they have the advantage of getting someone who will help to finance their business but who will not interfere with their decision making.*

This is a rather limited answer. Points should be made that a full partner may not be suitable due to (for example) lack of business knowledge or inability to get on with Arthur and Brian (partnership disputes are more likely with three partners). A full partner will also have the power to bind them by his or her business decisions.

(c) To what extent does the type of business ownership in the private sector determine who takes the business decisions? **(8)**

(c) *In a sole trader business, all decisions are taken by the single owner. There is nothing to stop the sole trader involving any staff in the decisions, but it is the sole trader's responsibility only. With a partnership, decisions could be on the basis of a majority vote unless it is a decision to do with any change in the nature of the partnership. Again, the partners can involve staff in decision making if they choose to do so. A private limited company's strategic decisions are carried out by the Board, who will delegate day-to-day decision-making to managers.*

Although the company is owned by shareholders, some of them may not be directors or otherwise work in the company, although they can attend shareholder meetings and take part in any votes. A public limited company will have more shareholders, who help take major decisions at shareholder meetings (e.g. Annual General Meetings and Extraordinary General Meetings). Again, there will be directors who are involved in the more strategic decision-making, with delegation of the more tactical decisions to their managers.

Accurate points. Mention could be made of two other forms: (a) franchises, where the franchisee takes basic business decisions but must follow the franchisor's strategic policy (e.g. on layout and decor) (b) co-operatives, where decisions are taken by the members who own it, normally by vote.

Exam practice question

Lucy uses her loaf

1 Lucy Lee is an unassuming individual who gets on with her work quietly and efficiently. Lucy owns a small bakery firm, Lee's Loaves, which she runs on her own. "My type of business they call a sole trader," Lucy says, "but if 'sole' means being on your own, that's a strange name to use since I'm hardly ever on my own here."

In fact, Lucy employs three full-time staff in the bakery, and two full-time – as well as three part-time – Saturday employees in her shop. Lucy admits: "It's a difficult one when you're talking to people, to try to explain the size of your business: you say 'sole proprietor', and they think you're doing it all yourself."

Lucy explains further: "They say I'm part of what they call the 'small firm sector', but my firm is big enough for me. In fact, it's been growing since before last Christmas. What we found in November was an increase in demand, which continued up to and beyond Christmas. I had to hire an extra couple of part-timers to help out on Saturday, and we're still doing so well that I'm pleased to say we could keep them on."

Lucy is one of the local success stories, but she admits that there are some areas of the business she leaves well alone: "Although I'm happy enough to do a lot of the administration myself, my background is one of baking bread and cooking cakes. I leave the specialist accounts work to my accountant, who comes in every Friday. And before you ask, the answer's no – he doesn't 'cook the books'!"

(a) Lee's Loaves operates as a sole trader. Why might a firm such as Lee's Loaves give a false impression if it uses 'number of employees' as the only indicator of its size? **(8)**

(b) Sole traders make up the majority of businesses in the United Kingdom, and dominate the 'small-firm sector'. Explain why a healthy small-firm sector is so important to the UK economy. **(8)**

2 Size and growth

The following topics are covered in this chapter:

- Business size
- Business growth
- Economies of scale
- The small firm

2.1 Business size

LEARNING SUMMARY

After studying this section, you should be able to:

- identify and explain four methods commonly used to measure the size of a business

Measuring size

Edexcel **M4a**
OCR **M1, M6**
WJEC **M1, M3**
CCEA **M1**

An organisation's size can be measured using different indicators. Some indicators are more suitable than others, depending on the nature of the organisation.

The level of **turnover** – annual sales – is the most widely used indicator of a firm's size. It suggests the ability to obtain finance and benefit from economies of scale.

		Revenues ($m)
1	Royal Dutch Shell	458 361
2	Exxon Mobil	442 851
3	Wal-Mart Stores	405 607
4	BP	367 053
5	Chevron	263 159

Global 500 2009, Fortune Magazine website

Figure 2.1 The world's largest companies by turnover (2009)

There are limitations of using turnover as the measure of size:

- An organisation's turnover often varies greatly from year to year.
- Firms that have similar turnover figures may have quite different profits, because profit margins vary between industries.
- Turnover is not necessarily an indicator of market share or market value.

Capital employed shows net investment and is compared with profit to assess profitability. It can be a difficult figure to measure – firms in the same industry may use different bases for valuing assets, which affects capital employed figures and can lead to inaccurate comparisons.

A firm's **profit** figure – such as profit before tax – may be used to indicate its size. One drawback of using this measure is that different firms in the same industry operate on different profit margins.

The number of **employees** is often a straightforward indicator to use, but firms in different industries will have differing capital/labour ratios. For example, a service sector firm is normally much more labour-intensive than one in the manufacturing sector.

	Tesco	J Sainsbury
Turnover (£) (including VAT)	59.4bn	20.4bn
Profit before tax (£)	3.1bn	466m
Capital employed (£) (balance sheet net assets)	12.995bn	4.376bn
Employees (full-time equivalent)	364 015	150 000 (estimate)

Figure 2.2 Size indicators for Tesco and Sainsbury's in 2009

KEY POINT

Firms in the same industry should be compared using the same indicator of size.

PROGRESS CHECK

1 List four ways in which the size of a business can be measured.

1 Turnover; profit; capital employed; number of employees.

2.2 Business growth

LEARNING SUMMARY

After studying this section, you should be able to:

- outline why growth is a popular business objective
- distinguish between internal and external growth
- define and distinguish between horizontal, vertical and lateral integration
- explain 'deintegration'
- describe typical problems associated with growth

Growth as a business objective

AQA **M3**
Edexcel **M4a**
OCR **M1**
WJEC **M1, M3**
CCEA **M1**

Many organisations adopt **growth** as one of their main business objectives. Most try to grow in size for specific reasons.

Global rank	Company	Market value $m	Turnover $m	Net income $m	Employees
1	PetroChina	329 260	149 303	15 144	539 168
2	Exxon Mobile	316 231	301 500	19 280	80 700
3	Microsoft	256 865	58 437	14 569	93 000

Figure 2.3 Global ranking by market capitalisation, 2010

Growth brings:

- improved survival prospects through larger market share, diversification into different markets, and greater finance
- economies of scale
- an increased feeling of status and power.

> ... we are also continuing to invest for future growth. This is a strategy that has served us well in the past; for example we entered Thailand and South Korea during the Asian economic crisis in the 1990s and emerged stronger once the economies started to recover. We are now market leader in Thailand... .
>
> *Tesco plc Annual Report and Financial Statements, 2009*

Internal and external forms of growth

AQA	**M3**
Edexcel	**M4a**
OCR	**M1, M6**
WJEC	**M1, M3**
CCEA	**M1**

An organisation can also grow by selling its products in new markets.

An organisation can grow through **internal expansion** – also known as **organic growth** – using its own resources to expand. This can be done by:

retaining its profits
↓
preserving its liquid assets
↓
using liquid assets to invest in additional fixed assets
↓
improving its productive capacity
↓
increasing its market share and growth

External growth (integration) occurs when one firm takes over – or merges with – another.

Mergers and **takeovers** remain the most popular way to grow quickly:

- A takeover occurs when one firm obtains a controlling interest in another – it does not normally involve agreement between the firms.
- A merger takes place when two (or more) firms agree to combine their assets – the firms are completely re-organised as a result of the merger.

Synergy – 'the whole is greater than the sum of its parts' – has often been used as an argument to justify taking over another business. Specific arguments include expected gains from economies of scale, and a reduced risk through diversification of products.

Types of external growth

Horizontal integration occurs when **firms making similar products or providing similar services join together**.

The car industry provides many recent examples:

- In 2009, Fiat sought to merge its car division with General Motors Europe and Chrysler to create a car manufacturer second only to Toyota in terms of production.
- In 2010, BMW owned Mini and Rolls Royce, Ford owned Volvo and a 13.4 percent share of Mazda, Peugeot owned Citroen, and Porsche owned a majority stake in Volkswagen, which in turn owned Bentley.

Horizontal integration could be the only way to substantially increase market share in saturated markets.

Such horizontal integration should result in larger-scale production and economies of scale. The new company will have greater market dominance since it now has the previous market share of the former companies.

Companies in the same industry may decide to establish links – co-operating with each other or setting up a separate business – rather than formally integrating.

Google, Sony, Intel and Logitech established links in a joint venture in 2010 by agreeing to launch a smart TV with built-in web browsing and search facilities.

These **joint ventures**:

- avoid the expense and permanent commitment of a formal merger
- help to reduce competition
- improve competitiveness by sharing resources and expertise.

Vertical integration occurs when **two firms in the same industry, but at different stages of production, amalgamate**. When a firm amalgamates with one of its outlets, for example when an oil company acquires a chain of petrol stations, it is **vertical forwards** integration. **Vertical backwards** integration occurs when a firm moves back down the production chain and obtains one of its suppliers (e.g. a food processing firm taking over an agricultural producer).

Motives for vertical integration include:

- protection – through the firm controlling its outlets or suppliers
- control – the firm can get closer control over quality, delivery and levels of supply, as well as greater control of its market
- profits – the profits of the previous supplier/outlet now belong to the firm, allowing greater flexibility on pricing and profit margins.

Lateral integration occurs when **firms in different industries and markets amalgamate**. There may be some link between the firms' products, or the conglomerate may own quite different companies.

This is also known as conglomerate or diversified integration.

The main advantage of lateral integration is **diversification**, i.e. not over-relying on a single product or market. Risk is spread over different products and markets – failure in one area should not lead to collapse. Also, companies that were in a saturated market are no longer limited by that market.

One example of lateral integration is British American Tobacco, which diversified to counter the contracting UK market for smokers' products.

The arguments against integration include the following:

- Reduced competitiveness – the growth resulting from integration may cause diseconomies of scale.
- Asset stripping – a predator company acquires another firm because it believes the market value of the firm's assets is greater than the firm's

stock market valuation. The predator then closes the bought firm to sell off the assets.

- Over-borrowing – increased financial costs (e.g. interest payments on loans taken out to finance the acquisition) may affect the company's profitability.

Deintegration

In 2010, Carphone Warehouse demerged, separating the broadband provider TalkTalk from its parent company.

A company may also reduce the scope of its activities. The main reason is financial – raising finance through selling a subsidiary, or cutting costs through the drive for efficiency. Deintegration occurs through **divestment** – selling a subsidiary that no longer fits into the company's long-term strategy – or **demerger**, where an existing company is split into two or more new groups/divisions. Reasons for demerging include a failure to achieve expected economies of scale, and the need to cut costs (e.g. in times of economic downturn).

KEY POINT

In the UK economy, takeovers and mergers are a popular way for firms to increase in size very quickly.

Problems associated with growth

AQA	**M3**
Edexcel	**M4a**
OCR	**M1, M6**
WJEC	**M1, M3**
CCEA	**M1**

There are a number of possible problems arising from growth:

- **Financial** – expansion brings pressure on a firm's liquidity, e.g. as a result of offering additional credit to encourage sales, and on its level of gearing.
- **Managerial** – although growth may have been planned efficiently by managers, they may find that this growth makes the firm's various functions/projects more difficult to co-ordinate and to control, and its communication procedures slower.
- **Organisational** – e.g. the growth from private limited to public limited requires the company to float its shares on the stock market. This brings added pressures, such as the publicity of its share price and financial analysts' opinions on performance.
- **International** – there is no guarantee that what is popular in the UK or other home market will become equally popular overseas, because of local and national differences (e.g. due to culture). Control and co-ordination also become more difficult as a result of international expansion.

KEY POINT

Diseconomies of scale often set the limits to growth.

PROGRESS CHECK

1 What is the difference between horizontal and vertical integration?

1 Horizontal: firms in the same industry and production stage join together; vertical: firms in the same industry but at different production stages join together.

2.3 Economies of scale

LEARNING SUMMARY

After studying this section, you should be able to:

- distinguish between internal and external economies of scale
- describe, with examples, how internal economies are gained by a firm
- explain, and give examples of, how diseconomies of scale typically arise

Internal economies of scale

AQA	**M3**
Edexcel	**M4a**
OCR	**M1, M6**
WJEC	**M1, M3**
CCEA	**M1**

Internal economies of scale are created when a firm's **unit cost of production falls as its output and scale of operation increases**. Because the increased volume of production does not normally increase fixed costs, these costs are spread over a larger output and as a result the average cost per unit falls.

The main types of internal economies of scale are summarised below:

- **Economies of increased dimensions** arise from an increase in size. For example, super tankers can carry many times the cargo volume compared to traditional tankers, more than offsetting their increased running costs.
- **Financial economies** arise because larger firms are assumed to be more stable financially and therefore find it easier to obtain loan capital and to negotiate lower interest rates on these loans.
- **Managerial economies** occur when growth in a firm's size allows specialist managers to be employed, bringing with them greater expertise into the firm.
- **Marketing economies** allow larger firms to buy the services of specialist marketing companies, e.g. advertising agencies – a wider range of promotion is possible, with the extra cost being spread over more sales, reducing the unit cost of promotion.
- **Purchasing economies** occur when larger firms receive bulk-buying discounts, thereby reducing unit material costs. These firms can also negotiate more favourable credit terms with suppliers.
- **Risk-bearing economies** arise when firms grow larger by increasing their product range. This diversification spreads risk across more products and markets.
- **Technical economies** arise where a larger firm is able to afford research and development, which may lead to improved products or savings from technological breakthroughs. The cost or use of efficient, sophisticated technological equipment can often only be met by larger organisations.

Larger plcs also have less expensive sources of finance available.

The division of labour principle leads to greater efficiency through specialisation.

KEY POINT

The main types of internal economies of scale are measurable financially – they can normally be quantified.

External economies of scale

AQA	**M3**
Edexcel	**M4a**
OCR	**M1, M6**
WJEC	**M1, M3**
CCEA	**M1**

External economies of scale arise from a growth in the size of the industry, and all firms in the industry benefit from them. External economies have often been found where the industry is/was concentrated in a particular area.

Japanese language courses are offered in Telford, the location of some Japanese multinationals.

These are the main types of external economies of scale:

- **Support** – local firms provide specialist services, such as car component manufacturers in the Midlands supplying the local car industry.
- **Training** – employees improve skills via local training providers who supply industry-specific courses. This skilled pool of labour is available to all firms in the area.
- **Information** – local trade associations and chambers of commerce develop and provide specialist information.

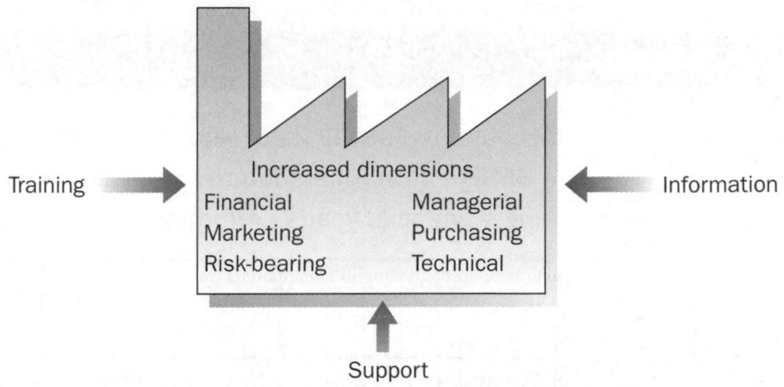

Figure 2.4 Internal and external economies of scale

Diseconomies of scale

AQA	**M3**
Edexcel	**M4a**
OCR	**M1, M6**
WJEC	**M1, M3**
CCEA	**M1**

There are practical limits to the growth that can take place. Beyond a certain point, an organisation finds that its unit costs increase – it starts to suffer from **diseconomies of scale**. The larger the firm, the more levels of hierarchy there tend to be for communication to flow through, leading to greater bureaucracy.

Communication may also become distorted, leading to a further increase in inefficiency.

Diseconomies of scale result in:

- worker dissatisfaction and poor labour relations, which in turn causes low morale, higher absenteeism, or actions such as overtime bans
- the chain of command lengthening, with decisions becoming slower to implement, which...
  - reduces efficiency and therefore raises costs
  - means a firm is slower to react to changing (e.g. market) conditions.

KEY POINT

These diseconomies are not as quantitative as economies of scale – they are more qualitative in nature.

PROGRESS CHECK

1. What is the difference between internal and external economies of scale?
2. Why must managers be aware of diseconomies of scale?

1 Internal: within the firm; external: available to all firms in the same area.
2 Increasing unit costs and inefficiency make the firm less competitive.

2.4 The small firm

LEARNING SUMMARY

After studying this section, you should be able to:

- define 'SME'
- outline typical strengths and weaknesses of small firms
- give reasons why small firms continue to exist

Defining 'small'

AQA **M1**
Edexcel **M4a**
OCR **M1**
WJEC **M1, M3**
CCEA **M1**

Other definitions exist in both the UK and the EU.

SMEs still have to prepare full statutory accounts for approval by their shareholders.

Accounting definitions of what constitutes 'small' and 'medium-sized' enterprises – **SMEs** – have been determined (Companies Act 2006) as follows, based on a single financial year's performance.

		Small	Medium-sized
Turnover	Not more than:	£6.5m	£25.9m
Balance sheet total	Not more than:	£3.26m	£12.9m
Employees	Not more than:	50	250

The value of being classed as a small or medium-sized company is that you are allowed certain filing exemptions with the registrar of companies. The accounts lodged – which will be available for public inspection – need not contain all the information that must be disclosed by large companies. As a result, an SME gains a competitive advantage from not having to disclose so much financial information to its competitors.

	Number and %	Employment (000) and %	Turnover (£m) and %
All enterprises	4 783 285 (100)	23 128 (100)	2 994 978 (100)
Employees: none*	3 545 720 (74.9)	3 888 (16.8)	231 698 (7.7)
1	192 055 (4.0)	438 (1.9)	31 323 (1.0)
2–4	617 130 (12.9)	1 868 (8.1)	210 984 (7.0)
5–9	223 585 (4.7)	1 551 (6.7)	177 975 (5.9)
10–19	116 645 (2.4)	1 612 (7.0)	190 499 (6.4)
20–49	55 415 (1.2)	1 720 (7.4)	251 897 (8.4)
50–99	17 105 (0.4)	1 189 (5.1)	171 373 (5.7)
100–199	7 985 (0.2)	1 113 (4.8)	164 183 (5.5)
200–249	1 620 (0.1)	363 (1.6)	70 893 (2.4)
250–499	3 070 (0.1)	1 061 (4.6)	269 371 (9.0)
500 or more	2 955 (0.1)	8 325 (36.0)	1 224 781 (40.9)

* 'Employees: none' comprises sole proprietorships and partnerships comprising only the self-employed owner-manager(s), and companies comprising only an employee-director.

Figure 2.5 Small and medium-sized enterprise statistics, 2008 (figures subject to rounding)

Survival of the small firm

The principle of economies of scale suggests that smaller firms should be driven out of the market as a result of their higher unit costs.

Other common competitive weaknesses include:
- reliance on a single product for survival
- a relative lack of business expertise
- limited financial resources to withstand competition or economic downturn, and to employ specialists.

There are a number of reasons why small firms continue to survive:
- They supply a local or limited market:
  - e.g. personal services such as hairdressing and plumbing
  - they operate in a particular segment of the market, e.g. domestic building extensions and improvements.
- They provide convenience (e.g. the 'corner shop').
- They concentrate on specialist or luxury items with limited demand, e.g. specialist firms for coin and stamp collectors.
- They work in areas where growth is naturally limited, e.g. the market for personal services.
- The owners might lack ambition, have a desire to remain in charge, or wish to avoid risk.
- Vertical 'disintegration' takes place, i.e. larger companies sub-contract out to small firms because they find it unprofitable to do the work themselves.
- They are attracted by entrepreneurship:
  - Some small firms are established by people wanting to work for themselves.
  - Small firms give people who dislike working for a large organisation the chance to work for themselves.

Two related factors are the increasing popularity of franchise operations, and the growth in the number of self-employed people.

Small firms also have a number of typical strengths that help them to survive. They are often quicker to respond to market forces, the communication between management and staff is normally more efficient, and labour relations tend to be good.

Encouraging survival

The growth of the small-firms sector has been encouraged by policies that attempt to stimulate the economy, and encourage entrepreneurism and employment.

The government supports the small-firms sector through policies attempting to:
- reduce bureaucracy – cutting statistical and other information required by government authorities
- help with taxation – e.g. by lowering corporation tax levels for small firms, and establishing a turnover threshold for VAT registration
- provide assistance – e.g. through various websites and other initiatives such as Business Link, which has web pages dedicated to helping small firms, and support networks such as Business Innovation centres

- encourage entrepreneurship in disadvantaged communities (e.g. through the Phoenix Fund 2000–2008) and in other contexts, such as the Enterprise Finance Guarantee scheme, which provides lenders to SMEs a government guarantee for 75 percent of their loan
- support EU schemes for small and medium-sized firms, e.g. the EU's Structural Funds (through its regional policy).

KEY POINT

Profit maximisation is a less important business objective for many small-scale entrepreneurs, who are often more concerned to stay independent.

PROGRESS CHECK

1 What competitive weaknesses do small firms often have?

1 No economies of scale; reliance on a single product; limited expertise and resources.

Sample questions and model answers

1. Steve is thinking of going into business on his own. He realises that this will be a major challenge for him, and is aware of the high failure rate of small firms.

Advise Steve on how small firms continue to survive in a competitive economy such as the UK. **(6)**

The examiner is likely to expect you to show your knowledge of the specific qualities of small firms, and these are relevant examples.

There are several reasons why Steve's small firm could succeed and why small firms in general continue to survive. First, the firm may supply a local or limited market, such as providing a personal service like hairdressing or plumbing. A small firm often provides convenience for its customers (such as the local 'corner shop'), or it may operate in a small segment of the market, such as domestic building extensions and improvements. It can compete successfully because the demand for its product or service is likely to be limited, for example where it is in a specialist or luxury market.

This section is related well to Steve's situation, recognising that it is not only the product or market, but could be the nature of the owner, that influences the size of the business.

The policy of some small business owners is to deliberately stay small. This may be due to reasons such as a lack of ambition, the desire to remain in charge, or the wish to avoid what is seen as unnecessary risk. As an owner, Steve may be attracted by the nature of entrepreneurship - if this is the case, the level of profits will not be as important to him as it is to a larger firm having external demands (e.g. shareholder expectations) to meet.

It can be useful to provide a summary of the overall situation.

Steve also needs to realise that small firms have a number of typical strengths which help them to survive. They are quicker to respond to market forces, communication between all levels tends to be efficient, and labour relations are often very good.

2. How might economies of scale be useful to a vehicle manufacturer? **(6)**

This answer starts with a simple definition of the term, which shows understanding that it is more than 'costs fall' (the word 'unit' is vital here). Examples are also given.

'Economies of scale' refers to the unit cost savings that are made as firms grow in size. Although total costs will increase, these are proportionately lower than the increase in output, because fixed costs do not automatically increase as output increases. Economies of scale may be internal to the firm, e.g. bulk-buying discounts which lower the price of materials, or external (e.g. improved provision of local training).

This section of the answer applies knowledge well to the context (vehicle manufacturer). Note how reference is made clearly to this context, i.e. 'new machinery' and 'advertising of the vehicles'.

An example of an internal economy of scale from which a vehicle manufacturer might benefit is the purchasing economy mentioned above. Other likely economies are financial (lower interest rates on loans for new machinery), marketing (spreading the cost of advertising over higher output can make TV advertising of the vehicles cost-effective), managerial (specialists in vehicle research, development, manufacture and sale can be employed), and technical (shop-floor employees can use specially developed machinery and equipment, making production more efficient).

Exam practice question

1 Demon Drinks plc makes and sells soft drinks, including a range of seven fruit drinks made in three factories spread throughout the UK. These fruit drinks are new to the market, having been launched within the last year. As yet, the drinks are not selling well and the directors of Demon Drinks plc are disappointed with the results. They propose closing two of the factories and concentrating all production in the third factory, which will be modernised and expanded.

The directors of Demon Drinks plc wish to diversify into other aspects of food and leisure, and have identified a business – LeisurePleasure – that owns and operates a number of leisure centres in the UK, which they would like to acquire.

(a) Describe **one** economy of scale likely to be gained by:

Demon Drinks plc **(4)**

LeisurePleasure **(4)**

(b) Explain how closing two of the factories and concentrating production in a modernised and expanded single factory is likely to affect Demon Drinks plc's costs. **(6)**

(c) If the directors go ahead with their plans to acquire LeisurePleasure, explain the type of integration that will occur. **(4)**

3 Business goals and strategy

The following topics are covered in this chapter:

- Goals and objectives
- Strategic planning
- Strategic analysis
- Corporate culture
- Change

3.1 Goals and objectives

LEARNING SUMMARY

After studying this section, you should be able to:

- outline the purpose and nature of a mission statement
- explain the value of corporate objectives to a firm
- define and describe 'SMART' objectives

Mission statements and corporate objectives

AQA	**M3, M4**
Edexcel	**M1, M4a**
OCR	**M1, M7**
WJEC	**M1, M3**
CCEA	**M3**

An organisation sets objectives in order to achieve long-term strategic plans.

Mission statements

The **mission statement** outlines why a business exists, stating its overall aim and purpose.

The mission statement is then translated into corporate objectives.

The purpose of the mission statement is to:

- communicate the objectives and values of the organisation
- influence employee behaviour and attitudes
- help in achieving congruence ('harmony' or 'balance' in the organisation).

KEY POINT

Mission statements are influenced by the organisation's culture and structure, the nature of its competition and markets, and the beliefs and attitudes of its owners.

The Body Shop's mission statement is on the next page.

Our reason for being is to:

- Dedicate our business to the pursuit of social and environmental change.
- Creatively balance the financial and human needs of our stakeholders: employees, franchisees, customers, suppliers and shareholders.
- Courageously ensure that our business is ecologically sustainable, meeting the needs of the present without compromising the future.
- Meaningfully contribute to local, national and international communities in which we trade by adopting a code of conduct which ensures care, honesty, fairness and respect.
- Passionately campaign for the protection of the environment, to defend human rights, and against animal testing within the cosmetics industry.
- Tirelessly work to narrow the gap between principle and practice, while making fun, passion and care part of our daily lives.

The Body Shop website, Values Report 2009

Mission statements – and business objectives generally – are influenced by the organisation's stakeholders.

A board of directors is an example of stakeholders having both high power (through control of the company) and high interest (e.g. through share ownership).

According to Mendelow's model (1991), stakeholders can be rated as a result of their:

- power – i.e. their ability to influence the organisation
- interest – i.e. their willingness to influence the organisation (which depends on their degree of interest in it).

A stakeholder with high power and high interest will be more influential than one with low power and/or low interest.

KEY POINT

Stakeholder power **×** Stakeholder interest **=** Stakeholder influence

Corporate objectives

Corporate objectives are set and often made measurable when developed into more detailed functional objectives, which are then expanded into individual objectives for employees to achieve. The objectives may be **commercial** in nature – for private sector firms – or **social**, often set by public sector and voluntary sector organisations. Such objectives support business **decision-making** – deciding between alternatives or on a course of action, and taking into account factors such as the level of risk.

Corporate objective	***Value to the firm***
Increase market share and become the market leader	*Greater control over market price, easier to get new products accepted*
Maximise profits	*Pleases shareholders and improves share price*
Ensure long-term growth and stability	*Economies of scale; helps protect the company from being taken over*
Stay a market leader through technological innovation	*Remain competitive in the market*
Diversify in order to develop new markets	*Exploit profitable markets; spread the risk by operating in different markets*

Businesses set measurable objectives to:

- monitor progress against targets
- help with decision making
- motivate employees
- co-ordinate the business functions.

SMART objectives

SMART objectives need to be set in terms of targets.

A SMART objective must be:

- **Specific** – state what it seeks to achieve
- **Measurable** against some yardstick, e.g. 'we will increase our total exports to the rest of the EU by 10 percent this financial year'
- **Attainable** (or achievable) – it must represent a target that is possible to achieve
- **Realistic** in relation to available resources
- **Time-related** – a time limit or deadline is set.

KEY POINT

Achievement of corporate objectives can be measured by appraising employees and by adopting a management by objectives (MBO) approach.

PROGRESS CHECK

1. What is a mission statement?
2. List the five elements of SMART.

1 A statement of why the business exists – its overall aim and purpose.
2 Specific; Measurable; Attainable; Realistic; Time-related.

3.2 Strategic planning

LEARNING SUMMARY

After studying this section, you should be able to:

- describe what is meant by 'strategy'
- outline typical key features of business strategy

'Strategy'

AQA	**M4**
Edexcel	**M1, M4a**
OCR	**M1, M7**
WJEC	**M3**
CCEA	**M3**

Henry Mintzberg has suggested that different organisations use 'strategy' to mean different things.

'Strategy' can be one of five Ps:

1. **A plan** – for finance, human resources, etc.
2. **A ploy** – a short-term strategy with very limited objectives.
3. **A pattern of behaviour** – where managers consistently act the same way (e.g. buying patterns, pricing behaviour).
4. **A position in respect to others** – how the firm obtains and then defends its position in the market (e.g. using its reputation for safety or good service).
5. **A perspective** – the core beliefs of the people running the organisation.

Professor Chandler of Harvard Business School defined 'strategy' as follows.

> The determination of the basic long-term goals and objectives of an enterprise, and the adoption of courses of action and the allocation of resources necessary for carrying out these goals.

The key features of business strategy are therefore:

- **long-term goals** being determined
- **courses of action** being adopted
- **resources** being allocated.

When carrying out their strategic planning, managers conduct both an internal audit and an external audit for an organisation. The overall audit is often built around a **SWOT** analysis, with the external audit having a **STEEPLE** ('STEP' or 'PEST') focus.

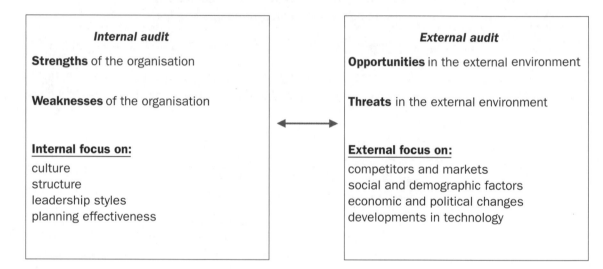

Internal audit		***External audit***
Strengths of the organisation		**Opportunities** in the external environment
Weaknesses of the organisation	↔	**Threats** in the external environment
Internal focus on: culture structure leadership styles planning effectiveness		**External focus on:** competitors and markets social and demographic factors economic and political changes developments in technology

KEY POINT

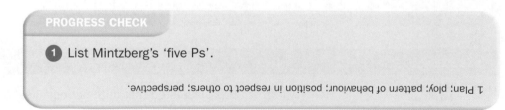

Other influences on strategic planning include Ansoff's matrix, investment appraisal and the use of decision trees.

PROGRESS CHECK

1 List Mintzberg's 'five Ps'.

1 Plan; ploy; pattern of behaviour; position in respect to others; perspective.

3.3 Strategic analysis

LEARNING SUMMARY

After studying this section, you should be able to:

- describe the nature and relevance of Porter's matrix
- outline Porter's framework of how to analyse the competitive environment
- explain the nature and purpose of benchmarking
- discuss the likely relevance of contingency planning to a business
- carry out decision tree analysis, commenting on the results and limitations of this analysis

Porter's matrix

AQA **M4**
Edexcel **M4a**
WJEC **M3**

'Value added' is the difference in the financial value of the output (the finished product) compared with the financial value of its inputs.

Professor Michael Porter of the Harvard Business School developed a generic strategy framework in which he argues that competitive advantage results from selecting the strategy that best fits an organisation's competitive environment. Once this is done, **value-adding** activities can be organised to support the chosen strategy.

Porter identifies three main options for a firm:

1. **Cost leadership** – being the lowest cost producer of a product.
2. **Differentiation** – creating consumer perception that the product is 'better' than those of competitors.
3. **Focus** – concentrating on either cost leadership or differentiation in markets/segments.

This analysis suggests that the entrepreneur must decide whether to sell differentiated products at premium prices, or to produce at a lower cost than competitors, and also whether to target the whole market or concentrate on a niche or segment.

KEY POINT

Porter's matrix framework summarises two key strategic decisions:

1. Should the scope of the organisation's strategy be broad or narrow?
2. Should the strategy focus on cost leadership or on differentiation?

Strategic scope	Strategic advantage: *Low cost*	Strategic advantage: *Differentiation*
Broad scope (whole market is targeted)	**COST LEADERSHIP**	**DIFFERENTIATION**
Narrow scope (a single segment is targeted)	**COST FOCUS**	**DIFFERENTIATED FOCUS**

Figure 3.1 Porter's generic strategy matrix

Porter argues that the best competitive situation is to be based in one of the four segments.

Many Japanese car manufacturers have successfully adopted this approach.

Limitations to his framework have been suggested:

- Businesses can succeed by adopting a 'hybrid' strategy, which combines elements of differentiation with cost- and price-competitiveness.
- Cost leadership does not guarantee product sales, because buying decisions can be made on the basis of the product rather than its price.

Analysing the competitive environment

Porter also developed a five-point framework for analysing the nature and extent of competition within an industry (1980).

He suggests there are five competitive forces a firm can analyse to determine the extent of its competition:

1. The threat of **new entrants** to the industry – this will vary according to the following barriers to entry:
   - the capital investment required
   - the degree of brand loyalty from the market's consumers
   - the economies of scale available
   - the amount of resistance from existing firms in the industry.
2. The threat of **substitute products** – the degree to which the substitute product's features (e.g. price, performance) match those in the industry, and how willing consumers are to switch to the substitute.
3. The power of **buyers or customers** – this depends on their number and the costs they face in switching to substitutes.
4. The power of **suppliers** – for example, the number and size of firms in the market and the degree of brand loyalty customers have to these firms' products.
5. **Rivalry** among firms in the industry – e.g. the level of price competition and non-price competition.

KEY POINT

It is important for a firm to repeat this 'five-forces' analysis – because of changes taking place in the industry – to help it gain a competitive advantage over others.

Benchmarking

AQA	M4	CCEA	M1
OCR	M6		
WJEC	M2		

The **benchmarking** process seeks out 'best practice' from other organisations, compares it with the firm's own practice, and therefore leads to an improvement in the firm's practice. It may be based on a simple comparative analysis, but is often used as a much wider **performance improvement tool** for the firm.

Benchmarking can be traced to the 1980s when Xerox sent a team to Japan to discover why Canon could sell its photocopiers at a lower price.

Benchmarking measures a firm's performance against the most competitive industry standards. By doing so, a firm focuses more on external competition than on its internal progress, and can adopt industry best practice.

Most benchmarking is external, but it can be carried out internally, e.g. where a multinational has a number of similar units and operations.

A typical benchmarking process involves the following steps:

1. Identify the subject for benchmarking.
2. Examine your own procedures.
3. Select the elements to be benchmarked.
4. Identify a benchmarking organisation.
5. Collect data on the organisation.
6. Undertake a comparative analysis of the data.
7. Compare results.
8. Plan changes to the elements/procedures.

Strengths and weaknesses of benchmarking

Research has suggested that the benefits of benchmarking include:

- setting more meaningful and realistic targets
- having an early warning of competitive disadvantage
- increased motivation – through involvement in the benchmarking process, and team work.

The limitations of benchmarking include the difficulty in selecting suitable performance measures and the most appropriate benchmark 'partner', and an inability to obtain suitable information for the benchmark process.

KEY POINT

Benchmarking can play an important role in strategic analysis, but its value depends on being able to choose a suitable benchmark partner and on obtaining relevant benchmark data.

Contingency planning

AQA	M4	WJEC	M4
Edexcel	M4a	CCEA	M3

In 2010, BA used contingency planning to try and counter industrial action taken by cabin crew.

An important part of planning and strategic analysis is to ask 'what if?' questions. **Contingency planning** encourages managers to consider alternative courses of action if an emergency or unforeseen event occurs. Examples of such crises include environmental disasters, selling dangerous products or contaminated foodstuffs, and the collapse of a major customer/market.

Any or all of an organisation's major business functions may be affected by a crisis. Staff representing each function should therefore be involved in contingency planning. Being involved in this way improves staff motivation, but illustrates the fact that contingency planning can be expensive.

If a crisis does occur, an organisation's public relations department is likely to manage it.

If an organisation's management recognises the value of contingency planning, the normal procedure for contingency planning is to:

- outline and examine all possible **crisis scenarios**
- **plan** for each crisis
- **test** the plan, e.g. by running a computer simulation.

KEY POINT

A firm's managers should measure the expected cost of contingency planning against (a) its likely effectiveness; and (b) the cost of not having suitable plans if a disaster occurs.

PROGRESS CHECK

1. What three options are identified in Porter's matrix analysis?
2. State the five points in Porter's competitive environment framework.

1 Cost leadership; differentiation; focus.
2 Threat of new entrants; threat of substitute products; power of buyers/customers; power of suppliers; industry rivalries.

Decision tree analysis

Edexcel	**M4a**	WJEC	**M4**
OCR	**M7**	CCEA	**M3**

Decision tree analysis creates tree-like diagrams to represent business situations where a series of decisions need to be made. Each decision has its own 'branch' on the tree, the branch leading to further branches that represent the outcomes of the decision.

The tree shows all possible outcomes (alternative courses of action) that can be taken under all conditions.

Each possible outcome is given:

- an estimated **monetary value**
- an estimated **probability** of it happening.

These values, weighted by their probabilities, are calculated as **expected values** (EVs). The decision taker will select the line of action that results in the highest EV (the 'expectation').

Constructing the decision tree

Here is a question with a step-by-step construction of a decision tree.

In the summer, Laura runs an ice-cream van. She finds that traffic congestion occasionally causes her delays and affects her sales, but she has the option of changing route to avoid the delay. Cold weather also affects her sales.

Laura now has the chance to rent, in her local town centre, a small kiosk where she can sell her ice cream. She knows that sales from the kiosk will also be affected by cold weather. Laura cannot run the kiosk and continue with her ice-cream van. Should she rent the kiosk?

1. **Start with the main decision**
   Laura's first decision – ice-cream van or kiosk? – is recorded ('D1').

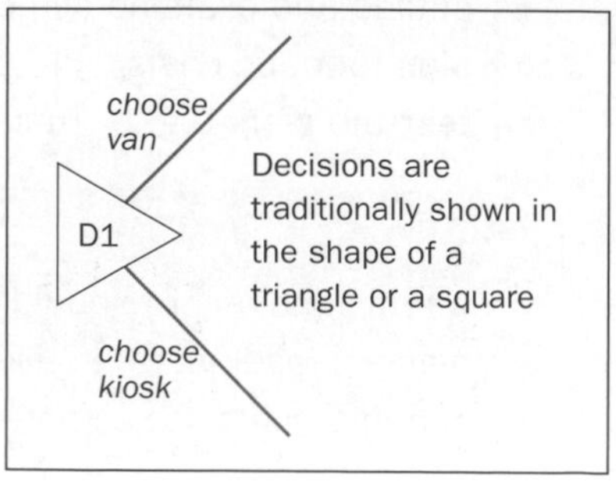

2. **Construct event circles**

Alternatives extending from this decision are now shown as event circles (and £ values are also recorded later in these circles).

Laura faces two alternatives with the van. First, whether there will be a traffic delay or not (event circle E1). If there is no delay (E3), the second alternative – warm or cold weather – can be plotted. If there is a delay, however, Laura has a second decision to make (D2) – this branch is developed later.

The only alternative Laura faces with the kiosk (E2) relates to the weather, and so this can be plotted.

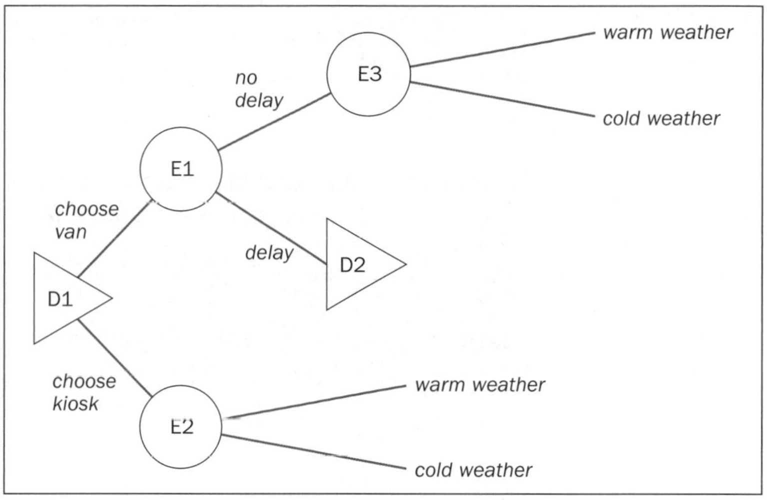

If there is a traffic delay, Laura must make her second decision – change the route or stay on the same route? This decision is plotted and the resulting event circles (E4 and E5) are given the alternatives of warm and cold weather.

The range of alternatives for Laura with her ice-cream van is therefore:

- no delay, with either warm weather or cold weather
- delay, but stay on same route, with warm weather or cold weather
- delay and change route, with either warm or cold weather.

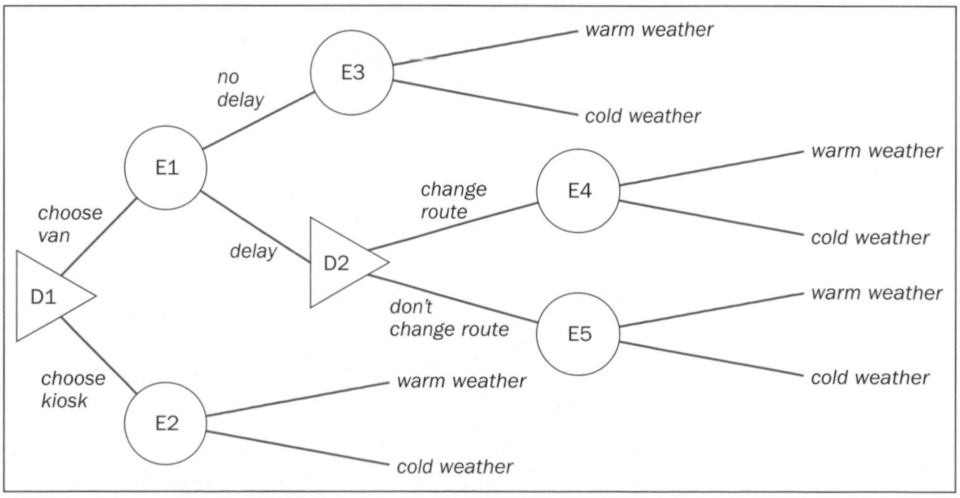

3. **Record the probabilities**

Laura believes that there is a 75 percent chance of any day being warm. She also thinks the probability of being delayed in the van on any one day is 30 percent. The weather probabilities (0.75 and 0.25) and the chance of traffic delay (0.70 and 0.30) are recorded.

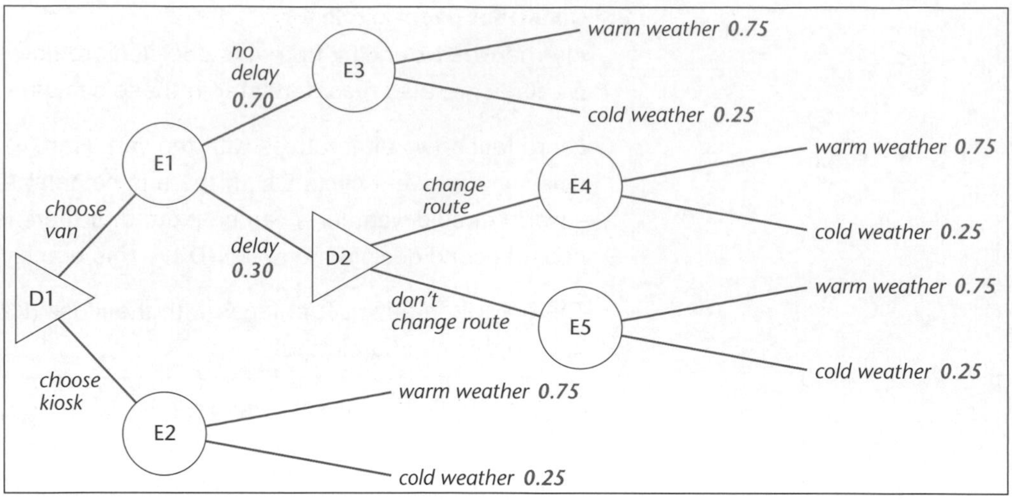

4. **Plot the values and calculate the results (the EVs)**
   Laura's estimated daily sales are as follows:

		£
Warm days	van, without experiencing any delays	140
	van, with delays and a change of route	110
	van, with delays and not changing route	100
	kiosk	125
Cold days	van, without experiencing any delays	90
	van, with delays and a change of route	75
	van, with delays and not changing route	65
	kiosk	80

Working from the right, the financial values are plotted and multiplied by the probability score.

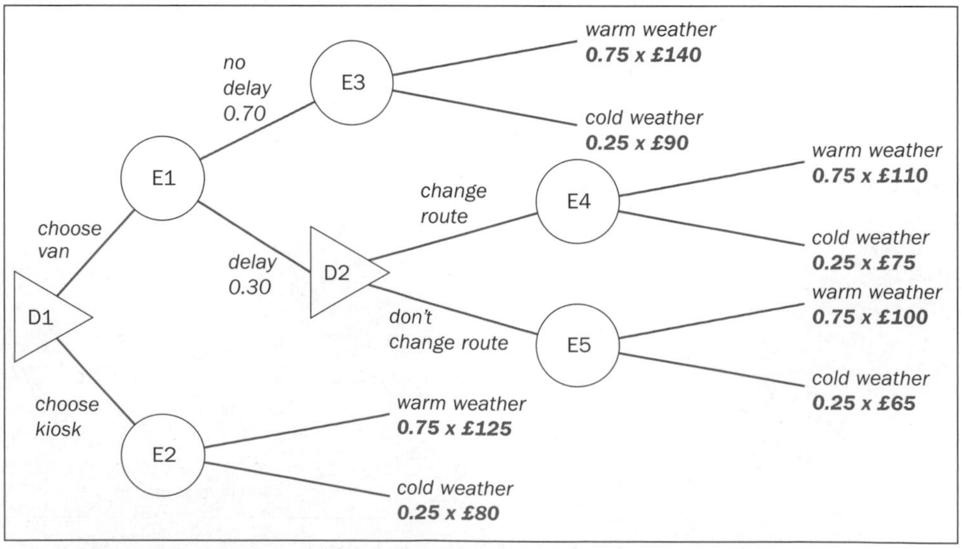

Kiosk calculation:

EV for E2 = (0.75 × £125) £93.75 + (0.25 × £80) £20 = £113.75

Van calculations:

EV for E3 (no delay) =

(0.75 × £140) £105 + (0.25 × £90) £22.50 = £127.50

EV for E4 (delay, change route) =
(0.75 × £110) £82.50 + (0.25 × £75) £18.75 = £101.25
EV for E5 (delay, no change) =
(0.75 × £100) £75 + (0.25 × £65) £16.25 = £91.25

D2 (change route or not) calculations show that Laura would decide to change the route, because of the higher sales income. This figure is therefore used to calculate E1.

E1 = (E3 £127.50 × 0.7) + (E4 £101.25 × 0.3) = £89.25 + £30.38 = £119.63

5. Show the calculation results in the decision tree, and make the decision

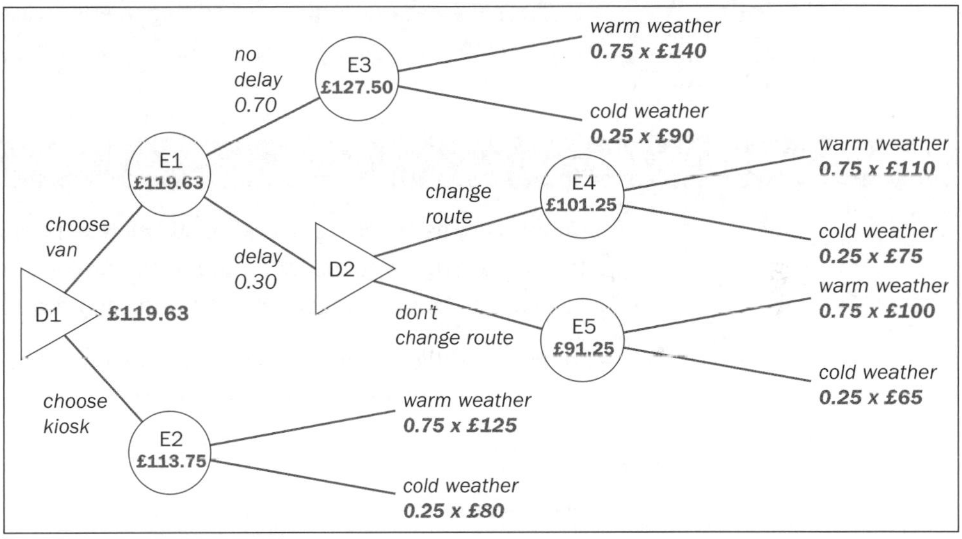

The calculations show that Laura should continue operating her ice-cream van. The 'choose van' option is worth £119.63 sales, whereas the 'choose kiosk' option is worth only £113.75 sales.

The value of decision trees

Examples of suitable use include deciding whether to buy or hire equipment, to develop and sell a new product, or to build a new factory.

Decision trees are suited to situations where there is a **logical sequence of events** or alternatives that are followed in **conditions of uncertainty**. They are most effective where a similar past event (e.g. launch of a product) provides quantitative information that can give **realistic estimates** for the new situation.

Decision tree analysis requires management to:

- allocate probabilities to events occurring, which makes them think logically and in quantitative terms
- set out these events in a logical manner, which assists their planning
- consider the expected costs of failure as well as of success.

The limitations of decision tree analysis are that:

- it cannot take full account of the uncertainty of business
- the information on which the tree is based is incomplete or inaccurate
- it ignores qualitative aspects of the decision.

As a result, the tree may give an inaccurate and incomplete overall picture.

KEY POINT

Constructing a decision tree encourages a full and logical analysis of a problem – covering all eventualities – before undertaking a project.

PROGRESS CHECK

1. List the steps in constructing a decision tree.

1 Record the main decision; construct event circles; record probabilities; plot values and calculate results; show the results in the tree; make the decision.

3.4 Corporate culture

LEARNING SUMMARY

After studying this section, you should be able to:

- discuss the nature of different management styles
- explain the term 'organisational culture' and its determinants

Management styles

AQA	**M4**
Edexcel	**M1**
OCR	**M2**
WJEC	**M2, M3**
CCEA	**M2**

Theorists such as Herzberg and Maslow analyse people's needs, rather than the job they are doing, by focusing on the social environment of the organisation. Such analyses help management carry out their functions efficiently.

Managers have four traditional functions, which are carried out within a framework of **management style** and **organisational culture**:

1. Planning.
2. Controlling.
3. Directing.
4. Organising.

Types of management style

The **democratic manager** type will guide and advise, but will allow the group or individual to make decisions. This style is more closely associated with the human relations theorists, notably McGregor's Theory Y approach.

Typical examples include many small firms, where the emphasis is on communication and employee involvement.

This management style is found in organisations that have:

- efficient and open communication procedures
- limited chains of command
- routine delegation.

The **autocratic manager** type might allow some individual and group involvement, but makes the final decision. Concentrating decisions in the hands of senior management encourages a 'top-down' centralised structure, influenced more by the work of classical theorists (such as Taylor). Traditionally, examples include state-operated services such as the police and armed forces.

The laissez-faire approach can be criticised if the manager avoids controlling and directing.

The **laissez-faire** ('let it be') manager type chooses not to interfere in the work of the group. This style of management can operate successfully if the firm has cohesive groups prepared to work together to achieve common objectives.

Another way to analyse management styles is to identify extreme situations. For example, an organisation's management might be seen in terms of the dimensions set out on the next page.

Autocratic	◀——▶	**Democratic**
Mechanistic (follows fixed procedures and routines)	◀——▶	**Organic** ('growing' as the organisation alters)
Entrepreneurial (proactive – uses new situations and events)	◀——▶	**Conservative** (reacting as and when necessary)

KEY POINT

Influences on management style include personal preferences, the amount of management training undertaken, the level of awareness of different management styles, the nature of the tasks being managed, the pace of change and the organisation's culture.

Organisational culture

AQA **M4** WJEC **M3**
Edexcel **M4a** CCEA **M4**

A '**culture**' is created from various beliefs, ideals, norms and values. Each organisation has a culture in much the same way that people represent different cultures.

An organisation's culture is expressed in:
- the actions of the people who make up the organisation
- the organisation's rules, procedures, structures and systems.

Culture is important to an organisation because it influences all of the organisation's activities. It has a particular influence on employee **motivation** (and therefore on output, quality and productivity), the **image/appeal** of the organisation (e.g. as an employer), its degree of **creativity**, and the nature and quality of **labour relations**.

Types of organisational culture

Four distinct organisational cultures can be identified: power culture, role culture, task culture and person culture. These are shown in the table on the next page.

Organisational cultures can also be classified as:
- **hierarchical** cultures – these are based on the formal hierarchy and chain of command and often have a 'mistake-free' philosophy
- **growth** cultures – these are associated with matrix- or product-based organisations that encourage a market-based approach
- **goal-oriented** cultures – where goals are followed 'at all costs'.

Determinants of an organisation's culture

In addition to management style, other influences on the culture adopted by an organisation include:
- the personal philosophy of the organisation's creators
- the type of industry in which the organisation is based
- the organisation's degree of dependence on capital/technology or on people
- the organisation's geographical location
- the organisation's structure ('tall' or 'flat').

Culture	Features	Advantage	Disadvantage
Power culture	• Mainly associated with small entrepreneurial organisations • Relies on a central source of power delegating to a surrounding 'web'	Few layers in the hierarchy, with wide spans of control	Control remains centralised at the top
Role culture	• Exists in organisations structured by function and specialism • Consists of chains of command and lines of authority	Roles, status and positions are known	Relies heavily on rules and procedures
Task culture	• Associated with matrix and project-based structures • Decentralised and flexible (team-based) organisations	Effective where flexibility and teamwork are important	Control may be difficult
Person culture	• Typical of small professional organisations • Clusters of people operate in a minimal structure	Creativity is encouraged, with a quick response time	Can be difficult to set targets and monitor achievement

Theorists such as R Harrison and C Handy argue that these organisational cultures exist.

Culture and conflict

A culture that is unsuitable for a firm and its employees – e.g. where a merger or privatisation has led to changes in the culture – will result in low levels of motivation, and potential **conflict** between the management and workforce.

The work of McGregor highlights the potential problems when a group of employees has one set of beliefs or expectations, and managers have a different set. If employees have Theory X attitudes but their managers expect Theory Y attitudes, the resultant delegation and involvement is likely to produce poor quality output and misdirected effort. Managers who use Theory X approaches with groups wanting to operate on a Theory Y basis will find that output and morale will again be adversely affected.

An organisation's culture helps determine the level of resistance to change.

KEY POINT

When changing an organisation's culture, managers must communicate the nature of these changes to other employees, and provide adequate training so that the employees can cope with new systems arising from these changes.

PROGRESS CHECK

1. How is an organisation's culture expressed?
2. Name four types of organisational culture.

1 Through its rules, procedures and people.
2 Power; role; task; person.

3.5 Change

LEARNING SUMMARY

After studying this section, you should be able to:

- give examples of how change affects organisations
- explain why people typically resist change
- discuss how change might be managed

Coping with change

AQA	**M4**
Edexcel	**M4a**
OCR	**M7**
WJEC	**M1, M3**
CCEA	**M4**

All organisations are affected by **change** taking place. Most causes of change are **external** to the organisation, and typically include the following.

New...	Examples
Legislation	Data Protection Act 1998; Companies Act 2006
Technology	Apple i-products; environmentally-disposable plastics
Owners	Volkswagen owning Skoda; Wal-Mart taking over Asda
Competition	Football pools and the National Lottery
Tastes	Organic and vegetarian foods; clothing fashions
Markets	Eastern European (former communist) countries now in the EU, e.g. Czech Republic; growth of the mobile telephone market

How change affects organisations

There are three key questions associated with business change:

1. Has it been **anticipated** by management?
2. If so, has it been **planned for** by management?
3. To what extent is it **controllable** by management?

Some unforeseen change can sometimes be anticipated, e.g. by undertaking contingency planning.

The most difficult form of change to cope with is change that is unforeseeable, and therefore uncontrollable. Examples of unforeseeable change include the financial markets, social and demographic trends, legislation and the actions of competitors.

Figure 3.2, on the next page, illustrates the change in consumer spending over time. Such changes have had a major impact on firms in the industries shown in the figure.

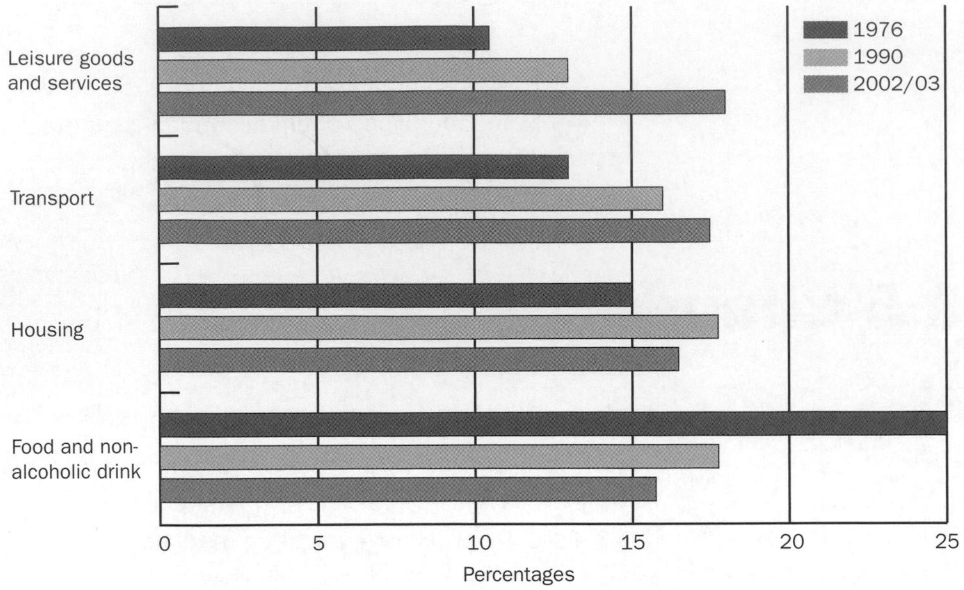

Source: ONS

Figure 3.2 Changes in spending patterns (United Kingdom)

This often occurs when a new chief executive and/or management team is appointed.

Change also takes place **internally**, e.g. when a firm decides to restructure its operations. The firm may restructure and alter its objectives if its management style or corporate culture changes.

Areas of business change can be analysed under headings taken from – or similar to – STEEPLE.

Economic	e.g. changing levels of unemployment and skills; balance of payments problems; single European currency
Legislative	e.g. new EU Directives; UK consumer protection laws; human rights legislation
Demographic	e.g. growth in the number of over 65s; fewer young people entering the job market
Technological	e.g. increased computer power; changed production processes
Social	e.g. increasing leisure time; greater awareness of health and fitness

There has been considerable change in customer shopping patterns over the last year as people have felt the need to manage household budgets more carefully.

J Sainsbury's plc Annual Report 2009

An example of change – particularly as a result of technological and social influences – is in the banking sector of the economy. Banks have had to respond to changes in society, e.g. customers' increased use of debit card transactions at the expense of cheques (Figure 3.3 on the next page shows trends such as the fall in cheque transaction volumes). Banks have also introduced change, for example cost-cutting methods – such as reducing their number of branches – and encouraging the greater use of Internet banking, which is also cheaper for the banks.

	1999	2009
Wages paid in cash	1 in 8	1 in 20
Transactions using cash	73%	59%
Cash spending in pubs	90%	40%
Debit card spending	£65bn	£264bn
Personal transactions using cheques	6%	2%

Payments Council statistics, 2010

Figure 3.3 Payment methods in 1999 compared to 2009

KEY POINT

PESTEL analysis is closely associated with the notion of change.

The pace of change

Step change and **incremental change** are the two main categories for the pace of change. They are influenced by:

- how urgent the need for change is
- what **inertia** there is in the firm's corporate culture – how sluggish or inactive it is.

Step change occurs rapidly – here, the benefit is that the firm responds quickly to change, but the speed can cause disruption and discontent amongst the staff. Incremental change takes place in stages over a longer time period. The change is therefore phased in more gradually, but the relative delay in making changes may cost the firm its competitive advantage.

Step change at Tesco
We have made a step-change in our work on climate change and environmental responsibility by taking clear leadership in these vital areas. In 2007, we set ambitious targets to reduce emissions in our own buildings....

Tesco Annual Report, 2009

Managing change

AQA **M4**
Edexcel **M4a**
OCR **M7**
WJEC **M1, M3**
CCEA **M4**

All people – entrepreneurs, managers, employees, suppliers and customers – may resist change.

Resisting change might be due to:

- **personal** reasons
  - fear of the unknown
  - a low tolerance of change
  - prejudice
  - dislike of the methods being used to implement the change
- **communication** reasons
  - not being given adequate reasons for the change
  - mistrusting or misunderstanding the reasons given

- **social** reasons
  - existing satisfaction with present colleagues, equipment and systems
  - initial dislike of new colleagues, equipment or systems
  - dislike of outside interference
- **economic** reasons
  - lack of belief in ability to acquire the new skills needed
  - an increased fear of unemployment.

Figure 3.4 summarises the requirements for the effective management of change.

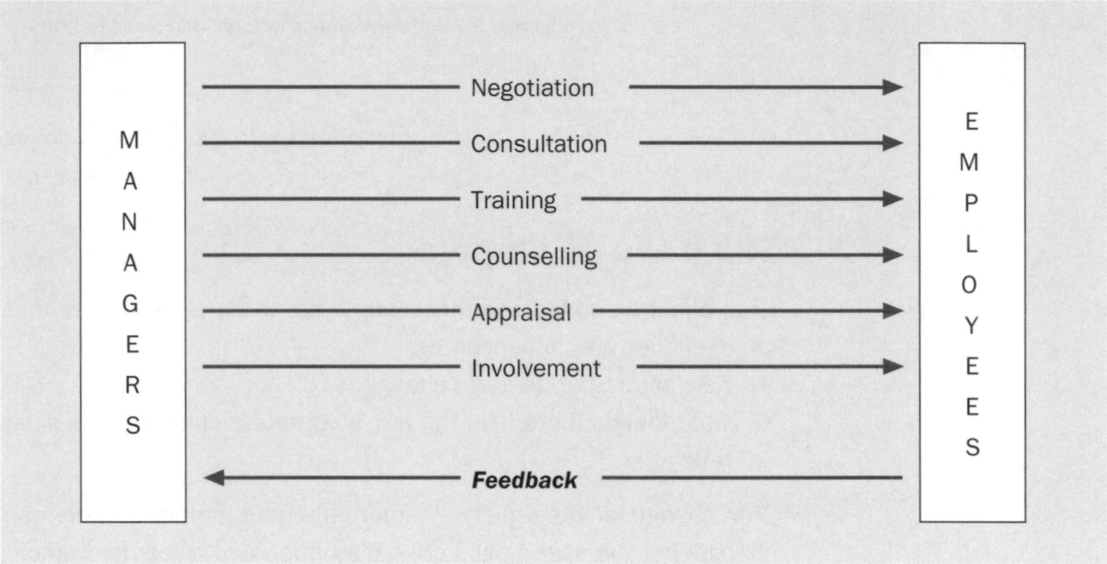

Figure 3.4 Managing change

Managers must:

- ensure that full and clear information is given about:
  - reasons for the change
  - method(s) proposed for implementing the change
  - likely disruptions to existing work routines
  - progress of implementation of the change
- give employees their own opportunity to evaluate the possible effects of the proposed change
- establish working parties, quality circles and training routines for all staff affected by the change
- provide a system to monitor the implementation, which allows employees to give feedback
- continue to monitor the effects of change once the new systems have been fully implemented.

KEY POINT

Managing change involves planning, preparing for, and implementing it. Once the change has been implemented, it will need evaluating.

The chances of success

The leadership style adopted may affect whether a change is successfully managed. Involvement of staff, e.g. through McGregor's Theory Y approach, should increase motivation levels and ensure communication takes place.

KEY POINT

The greater the level of employee participation and involvement in the process, the more effectively change will be implemented.

PROGRESS CHECK

1. State four reasons why people may resist change.

1 Personal; communication; economic; social.

Sample question and model answer

1. O'Brien Ltd is a company in the food processing industry. It is a market leader in the manufacture of processed dairy products such as cheese and yoghurt.

At a recent board meeting, the directors discussed the contents of this article (extract below).

> **Difficulties at Depps**
> Depps Ltd, one of the leading suppliers of processed foodstuffs, was today found guilty of supplying contaminated products to Britain's leading supermarkets...
>
> ... At the press conference, the Managing Director for Depps Ltd, Jules Binoche, apologised but maintained that there had never been any danger to public health.
>
> When asked how Depps Ltd would recover from this setback, he stated: "Our contingency planning is robust, and we remain confident that we shall soon re-establish ourselves as a leading player in the marketplace..."

At the O'Brien Ltd board meeting there was substantial discussion concerning the nature and value of contingency planning. The Production Director commented: "In some ways, this Depps business will be a boost to us, and we have spare productive capacity if necessary. However, in the light of the food contamination problem faced by Depps, we need to review our own contingency planning. I'm concerned that our plans don't consider such an eventuality in sufficient detail."

The Sales Director replied: "There's hardly any need to panic, given our excellent track record in food production. Where's the problem? The bottom line for me is that, whilst it's all very well to talk about reviewing, developing and improving our own contingency planning, this contingency planning business is very expensive, and there's no guarantee that it will work. Why bother?"

(a) What is 'contingency planning'? **(4)**

Contingency planning occurs when an organisation such as O'Brien Ltd prepares for unplanned eventualities. Typical situations that would benefit from contingency planning include preparing for a possible general economic downturn (recession) or a sudden change in demand due to a specific event such as the financial collapse of a customer, or if a competitor is suspected of introducing a technological development.

A detailed and thorough answer – a clear definition supported by relevant examples. The answer need not apply specifically to O'Brien Ltd, but mention has been made of this company.

(b) If "...this contingency planning business is very expensive, and there's no guarantee that it will work...", why do companies like O'Brien Ltd commit resources to it? **(8)**

Contingency planning will help identify weaknesses such as over-reliance on a single supplier or customer - as a result, the organisation can take appropriate action (e.g. use another supplier, diversify into another market/segment). By doing so, the risk of a future major problem is reduced, and - as a result - the organisation may regard the investment in contingency planning as a form of 'insurance', even though it will be expensive because it tends to be based on computer modelling (the computer program answering 'what if?' questions).

This is quite a good answer. It contains balance (the acknowledgment that contingency planning is expensive), but emphasises why contingency planning is often undertaken. Perhaps the increasing pace of change and uncertainty in our economy could also have been mentioned as a reason why this type of planning is undertaken.

Exam practice question

1 WJ plc is a large multinational based in the UK. Below are extracts from its most recent Annual Report.

> 'The board of directors of WJ plc has created a Remuneration Committee, which will consist of all non-executive directors in the company. The Remuneration Committee's terms of reference include determining on behalf of the board a fair remuneration level for the executive directors. This will be based on what the company can afford and will recognise their individual contributions to the company's overall performance. In addition, the Remuneration Committee will assist the board in ensuring that the current and future management of the group is suitably recruited and remunerated.'
>
> 'The remuneration policy of WJ plc consists of setting a basic salary in line with the average salary for each director's responsibilities as advised by independent financial consultants.'
>
> 'WJ plc recognises the value of its employees. The company's policy is to recruit and develop employees at all levels in order to meet the company's corporate objectives.'

The most recent Annual Report and Accounts shows that the executive directors of WJ plc received an average of over £550 000 each in the form of directors' emoluments (i.e. basic salary plus bonus and benefits). This level of payment to the executive directors of a large plc is not unusual.

(a) How can the size of payment received by these and other executive directors of large plcs be justified by the role that they play in the success of firms such as WJ plc? **(6)**

(b) WJ plc's management culture is based on a democratic management style. To what extent could this management style fit with the existence of large incomes for these directors? **(8)**

4 International business

The following topics are covered in this chapter:

- **International trade**
- **The UK and Europe**
- **Multinational corporations**

4.1 International trade

LEARNING SUMMARY

After studying this section, you should be able to:

- describe the effects of countries specialising
- outline the work of some of the main international trading organisations
- give examples of the benefits of free trade
- explain the main measures used in protectionism
- describe and distinguish between fixed and floating exchange rates
- describe how the IMF and WTO support world trade

Specialisation and trade

AQA	**M4**
Edexcel	**M1, M3**
OCR	**M2, M7**
WJEC	**M3**
CCEA	**M4**

Just as people specialise (i.e. **division of labour**), so do countries. Influences on specialisation include land and climate, availability of raw materials, and the level of training and expertise of the workforce. Firms generate mass production by specialising and surpluses are traded with other countries. **Interdependence** between trading countries exists because specialisation means a country's resources are not being used by firms to make the other items it needs.

The UK is noted for specialising in (for example) manufactured products and financial services.

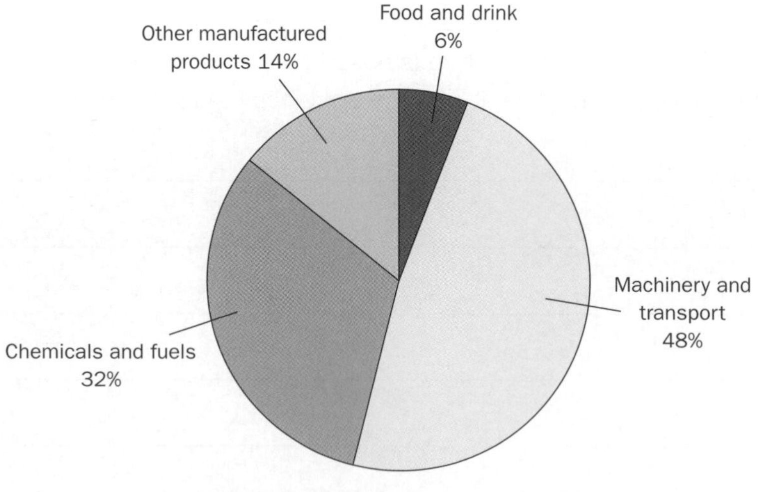

Figure 4.1 UK export of goods by category, 2009

Trade areas and trading blocs dominate international trade:

- **NAFTA** (the North American Free Trade Agreement) was formed in 1994 between the USA, Canada and Mexico, and created the world's largest free trade zone with a population of about 400 million and a GDP amounting to a third of the world's total GDP.
- **ASEAN** (the Association of Southeast Asian Nations) consists of countries in Southeast Asia, with nearly 600 million people and a combined GDP of about £1 trillion.
- **OPEC** (the Organisation of the Petroleum Exporting Countries) is a cartel of 12 countries (2010) seeking to protect the cartel members' interest by, for example, ensuring stable oil prices in order to avoid unnecessary fluctuations in income.
- **BRIC** (Brazil, Russia, India and China) comprises more than a quarter of the world's land area and about 40 percent of its population, although they do not have a formal political or economic alliance like the European Union (EU), and do not form an official trading bloc. The growing middle class in these countries is demanding more consumer goods and services; and the speed of improving the infrastructure, and developing advanced telecommunications, is increasing the demand for raw materials. Russia and Brazil are expected to become major world suppliers of raw materials such as iron ore (Brazil) and oil and natural gas (Russia). China and India are expected to be dominant in manufacturing.

Some analysts speculate that, if Russia and Brazil become major commodity suppliers to China and India, the four countries will form a closer economic alliance.

Country	Exports (£m)	Imports (£m)	Balance (£m)
Brazil	1 786	2 526	– 740
Russia	2 403	4 609	– 2 206
India	2 948	4 560	– 1 612
China	5 398	24 305	– 18 907

Source: ONS

Figure 4.2 UK exports to, and imports from, BRIC countries (£m) 2009

Free trade and protectionism

Free trade agreements continue to be created, for example the 2009 free trade agreement between the EU and South Korea.

Countries cannot produce certain items efficiently (e.g. tropical foodstuffs in the UK's climate) and so trade leads to greater consumer choice. **Free trade** occurs when the movement of goods and services between countries is not restricted in any way. Specialisation and free trade allow firms to gain productive efficiency through economies of scale.

Countries may restrict free trade from taking place.

The government of a country uses **protectionism** for one or more purposes, as the table on the next page illustrates.

Purpose of protectionism	Possible approach
To improve the country's balance of payments by reducing imports	**Quotas** – physical limits placed on amounts allowed into the country
To protect the exchange rate	**Exchange controls** – limit on the amount of foreign currency bought by firms/individuals
To raise revenue	**Tariffs** – taxes on imports making them more expensive than home-based goods
To safeguard domestic employment and 'infant industries' not yet strong enough to compete with imported competitor products	**Subsidies** – financial support to industries to improve their competitive position

A government may also need to protect against the 'dumping' of goods from overseas competitors who are exporting at low prices to establish market penetration. A government also has available the other protectionist methods of **embargoes** (refusing to trade in certain items for political or military reasons) or **procurement policies** (to 'buy from within').

The EU's Common External Tariff is applied to goods or services entering the EU to encourage member states to import from other members due to the relative price benefit.

Protectionism counters the benefits of free trade – there can be less choice, higher prices for consumers and reduced competition from inefficiency. There is also a danger that if one country adopts protectionist measures, other countries will follow, thereby reducing overall world trade.

KEY POINT

A government's foreign policy – its relations with other governments – affects trade. For example, if the UK has a dispute with another country, trade between businesses in the two countries may be halted.

Exchange rates

The **exchange rate** of a currency is expressed as its value in other currencies. This is particularly important for importers and exporters, who could find that their profit margins are affected by the change in the relative prices of the different currencies they use in international trade.

Under a **floating exchange rate** system, the rate (price) is determined by market forces, i.e. the demand for – and supply of – the currency on the foreign exchange market. A government will sell or buy some of its reserves of foreign currency to influence the exchange rate and even out major fluctuations. It may also alter domestic interest rates to control short-term speculative capital movements.

A floating exchange rate should solve balance of payments problems.

If the UK becomes less competitive internationally:

it suffers a deficit in its balance of payments →	increased imports will increase the supply of, and lower exports will reduce the demand for, sterling →	so the value of sterling will fall, raising import prices and reducing export prices →	which leads back to equilibrium.

The advantage of a fixed exchange rate to firms trading in overseas markets is greater certainty that profit margins will be maintained.

However, floating exchange rates encourage **speculation** – speculators gamble on future changes in these rates, their actions affecting the rate which is the focus for speculation. A **fixed exchange rate** system is the alternative, and has often been tried – e.g. the EU's Exchange Rate Mechanism (ERM). Under this system, governments agree the rate at which their currencies are fixed and exchanged, within set limits.

Globalisation of markets

AQA	**M3, M4**
Edexcel	**M3**
OCR	**M2, M7**
WJEC	**M1, M3**
CCEA	**M4**

The following factors influence how an entrepreneur assesses the nature and attractiveness of an overseas market.

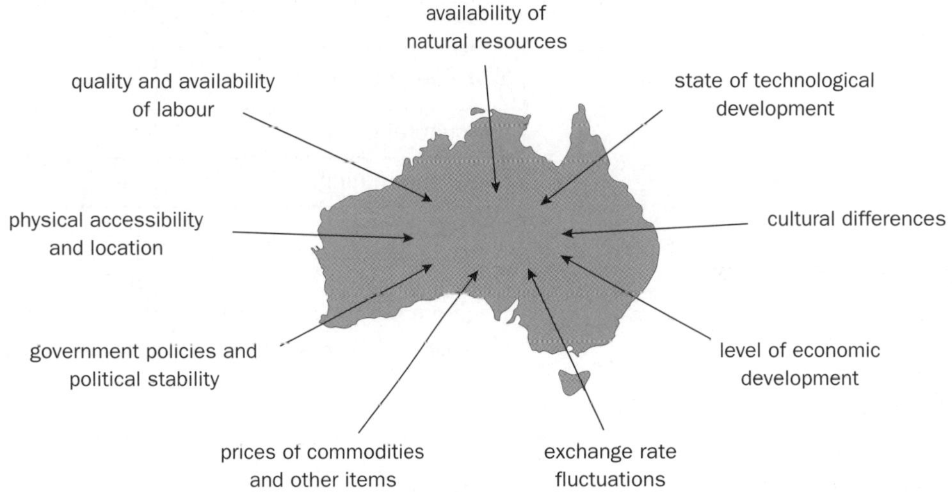

An effective **global strategy** can help a firm to gain competitive advantages when entering overseas markets.

Global strategies include:

- **greater efficiency**
  - product life cycles can be extended by selling in new growth markets
  - greater operational flexibility – production costs can be moved, e.g. as exchange rates fluctuate
  - economies of scale
  - cross-subsidisation between countries
- **reduced risk**
  - increased diversification
  - stronger trading position.

Global marketing requires firms to co-ordinate the 'four Ps' (especially products and prices) across international markets.

Firms that limit trading to home markets only are involved in **domestic marketing**. This strategy carries the risk that a firm – by ignoring overseas market activity – may suddenly find that an emerging global competitor launches its products in the home market. Global strategy requires **global marketing**, where firms need to identify, reconcile or take advantage of differences from market to market. As in home markets, a firm may concentrate on a market niche.

KEY POINT

A global strategy is typically suitable for firms that can make and sell standardised products worldwide.

Supporting world trade

The UK contributes to – and benefits from – a number of international trade organisations. The role of the **International Monetary Fund** (IMF) is to encourage greater co-operation between countries in formulating economic policy. It was created following a worldwide economic depression in the 1930s in an attempt to stop such an event happening again, and to avoid protectionism. It has about 200 member countries who agree to be open about how they determine their currency's value – the IMF monitors exchange policies.

The main function of the **World Trade Organization** (WTO) is to help trade flow as freely as possible, e.g. by removing tariffs. The WTO is also a forum for trade negotiations and it handles trade disputes.

World merchandise exports	% increase 2000–2008
Agricultural products	4.0
Fuels and mining	3.0
Manufactures	6.0
Overall	5.0

Figure 4.3 Increase (%) in world merchandise exports 2000–2008

Region	% increase in exports 2000–2008
North America	2.5
South and Central America	5.5
Europe	3.5
Asia (total)	10.0
India	12.5
China	20.5

Figure 4.4 Increase (%) in exports by region 2000–2008

From the late 1940s to date, the WTO and its predecessor (GATT) have worked to liberalise trade through a set of talks, or Rounds. Recent ones include the Uruguay Round and the Doha Round, which have resulted in tariff reductions.

PROGRESS CHECK

1. How does protectionism disadvantage consumers?
2. What is the 'exchange rate' of a currency?

2 Its value when expressed in other currencies.
1 Less choice and higher prices are likely.

4.2 The UK and Europe

LEARNING SUMMARY

After studying this section, you should be able to:

- explain the nature and purpose of the European Union
- discuss the influence of the Single Market on UK businesses
- examine the arguments for and against the UK joining the Eurozone

The European Union

AQA **M4**
Edexcel **M3**
OCR **M2, M7**
WJEC **M3**
CCEA **M4**

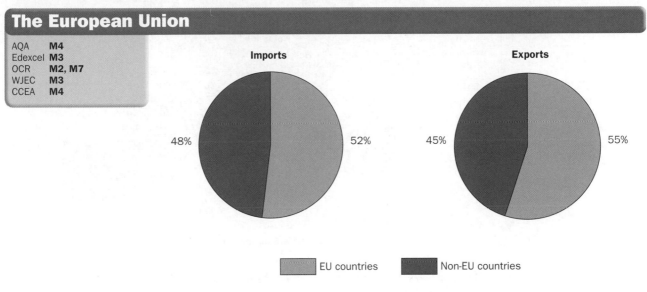

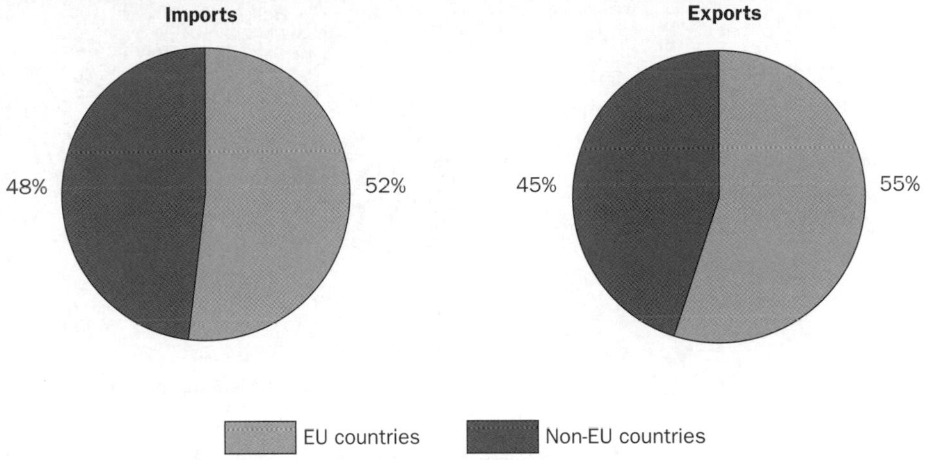

Figure 4.5 UK imports and exports, 2009

In 2010, 7 of the world's 12 largest industrial economies were EU members.

The **European Union** (EU) is an example of a customs union, with common institutions and common policies on trade between members and with the outside world. Although the USA and Japan have been the world's dominant industrialised economies, the EU as a whole is larger than either. The EU itself is a member of the G20 group, and the UK, France, Germany and Italy are individual members. These four members are also part of the G8 group of industrialised economies.

Croatia, Macedonia and Turkey are official candidates to join the EU.

The 27 EU countries (2010) are as follows (the year they joined is in brackets):

- Belgium, France, (West) Germany, Italy, Luxembourg, Netherlands (1958)
- Denmark, Ireland, UK (1973)
- Greece (1981)
- Portugal, Spain (1986)
- Austria, Finland, Sweden (1995)
- Cyprus, Czech Republic, Estonia, Hungary, Latvia, Lithuania, Malta, Poland, Slovakia, Slovenia (2004)
- Romania, Bulgaria (2007).

Figure 4.6, on the next page, shows the location of these EU countries.

Figure 4.6 EU membership, 2010

The Single Market and UK businesses

Promotion of trade between members was a major reason behind the formation of what is now the EU. The 'Common Market' has become the **Single European Market** following the 1986 Single Market Act.

The Single Market Act sought to:

- **remove**
  - administrative barriers to trade
  - controls on the flow of capital
  - the abuse of market power
- **establish**
  - free movement of labour
  - free movement of goods
  - common technical standards
  - parity of professional qualifications.

The Single Market has influenced UK businesses by:

- establishing common standards
- creating open markets
- allowing the free movement of labour and goods
- regulating anti-competitive practices.

CE mark

Common standards of quality and safety are set throughout the EU. UK manufacturers must ensure that their products meet standards set in Directives on, for example, food labelling and product safety.

Open markets now exist in areas such as information and communications technology, and in financial services. UK firms face increased competition as a result of open markets with common standards.

The **free movement of labour and goods** are basic EU principles:

- The free movement of labour is in the EU's Social Charter, and the increased recognition and standardisation of professional qualifications has improved employment prospects for UK nationals, and influenced employment policies of UK firms.
- The use of the Single Administrative Document and simplified border formalities have reduced the delay in moving goods throughout the Union, with transport services being liberalised, for example by abolishing road haulage permits and quotas.

Free and fair competition is a fundamental EU policy to ensure control of prices and improve choice of products.

Anti-competitive practices have been regulated as a result of EU anti-competition rules that seek to allow competition to flourish. Between 1990 and 2010 the EU has blocked over 20 mergers/takeovers for being anti-competitive, e.g. Ryanair's bid for Aer Lingus, the other major Irish airline.

KEY POINT

The Single Market remains the greatest assistance provided to competitive firms by the European Union. The objective – to remove trade barriers and allow free access to markets – means that companies have access to a market with a spending power even larger than that of North America.

European monetary union

AQA **M4** WJEC **M3**
Edexcel **M3** CCEA **M4**
OCR **M2, M7**

Euro area	108	Ireland	139	Lithuania	61	Portugal	75
Belgium	115	Greece	95	Luxembourg	253	Romania	46
Bulgaria	40	Spain	104	Hungary	63	Slovenia	90
Czech Republic	80	France	107	Malta	76	Slovakia	72
Denmark	118	Italy	100	Netherlands	135	Finland	115
Germany	116	Cyprus	95	Austria	123	Sweden	121
Estonia	67	Latvia	56	Poland	58	UK	117

Source: Eurostat

Figure 4.7 GDP per head, 2008 (EU = 100)

By 2010 there were 16 EU countries, with a population of 330 million, in the Eurozone – or euro area.

On 1 January 1999, 11 member states adopted the **euro** as their common currency. The conversion rates between the euro and national currencies were fixed – the currencies were withdrawn in 2002 and replaced with euro notes and coins. All transactions in the various financial markets – capital, money and foreign exchange – are carried out in euros.

Studies on the effect of introducing the euro suggest it has increased trade within the Eurozone by up to 10 percent.

The trade of goods and services within the **Eurozone** (the euro area) is no longer 'foreign' trade – it is now domestic trade. This should eliminate any related balance of payments problems for the member states, and also exchange rate instability within the euro area.

In March 2010, the euro area reported an external trade surplus of 4.5 billion euro, though the EU as a whole showed a 7.1 billion euro trade deficit.

The euro has led to a transfer of monetary policy from Eurozone member countries to the **European Central Bank**. Using interest and exchange rates to help control national monetary policy is no longer available to the member governments. There is, therefore, a single currency and monetary policy in the Eurozone.

The euro in foreign exchange transactions

The euro's role as an international investment currency and part of a country's official reserves has only recently developed. It is a serious competitor to the dollar and sterling as an international currency, even though the dollar's wide acceptance and use makes it the major trading currency.

Instability in one Eurozone country affects the euro. For example, the collapse of global credit markets in 2008, followed by economic difficulties experienced by Eurozone countries such as Greece, Spain and Portugal, put pressure on the value of the euro in the international currency markets.

The European System of Central Banks

The **Eurosystem** consists of the ECB and the central banks of the Eurozone members only.

The European Central Bank (ECB) is responsible for the euro area's monetary policy. The European System of Central Banks (ESCB) consists of the ECB and the national central banks of all EU member states. The ESCB is independent of national governments and therefore monetary policy can be removed from the control of the individual governments making up the euro area.

The ESCB's main tasks are to:

- carry out monetary policy for the euro area
- conduct foreign exchange transactions
- manage the official currency reserves of the countries in the euro area.

The UK and monetary union

€
The euro
Now in business

EMU – Economic and Monetary Union – is closely associated with the establishment of the Eurozone. UK governments have supported the principle of joining if the economic benefits of doing so are clear. They have created a dedicated unit in the Treasury – the Euro Preparations Unit (EPU) – to help UK firms prepare for the effects of the euro.

The existence of the single currency influences EU markets in three main ways:

1. **Exchange rates** – all uncertainties in exchange rate movements are removed for trade within the euro area when trade is valued in the single currency.
2. **Transaction costs** – there is no need to change national currencies in the Eurozone; as a result transaction costs are reduced and firms find it cheaper to make payments between countries.
3. **Transparency** – price differences are more transparent to consumers as a result of the single currency.

UK businesses that prepared early for the introduction of the euro – such as those in the financial sector of our economy – gained a competitive advantage.

The UK businesses most affected by EMU are exporters and importers dealing with the euro, multinationals with UK bases (some use the euro to simplify their accounting procedures), the financial sector (banks and other financial institutions, and financial markets), and retailers (for example, the major retailers based in tourist areas).

Evidence for and against the UK joining the Eurozone

Here are some of the arguments for and against the UK joining the Eurozone:

- Although many manufacturers have faced problems since the euro was established (due to the strength of the pound against it), any raw materials they import are very competitively priced as a result.
- Companies like Nissan, Toyota and Ford have either cut jobs, announced closures or warned that future investment is put at risk when sterling is high against the euro. Although part of their argument that the UK should join the Eurozone may be influenced by other factors – such as overcapacity in vehicle production – in recent years:
  - Toyota, Nissan and Honda have reduced their dependence on UK-made components
  - Matsushita (makers of Panasonic and National televisions) moved production of its flat-screen TV sets to the Czech Republic, and started importing more TV components from Germany
  - Hitachi ceased making personal computers in the UK
  - jobs in Scotland in Wales were cut by Canon.
- Concern has been expressed that inward investment will be lost if the UK does not join the single currency, although in recent years there has been substantial new inward investment. The UK is seen by some international companies as a gateway to mainland Europe, and much of this investment will probably be maintained if the UK does not join the single currency in the near future.
- UK firms need to consider the extent to which the single currency and euro area will create or affect:
  - increased cross-border competition – UK firms are disadvantaged compared with Eurozone-based firms that share the same currency
  - raising finance – euro-based financial markets may become more attractive
  - buying and moving goods – firms located in the Eurozone should find that buying, transport and distribution costs are reduced due to the more transparent competition and the lack of fluctuating exchange rates
  - selling – pricing UK firms' products in both sterling and euros
  - greater competition from growth or co-operation – the single currency and increased competition for firms within the euro area may encourage mergers, closer co-operation and joint ventures for these firms.

How one limited company was influenced by EMU

Overall, the euro simplifies our business, reduces administration and transport costs and makes it much easier to deal with exchange rate risk. Accordingly, we will trade in the currency as much as we are able... . With an annual price list system, we are always going to be vulnerable to changes in exchange rates but now we have just the one euro list, it is much easier to monitor and to be aware of the exact position... . The mechanics of setting up euro accounts and contacting customers and suppliers were not difficult or particularly time consuming. Plus, getting ready for the euro has given us a chance to think through our business. Price transparency will undoubtedly have an impact. In some ways, it will make it easier to plan but it is also likely to make Europe a more competitive market.

KEY POINT

UK firms have had to change their accounting and IT-based systems to accommodate the euro, reconsider their pricing policies so their goods are competitively priced in euros, and train staff to handle euro-based transactions.

PROGRESS CHECK

1. In what ways does the Single Market influence UK business?
2. How are EU markets affected by the existence of the Eurozone?

1 Establishing common standards; creating open markets; allowing free movement of labour, capital and goods; regulating anti-competitive practices.
2 Uncertainties are removed in exchange rates; transaction costs are reduced or eliminated; price differences are more transparent.

4.3 Multinational corporations

LEARNING SUMMARY

After studying this section, you should be able to:

- describe the role and importance of multinationals in the global economy
- discuss the benefits and problems that multinationals bring to their host economy

The importance of multinationals

AQA	**M3**	WJEC	**M3**
Edexcel	**M3**	CCEA	**M4**
OCR	**M7**		

Multinational corporations (MNCs) are also known as transnational corporations (TNCs) or multinational enterprises (MNEs).

A multinational corporation operates internationally, although its ownership is based in a single country. The ownership may be in the form of a **holding company**, which 'holds' (controls) the different subsidiaries.

Many of the UK's best-known companies are multinationals.

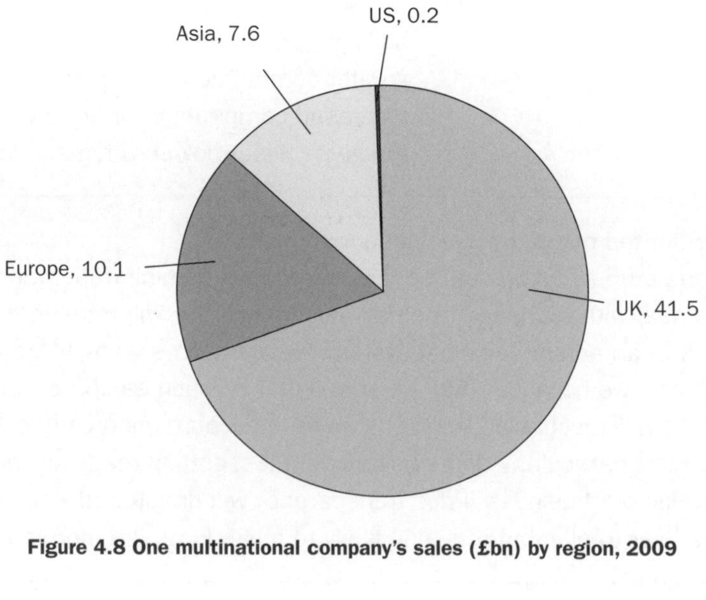

Figure 4.8 One multinational company's sales (£bn) by region, 2009

Operation centres	
Role	**Location**
Licensing, manufacturing, operations and logistics	Ireland (Dublin)
Manufacturing	Puerto Rico (USA)
Licensing and operations	Reno, Nevada (USA)
Operations and logistics	Singapore

Figure 4.9 Microsoft manufacturing, distribution and logistics organisation, 2009

MNCs have played a key role in globalisation.

Multinationals contribute up to one-half of world production, and the larger multinationals generate output and turnover levels that exceed the GDP of many countries. As a result, many governments offer a range of (financial) incentives to encourage multinationals to base their operations in the countries concerned.

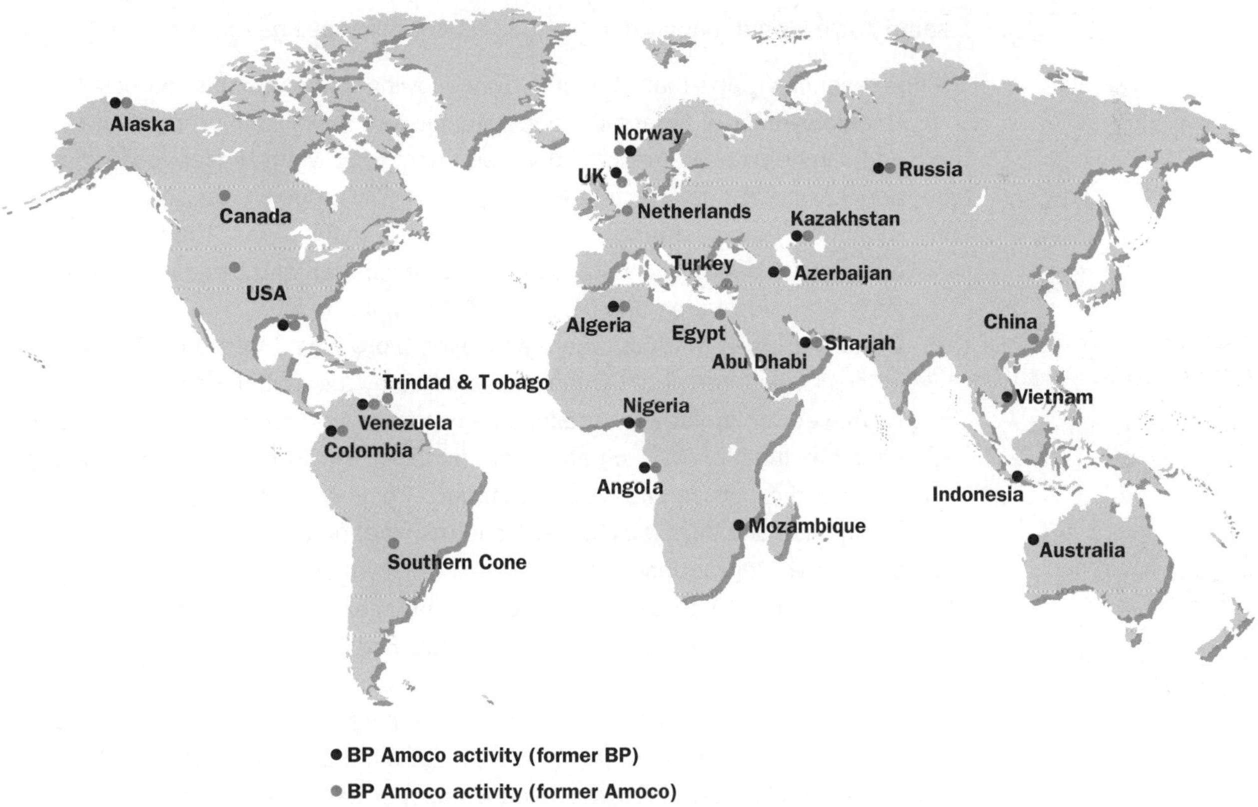

Figure 4.10 Worldwide involvement of BP and Amoco following their merger

Some analysts have calculated that the labour–cost element of a fashion shoe retailing at £50 can be less than 10p.

Multinationals have grown in number and importance because they gain from several benefits:

- **Cheaper labour or materials found in different countries** – General Motors relocated production from the USA to Mexico; footwear/sportswear multinationals such as Nike also gain labour–cost benefits from manufacturing in the Far East.
- **Entering tariff-protected markets** – one way round the EU's Common External Tariff is to set up production in one of its countries. Overseas multinationals like Nissan, Toyota, Epson, Tatung and Ricoh have located in the UK and now form part of the 'home' economy.
- **Avoiding regulation in the home country** – legislation and other restrictions (e.g. through the Competition Commission in the UK) can be avoided by the multinational basing some of its operations in a different country.

Benefits of multinationals to the host economy

Advocates of the free market system argue that multinationals are subject to the same basic laws of supply and demand as any other business.

A host economy gains many benefits from allowing multinationals to operate:

- **Unemployment is reduced** – multinationals are major employers of labour, and can help reduce regional unemployment (e.g. when Nissan located in north-east England, which at the time was badly hit by the decline of traditional manufacturing and construction). Support firms – such as component manufacturers and suppliers of canteen and cleaning services – grow in the local area and provide further employment.
- **Other factors of production are employed more fully** – they are used more efficiently as a result of competition created by the multinational.
- **Advanced technology** is introduced – examples in the UK include technology-based multinationals such as Epson (printers) and Toyota (vehicles) bringing ideas and expertise into the UK economy. Training in more advanced techniques and skills also develops in the local area.
- **Modern work practices** are introduced – many multinationals have work practices that emphasise team work, shared goals and employee participation in decision making. They may also operate no-redundancy policies.
- **Greater choice and higher income** – consumers benefit from wider product choice, and the economy gains through the multinational's activities, both at home (employment rises, tax revenue is generated and greater expertise improves economic competitiveness), and by exporting (balance of payments benefits).
- **Improved infrastructure** – one common side effect of multinationals setting up in a country is an improvement to the local infrastructure, sometimes financed by the multinational itself.

Examples include the introduction of Japanese-originated working practices into the UK economy.

Problems that multinationals bring to the host economy

The policies and actions of a multinational may also create tensions as a result of its economic power:

- A multinational may concentrate on its own interests rather than those of the host country.
  - It may move production out of the country, causing problems to the areas affected (e.g. unemployment), the host country's balance of payments and level of economic growth.
  - It can adjust its costs between its various subsidiaries to gain maximum benefits from one country's lower taxation requirements.
  - It has the power to move its reserves between different countries, gaining financial advantage but causing currency fluctuations.
- A multinational may also use its economic power in ways that are **socially undesirable**. Accusations of bribery, corruption, financial irregularity and the exploitation of cheap labour have been levelled against some multinationals, and raw materials may be obtained with only limited regard for the environmental impact or long-term stability and growth of the countries concerned.

Some UK-based multinationals have moved production elsewhere in the EU, partly as a result of the UK not having joined the Eurozone.

KEY POINT

The importance of multinationals lies in their significant economic contribution to a country's economy.

PROGRESS CHECK

1 What are the **(a)** benefits and **(b)** problems presented to the host country as a result of multinational operations?

1 **(a)** Reduced unemployment; efficient use of factors of production; introduction of advanced technology and modern work practices; greater consumer choice
(b) Concentration on the multinational's interest rather than the host country's; possible socially undesirable practices.

Sample question and model answer

This answer, although correct, is much too brief. It should outline the fact that there is free movement of goods in the EU and not elsewhere in Europe, the simplified border formalities, and the use of a Single Administrative Document. Furthermore, the EU's regulation of anti-competitive practices helps a business compete on a more 'even playing field' in the EU.

A good point, well explained, but the answer should go further, e.g. by referring to the reduction in costs such as transaction costs (no need to change national currencies), and the greater transparency of prices in a single currency area.

Correct points are made, but there are other issues. For example, the transfer of monetary autonomy to the ECB may affect the UK economy and therefore UK businesses (e.g. interest rates), it is harder for the UK government to support UK firms (e.g. by devaluing the currency and increasing exports), and business taxes may be increased to support poorer Eurozone countries.

1. McLea Ltd is a company making and selling glues and other solvents. The company is based in Birmingham, employs about 50 people and sells its products exclusively in the United Kingdom.

The directors of McLea Ltd wish to sell their products throughout Europe. They have recently appointed a new Marketing Manager who has experience of working for a company selling its products in the EU, although not in other European countries.

(a) Outline why McLea Ltd will find it easier to sell its glues and solvents to EU countries rather than non-EU countries. **(4)**

It is easier because the United Kingdom is a member of the European Union and therefore benefits from easier access to the EU markets.

(b) The new Marketing Manager is an advocate of the UK adopting the euro and joining the Eurozone.

(i) Describe the main advantages to McLea Ltd if the UK adopts the euro and joins the Eurozone. **(6)**

The main advantages to McLea Ltd will be that exchange rate movement uncertainties cease to exist, so it does not have to worry about the pound-euro relationship and how changes in the value of these currencies will affect its profits.

(ii) Why do many other business people disagree about the UK adopting the euro and joining the Eurozone? **(6)**

Businesses will be disrupted by the switch to the euro - they will need to prepare to cope with issues such as paying employees in a new currency, as well as buying and selling in this currency.

Exam practice question

1 RedShed Ltd is a manufacturing business that makes wooden buildings used as holiday chalets. It imports wood and many of its other raw materials, and sells its finished buildings overseas.

(a) How will a fall in the value of sterling affect RedShed Ltd? **(4)**

(b) The owner of RedShed Ltd believes that his company and other UK firms would gain from greater protectionism.

Outline the arguments for and against protectionism, and explain why the owner is likely to be wrong in his belief that RedShed Ltd would gain from greater protectionism. **(8)**

5 External influences (1)

The following topics are covered in this chapter:

- Social influences
- Technological influences
- Economic influences

5.1 Social influences

LEARNING SUMMARY

After studying this section, you should be able to:

- explain the nature and role of corporate social responsibility
- describe the influence of demographics on business activity
- outline how attitudes, tastes and fashions affect firms

Corporate social responsibility

AQA	**M4**
Edexcel	**M1, M3, M4**
OCR	**M7**
WJEC	**M3**
CCEA	**M4**

Modern-day organisations are aware of the importance of their image, and of the relationships they have with the wider community. They acknowledge their responsibilities to employees, customers, shareholders and other stakeholders. Most businesses, particularly the larger firms, operate using a **corporate social responsibility** (CSR) philosophy. (CSR is known by various names, such as responsible business, corporate citizenship and sustainable business.)

Firms with a CSR philosophy should make sure that their business activity operates in the public interest by:

- following appropriate laws, initiatives and guidelines through (self-)regulation
- acknowledging their effect on the human and wider environment.

Examples of specific responsibilities include:

- **equal opportunities (EO)** – as well as obeying legislation, firms publicise their commitment to EO
- **health and safety** – most firms do not limit themselves to the minimum legal requirements, believing that a good health and safety record helps create a positive image, which can be used to develop their business
- **ethical trading** – firms balance moral and ethical stances with the need to make an adequate return on investment (i.e. an adequate profit)
- **environmental awareness** – firms realise the negative effect of bad publicity.

The Body Shop's reputation and image has been largely created through its ethical business stance, and is strongly reflected in its advertising and publicity.

Corporate social responsibility at work

In 2007, Marks & Spencer launched its five 'Plan A pillars': Climate change, Waste, Natural resources, Fair partnership and Health and wellbeing. The following extract from the company's 2010 Plan A Commitments report illustrates how social responsibility can operate effectively and also bring commercial benefits.

Plan A today

In the last three years, thanks to Plan A, we've made a number of groundbreaking innovations that have changed the way we do business:

- We've motivated one million M&S customers to raise over £2.2m for Oxfam and saved 4 million items of unwanted clothes from going to landfill.
- We've improved energy efficiency by over 10% in our stores.
- We've reduced packaging on our foods by 16%, without compromising freshness, quality or shelf life – and cut costs in the process.
- We've improved fuel efficiency by over 20% and introduced our instantly recognizable 'tear drop' aerodynamic lorry trailers.
- We've made clothes hanger recycling 'mainstream' – with 120 million re-used or recycled each year.
- We've reduced the number of food carrier bags we give out by 400 million each year.
- We've purchased GreenPalm Certificates to cover all of the palm oil used in our M&S products. By doing this we are rewarding palm oil producers for working in a sustainable and responsible way.

Extract taken from Marks and Spencer Group plc 'Our Plan A Commitments 2010–2015' report, 2010

The range of social influences

AQA **M4** WJEC **M1, M3**
Edexcel **M3** CCEA **M4**
OCR **M1**

Social influences are linked closely to changes in the culture and habits of a country's population.

These influences relate to changes in:

- **demographics** – population trends
- **attitudes** – issues such as tastes and interests, eating habits, fashion, work and religion.

Demographics

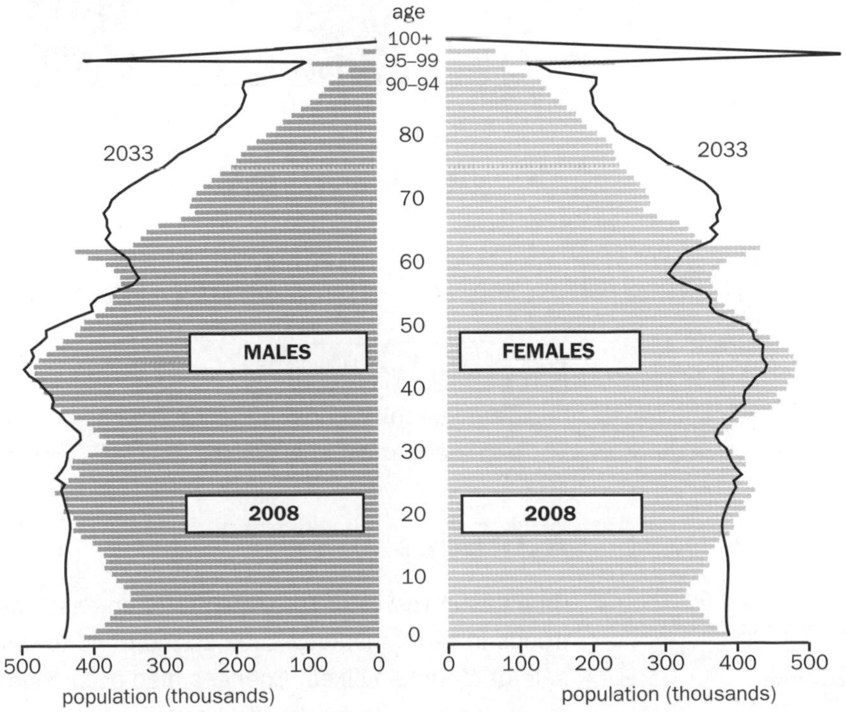

Source: ONS

Figure 5.1 UK population projections: 2008–2033

Business is affected greatly by demographics in terms of the size, structure and growth of the population.

The present UK population (2010) **size** is about 62 million people. It has grown steadily over time – the 1901 Census put it at just under 38 million. This effectively gives a modern business a market that is half as big again as that of just over 100 years ago.

More important, perhaps, are changes in the **structure** of the population – the number of each sex and in each age group. If, for example, many of the population were in their teens or early twenties, demand would shift towards products aimed at this sector (e.g. fashionable clothes and popular music). At present, the UK has an ageing population, which means there is greater demand for products aimed at the older person, so businesses will provide for those demands.

The UK now has more people aged over 60 than under 16, and by 2034 it is estimated that 23 percent of the population will be 65 and over, compared to 18 percent aged 16 or younger.

Since the 1980s, the percentage of people aged 65 and over has increased from 15 percent (1984) to 16 percent (2009), an increase of 1.7 million in this age group. In the same period the percentage aged 16 and under fell from 21 percent to 19 percent. This is projected to continue.

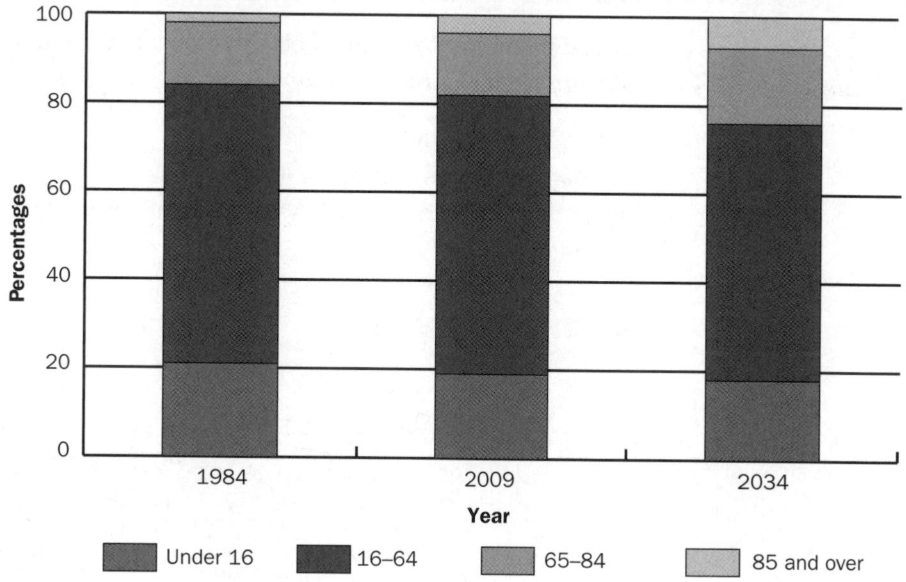

Source: ONS

Figure 5.2 The UK's ageing population

KEY POINT

Demographic trends influence not only demand but also labour supply – e.g. recruitment and training policies – and therefore HR costs.

Attitudes

The effect on demand can be either short term or long term.

Changes in **tastes or fashions** are often associated with clothing or particular trends in youth markets, such as the trend towards off-road cycling increasing the sale of mountain bikes. Changes also occur when health-related information is made available on foodstuffs or other products such as tobacco. The effectiveness of a product's promotion in shaping consumer tastes can influence tastes and fashions.

Some reports in 2010 stated that 1 in 8 people under 21 are vegetarian.

As an example, there has been a steady increase in demand for vegetarian foods. This niche market demand has led to the development of specialist vegetarian food outlet chains such as Otarian, which in 2010 launched its first restaurant in London.

PROGRESS CHECK

1. What is the purpose of CSR?
2. Name two types of social influence on firms.

1 To ensure a firm operates in the public interest.
2 Demographics; attitudes, e.g. changes in tastes/fashions.

5.2 Technological influences

LEARNING SUMMARY

After studying this section, you should be able to:

- give examples of major technological changes affecting business
- explain how technological influences affect the work of firms

Importance of technological influences

AQA	**M4**
Edexcel	**M3**
OCR	**M1, M7**
WJEC	**M1, M3**
CCEA	**M4**

Changes in **technology** often act as the major influence on an organisation. Any business that fails to keep pace with technological change will find that its competitive position is affected through (for example) operating outdated production equipment, using slow or inefficient communications equipment, or failing to use the Internet and other e-commerce technological developments.

New products, markets or segments are created through technological developments.

Examples include:

- the worldwide mobile phone market
- electronic downloads of music files that replace CDs being bought
- developments in videoconferencing, avoiding the need to meet face to face
- solar panel and wind technologies being used for power and heating.

Developments such as wireless Internet access support this growth.

This has resulted in technological advances revolutionising certain industries. Examples include the financial sector's use of electronic funds transfer (EFT), telephone banking and e-banking, and manufacturers using CAD/CAM equipment. By 2008, the Office for National Statistics (ONS) estimated that nearly half (45.5 percent) of all employees had access to the Internet at work, and nearly three-quarters (73.5 percent) of all businesses had a website. As a result, more and more is being bought and sold over the Internet, as shown in Figure 5.3 on the next page.

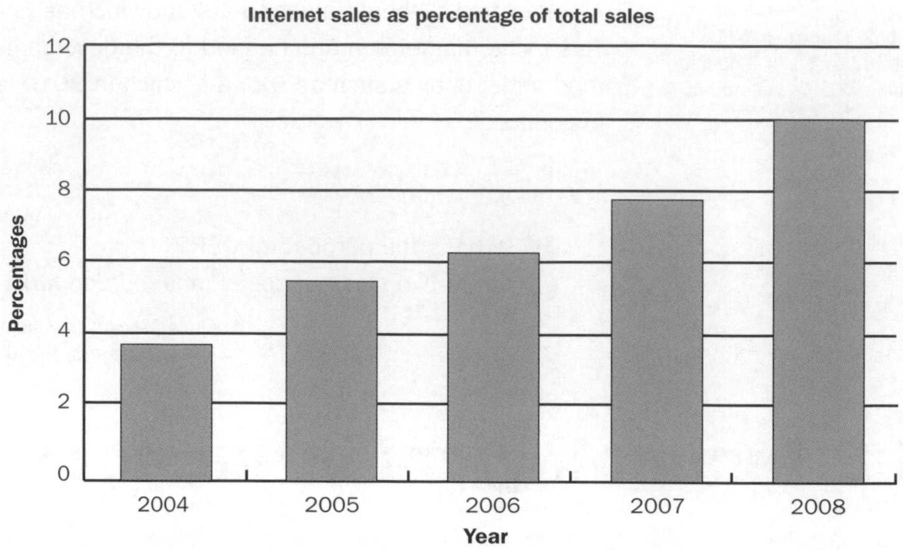

Figure 5.3 The growing influence of e-commerce

KEY POINT

Benefits to firms from technological developments include lower costs, greater speed of production and sale, marketing opportunities, and improved customer satisfaction.

PROGRESS CHECK

1. Identify two examples of technological developments influencing firms.

1 Mobile phone technology; wireless Internet use (**accept any other suitable answers**).

5.3 Economic influences

LEARNING SUMMARY

After studying this section, you should be able to:

- name the major economic influences on a firm in the UK
- describe the four stages of the business cycle
- state the key UK government economic objectives
- discuss the effects of inflation and unemployment on UK business
- distinguish between monetary and fiscal policy of the UK government
- explain the influence of interest and exchange rates on organisations
- give examples of how government supports UK business

The government and the economy

AQA	**M4**
Edexcel	**M1**
OCR	**M7**
WJEC	**M1, M3**
CCEA	**M4**

Local and central government, together with the EU, influence many decisions that a firm makes. Examples are shown in the table on the next page.

Area of influence	Examples of influence
Location	Granting planning permission; creating the Single Market
Workforce	Passing employee protection and health and safety legislation; allowing free movement of labour in the EU
Trade links	Removing tariff barriers; giving help to exporters
Expansion	Passing legislation controlling monopolies and mergers
Income	Altering tax rates
Finance	Influencing the level of interest rates

However, government and the EU are not the only external influences on business, as Figure 5.4 illustrates.

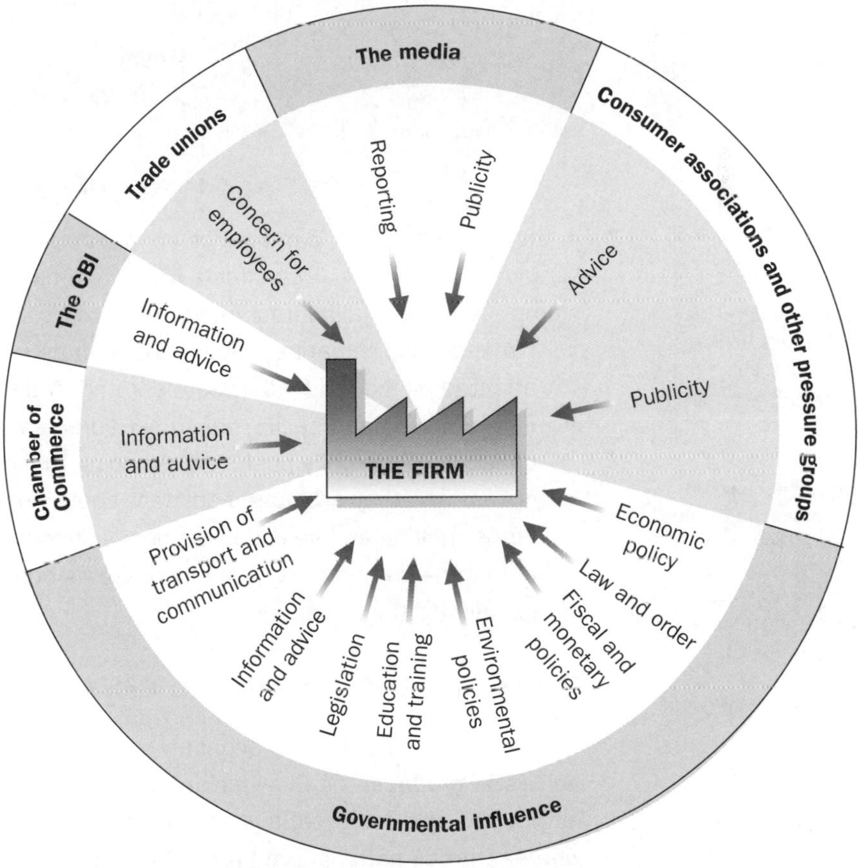

Figure 5.4 External influences on a firm

The business cycle

Figure 5.5 shows how the **business cycle** operates.

Stage	*Firms...*
Recession Contracting output; gloomy outlook	experience falling demand and so cut prices and dismiss staff; losses are made; investment falls; some go out of business.
Recovery The economy starts expanding; rising, but limited, expectations	experience increase in demand; review their employment and investment positions, but still lack confidence.
Boom Rapid growth in output; high confidence but fear of inflation	invest and take on staff; may find skill shortages; increase prices and profit margins; utilise spare capacity.
Downturn (recession) Growth slows again	experience falling demand and profits; start reducing output and investment.

Figure 5.5 Stages in the business cycle

To survive through a recession, a firm will be forced to overcome some of the weaknesses in its product range, expertise, organisation, etc.

In the business cycle, personal consumption normally fluctuates less than business investment. This affects firms in different ways when a recession or slump – a time of falling real incomes – occurs:

- Firms producing capital equipment such as industrial machinery will be badly affected by the reduced investment undertaken by other firms.
- Firms making and selling consumer durables will also be badly hit because consumers normally postpone replacing these items until an economic upturn occurs and they are more confident about employment and income.
- Firms making and selling basic necessities will experience less of a fall in demand – demand may even increase as consumers switch expenditure from luxuries to these items.

In 2009, the discount store Poundland opened 60 new stores in the UK, largely because the continuing recession encouraged consumers to make low-price purchases.

Government economic objectives

The performance of the UK economy can be assessed by measuring its **gross domestic product** – GDP – which represents the total value of the UK economy's output over the course of a year. (GDP does not include net income from abroad, whereas **gross national product** – GNP – does.)

When trying to improve the performance of the economy, the government has four main economic objectives:

1. Control **inflation**, e.g. through interest rate and tax policies.
2. Sustain **employment**, e.g. through regional policy.
3. Encourage controllable **economic growth**, e.g. by stimulating demand through interest rate cuts.
4. Keep a stable **balance of payments**.

Government policies used to achieve these aims have an impact on businesses.

The challenge the government faces is to balance these economic objectives. As an example, a high level of economic growth creates employment, but may also increase inflation through increasing demand levels and by attracting imports into the UK – a balance of payments deficit may result. In times of recession, low demand levels stimulate competitive action such as cutting prices, thereby lowering inflation but also creating unemployment.

Inflation and unemployment

AQA **M4** WJEC **M1, M3**
Edexcel **M1** CCEA **M4**
OCR **M7**

Causes of inflation

Inflation is defined as a persistent tendency for prices to rise over time. Because of the effect of inflation on firms and people, its control becomes a high priority for any government. Most western governments (including the UK) believe that economies have 'speed limits' – output cannot grow at a certain speed without causing price rises.

Cost-push inflation occurs when production costs increase, perhaps due to pay rises not being supported by productivity increases, or through costs of imported items rising due to the pound falling on the foreign exchange market. **Demand-pull inflation** occurs when aggregate (total) demand in the economy exceeds aggregate supply.

Deflation occurs when a downward pressure on economic activity produces falling demand and prices. The danger is that, as a result, firms reduce output and employment. Deflation can also cause problems for the government. For example, when state pensions are linked to a price index, at times of falling prices it is politically impossible to reduce pensions, but maintaining the level of pensions stretches the government's finances.

A major influence on the inflation rate in the euro area is the differences in real incomes across its members.

Ireland	–2.5%
France	1.9%
UK	3.4%
Hungary	5.7%
Euro area	1.5%
The EU	2.0%

Source: Eurostat

Figure 5.6 Inflation rates in the EU, Eurozone and some member states, April 2010

For most of the 2000s (from 2003), the target rate was 2 percent.

Inflation targeting is carried out by the Bank of England's Monetary Policy Committee. A target inflation level is set and interest rates are manipulated to meet this target.

The Bank of England bases its inflation target on the **Consumer Prices Index** (CPI – also known as HICP, the Harmonised Index of Consumer Prices). The CPI calculates the average price increase from a 'basket' of about 600 goods and services.

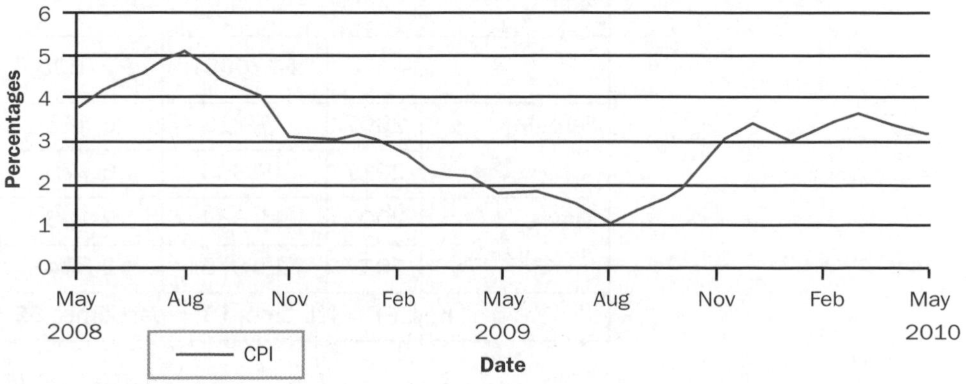

Figure 5.7 The CPI measure of inflation 2008–2010

The importance of inflation

The action of firms can counter inflation, e.g. where cut-throat competition occurs, such as the occasional 'price war' amongst supermarkets.

Entrepreneurs normally have **inflationary expectations** – their business plans are influenced by what they expect to happen to inflation in the future. The actions they take as a result may help fulfil these expectations. For example, if the rate of inflation is expected to increase, entrepreneurs may buy goods now, increasing present demand levels and reinforcing any demand-pull inflation. Their employees may seek higher wage increases on the basis of the expected rise in inflation, increasing costs and adding to any cost-push inflation in the economy.

Inflation affects firms' behaviour and chances of survival:

- Long-term planning becomes more difficult.
- Profit margins may be squeezed, since firms cannot always pass prices on (if they do, their selling prices become uncompetitive).
- The increase in interest rates during inflationary periods hits firms with high debt borrowing and may encourage them to pay higher dividends (which reduces their cash levels).
- UK exporters may find that their increased prices due to inflation makes them uncompetitive overseas.

The UK's inflation rate is kept low partly by increased globalisation, which has led to increased competition.

Firms may benefit from inflation. For example, those with high borrowing find that the sum owed is falling in real terms, making it easier to repay the loan at the end of its life.

Inflation also hits those on a fixed income, for instance pensioners (though indexing of pensions may counter this), and therefore affects the demand level for firms supplying these consumers. It may also distort general economic behaviour (high inflation often encourages saving and reduces spending, leading to an economic downturn – low inflation tends to encourage spending and fuels output and recovery).

KEY POINT

Governments try to control inflation by monetary policy (controlling credit by reducing its availability or increasing its cost) and fiscal policy (increasing taxation to reduce spending power or cutting government spending to reduce demand).

Unemployment

Full employment is another typical key government objective (although there are various ways of interpreting what is meant by 'full').

		FT (000)	PT (000)	SE (000)	Total (000)
Female	2007	7 018	6 465	1 231	14 715
	2017	7 303	6 775	1 387	15 094
Male	2007	11 384	2 163	2 973	16 520
	2017	11 875	2 834	3 010	17 719
Key: **FT** = full time; **PT** = part time; **SE** = self-employed					

Figure adapted from UK Commission for Employment & Skills

Figure 5.8 Actual (2007) and predicted (2017) employment

Unemployment can be:

- **structural** – where industries face structural decline through lack of competitiveness, e.g. the old 'staple' industries such as shipbuilding and mining (this has continued with the trend towards de-industrialisation)
- **frictional** – caused by the time lag between moving from one job to another; it is linked to labour's **geographical immobility** where a person will not move to another area (e.g. the high cost of housing in south-east England) and its **occupational immobility** (e.g. lack of skill to do the jobs available)
- **casual** or **seasonal** – found in sectors such as agriculture and tourism
- **cyclical** – due to a downturn in the business cycle.

	Males (%)	Females (%)	Total (%)
EU overall	9.4	9.1	9.3
Euro area	9.7	9.9	9.8
UK	9.0	6.5	7.8
Germany	8.2	6.8	7.5
Italy	7.1	9.2	8.0
Norway	3.7	2.8	3.2
USA	11.0	8.5	9.8
Japan	5.6	4.9	5.3

Source: Eurostat

Figure 5.9 Examples of percentage unemployment rates in the EU and elsewhere, September 2009

Unemployment rates vary considerably across the UK. Areas that used to rely on heavy industries and which have since declined often have some of the highest rates of unemployment. For example, north-east England was traditionally a strong shipbuilding area before this industry experienced a decline, and Yorkshire was a prosperous coal-mining region. ONS figures state that by spring 2010 these areas had unemployment rates well above the UK average (8 percent), at 9.6 and 9.7 percent respectively.

KEY POINT

In the economy, structural changes, in particular, lead to expansion of some sectors and/or areas at the expense of others, and these changes influence employment patterns.

Government economic policies and UK firms

AQA	**M4**	WJEC	**M1, M3**
Edexcel	**M1**	CCEA	**M4**
OCR	**M7**		

Government economic policies affect different firms in different ways. Firms selling products with a high income elasticity of demand (for instance, many luxuries) are often hit hard by a downturn in the economy, with consumers choosing to postpone their purchase of these products. Other firms that produce capital equipment are also badly affected when their customers cannot invest in new machinery and equipment.

Monetary and fiscal policy

The UK government seeks to achieve its economic aims through the use of different types of economic policy.

The main types of economic policy are monetary policy and fiscal policy:

- **Monetary policy** is based on changing the amount of money in the economy and the cost of borrowing it.
  - Lowering interest rates stimulates demand by making capital (and therefore investment) less expensive – firms are more likely to try to expand by investing and as a result they create more demand for labour. Demand will also be stimulated by consumers having more money to spend as a result of lower interest rates.
  - Increasing interest rates increases the cost of borrowing, hitting firms' cash flow through higher interest charges. Sales will also be hit as consumers face higher bills.
- **Fiscal policy** is based on changing government taxation and expenditure levels.
  - Lowering business direct taxes (corporation tax) increases the amount of profit retained and therefore available for re-investment – as firms grow they increase output and employment. Lowering indirect tax (VAT) cuts prices for consumers and therefore stimulates demand.

Joining the single currency would remove the UK government's direct control of monetary policy.

Interest rates

An **interest rate** indicates the cost of borrowing money – from the lender's viewpoint it is the cost of not having the money available, or 'lost liquidity'. Interest rates and borrowing decisions are influenced by **opportunity cost**. For the borrower this is the cost of not taking out the loan (i.e. going without the item bought by the loan) and for the lender it is not having the cash to spend.

The theory is that growth means more inflation, and more inflation means higher interest rates.

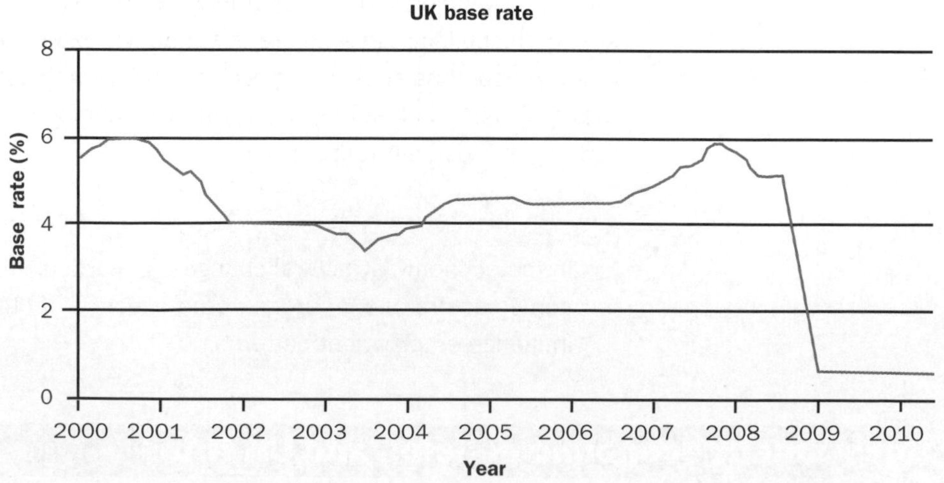

Figure 5.10 UK base rate history from 2000–2010

KEY POINT

If interest rates increase, borrowing – and so spending – falls, taking demand-led pressure out of the economy and reducing inflation. Firms face not only the direct cost of increased interest payments, but also a falling demand for their goods and services.

Exchange rates

High UK interest rates encourage an inward flow of capital (seeking these higher rates) into the UK. Demand for sterling increases, which pushes up its exchange rate. This in turn increases the price of UK exports, making them less competitive, and so lowers output and affects employment.

Falling exchange rates benefit exporters but disadvantage importers.

A rising exchange rate means:
- for an **importer**, lower costs for imported items
- for an **exporter**, reduced price competitiveness and profit margins.

Fluctuating exchange rates cause importers and exporters concern, and may discourage an entrepreneur from entering an overseas market.

Exchange rates therefore affect business decision-making. Entrepreneurs seek to increase profit margins by increasing sales and/or cutting costs. The choice of where to sell and where to buy from is influenced by exchange rate fluctuations. Multinationals are in a stronger position to cope with these fluctuations compared with firms based only in a single country, because they can move resources and accounting procedures from country to country in order to take advantage of the fluctuations.

KEY POINT

Firms find it difficult to remain competitive if exchange rates alter. Exporters must consider whether to change price or accept different profit margins, and importers whether to maintain overseas or home sources of supply.

Government support for business

AQA	**M1, M4**
Edexcel	**M1**
OCR	**M7**
WJEC	**M1, M3**
CCEA	**M4**

The UK government provides support to help businesses in four main ways, as shown below.

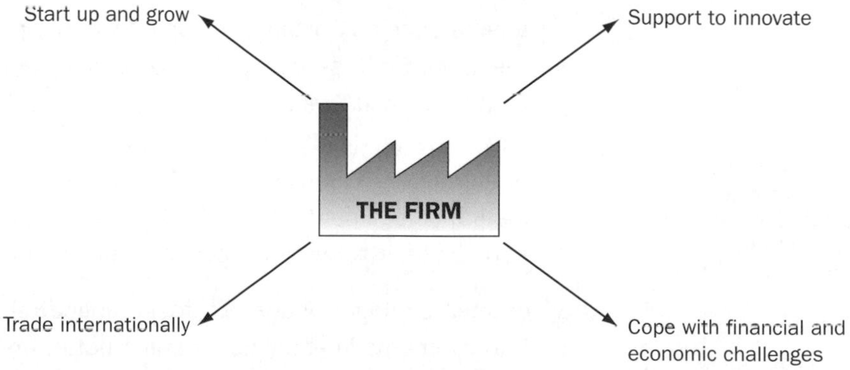

Examples of government support

The **Department for Business Innovation & Skills** (BIS) is the government department that works to build a dynamic and competitive UK economy by creating the conditions for business success.

Some BIS policy areas (2010)

We are committed to fostering competitive markets through the right business law framework, enabling companies to compete freely and giving consumers choice and value.

Consumers should be treated fairly, know their rights and be able to use them effectively, and consumer law should be fair to both consumers and businesses.

We believe employment matters and are working to promote best practice and effective employment relations.

Through enterprise and business support we are strengthening the enterprise environment for small businesses and enabling more people and communities to set up in business.

We are committed to helping British industry increase its productivity and develop world-class competitiveness by supporting strategically important business sectors.

Britain is a trading nation, and we help UK firms to trade with other countries in three key areas of importance to companies trading and exporting internationally: Europe, trade and export control.

Extract from 'What we do' page, BIS website, 2010

Governments encourage businesses through grants and other **financial support** (for instance, for small businesses). Grants for specific business purposes also come from local authorities, UK regional development agencies and the EU.

Examples of financial support available in 2010 include:

- the Grant for Business Investment (GBI), allowing businesses to acquire key assets such as buildings, machinery and equipment
- the Grant for Research and Development, which provides finance to individuals and SMEs in England to research and develop technologically innovative products and processes
- help from the **Export Credits Guarantee Department** (ECGD), which provides insurance against loss and facilitates the provision of finance for exporters to support their sales of UK services and capital goods.

In 2008/9, the ECGD issued guarantees and insurance policies to the value of £1.46bn.

Governments support industry through **education** and **training**:

- Improvements in education mean a better educated and trained workforce for UK organisations, e.g. the National Curriculum seeks to give pupils a good grounding in core subjects.
- Government-funded ICT training and upgrading of vocational courses improves employee skill levels.
- Because of the pace of change, workers need to be more flexible and adaptable, so the government provides support to businesses needing to re-train employees.

An aim of educational reform is for the workforce to be more effective.

Governments provide businesses with **information**:

- **Business Link** is an online information source for businesses – it covers areas including finance and grants, taxes, employing people, and health and safety matters.
  - An example of the support provided on the Business Link website is the government-introduced 'Solutions for Business' scheme, which offers English firms:
    - financial support, e.g. the Small Loans for Business scheme
    - information and advice on exploiting a business idea and starting up a business, employing people, improving resource efficiency, and accessing international markets.

ONS publications include Regional Trends, Social Trends and Economic Trends.

- The **Office for National Statistics** (ONS) is the government agency responsible for compiling many of the UK's economic and social statistics used by firms to analyse market and other trends.

Governments support businesses through their **regional policies**, which influence where a business locates and employs labour:

- Both the UK government and the EU seek to correct economic imbalances between regions by stimulating the economy in less well-off areas, in order to:
  - reduce inequality of income and employment
  - help firms in these areas compete more effectively
  - counter problems of unemployment due to factors such as structural decline and geographical immobility of labour.

ERDF-funded projects include the Eden Project (£12.8m) and Liverpool's King's Dock re-development (£48m).

- The **European Regional Development Fund** (ERDF) helps stimulate economic development and regeneration in the least prosperous EU regions. From 2000 to 2010, England benefited from more than £5bn of ERDF funding, creating some 200 000 new jobs and helping more than 200 000 SMEs.

KEY POINT

Government support for (and control of) business undergoes regular change, as governments themselves have to respond to change.

PROGRESS CHECK

1. State the four main macro-economic objectives of the UK government.
2. Distinguish between interest and exchange rates.
3. What is the difference between cost-push and demand-pull inflation?
4. In what ways can a firm benefit from government assistance?

1 Economic growth; control of inflation; control of unemployment; stable balance of payments.
2 Interest rates determine the cost of borrowing money; exchange rates show the relative cost of currencies.
3 Cost-push is when higher input (production) costs are translated into higher prices; demand-pull is when the demand for goods exceeds their supply.
4 Financial; education and training; information; regional policy.

Sample question and model answer

Taxation rates are likely to change, but this answer is very limited. Potential tax changes need to be explored in more detail (e.g. how VAT increases affect cost and demand; what if direct taxes on businesses and/or individuals are changed?). Many other points on possible changes in government support (e.g. relating to information, financial support) should be included.

A good point because the unemployment talked about at the start of the question is not necessarily limited to the area where Mercante Ltd is located. The answer needs to look at exactly how demand will be affected.

Some valid points made, although these points should be more closely linked to the idea of improved efficiency (so, for example, how does the ease of linking with other packages actually improve efficiency?). This is a 'To what extent' type of question, so a balanced answer is normally expected – mention should be made of issues such as problems of ensuring security, obsolescence of the system, and the need for a back-up system in case of computer problems.

1. Mercante Ltd is a medium-sized business making components used in the manufacture of televisions and radios. It is based in north Wales, in an area of relatively high unemployment.

(a) How might a change of government policy, following the 2010 general election, affect Mercante Ltd? **(6)**

The new government might change the rates of tax. This will affect costs and demand, for example if VAT is increased.

(b) Explain how a continuing high level of unemployment is likely to affect:

(i) Mercante Ltd

(i) Heavy unemployment in general could affect demand for TVs and radios.

Pricing policy might have to be changed because of the lack of demand, so Mercante's margins will be small, affecting profitability. It might have to review the product range, rationalising production to save costs.

Again good points, but more could be made of other actions such as reviewing labour costs (supply of labour exceeds demand).

(ii) the area in which Mercante Ltd is based. **(8)**

(ii) As unemployment is high, income in the region is low and so spending is also likely to be low, keeping demand for TVs and radios low. It may be that skilled workers will move away, and social problems arise.

Well outlined, though the answer would be strengthened by reference to possible government or EU support from which Mercante could benefit.

(c) The directors of Mercante Ltd are aware that the company might benefit from using more advanced ICT systems. In particular, the invoicing system presently used is regarded as inefficient and is not computerised.

To what extent is computerising the invoicing system and other documents used by Mercante Ltd likely to improve efficiency? **(6)**

The advantages of computerising the invoice system and other documents include speed of access to individual records, the ability to sort and save vast amounts of data, and the ease of linking with other computer-based packages (e.g. the mail merge facility). The system is also likely to be easily expandable when compared with a paper-based system.

Exam practice question

1 The UK government has encouraged foreign-owned car and other manufacturers to set up manufacturing plants in the UK. It has at the same time provided support for other manufacturers, such as Ford and Vauxhall, that are already based in the UK.

What objectives might the government have in giving financial or other support to encourage manufacturing firms either to establish a base in the UK or to remain in the UK? **(10)**

6 External influences (2)

The following topics are covered in this chapter:

- Environmental influences
- Political influences
- Legal influences
- Ethical influences

6.1 Environmental influences

LEARNING SUMMARY

After studying this section, you should be able to:

- give examples of sustainable business activities
- describe the nature and importance of environmental management in business
- outline the steps involved in environmental management

Influence of the environment

AQA	**M4**
Edexcel	**M3**
OCR	**M7**
WJEC	**M1, M3**
CCEA	**M4**

Environmental influences relate to how businesses reduce their impact on the environment. One recent development has been the **sustainable business**, i.e. a business which does not have a negative effect on the environment. Sustainable businesses do make profits, but also undertake environmentally friendly initiatives relating to their goods, services, production processes and other business activities.

Examples of sustainable business activities include:

- making products 'greener', such as the development of 'hybrid' (petrol and electric) and purely electrically-powered cars, and replacing standard electrical bulbs with 'long life' versions
- cutting usage of resources, e.g. electronic storage and transmission of data to reduce paper
- removing harmful substances from production processes or consumer use, such as manufacturing 'eco friendly' household products
- recycling, e.g. re-using packaging, and using paper made from recycled matter.

These activities present challenges to firms (e.g. controlling costs), but also opportunities in terms of new products and markets.

Environmental management

Organisations have become increasingly aware of the impact they have on the environment and their local communities. They can use this awareness to gain a competitive advantage through efficient **environmental management**.

Businesses promote their contribution to the environment through corporate responsibility statements and public relations.

Specific benefits and financial savings result from:

- reduced risk of legal action
- an improved image
- improved energy efficiency
- better waste management
- improved relationships with actual and potential investors.

When carrying out environmental management, an organisation has to consider internal and external influences. Externally, the organisation considers supply chain environmental impacts, seeking to 'green' the supply chain, which enables it to advertise this benefit.

Internally, the normal procedure is to carry out three steps:

1. Undertake an **environmental audit** to establish the current level of environmental performance and achievement, through managers and employees assessing the present impact on the environment, together with how it is being influenced by current legislation.
2. Create an **environmental policy** from the environmental audit – e.g. by documenting environmentally friendly work procedures and setting environmental objectives – and communicate it to all staff (continuing to involve and motivate them).
3. Monitor **environmental performance** against set objectives to improve the firm's environmental performance.

Environmental management at Morrisons

Our strategy for environmental management focuses on cutting carbon and preventing waste. As one of the country's largest supermarket chains with stores, manufacturing and logistics operations, these environmental issues are material impact areas. Reducing our carbon footprint and our waste is an important part of running a responsible and commercially efficient business.

Transport efficiency

Target	**Progress**
Reduce road kilometres travelled per pallet of stock by 6% by 2010.	11.7% reduction compared to 2006.
Achieve an 8% reduction in empty road miles travelled.	22.8% reduction compared to 2006.

2009/10 Morrisons CSR report extracts

Firms can use an improvement in environmental image as an effective marketing tool.

Although there are financial costs associated with an environmental management policy, saving waste can avoid penalties. For example, the UK has adopted the EU Packaging and Packaging Waste Directive, which has imposed charges on firms creating packaging waste.

KEY POINT

There are close links with other external influences, such as UK legislation and developments in 'clean technology' that combat pollution.

PROGRESS CHECK

1. Give two examples of sustainable business activities.
2. List the steps in establishing an effective environmental policy.

1 **Accept two from:** cutting resource usage; recycling; making products 'greener'; removing harmful substances from production processes or consumer use.
2 Carry out environmental audit; set environmental policy; monitor environmental performance.

6.2 Political influences

LEARNING SUMMARY

After studying this section, you should be able to:
- give examples of the scope of political influences
- explain the nature and importance of pressure groups to business

The nature of political influences

AQA	**M4**	WJEC	**M1, M3**
Edexcel	**M3**	CCEA	**M4**
OCR	**M7**		

A key challenge for entrepreneurs is to identify and manage risk. They have traditionally concentrated on risks associated with technology, finance and the market, but increasingly have to consider how political influences can seriously disrupt the work of their business.

Any SWOT analysis of external opportunities and threats should assess politically influenced risks and opportunities.

The scope of political influences includes impacts on:
- **operations** – e.g.
  - work-based legislation such as the minimum wage, equal pay and non-discrimination, which affects cost levels
  - political decisions on grants and planning regulations, which influence location decisions
- **products** – restrictions on product development (e.g. environmental controls, health and safety regulations)
- **image** – e.g. the Labour government 1997–2010 had a policy of 'naming and shaming' organisations of which it was critical (e.g. some railway companies and financial sector firms).

An example of a politically-based campaign is the criticism made about bonuses of some 'fat cat' directors.

The costs of political influences to some firms may present opportunities to others. For example, the decision to introduce new savings (e.g. ISAs) and pensions (e.g. the 'stakeholder pension') brings opportunities for financial services firms.

Entrepreneurs may carry out **political audits** to judge the nature and extent of the political risks they face. They also need to assess expected or actual political influences when making major strategic decisions, such as relocation or the manufacture of a new product.

Pressure groups

Pressure groups are organised groups of people with similar interests who attempt to influence others, notably government and industries. They range in size from international organisations such as Greenpeace and Amnesty International to small community groups concerned with local matters only. **Sector groups** (e.g. British Medical Association) represent a particular sector of interest, and **cause groups** (e.g. ASH – Action on Smoking and Health) promote a particular cause.

The following examples show how pressure groups can affect firms:
- Trade unions act on behalf of their members.
- Motoring organisations, such as the AA, influence vehicle manufacturers on issues such as safety and fuel economy.
- Media influences, e.g. TV campaign-style programmes such as 'Watchdog', affect costs (e.g. correcting faulty product lines) and sales (through good or bad publicity).

A pressure group's success largely depends on the level of financial, public and political support, as well as on the organisational ability of the group itself.

KEY POINT

An increasingly important trend is for politically influenced organisations – such as pressure groups – to create 'virtual' communities of activists through the use of social networking using the Internet.

PROGRESS CHECK

1. Give two examples of the scope of political influences.
2. What is a pressure group?

1 **Accept two from:** business operations; business products; image.
2 An organised group of people with similar interests who attempt to influence others.

6.3 Legal influences

LEARNING SUMMARY

After studying this section, you should be able to:

- explain how employment protection operates in the UK
- outline the nature and relevance of anti-competition legislation
- describe a range of consumer protection laws
- discuss how each of these areas influences the work of UK businesses

Legal regulation

AQA	**M4**	WJEC	**M1, M3**
Edexcel	**M3**	CCEA	**M4**
OCR	**M7**		

The UK parliament passes 'home' legislation. In the EU, Regulations apply directly in all member states and do not have to be confirmed by national parliaments to be legally binding – if there is conflict between a Regulation and existing national law, the Regulation prevails. Directives bind member states, but leave the method of implementation up to national governments.

The main areas of legal regulation affecting firms are employee and employment protection, consumer protection and competition policy.

KEY POINT

Legislation has a two-fold effect on business – it acts as a constraint on firms, and as a framework within which firms operate.

Employment protection

AQA	**M4**	WJEC	**M1, M3**
Edexcel	**M3**	CCEA	**M4**
OCR	**M7**		

The Health and Safety at Work Act (HASAWA) 1974

Under **HASAWA**, employers must take all reasonable care to ensure the safety of their employees.

Employers must provide appropriate training and instruction on health and safety matters, and are obliged to provide safe:

- working environments
- entry and exit arrangements
- plants and systems of work
- working processes (e.g. for unsafe materials).

The obligations of **employees** under HASAWA are:

- to co-operate with their employer on health and safety matters
- to take reasonable care of themselves and others at work
- not to interfere with anything provided for their safety
- to report defects in workplace equipment and processes.

A breach of HASAWA can result in a verbal warning, issuing an improvement notice on the employer, or prosecution.

Enforcement of HASAWA is carried out by the **Health and Safety Executive** (HSE), which carries out investigations by its inspectors, develops new health and safety laws and standards, and publishes guidance and advice. The HSE also oversees the **Control of Substances Hazardous to Health** (COSHH) regulations, which require employers to control, monitor and carry out training associated with substances hazardous to employees' health.

European Union health and safety protection

The European Agency for Safety and Health at Work is the main EU reference point for safety and health at work.

EU member states have harmonised health and safety provisions within a legal framework, adopting measures to ensure that employers adopt safe practices. For example, the **Framework Directive** outlines the responsibilities of employers and employees to encourage workplace health and safety improvements.

The Framework Directive and other EU Directives include protection on:

- workplace requirements – e.g. fire safety and structural stability
- visual display units (VDUs) – covering design features of VDU work stations
- manual handling of heavy loads – e.g. making employers provide mechanical assistance for handling heavy loads
- machinery safety – safety must meet harmonised EU standards.

The UK has adopted EU regulations on **working time** that set minimum standards for employees (with some exceptions) for a maximum working week – an average, including overtime, which does not exceed 48 hours.

These EU regulations also establish minimum:

- rest periods – a 20-minute break if a shift lasts for more than 6 hours, and working no more than 6 days out of every 7
- annual leave – 5.6 weeks' holiday a year.

Country	Hours worked
United Kingdom	43.0
Austria	44.0
Belgium	40.9
Czech Republic	42.7
Germany	41.7
Ireland	40.0

Source: Eurostat

Figure 6.1 Hours worked per week, 2008 (full-time employment)

KEY POINT

Whilst health and safety regulations impose additional costs, firms can also gain because a safe environment improves morale, enhances a firm's reputation and avoids bad publicity.

Employment contracts

Although an **employment contract** need not be in writing, an employer must give a written summary – the 'principal statement' – to an employee within three months of starting work.

Details included are:

- names of the parties and the date that employment commenced
- job title, hours of work and pay rate
- pensions and pension schemes
- length of notice
- holidays and holiday pay
- sick pay arrangements.

Remedies for unfair dismissal include reinstatement if the employee wishes, re-engagement in a comparable job, or compensation.

Workers employed under a contract of service are protected against **unfair dismissal**. The employee can be dismissed for incompetence, gross or serious misconduct (e.g. assault, dishonesty), or the post becoming redundant.

Other employment protection measures now implemented in the UK include:

- the EU's **Part-time Work Directive**, which gives part-time workers equal treatment with full-time employees
- **parental leave and flexible work** regulations, which give working parents the right to request flexible work and to take set amounts of maternity and paternity leave on the birth or adoption of a child.

Anti-discrimination

In 2010, it was reported that only 12 percent of directors of the FTSE-100 companies were women.

In practice, men generally earn more than women in the UK. In 2009, the highest pay difference was for skilled trade occupations (26 percent) and the lowest for professional occupations (3.8 percent). The Equality and Human Rights Commission has expressed concern over discrimination in UK pay systems and a lack of objectivity in setting rates of pay.

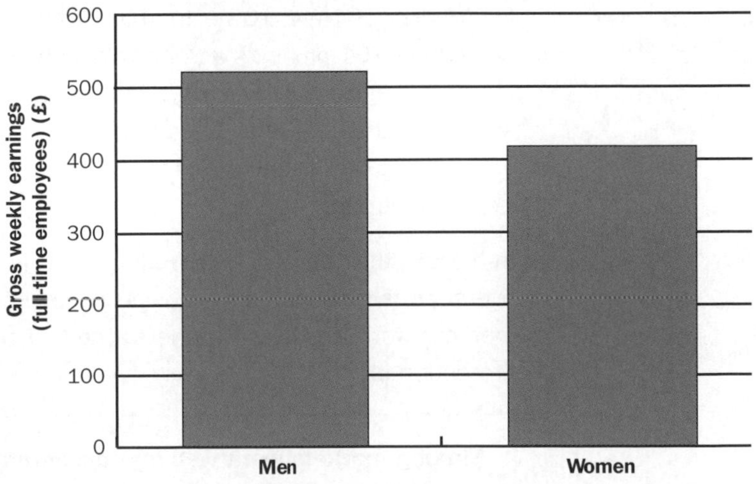

Graph adapted from ONS statistics, 2009

Figure 6.2 Disparity in earnings, April 2009

Although in general men earn more than women, UK law includes the **Equal Pay Act**, which requires employers to pay equal rates of pay to men and women for **doing the same job** (or work of equivalent value). The EU has reinforced this principle in its Directive on equal pay and it also requires UK businesses to offer equal treatment on issues such as training and social security rights.

Employment statistics tend to show non-white workers' unemployment rates to be higher than those of white workers.

It is also illegal for an employer to discriminate on the grounds of sexual orientation, religion, or certain other beliefs.

Other anti-discrimination legislation includes:

- the **Sex Discrimination Act**, which makes it unlawful for employers to discriminate on the grounds of sex when they advertise a job, recruit staff and set retirement dates
- the **Race Relations Act**, which makes it unlawful for an employer to discriminate on the grounds of race, colour, nationality and ethnic origin
- the **Disability Discrimination Act**, which makes it unlawful for disabled persons to be treated less favourably than others – employers must also review the work environment to help overcome problems faced by those with disabilities
- the **Employment Equality (Age) Regulations**, which make it unlawful to discriminate against employees, job seekers and trainees because of their age.

KEY POINT

Issues of discrimination in business relate to an organisation's social responsibility and ethical stance. Evidence showing that discrimination still persists indicates that some firms must be criticised for their lack of social responsibility and inappropriate ethical behaviour.

Competition policy

AQA	**M4**	WJEC	**M1, M3**
Edexcel	**M3**	CCEA	**M4**
OCR	**M7**		

In the UK and the rest of the EU, monopolies and anti-competitive practices are deemed to be against the public interest – prices tend to be higher than in a competitive market, and there can be less consumer product choice. Through its 'competition policy' and Merger Control Regulation, the EU seeks to ensure that trade between member states is based on **free and fair competition**.

Price fixing or market sharing are characteristics of cartels (agreements between businesses not to compete with each other).

Anti-competitive behaviour that may affect trade inside the UK is prohibited by the **Competition Act** and the **Enterprise Act**.

EU Articles 101 and 102 extend this to the rest of the EU:

- Article 101 prohibits agreements between two or more firms that restrict competition, e.g. by fixing prices, controlling production and sharing markets.
- Article 102 prevents firms that are in a dominant market position from abusing that position by, for example, using predatory pricing to eliminate competitors.

Regulatory bodies such as OFGEM and OFWAT enforce competition laws in their own industries.

In the UK, the **Office of Fair Trading** (OFT) is the main enforcement authority that oversees fair competition amongst businesses. It has the mission to make markets work well for consumers. The OFT also helps enforce consumer protection law.

Making markets work well for consumers – the OFT's mission

The OFT's mission is to make markets work well for consumers. We achieve this by promoting and protecting consumer interests throughout the UK, while ensuring that businesses are fair and competitive.

OFT website, 2010

The OFT can refer proposed mergers (which may lead to a monopoly) or restrictive practices (such as agreements to fix prices, which is against the interest of consumers) to the **Competition Commission**, which conducts in-depth inquiries into mergers, markets and the regulation of the major regulated industries.

Consumer protection

AQA	**M4**
Edexcel	**M2, M3**
OCR	**M7**
WJEC	**M1, M3**
CCEA	**M4**

Consumers enter **contracts** when buying goods or services. To support contract law, UK governments and the EU have a range of consumer protection laws.

Examples of consumer protection laws include the following:

- The Unfair Commercial Practices Directive, implemented in the UK, prevents business practices that are unfair to consumers.
  - Businesses have a general duty to follow acceptable trading practice.
  - Misleading or aggressive practices are not allowed, and certain practices (e.g. falsely stating that a product will only be available for a limited time) are banned.
- Traders have a legal duty not to use unfair terms – such as those that deny the consumer full redress – in the contracts they have with consumers.
- The Distance Selling Regulations protect consumers buying online or at a distance (e.g. by mail order).
  - For example, a seven working-day 'cooling off' period is allowed, during which time the customer can cancel the contract.
- Sale of goods legislation ensures that goods – and now services – must be of satisfactory quality (fit to be sold), fit for the purpose for which they were bought, and when sold by description they should match that description.
- The Consumer Protection Act introduced liability for damage arising from defective products.
- Businesses offering credit to consumers must be licensed and set out credit agreements in a particular way, ensuring they contain particular information.
- The Food Safety Act consolidates earlier law relating to the supply of food products, and protects consumers against the sale of unfit food.
- Laws on weights and measures protect consumers by making it an offence to sell goods underweight or short in quantity.

Certain goods, e.g. milk, must be sold in fixed weight/volume so prices can be compared.

EU influences

EU Directives in this area seek to establish **common levels of consumer protection** throughout the Union. Some Directives have removed trade barriers and others concentrate on transport arrangements to ensure free movement of goods.

The CE Marking Directives set out various requirements that have to be met before products can be sold in member states (e.g. relating to safety). Products meeting these requirements carry the CE mark, which means they can be sold anywhere in the Community. Such Directives control product design and give a 'level playing field' for product safety requirements across the EU.

The CE Marking Directives have had a major impact on many industries (page 76 shows the CE safety mark).

Figure 6.3, on the next page, illustrates the general framework for EU activities in favour of the consumer.

Education and consumer information	Consumer requirements	Protection of consumers' interests
Product packaging: e.g. – pre-packaged products – quick-frozen foods **Product labelling**: e.g. – household appliances – beverages – footwear – tobacco **Special indications**: e.g. – designation of origin **Price indications**: e.g. – foodstuffs*1 – gas and electricity **Advertising**: e.g. – misleading adverts*2 – advertising medicines	**Product safety**: e.g. – general product safety*3 – toy safety*4 – dangerous imitations **Consumer health**: e.g. – food safety – veterinary inspections – genetic modification **Quality of goods and services**: e.g. – cosmetic products – foodstuff quality – quality of the environment	**Electronic commerce**: e.g. – legal aspects **Contracts**: e.g. – contracts away from business premises – unfair contract terms*5 – guarantees **Transport**: e.g. – package travel*6 – air transport **Financial and insurance services**: e.g. – electronic payments – consumer credit **Legal redress**: e.g. – access to justice

(* indicates specific numbered example – see below)

Figure 6.3 The general framework for EU activities in favour of the consumer

1. It is compulsory for traders to indicate the selling price and unit price of all products offered to consumers, for both food and non-food items.
2. The Misleading and Comparative Advertising Directive protects consumers and competitor firms from the consequences of misleading advertising. This Directive covers comparative advertising, which identifies a competitor or the products of a competitor, and protects firms from being unfairly discredited.
3. The General Product Safety Directive requires producers to place only safe products on the market. It applies entirely to a product if no CE Marking Directives apply.
4. The Toy Safety Directive ensures that every toy sold in the EU fulfils, to the highest level, the newest health and safety standards.
5. The Unfair Contract Terms Directive introduces a notion of 'good faith' to ensure greater balance between the rights and duties of consumers, and those of sellers. Contractual terms found to be unfair under this Directive are not binding on consumers.
6. The Package Travel Directive protects consumers who enter a contract for package travel, whereby package organisers and retailers must accept responsibility for the performance of the services offered.

The underlying principle behind these and other Directives is the free movement of goods.

Relevance of consumer legislation to business

The effects of consumer legislation on firms relate to:

- **protection** – e.g. against comparative advertising, which could exploit a trade name or which presents a firm's goods as replicas of goods protected by a trade name
- **costs** – e.g. food safety laws requiring hygiene-related costs to be met
- **customer satisfaction** – by meeting customer expectations, as well as legal requirements, the firm's products are more saleable
- **internal systems** – e.g. firms seek to improve quality control and to develop a 'quality culture'.

KEY POINT

Firms have become increasingly customer-oriented, using market research and public relations as key departments for providing feedback.

PROGRESS CHECK

1. What forms of discrimination still exist at work?
2. Why does the UK legislate against anti-competitive practices?

1 Sexual, e.g. unequal pay, sexual orientation; employment; racial; age-based; disability-based; religion and other beliefs.
2 In the public interest, to stop consumers being exploited by, for instance, monopolies.

6.4 Ethical influences

LEARNING SUMMARY

After studying this section, you should be able to:

- define the term 'ethics'
- outline the purpose of an ethical code of practice in business
- explain the benefits and drawbacks to a business of having an ethical policy

Business ethics

AQA	**M4**
Edexcel	**M3, M4**
OCR	**M1, M7**
WJEC	**M1, M3**
CCEA	**M4**

Ethics refers to a code of morally correct behaviour. For example, concerns over excessive drinking led businesses such as Tesco, in 2010, to support the introduction of minimum pricing for alcohol. Organisations nowadays make ethical statements that outline the moral stance they take in business.

The Body Shop's ethical statement about animal testing

Since the beginning The Body Shop has campaigned passionately to end animal testing for cosmetics purposes. In the EU, we pride ourselves in being part of the movement that saw the Cosmetics Directive amended to ban animal testing of finished cosmetic products from 2004. The ban on the testing of ingredients came into force in March 2009.

...The Body Shop has not tested finished cosmetic products on animals since its inception and we do not ask others to test on our behalf.

Suppliers must certify that they have not carried out animal tests on ingredients to support their use for a cosmetics purpose... .

The Body Shop website, Values Report 2009

An **ethical code of practice** is normally drawn up to clarify a firm's ethical policy. This document outlines the way that the firm and its employees are expected to behave in certain situations and is tailored to the nature of the business.

Organisations such as The Body Shop – which takes pride in its ethical stance – may concentrate on general human rights issues; manufacturing firms may focus on the environment; financial institutions on honesty and integrity, and so on.

Legal controls, including the **Human Rights Act**, are available if firms fail to make a commitment towards acceptable business ethics. There are also voluntary agreements – for example, an OECD (Organisation for Economic Co-operation and Development) voluntary code of conduct for multinationals includes human rights standards where, under the code, a multinational is accountable for abuses of its employees and the environment throughout the world. Many businesses follow **voluntary codes of practice** – guidelines to be followed – for their industry. The codes are often written up after consulting a range of stakeholders, such as suppliers, customers and employees.

KEY POINT

The ethical behaviour and policy of an organisation is influenced by the ethical stance of the people who make up that organisation, because employees can nowadays impose their own ethical views. For example, the Public Interest Disclosure Act protects employees who wish to raise concerns about issues at work.

Benefits and drawbacks of an ethical policy

Many pressure groups adopt ethical stances and encourage organisations to adopt a similar viewpoint.

There are a number of benefits to an organisation from having an ethical policy:

- **Marketing benefits** – a firm may find many of its customers will only buy its products if it has an acceptable ethical policy. So, having drawn up an ethical code of practice, the firm will publish it to communicate its policy to customers and to support its marketing strategy.
- **Employee benefits** – firms adopting positive ethical practices often find their employees are more motivated to work for them.

The problems associated with an ethical policy include lower profits, because ethical behaviour is likely to lead to higher costs, and potential conflict with existing objectives such as profit maximisation and market share. For example, an objective based on profit maximisation may encourage a firm to act in a way unacceptable under its ethical policy, for instance in relation to exploitation of labour or the environment.

KEY POINT

Although environmental and ethical policies commit a firm to expenditure and increase overall costs, they are of great benefit to the firm's image and its marketing strategy.

PROGRESS CHECK

1 State two benefits to a firm of having an ethical policy.

1 The firm can use the ethical policy as part of its marketing strategy; more motivated employees.

Sample question and model answer

1. HavaGo plc is a major retailing 'do it yourself' (DIY) store. It is aware that all its major competitors are publicising their ethical policies. The management of HavaGo plc is in the process of reviewing the company's ethical policy to establish a more clearly defined ethical code. As a result of the review it has been decided to implement a much clearer and more aggressive ethical policy.

(a) What is an 'ethical policy' and an 'ethical code'? **(4)**

'Ethical policy' refers to the code of behaviour adopted by a business. They give a sort of moral guideline on what it does. An 'ethical code' is the document that actually sets out the way the business and its staff act in certain situations.

A good answer. The candidate could also include the point that an organisation's ethics are shaped by (a) its culture, and (b) the nature of its business.

(b) Describe **two** types of ethical policy that might be adopted by the managers of HavaGo plc. **(6)**

The first policy I would recommend is for HavaGo plc to consider the effects of its policies on the environment. It could, for instance, encourage customers to re-use plastic bags, it should only sell 'environmentally friendly' and 'repeat-use' products where possible, and it shouldn't trade with any firms that exploit their local environment.

The second ethical policy I would recommend would be to support equal opportunities. HavaGo should make sure it applies all the UK and EU legislation on anti-discrimination and it should also support local and national equal opportunities initiatives.

This answer includes some relevant policies, although it could outline some relevant illustrations, e.g. by including mention of how anti-discriminatory practices (race, sex and disability) affect specific functions (human resources, customer service, shop layout, advertising images, etc.).

(c) Evaluate the costs and benefits of one of these policies to the employees of HavaGo plc. **(10)**

The benefits of Policy 2 to employees are that it will give them a greater sense of worth and self-esteem (Maslow), and the business may also prosper - its enhanced reputation and goodwill will lead to positive publicity and more sales, and also help frame advertising campaigns that will again increase sales. If this happens, higher profits should result, which could ensure jobs are secure and also benefit employees through share schemes/profit sharing.

The cost of this policy to employees is that monitoring and applying laws have a financial cost that will affect HavaGo's profits. Also, prices charged by 'acceptable' suppliers may be higher - as a result, some customers may go elsewhere for lower prices if HavaGo's price competitiveness suffers. This may put pressure on keeping jobs for employees, and reduced profit margins may lead to lower share prices and lower dividends if they are part of an incentive share scheme.

It is important to refer to motivation theory – other theorists such as Herzberg could also be included.

Exam practice question

1 **(a)** Outline how the finance, human resources, marketing and operations management (production) functions of an organisation might be influenced by an increased awareness of environmental matters. **(10)**

(b) NAM Ltd makes components for the vehicle industry. The directors of NAM Ltd are considering whether to change their policy on how their industrial waste is disposed of. The company is based in an area formerly used for mining and quarrying – as a result, this waste is used as landfill to help fill the old mining and quarrying sites. The directors are proposing to buy and use large machinery to crush and burn the waste.

Identify the main costs associated with such a decision. **(10)**

7 Markets and marketing

The following topics are covered in this chapter:

- Market types
- Market demand, supply and price
- Elasticity of demand
- The marketing concept
- Marketing strategy and planning
- Market segmentation

7.1 Market types

LEARNING SUMMARY

After studying this section, you should be able to:

- define the term 'market' in the context of business
- give examples of real-life markets
- distinguish between consumer markets and industrial markets

The nature of markets

AQA	**M1, M2**	WJEC	**M1**
Edexcel	**M1**	CCEA	**M1**
OCR	**M1**		

The term 'market' features in our everyday language, but in Business Studies a market can be defined as a place where buyers and sellers come together. It can be a physical location, such as a town or village market, but need not be. Firms need to understand their markets in order to be successful, and to market their products effectively to make profits.

Markets can be regional, national or international. Examples include the labour market, the market for vehicles and the international capital market. Specialist markets exist for some products, such as a stock exchange which specialises in buying and selling stocks and shares.

The degree of **competitiveness** varies from market to market. Some markets, such as the grocery market, are dominated by a few large firms, whereas others – such as the market for personal services, e.g. hairdressing and electrical maintenance – have no dominant firm.

KEY POINT

A firm can improve its market competitiveness through strategies such as staff training, improving product quality and cutting costs.

There are two main types of markets: **consumer markets** and **industrial markets**.

Consumer markets

Consumer markets exist for consumer goods, which are bought for their own satisfaction:

- Single-use consumer goods have short lives and are income-inelastic. Often called FMCGs (fast-moving consumer goods), they satisfy physical (e.g. food), psychological (e.g. cosmetics), or impulse (e.g. sweets) needs.
- Consumer durables such as televisions and washing machines have an income-elastic demand (see page 122). They are long lasting, expensive, bought infrequently and with care.
- Consumer services (e.g. hairdressers and plumbers) are used more often as income grows, and tend to satisfy basic physical and safety needs.

Industrial markets

Industrial markets are also known as B2B (business to business) markets.

Industrial markets exist for products used by industries in their production.

Industrial products can be classified as:

- capital goods, e.g. new equipment
- industrial consumables, e.g. fuel, stationery
- industrial services, e.g. cleaning.

	Consumer markets	*Industrial markets*
Customers	Many: allowing price to be set by the firm	Few: firm negotiates price and terms with the customer
Channel	Various, e.g. through wholesalers and retailers	Usually direct to customer
Product	More standardised: some differentiation	More personalised: may be made to end-user requirements
Methods	Resources concentrated on advertising: mass media used	Less generalised: more personal selling, use of specialist journals

KEY POINT

Some products can be both consumer and capital goods, depending on their use. For example, laptop computers are used for games and for business.

PROGRESS CHECK

1. Give an example of a local market and an international market.
2. How do consumer markets differ from industrial ones?

1 Corner shop (local); televisions (international) (**accept any other suitable answers**).
2 Number of customers; channel and product type; marketing methods.

7.2 Market demand, supply and price

LEARNING SUMMARY

After studying this section, you should be able to:

- state what is meant by 'effective demand'
- describe the laws of demand and of supply
- distinguish between a change in quantity demanded and a change in demand
- distinguish between a change in quantity supplied and a change in supply
- illustrate the effects of these changes diagrammatically

The nature of demand

AQA	**M1**	OCR	**M1**
Edexcel	**M1**	CCEA	**M1**

Buyers purchase from the range of goods and services available from producers. In order to supply products, producers must themselves buy factors of production – land, labour and capital – which are for sale in the marketplace. In the private sector, the price mechanism determines what firms produce, and how they use the different factors of production.

The laws of demand

It is assumed that this is **effective demand**, i.e. it is backed by money and an ability to buy.

The fundamental laws of demand are that:

- as price increases, the quantity demanded falls
- as price falls, the quantity demanded rises.

The demand curve

When a demand curve is plotted to show consumer behaviour in a single market, it appears as in Figure 7.1.

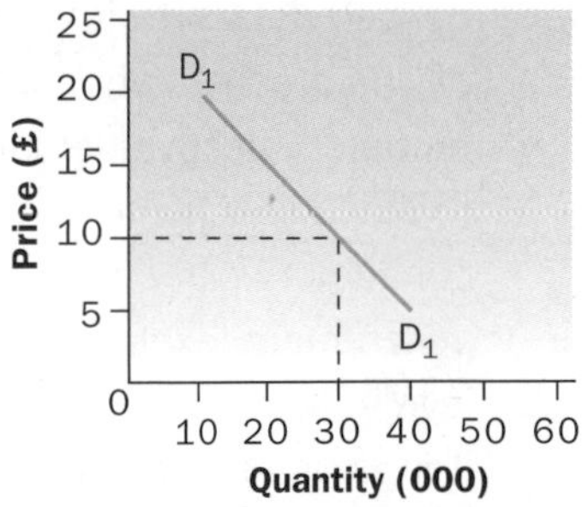

Figure 7.1 The demand curve

The graph shows that 30 000 items are demanded at a price of £10. The gradient of the curve's fall from left to right varies according to the elasticity of demand for the item (see page 121). The downward slope of the demand curve confirms that consumers demand more of the item as its price falls. In Figure 7.1, an expansion of quantity demanded occurs if the price falls from £10 (when 30 000 are demanded) to £5 (when 40 000 are demanded). A contraction of quantity demanded occurs when the price increases.

The demand curve does not change position on the graph.

These movements along the demand curve are due solely to price changes for the product, and are referred to as changes in quantity demanded.

Shifts in the demand curve

Changes in demand also occur, resulting in the demand curve moving position. These are known as **shifts in demand** – the curve moves to the right (an increase in demand) or to the left (a decrease in demand), as shown in Figures 7.2 and 7.3.

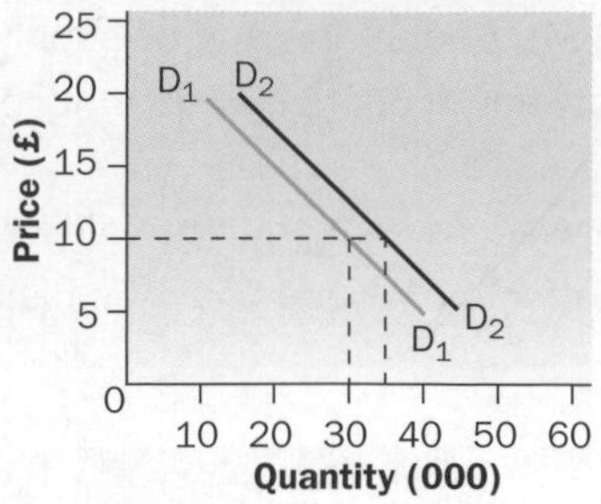

Figure 7.2 Increase in demand

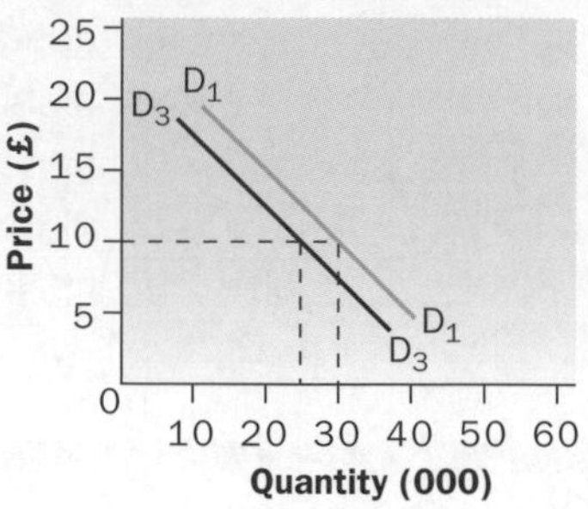

Figure 7.3 Decrease in demand

In Figure 7.2, the demand curve has moved to the right. The increase in demand (shown by curve D_2) at a price of £10 is from 30 000 to 35 000. Figure 7.3 represents a fall in demand. At a price of £10 demand has fallen from 30 000 to 25 000 (see curve D_3).

The growth in the number of vegetarians in the UK has increased demand for vegetarian foods.

Shifts in the demand curve are due to changes in the following:

- **Tastes or fashion**. Tastes change over time, new trends arrive and fashions go out of date. The effect on demand can be either short-term or long-term.
- **The price of substitutes**. Many products have close substitutes. This applies to foodstuffs (meat, spreads, etc.) and many branded products such as soap, toothpaste and washing-up liquid. In such cases an increase in the price of one alternative is likely to increase the demand for its substitute; the demand curve for the substitute will shift to the right even though its price has not altered.
- **The price of jointly-demanded products**. When one product is in joint or derived demand with another (e.g. vehicles and petrol), a change in the price of one product can affect the demand for its joint product.
- **Income**. Effective demand must be backed by money, and so any increase in real disposable income normally shifts the demand curve to the right because consumers can afford more of the product. Disposable income is affected by government taxation policies or changes in employment and general wage levels. Increases in income might result in less of a good being demanded if it is an inferior good. Consumers switch their attention to substitutes felt to be superior, for example by buying cars (private transport) to replace the use of public transport.
- **Innovation**. As new goods and services are introduced, they influence the demand for products currently on the market. Good examples come from the technology sector, where Apple's iPod and similar developments have lowered the demand for other media such as compact discs.
- **Population**. The UK population movements towards urban areas and away from the countryside have changed the demand for public and private transport in different parts of the country. Changes in society and attitudes also affect demand. For example, an increase in the number of one-parent families can increase the demand for smaller properties. The UK has an ageing population, which has caused increasing demand for health care and other products used by the elderly. A fall in the school-age population will lead to a reduced demand for a range of education services.

Firms create demand for labour, capital and land. Therefore, the relative level of firms' income is important.

Changes occur in the total population, its age or other structure, and its geographical location.

KEY POINT

A change in quantity demanded is different to a change in demand.

The nature of supply

AQA **M1** OCR **M1**
Edexcel **M1** CCEA **M1**

Figure 7.4 shows that the direction of the supply curve is opposite to that of the demand curve, because:

- as price increases the quantity supplied rises
- as price decreases the quantity supplied falls.

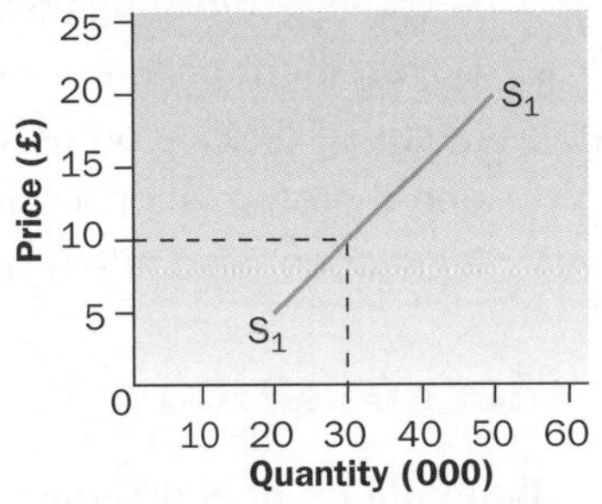

Figure 7.4 The supply curve

The higher the price, the greater the quantity supplied. Higher prices mean higher profit margins, so existing firms in the market are encouraged to produce more and new firms are encouraged to enter the market. The market supply curve in Figure 7.4 shows the amount that will be supplied at any given price. For example, at a price of £10 firms are prepared to supply 30 000 items.

Shifts in the supply curve

Movements along an existing supply curve – expansions or contractions of the quantity supplied – occur when the price of a product changes. The supply curve itself might also move, due to a number of factors. When this occurs it is referred to as a **shift in supply**, and it is due to non-price factors. Figures 7.5 and 7.6 show shifts in supply.

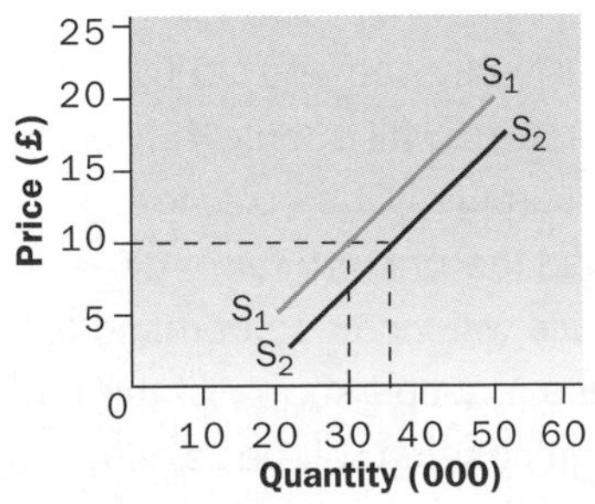

Figure 7.5 Increase in supply

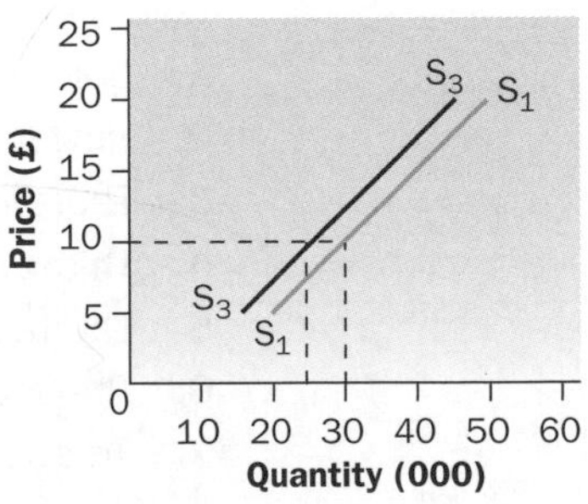

Figure 7.6 Decrease in supply

A change from supply curve S_1 to S_2 illustrates that, at a price of £10, firms are now prepared to supply 35 000 items. Where supply changes from S_1 to S_3, firms will supply 25 000 rather than 30 000 items.

Improvements in the quality of an individual factor, e.g. by training labour, has the same effect.

Shifts in the supply curve are due to changes in the following:

- **Factor inputs**. A change in the price of the individual factors of production used, their quality, or the ratio in which they are used all result in a change in production costs, which in turn affects profit margins. A good example is technological developments, where cost-saving new machinery and automated processes reduce labour costs and lead to increased productivity.

- **Competition**. The existence of major competitors should lead to increased efficiency in the use of resources. This in turn leads to higher output at given cost levels and increases the supply of the product.
- **Other products**. Where jointly-supplied products exist (for example, petrol, paraffin and other oils share many production processes), an increase in the price of one product leads to increased supply of both it and the other joint products.
- **Natural factors**. The UK's exploitation of North Sea oil illustrates how discovering a new source of a primary product increases its supply. Changes in climate through global warming influence agricultural production levels.
- **Government policies**. Taxation levels affect firms as well as individuals because direct (corporation) and indirect (VAT) tax changes affect total costs and therefore supply levels. Changes in the law, such as new environmental legislation, also affect production methods and costs.

Market price

The market – or **equilibrium** – price is established when supply equals demand. If the demand and supply curves in Figures 7.1 and 7.4 are combined, the equilibrium price will be £10 (see Figure 7.7). At this price, consumers demand 30 000 items and producers supply 30 000 items.

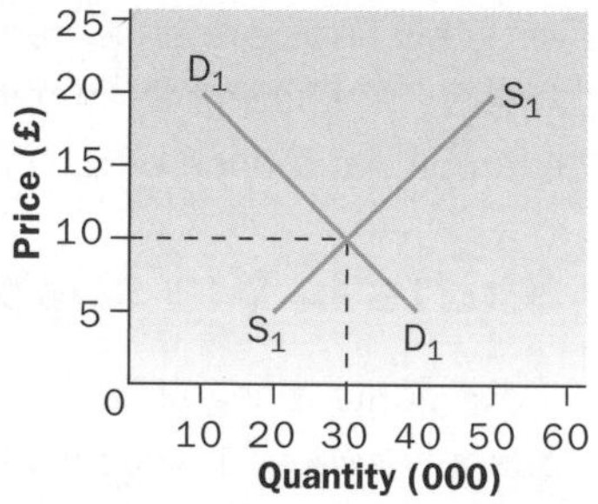

Figure 7.7 Equilibrium

Prices can change. For example, if the price rises to £15, the following is likely to take place:

1. Consumers will only demand 20 000 items.
2. However, producers will supply 40 000 items.
3. Therefore, a surplus will be created.
4. This will cause the price to fall.
5. The fall in price will increase demand for the product.
6. There will be a reduced supply of the product.
7. An equilibrium position will be re-established.

KEY POINT

The role of the market is to act as a **system of exchange based on demand, supply and price**.

PROGRESS CHECK

1. Movement along the same demand curve results from a change in what?
2. Give two examples of why a supply curve might shift.

1 Quantity demanded.
2 **Accept two from:** change in factor inputs; change in competition; change in other products; natural factors; government policies.

7.3 Elasticity of demand

LEARNING SUMMARY

After studying this section, you should be able to:

- distinguish between price and income elasticity of demand (PED and IED)
- state the formulae for calculating PED and IED
- calculate elasticity of demand from given information

Influences on elasticity

AQA	**M2**	WJEC	**M4**
Edexcel	**M2a**	CCEA	**M1**
OCR	**M1**		

The measure of the change taking place in the quantity demanded or supplied as a result of some external factor is know as **elasticity**.

Elasticity of demand is affected by:

- changes in **price** = **PED**
- changes in **income** = **IED**.

Price elasticity of demand

The PED for a product measures the responsiveness of the quantity demanded to a change in its price. **Movements along the demand curve** are being analysed, not changes in demand.

The following formula is used to calculate PED:

$$\text{PED} = \frac{\text{Percentage change in quantity demanded}}{\text{Percentage change in price}}$$

Applying this formula, if, for example, there is a rise in price from £20 to £30, with a fall in the quantity demanded from 400 to 300, PED = $\frac{25}{50}$ = 0.5. If PED is below 1, as in this case, demand is **price-inelastic**. When PED is greater than 1, the supplier knows that a change in price will bring about a more than proportionate change in the quantity demanded. The product is **price-sensitive** and demand is said to be **price-elastic** as a result. Where PED = 1, it is known as **unitary elasticity**. Any given percentage price change results in the same percentage change in the quantity demanded.

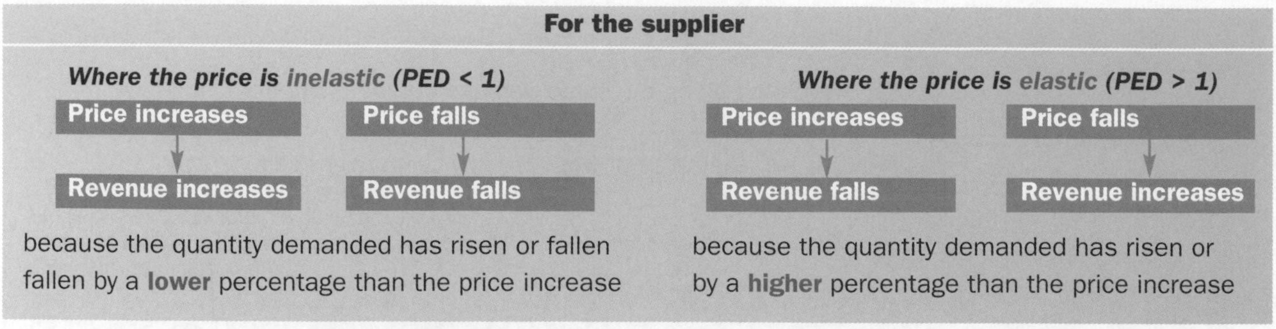

Figure 7.8 Price elasticity and the supplier

Price elasticity is influenced by the following:

- **Availability of substitutes**. If a product has a close substitute, e.g. margarine and butter, demand tends to be elastic because the user can move easily between the substitutes. Where substitutes do not exist, there is less competition and demand is therefore more inelastic.
- **Percentage of income spent on the product**. Inexpensive products often have inelastic demand because price increases have little effect on consumers' spending plans. With higher-priced products, consumers often search harder for substitutes or alternatives, or go without the item.
- **Addiction**. Where consumers are prevented from making price-rational decisions, for instance through alcohol or other drug addiction, price movements have less effect and prices tend to be inelastic.

KEY POINT

Price elasticity is an important measuring tool because it influences producers' decisions.

Income elasticity of demand

IED measures how demand responds to changes in consumer incomes.

IED is measured using the following formula:

$$\text{IED} = \frac{\text{Percentage change in quantity demanded}}{\text{Percentage change in income}}$$

So, if consumer income rises by 3% and demand for a product rises by 9% as a result:

$$\text{IED} = \frac{9}{3} = 3.0$$

A positive result is normal because demand for most products rises and falls with income. Inferior goods, e.g. some staple foodstuffs, may have a negative IED because the amount demanded falls as real income rises and people can afford more appealing alternatives.

Demand is **income-elastic when IED is greater than 1**, and **income-inelastic when IED is less than 1**. The higher the percentage of income spent on the product, the more income-elastic the product tends to be.

PROGRESS CHECK

1. State how income elasticity of demand is calculated.
2. Identify two influences on the price elasticity of demand for a product.

1 The percentage change in quantity demanded over percentage change in income.
2 **Accept two from:** availability of substitutes; percentage of income spent on the product; addiction.

7.4 The marketing concept

LEARNING SUMMARY

After studying this section, you should be able to:

- describe the roles of the marketing function
- distinguish between the focus of a product-oriented and a market-oriented business
- outline the nature of the marketing concept
- state the purpose of marketing objectives

The role of marketing

AQA	**M1, M2**
Edexcel	**M1, M2a**
OCR	**M1, M3**
WJEC	**M1**
CCEA	**M1**

The marketing function undertakes three key roles within an organisation:

1. It supports the exchange process through techniques aimed at the consumer.
2. It collects and analyses data on both the consumer and the market.
3. It acts as a co-ordinating function for the organisation.

Marketing is the one function in an organisation that looks outwards. It integrates and co-ordinates by collecting – then disseminating – information on the consumer and the market throughout the organisation.

Product-oriented business

The traditional production-led (or asset-led) approach to manufacturing focused on making the product. This approach to manufacturing, as a result of concentrating on the product, used production processes that were heavily cost-influenced. This led to the end products tending to be standardised, and the firm placing the product on the market in the hope that it would sell.

Product-oriented businesses are likely to struggle to survive in today's competitive world.

Market-oriented business

Production methods and cost-efficient processes remain important, but the emphasis is on the consumer and the market.

A **market-oriented** organisation recognises the importance of meeting the consumer's wants and wishes, and provides choices in order to satisfy consumers. Such a marketing-led approach requires an organisation to analyse its market and to meet what is demanded by the market. It seeks to differentiate products on the basis of market requirements, and to meet the needs of customers.

A market-led firm examines its activities through the eyes of its customers. It will set clear marketing objectives, and review its other objectives in the light of these. For example, a marketing objective to increase market share will affect other objectives, such as those based on production and cash flow.

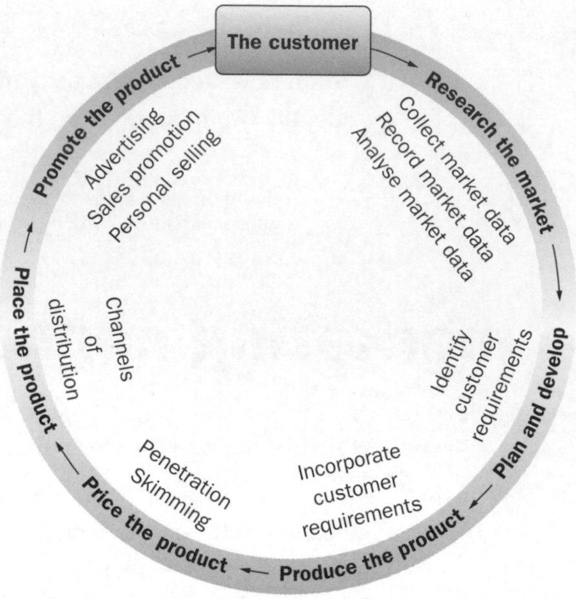

Figure 7.9 Marketing influence on the business cycle

> **KEY POINT**
>
> The basis of the 'marketing concept' is that the customer is seen as the start of the business cycle, rather than its end.

Marketing objectives

By focusing on the market, a market-led firm will use marketing objectives as targets to achieve. The targets set will be linked to the firm's mission statement. Marketing objectives often focus on product differentiation and innovation, on market growth, or on specialist features of a product range, as in the following example.

> The Fairtrade mark guarantees products are produced by workers in safe, decent conditions. We're so passionate about Fairtrade at Asda we have a dedicated team who work closely with the Fairtrade organisation to promote their licensed products.
>
> *Asda website, 2010*

> **PROGRESS CHECK**
>
> 1. State two roles undertaken by the marketing function.
> 2. What does a product-oriented business concentrate on?
>
> 1 **Accept two from:** collects and analyses consumer/market data; co-ordinates other business; supports the exchange process through techniques aimed at the consumer.
> 2 How to make the product using standardised processes.

7.5 Marketing strategy and planning

LEARNING SUMMARY

After studying this section, you should be able to:

- explain the nature of a typical marketing strategy
- illustrate and describe Ansoff's matrix

Marketing strategy

AQA	**M2, M3**
Edexcel	**M2a, M4a**
OCR	**M1, M3, M7**
WJEC	**M4**
CCEA	**M1, M3**

A firm's **marketing strategy** translates its marketing objectives into action. It is a medium- to long-term approach that balances the marketing and other objectives with the resources available and the practical realities of the market.

Competitor and government actions are important influences on strategy.

The strategy selected will be influenced by a number of factors, including:

- SWOT results – an evaluation and audit of the firm's (internal) **S**trengths and **W**eaknesses, and its (external) **O**pportunities and **T**hreats
- market research data, e.g. on consumer buying behaviour
- past sales statistics
- marketing audits – reviews of the efficiency of the marketing function
- resource availability.

Ansoff's matrix

Igor Ansoff's **product–market framework** is widely used to analyse the strategic direction of a firm. The matrix identifies four options:

The first two options focus on the market and the second two on the product.

1. **Market penetration** – increasing the firm's market share in its existing markets through its existing products.
2. **Market development** – the firm seeks to enter new markets or segments with its existing products.
3. **Product development** – new products are developed for existing markets.
4. **(Product) diversification** – new products are developed for new markets.

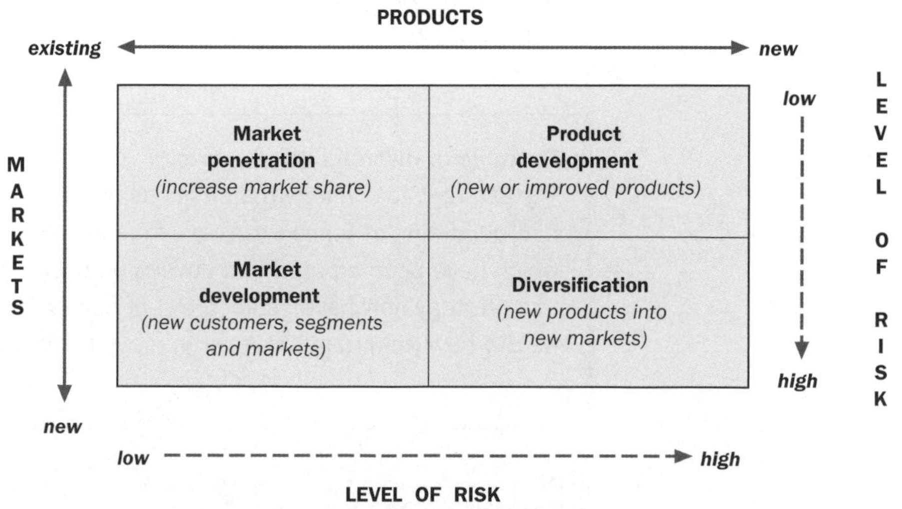

Figure 7.10 Ansoff's matrix

The lowest-risk strategy for **market penetration** is to increase market share using existing products within existing markets. Growth markets are easier to penetrate than mature or declining ones. To expand in mature and declining markets involves heavy advertising in order to take sales away from competitors.

Example of market penetration strategy

In 2010 Morrisons reported year-on-year sales increases, which were helped by promoting existing products through price cuts and by activities such as 'Essentials For Less' promotions.

Morrisons Annual Review, 2010

Although a product's strengths and weaknesses are known to a firm, **market development** is a higher-risk strategy, especially since the growth of globalisation has led to many firms marketing their existing products in new, international markets.

Example of market development strategy

The Group has made good progress in its plans to become a truly nationwide retailer. During the year we opened 43 new stores....

Morrisons Annual Review, 2010

The modern tendency is for products to have shorter life cycles, so **product development** strategies are widely found. Compared with market development, this strategy brings the advantage that a firm will be dealing with consumers about whom it has some knowledge and experience, and a firm may be able to use existing brand names successfully.

Example of product development strategy

This year, we intend to build on our success by bringing our leading HD box technology to even more customers. From today, we will start selling HD-enabled boxes as standard....

BSkyB Interim Management Report, 2010

Diversification is the highest-risk strategy for a firm. The diversification may be related (where new products and markets are similar to existing ones) or unrelated (growth into products and markets that have little in common with the firm's existing ones).

Example of diversification strategy

The strategy to diversify the business was laid down in 1997 and has been the foundation of Tesco's success in recent years. The new businesses which have been created and developed over the last 12 years as part of this strategy now have scale, they are competitive and profitable – in fact we are now [the] market leader in many of our markets outside the UK.

'Our strategy', Tesco website, 2010

KEY POINT

Ansoff's matrix is a management tool that can be used to discuss the effects of change on a business.

The marketing plan and budget

Many promotional strategies are based on AIDA (Awareness, Interest, Desire, Action) – see page 163.

A firm's promotional strategy is influenced by the product, its stage in the product life cycle, and the budget available. To implement the strategy, a **marketing plan** must be drawn up. The plan is important because it integrates the various parts of the marketing mix, and it communicates the strategy to all staff.

The marketing plan needs resources, and these are costed in the marketing budget, which expresses the marketing plan in financial terms. Some budgets are set by taking last year's budget and adding an increase to account for inflation.

As with any budgeting, variances can be calculated and compared against actual, allowing management by exception to take place.

Other influences on the budget are:

- the sales forecast
- the competition – 'competitor parity' budgeting seeks to ensure that the firm's budget is in line with its competitors.

KEY POINT

The more a firm moves away from its present products and markets, the greater the risk it is taking.

PROGRESS CHECK

1. What are the major influences on how a firm selects its marketing strategy?
2. What are the four options in Ansoff's matrix?

1 SWOT results; market research data; past sales figures; marketing audits; resource availability.
2 Market penetration; market development; product development; (product) diversification.

7.6 Market segmentation

LEARNING SUMMARY

After studying this section, you should be able to:

- explain the nature of market segmentation
- illustrate how firms typically segment their market
- distinguish between mass and niche markets

Segmenting a market

AQA	**M1, M2**	WJEC	**M1**
Edexcel	**M1**	CCEA	**M1**
OCR	**M1, M3**		

Market segmentation involves dividing a market into **distinct subgroups**. By doing so, products can be made and marketed to meet the needs of each subgroup.

The product or the consumer is the normal base for segmentation.

Example of how a bank segments its customer accounts

If you're between 11 and 18 years old, we've made it easy for you to make the most of your money. Our under 19s account offers you instant access....

KEY POINT

Banks, holiday firms, leisure businesses and clothing manufacturers are good examples of businesses targeting different age-related segments.

Influences on segmentation

Products are often segmented according to the following consumer – or other – characteristics:

People's saving and spending habits tend to change as they grow older.

- **Age**. The age of a person influences product features, such as the way that fashion typically influences clothing worn by different age groups.
- **Sex**. Some products, such as cosmetics, are gender-influenced. Others may be targeted at one sex (e.g. brewers targeting certain brands of drinks at men, and other brands at women).
- **Socio-economic status**. Marketers often use a scale to summarise occupational and social class groupings, identifying consumer groups by income and other characteristics (e.g. education, leisure interests). For example, ACORN (A Classification Of Residential Neighbourhoods) segmentation links population with geographical information to categorise UK postcodes using information such as lifestyle surveys and census data – the population is divided into five main categories, from Wealthy Achievers to Hard Pressed. Two further examples of socio-economic groupings used in the UK are shown below.

Socio-economic groupings influence how advertising is targeted, for instance at readers of either tabloids (e.g. *The Mirror*) or 'quality' dailies (e.g. *The Guardian*).

		% of population (NRS 2008)
A	Higher managerial, administrative and professional	4
B	Intermediate managerial, administrative and professional	23
C1	Supervisory, clerical and junior managerial, administrative and professional	29
C2	Skilled manual workers	21
D	Semi-skilled and unskilled manual workers	15
E	State pensioners, casual and lowest grade workers, unemployed with state benefits only	8

Taken from National Readership Survey social grade definitions

It is not necessary to memorise the groupings and categories in this table, or in the table above.

Classification	Major group
1	Managers, directors and senior officials
2	Professional occupations
3	Associate professional and technical occupations
4	Administrative and secretarial occupations
5	Skilled trades occupations
6	Caring, leisure and other service occupations
7	Sales and customer service occupations
8	Process, plant and machine occupations
9	Elementary occupations

- **National, regional and local factors.** Income, tastes and leisure vary between cultures, and from area to area. For example, income levels in south-east England are, on average, higher than those in Wales. An example of cultural and religious influence is McDonald's adapting its products to respect different cultures; for example, restaurants in Arab countries maintain Halal menus complying with Islamic laws for food preparation, in Israel the kosher outlets do not serve dairy products, and in India the Big Mac is made with lamb rather than beef.
- **Psychographic profiling.** This uses lifestyles to segment consumers and products, for example differentiating a car by emphasising different features (safety, economy, styling, power, carrying capacity) to different 'lifestyle' customers (e.g. young single driver, family of four).

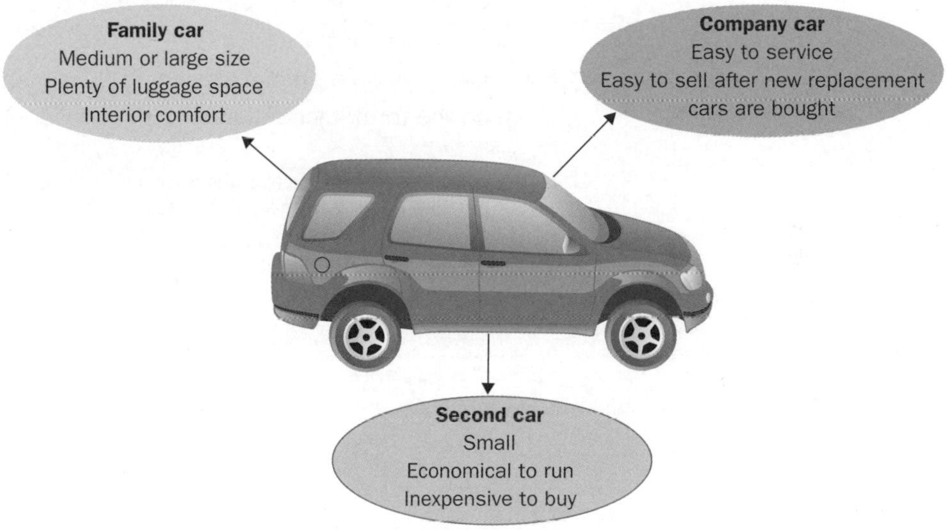

Figure 7.11 Segmenting the car market

Mass and niche markets

An organisation's **market share** is the proportion of the total available market – or of an individual market segment – that is held by the organisation's product(s). **Market size** is indicated by the number of firms in the market, and **market growth** can be measured by calculating the percentage year-on-year increase in the market's sales.

Other examples of niche marketers include Tie Rack and Sock Shop, which both concentrate on niche clothing markets.

A firm might target as large a market as possible – a **mass market** such as that for mass-produced vehicles. Alternatively, a firm may target a **niche market** where it concentrates on small market segments. Such firms create a known name and image, and establish a market position. A small firm can compete in a market dominated by larger firms – for example, the Morgan Motor Company produces hand-made cars for a niche market – and is likely to find that consumers will pay premium prices for its 'exclusive' product.

Problems for niche marketers include:

- a firm potentially having to remain small because overheads need to be kept low (if competitors benefit from economies of scale, they will be price-competitive)
- there being no diversification – a single-product approach depends for its success on consumers' demand levels and tastes remaining at least constant.

KEY POINT

The targeted market segments influence the nature of the marketing mix used.

PROGRESS CHECK

1. In what ways do marketers segment their market?
2. Define the term 'niche market'.

1 Product characteristics; consumers (e.g. age, sex, lifestyle, income).
2 A small focused section of the market for a particular product.

Sample question and model answer

1. Many large retailers are linked to loyalty card schemes. Sainsbury's launched the Nectar loyalty card in 2002, together with other suppliers. In 2010, Nectar announced that it had overtaken the Tesco Clubcard as the UK's most popular loyalty card.

(a) Outline two reasons for retail businesses to issue loyalty cards and two benefits of loyalty cards for consumers. **(8)**

For the retailers, loyalty cards allow segmentation to take place and provide Sainsbury's and Tesco with information about the shopping and buying habits of their customers. Second, loyalty cards support non-price competition, with the retailer finding that customers are retained because of 'loyalty' rather than lost. Consumers gain a small discount on goods bought from the retailer.

A good answer for retailers, though it would be strengthened by emphasising that, as a result of obtaining information, retailers can target their marketing more effectively. One valid benefit is given for consumers. A second benefit is the improved communication from the retailer (e.g. through a mailshot to loyalty card holders).

(b) Analyse the benefits and drawbacks to large retailers, such as Sainsbury's and Tesco, of emphasising segmentation in their marketing strategies. **(12)**

'Market segmentation' involves breaking the market into its constituent elements, e.g. on the basis of age, sex or gender, or other relevant characteristics.

A good start, defining segmentation briefly.

As a result of segmentation, retailers such as Tesco can target different groups who have similar needs or wants, and can develop and promote their products focused on these different groups. Segmentation also encourages a policy of diversification, which is a safer policy for a firm than over-reliance on a single-market product.

These points are well made and are relevant to large retailers.

One drawback to segmentation is that it may be more difficult to produce a standardised product for the mass market, and so the firm may lose economies of scale.

Although correct, the answer should refer to retailers and not manufacturers. The answer could mention factors such as the cost of analysing segmentation and that the information is not likely to be 100 percent accurate.

Exam practice question

1 TJE Ltd is a company that manufactures plastic household goods such as dustpans and brushes. These products are sold to retailers based in the United Kingdom. The company faces strong competition from firms both at home and abroad.

The managers of TJE Ltd believe that the company needs to review where to position its products in the market. They have recently appointed a marketing specialist to help review the company's marketing. This specialist has suggested the company considers new target markets. She also wants to review the company's market segmentation strategy.

(a) State what is meant by:

(i) positioning its products in the market **(2)**

(ii) target markets **(2)**

(iii) market segmentation. **(2)**

(b) The new marketing specialist has studied marketing theory and is aware of Ansoff's matrix. She has applied Ansoff's matrix to TJE Ltd, and as a result has suggested that the company adopts a 'product diversification' marketing strategy.

(i) What is meant by 'product diversification' in the context of Ansoff's matrix? **(2)**

(ii) Assess the likely effects on TJE Ltd of adopting this strategy. **(12)**

8 Market research and analysis

The following topics are covered in this chapter:

- **Market research**
- **Sampling**
- **Analysing market performance**
- **Forecasting market performance**

8.1 Market research

LEARNING SUMMARY

After studying this section, you should be able to:

- outline the purpose of market research
- give examples from the four areas that market research concentrates on
- distinguish between internal and external information
- explain the nature and strengths of primary and secondary research
- describe collection methods for primary research data

Purpose and types of market research

AQA	**M1**	WJEC	**M1**
Edexcel	**M1**	CCEA	**M1**
OCR	**M1, M3**		

The purpose of market research is to **obtain information on market conditions for the firm's products**. Information is collected from – and about – customers, and analysed.

Market research concentrates on four areas: the customer, the product, the market and the competition.

These are the main questions relating to **the customer**:

- Who buys the product at present?
- How often do they buy it?
- Who else might be persuaded to buy it?

These are the main questions relating to **the product**:

- What stage is the product at in its life cycle?
- How does it fit into the product portfolio?
- Can it be improved or can its life be extended?
- Is its price a competitive one?
- How effective is its promotion and distribution?
- How should any new products be:
  - tested?
  - packaged?
  - launched?

These are the main questions relating to **the market**:

- What is its overall size?
- Is it local, national and/or international?
- How is it segmented?
- Is it, or any of its segments, expanding or contracting?

- Are there seasonal influences?
- Is it easy for new firms to enter?

These are the main questions relating to **the competition**:

- Who are the main competitors?
- What are their pricing policies?
- What promotions do they use?

Some marketers use the 'seven Os' to structure and analyse market research:

1. Opposition	Who is in the market?	*Competition*
2. Objects	What do consumers buy now?	*Competitor products*
3. Occupants	Who is buying these products?	*Consumers*
4. Organisation	Who makes the buying decision?	*Social groups*
5. Objectives	Why do they buy?	*Buyer behaviour*
6. Occasions	How frequently do they buy?	*Buying frequency*
7. Operations	How do they buy?	*Distribution channels*

Figure 8.1 The 'seven Os' of market research

Market planning

Market planning seeks to discover as much as possible about a market so that the timing of marketing expenditure and events such as product launches is appropriate. Market planning requires information to be collected.

Information sources can be:

- **internal** to the firm from its own records – for example, accounts and other financial information, till and stock records
- **external** to the firm – the market, competitors and their products.

Internal information is from the organisation and is therefore exclusive to it. External information is also likely to be accurate and is wider ranging, but is not drawn exclusively from the organisation undertaking the research.

Primary research

Primary research is also known as field research.

Primary research collects original data using various techniques:

- **Questionnaires**. These are designed specifically for the task, and completed face to face, by telephone, sent through the post or by e-mail. These different methods produce different response rates. Face-to-face interviews can be expensive, telephone interviews are easily avoided, and postal and e-mailed questionnaires generate low response rates, though are relatively inexpensive.
- **Test marketing**. A potential new product is marketed (e.g. regionally) to gauge reaction to it, before committing the firm to full production and a national launch.
- **Consumer panels**. Consumers volunteer to receive the product and comment on it. Examples include tasting panels who comment on the taste of a planned new flavour or food, and testing panels who test the durability and/or reliability of a new product.

- **Observation**. People's reactions are observed whilst they shop, to provide information from the marketplace. Examples include observing buying patterns, shop layouts and reactions to a new display or form of packaging.
- **Surveys**. Consumers volunteer to contribute to a survey, e.g. when viewing an organisation's website, and contribute survey information when communicating with the organisation (e.g. by completing a guarantee registration card).

Primary research has the advantage that it is tailored exactly to a firm's requirements – the information obtained relates exclusively to a firm's customers and/or products. However, it is often expensive to obtain and – because it relies on a sample – there is no guarantee that the **sample** on which it is based will be a true reflection of the market.

Secondary research is also known as desk research.

Secondary research

Secondary research uses existing information, such as:

- a firm's own sales figures
- official (e.g. Office for National Statistics) publications
- information from trade associations and chambers of commerce
- market research agency reports, websites and newspaper reports.

Because information from desk research has been collected for purposes other than market research, it is not always relevant, although it is usually cheaper than primary (field) research and normally quicker to obtain.

KEY POINT

The cost of collecting the data and the time taken to collect it are key factors when deciding on the type of research.

Quantitative and qualitative research

Market research generates either quantitative or qualitative data.

Quantitative research	Qualitative research
concentrates on *factual information* (e.g. units sold, percentage market share)	concentrates on *attitudes and opinions* (consumers' tastes, likes and dislikes)

Different question types are associated with each type of research:

- **Closed questions** provide quantitative data because they can be analysed easily and presented as statistics. They require respondents to make a choice (e.g. a 'yes/no' question).
- **Open questions** provide qualitative data, typically requiring more detailed answers and allowing views and opinions to be expressed.

PROGRESS CHECK

1. What is the key difference between primary and secondary research?
2. Name three methods of collecting primary data.

1 Primary is tailored exclusively for a firm; secondary is not.
2 **Accept three from:** questionnaires; test marketing; consumer panels; observation; surveys.

8.2 Sampling

LEARNING SUMMARY

After studying this section, you should be able to:

- explain why organisations need to carry out sampling
- distinguish between sample size and sampling method
- explain random, quasi-random and non-random sampling methods
- outline how sampling results can be processed statistically

The need to sample

AQA	**M1**	OCR	**M1, M3**
Edexcel	**M1**	CCEA	**M1**

Primary research has to be limited in scope because of cost, time and other practical considerations – it is usually impossible to interview every consumer in a given market. For primary research to provide relevant information it must use a **representative sample**. Consumers who form the sample must represent the market as a whole.

Sampling method and sample size

Key decisions for the firm are to select:

- the right people – the **sampling method**
- a sufficient number of the right people – the **sample size**.

An adequate number of people must be selected. The larger the sample size, the greater the confidence in the results generated by the sample, but the higher the cost and the more time-consuming the research will be.

The sampling method used may be random (where everyone in the population has an equal chance of selection), quasi-random or non-random.

Random sampling

Random sampling is used when a completely representative selection is required. Everyone in the population must have an equal chance of being selected. This requires a **sampling frame** (a numbered list of all items in the population), e.g. using random number tables, electoral registers or council tax lists.

There are advantages and disadvantages to random sampling:

- The main advantage is that it means there is a completely random selection.
- A big downside can be cost (a large sample is often needed); in addition, a sampling frame may not exist or may not apply (e.g. an electoral register does not segment clearly by age or income).

Quasi-random sampling

Quasi-random sampling methods include the following:

- **Systematic**. A random start is made, then every nth item is selected. For example, if a sample of 100 people is needed from a population of 20 000, the **sampling interval** is every 200th person, $\frac{20\,000}{100}$, selected following a random start.
  - **Advantages**: once the sample frame is sorted it is easy to select the items; it is reasonably random.

  - **Disadvantages**: the systematic method needs a sampling frame; it can be costly; the whole population needs to be accessed.
- **Stratified**. The population is divided into groups/categories/strata, for example by type of business or type of employment, or by age/sex/social class. The sample is proportional to each group, the sampling frame being constructed accordingly, and a random sample is taken from each group.
  - **Advantages**: it gives a representative sample because all categories are included; the structure of the sample represents the structure of the population; each category is represented by a randomly chosen sample.
  - **Disadvantages**: cost; the sampling frames may not contain information that allows this method to be used.

Quasi-random sampling methods give a good approximation to random sampling and also need a sampling frame.

- **Multi-stage**. The population is divided and a small sample of areas selected at random. Each area is subdivided, a small number of these subdivisions being selected randomly and so on until a random selection of the population in each of the smallest units is taken.
  - **Advantages**: it can cut costs; it can be quick; gives a good approximation of a random sample; does not require a sampling frame of the whole population.
  - **Disadvantages**: it is not truly random; a small number of areas/units may introduce bias.

Non-random sampling

Non-random sampling methods include the following:

- **Quota**. The population is stratified by dividing it into groups, and the sample is restricted to a fixed number in each group. For example, interviewers must interview all people until their quota is met, and the interviewer chooses the people to interview (which makes this method non-random and therefore different from stratified).
  - **Advantages**: it cuts costs and is easy to administer; a large sample is obtained quickly.
  - **Disadvantage**: problem of bias, e.g. if interviewing in a single location certain people may never visit that location.

These methods are relevant when a sampling frame is not – or cannot be – used.

- **Cluster**. One definable subsection of the population is taken as the sample, and this subsection is assumed to reflect the whole population.
  - **Advantages**: low cost; an alternative to multi-stage sampling if there is no sampling frame; little administration is needed.
  - **Disadvantage**: greater chance of bias.

KEY POINT

The larger the sample size, the more accurate the results, but the more expensive and time-consuming it is to collect the data.

Analysing the results

AQA **M3**
OCR **M3**

> Research from Tesco Mobile showed that ... 59% of Brits said they would spend more time on the phone if they had unlimited minutes ... . Over half of all respondents (52%) also claimed they had friends or relatives who cut short phone calls to keep costs down.
>
> *Tesco Mobile website, 2009*

Marketing managers (and other managers) need to summarise and describe the results of the sampling process. They are likely to be interested in what is average, or typical. The data generated by a sample may contain a number of properties that enable managers to determine what 'average' is.

Three important properties are:

- **central tendency** – a measure of 'average'
- **dispersion** – a measure of the 'spread' of the data, i.e. how widely dispersed the numbers are
- **skewness** – how symmetrical the raw data are ('skewness' is the term used to describe a lack of symmetry in the raw data).

Measuring central tendency

The three primary measures of central tendency are the **arithmetic mean**, the **median** and the **mode**.

The arithmetic mean is a simple average of the total values of the data, and is calculated by totalling the values and dividing this total by their number. The median is the middle value of an ordered set of data (an **array**). The mode is the value occurring most frequently in the data.

The measure that is used depends on the data and the situation:

- The mean is best used to determine what would result from an equal distribution (e.g. consumption per head of a product). The mean may give a distorted answer where there is a large fluctuation in sales, due to the extreme values. Here, the median may be more appropriate.
- The median is used when order or ranking is important (e.g. the product's sales compared with competitor sales).
- The mode is used to determine the most commonly occurring values.

The mode is used by retailers to discover the most popular sizes or models sold.

Measure	Advantages	Drawbacks
Mean	• Easy to understand • Uses every value • Can be used for further analysis	• Distorted by extreme values • The answer may be a value not found in the original analysis
Median	• Easy to understand • Not influenced by extreme values in the data	• Needs the data to be organised • May be unrepresentative with only a few values
Mode	• Easy to understand • Not influenced by extreme values in the data	• Needs the data to be organised • Cannot be used for further mathematical processing

KEY POINT

The 'right' average to use depends on the situation and on the nature of the data.

Measuring dispersion

Measures of location – the mean, median and mode – give an average or typical value.

A market researcher or manager may also wish to know how the sample population is spread – **dispersed** – around the central value:

- The **range** is the difference between the smallest and largest values in the population. It is easy to understand and calculate, useful in providing a quick measure of dispersion, and can be used effectively when there are only a relatively few values in the population. However, it ignores all but two values (the largest and smallest) and is affected by an extreme value.
- The **quartile deviation** is often used as the measure of spread when the median is selected as the measure of location. Quartiles divide the data into four equal parts. The interquartile range is the difference between the first and third quarters, and the quartile deviation is half of this amount. It therefore concentrates on the most representative 'middle 50 percent' and is therefore not affected by extreme values, although it is more difficult to calculate than the range.
- The **standard deviation** is used to measure dispersion when the mean is used for location. It represents the average deviation from the mean. The standard deviation can be developed further mathematically, but can be distorted by extreme values. The following formula is used to calculate standard deviation.

In practice, the standard deviation is easily calculated by using a calculator.

$$\sigma = \sqrt{\frac{\Sigma(x - \bar{x})^2}{n}}$$

Where σ = the standard deviation
Σ = the sum of
x = a value
$\bar{x}$ = the mean
n = number of values

Results of research

One way of classifying market research is to examine the information that it generates.

This information may be:

- **controllable** – i.e. it is within a firm's power to alter a variable identified through research, such as poor packaging or an unsuitable method of promotion
- **uncontrollable** – i.e. the research identifies factors that are beyond the control of a firm, such as an economic downturn affecting sales and market size, or a new technological development influencing sales of its present model.

An example of controllable research information is Tesco's introduction, in 2009, of a new policy to let customers remove – and leave – plastic and paper packaging from products purchased in store. By making a note of the products that consumers remove the packaging from, the company knows which products can potentially have less packaging.

PROGRESS CHECK

1. Name four sampling methods.
2. In what situations should a firm use **(a)** the mean **(b)** the median and **(c)** the mode?

1 **Accept any four from:** random; systematic; stratified; multi-stage; quota; cluster.
2 **(a)** to determine the average of an equal distribution **(b)** when order is important **(c)** to identify the most commonly occurring items.

8.3 Analysing market performance

LEARNING SUMMARY

After studying this section, you should be able to:

- outline the four elements in SWOT analysis
- give an example of how SWOT analysis is used in business
- describe the 'Boston Box' Matrix
- comment on the nature and effectiveness of analysis using this matrix

SWOT analysis

AQA	**M2**
Edexcel	**M2a**
OCR	**M3**
WJEC	**M3**
CCEA	**M1, M3**

SWOT analysis is a tool used to assess a firm's strengths and weaknesses (which are mainly internal to the firm), and its opportunities and the threats to it (which are mainly external).

For example, a company selling garden sheds, which plans to diversify into greenhouses, could find that a SWOT analysis identifies these factors:

S existing contacts/outlets; a known trade name; reputation for a quality product; existing suppliers of glass and wood; well-motivated employees.

W employees lack suitable skills; no experience making glass-based products; no knowledge of the market for greenhouses; limited capital for expansion.

O diversifying will spread risk; expansion of capital through new share issue; reduction of the seasonal effect of shed sales; no major local or regional competitor.

T most competitors are large, so it will be difficult to compete (fewer economies of scale) on price; uncertainty of climate change affecting long-term demand.

Internal and external audits

Managers audit the business environment through an internal audit of strengths and weaknesses and an external audit of opportunities and threats.

An internal audit assesses what a firm does well (strengths) and what it could do better (weaknesses). Although the main emphasis is on marketing, other functions play an important role in this analysis.

The following are examples of questions that may be asked:

- Are there any new products planned?
- Is distribution efficient?
- What is the firm's reputation with its customers?

These external influences are known as 'PESTEL' – political, economic, social, technological, environmental, legal (see chapters 5 and 6).

An external audit assesses outside influences such as the wider economy (e.g. likely tax or interest rate changes, its stage in the business cycle), and changes such as new technological developments that result from these external influences.

KEY POINT

An organisation needs information about its consumers, products, markets and the organisation itself.

The Boston Growth and market share Matrix

AQA	M2	WJEC	M2
Edexcel	M2a	CCEA	M3
OCR	M3		

Boston Box analysis is particularly suitable for larger companies with a wide product range.

The Boston Box analyses the product element of the marketing mix.

The Boston Consulting Group (BCG) 'Boston Box' Matrix groups and analyses products under four headings:

- **'Stars'** are potentially highly profitable – large investment is needed to develop and promote them, and this should develop them into 'cash cows'.
- **'Problem children'** compete by plugging a hole in the product range in a slow-growth segment, but if not disposed of they can turn into 'dogs'.
- **'Cash cows'** are the key to a firm's profits and sales, and a firm will keep investing in them. They help finance the development of 'stars', but if not managed properly they risk becoming 'dogs'.
- **'Dogs'** are heavy users of resources, but remain unprofitable. A firm rids itself of 'dogs' unless there is a chance to make them profitable or if they are being held for strategic reasons (e.g. to maintain market share).

Although Boston Box analysis provides a framework for allocating resources amongst competing areas, it is limited because:

- the Matrix ignores factors such as other determinants of profitability
- it does not fully consider the relationship between market share and profitability (increasing market share can be costly).

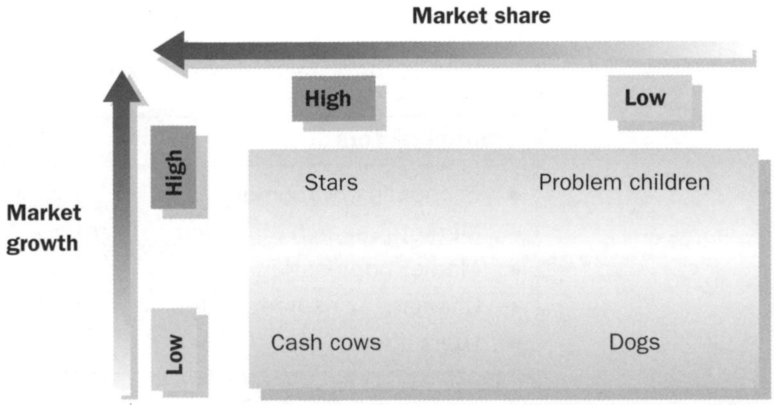

Figure 8.2 Boston Box analysis

KEY POINT

The Boston Box is not a one-off approach to product analysis, since a product's status changes over time. It therefore illustrates the importance of a balanced product portfolio.

PROGRESS CHECK

1. How is SWOT analysis used by a firm?
2. What are the four headings in the BCG Matrix?

1 To analyse internal strengths and weaknesses, and external opportunities and threats.
2 'Stars', 'problem children', 'cash cows', 'dogs'.

8.4 Forecasting market performance

LEARNING SUMMARY

After studying this section, you should be able to:

- explain the purpose of sales forecasting
- outline how sales forecasting is carried out
- explain the elements in time series analysis
- undertake time series analysis

Sales forecasting

AQA **M3** OCR **M7**
Edexcel **M2a** WJEC **M4**

Sales forecasting seeks to estimate a firm's future sales, together with the related cash flows and profits. It can be used for short-term tactical reasons such as production planning, or for longer-term strategic purposes such as estimating future staffing requirements.

Forecasters use external data by studying the industry as a whole and calculating the firm's estimated share of the total market. They use internal sales statistics as a basis for the forecast.

Sales forecasting is complicated by the number of factors to be considered.

Examples of these factors are listed below.

External factors	Internal factors
• Economic environment • Market research statistics • Market competition • Changing consumer tastes • Legislation	• Previous sales statistics • A firm's pricing policies • A firm's policies on offering discounts • A firm's distribution methods

Techniques for forecasting sales

Quantitative techniques for forecasting sales include mathematical techniques such as **time series** forecasting. Other quantitative techniques include linear regression analysis and mathematical models that can be created and manipulated by computer.

A simple quantitative approach to forecasting is to use the **scattergraph** method:

- Collect the data.
- Plot the data on a graph.
- Draw a line of best fit through the points.

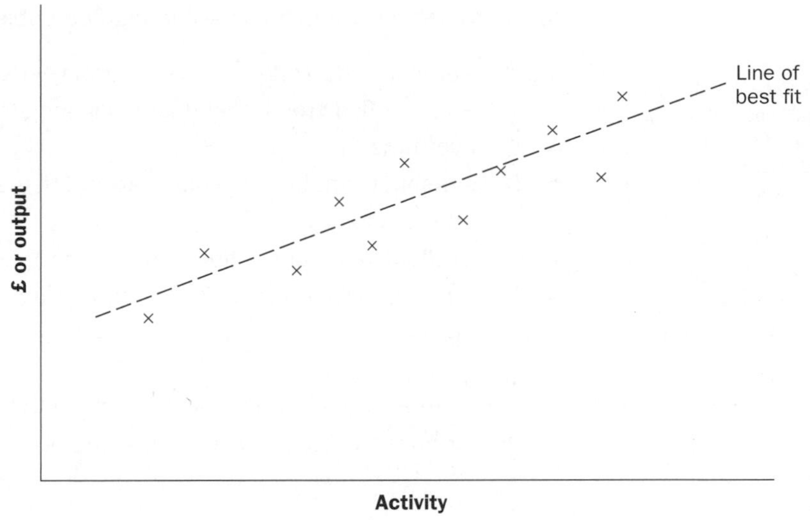

Figure 8.3 Example of a scattergraph

The main advantages of the scattergraph method are its simplicity, and its visual display of any correlation (relationship) between the items being plotted. Its major disadvantage is that it only gives an approximation of the exact position.

Qualitative techniques for forecasting sales include:

- test marketing
- forecasting panels, drawn from sales force employees or other experts who give opinions on the likely sales, which are then used to create a single forecast
- user surveys of existing customers and their expected future requirements.

Difficulties with sales forecasting

One of the difficulties with sales forecasting is that trend and seasonality patterns are not guaranteed to continue. Random factors that may be affecting trend and seasonal variations are ignored. The less data available on which the forecast is based, the less reliable the forecast will be.

STEP (social, technological, economic and political) changes also affect sales – and other – forecasting:

- Social changes (tastes, fashion, environmental awareness, etc.) make it difficult to forecast demand levels.
- Technological changes in production methods affect costs and cost behaviour, making existing output and related statistics unsuitable to use for forecasting.
- Economic and political changes (e.g. in interest rates, employment levels and policy) affect the forecasts that are made.

Environmental, ethical and legal influences can also be included here.

KEY POINT

All forecasts are subject to error – the further that the forecast is into the future, the more likely the error.

Time series analysis

AQA **M3**
Edexcel **M7**

A **time series** records figures over time. Time series analysis in a firm might involve analysing sales and factory output. Economic activity – recession, downturn, recovery and boom – can also be subjected to time series analysis.

Examples may relate to seasonal times of the year (e.g. increase in sales of toys at Christmas) or may be shorter term, e.g. weekly (Saturday sales are often higher than sales on other days).

The elements in time series analysis normally include:

- **T** an identified **trend** – an underlying long-term movement in the data over time
- **S** **seasonal** variations – shorter-term fluctuations due to seasonal or other factors
- **C** **cyclical** variations – fluctuations that take place in the longer term
- **I** **random** variations that arise through unforeseen 'one-off' events.

KEY POINT

Time Series Y = T + S (+ C + I) (normally the cyclical and random elements do not have to be calculated in questions).

The data are recorded on a historigram, which shows time on the horizontal axis and value on the vertical axis.

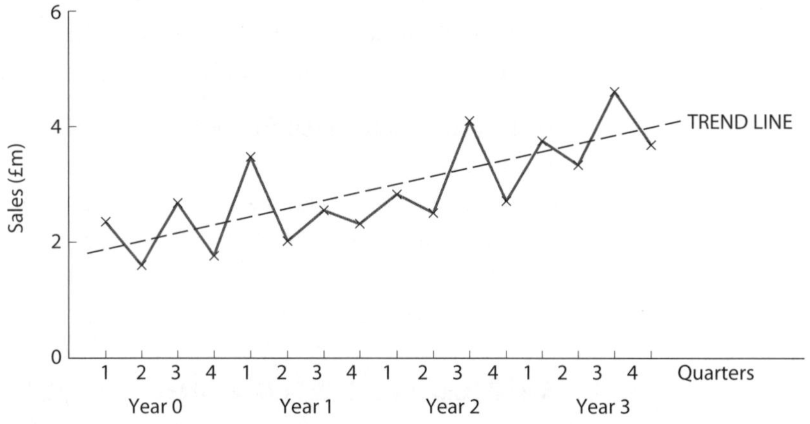

Finding the trend using moving averages

A **moving average** is the average of a set number of periods. It refers to the mid-point of the overall period. Here is an example.

Month	***Production (units)***
0	3 400
1	3 200
2	4 200
3	3 700
4	3 500
5	4 500

A three-month moving average of monthly production is:

- months 0–2 (3 400 + 3 200 + 4 200) divided by 3 = 3 600, which is located in the middle of the 3-month period (i.e. the middle of month 1)
- months 1–3 (3 200 + 4 200 + 3 700) divided by 3 = 3 700 (the middle of month 2)
- months 2–4, 11 400 divided by 3 = 3 800, located at the middle of month 3
- months 3–5, 11 700 divided by 3 = 3 900.

This is how the information can be displayed.

Month	Production (units)	Moving total (3 months' sales)	Moving average
0	3 400		
1	3 200	10 800	3 600
2	4 200	11 100	3 700
3	3 700	11 400	3 800
4	3 500	11 700	3 900
5	4 500		

The upward trend in monthly production can be seen clearly, because the **moving average column indicates the trend line**.

Taking a moving average of an even number of time periods means the mid-point of the overall period will not refer to a single period. Here is an example.

January	Sales	
Week 1	48	
Week 2	44	→ average 46
Week 3	47	
Week 4	45	

The average refers to the mid-point, between week 2 and week 3.

KEY POINT

The length of the moving average period has to be selected. If there is a known cycle of seasonal variations (e.g. a year), the moving average should cover that cycle.

Finding the seasonal variation

Once the trend has been established, the seasonal variation can be calculated.

Since Y = T + S + I, then Y – T = S + I
(deducting the trend leaves the seasonal and random variations)

By assuming that the random variation is small and so can be ignored, the seasonal variation is:

S = Y – T

The seasonal variation is therefore the difference between the actual results and the trend.

For example, the following data refers to a company's sales (in units).

	Quarter			
	1	2	3	4
Year 0	103	55	160	120
Year 1	107	59	167	130
Year 2	110	62	170	139

To calculate the moving average of the quarterly sales, a four-quarter moving total should be selected. As the moving average first calculated will not be located against an actual quarter, a second moving average is taken based on the mid-points of two moving averages, as shown below. (The average has been rounded to the nearest whole number.) The seasonal variation is calculated as the difference between the actual sales and the trend.

Year	Quarter	Sales	Moving total (4 quarters)	Moving average (4 quarters)	Mid-point (of two moving averages) (TREND)	Seasonal variation
0	1	103				
	2	55				
			438	109.50		
	3	160			110	+50
			442	110.50		
	4	120			111	+9
			446	111.50		
1	1	107			112	-5
			453	113.25		
	2	59			114	-55
			463	115.75		
	3	167			116	+51
			466	116.50		
	4	130			117	+13
			469	117.25		
2	1	110			118	-8
			472	118.00		
	2	62			119	-57
			481	120.25		
	3	170				
	4	139				

The average seasonal variation can be shown by re-displaying the calculations.

Year	Quarter 1	Quarter 2	Quarter 3	Quarter 4
0			+50	+9
1	–5	–55	+51	+13
2	–8	–57		
Total	–13	–112	+101	+22
Average	–6.5	–56	+50.5	+11

To deseasonalise (seasonally adjust) time series data, seasonal variations are removed to leave the trend.

Variations should cancel each other out, but –6.5 and –56 = –62.5, whereas +50.5 and +11 = +61.5. (The difference of 1 should be spread between the four unadjusted averages, to convert them to adjusted averages.)

KEY POINT

One weakness of calculating the moving average can be that it assumes components remain independent, e.g. an increasing trend does not also increase the seasonal variation.

Using time series information for forecasting

Time series analysis provides information to use in forecasting by:

- calculating moving averages to find the trend
- **extrapolating** the trend, i.e. projecting it forwards, outside the range of the data used
- using the seasonal variation to adjust the trend.

Using the above example, the trend line can be plotted and extrapolated, and the seasonal variations added to obtain forecast sales for year 3.

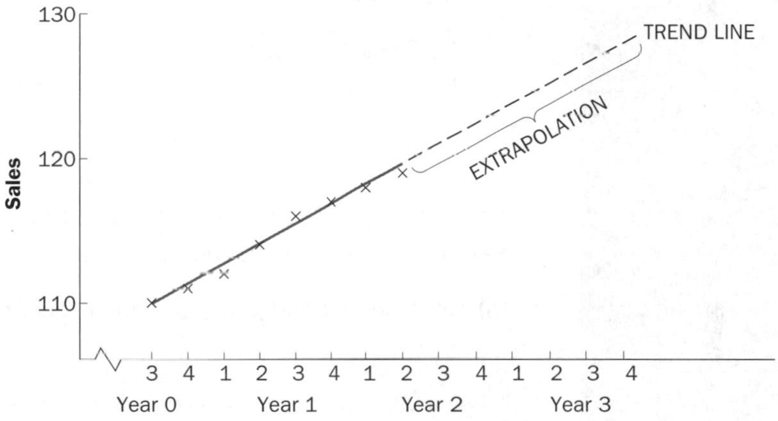

Forecast for year 3	**Extrapolation**	**Seasonal adjustment**	**Forecast sales**
Quarter 1	123	–6.5	116.5
Quarter 2	125	–56	69
Quarter 3	126	+50.5	176.5
Quarter 4	128	+11	139

PROGRESS CHECK

1. How is sales forecasting likely to prove limited and/or inaccurate?
2. How are time series seasonal variations calculated?

1 Trend and seasonal patterns may not continue; random variations are ignored; the further the forecast into the future, the less accurate; external changes affect the forecast.
2 S = Y – T.

Sample question and model answer

These are generally weak answers: (i) should clarify that the same product is bought by the same consumer, (ii) should state that brand loyalty means repeat purchases, and (iii) should mention that sales vary on a regular (seasonal) basis.

An attempted overview of primary and secondary research, but it is not applied to the situation. Examples could be given (primary: interviewing customers, assessing local competition; secondary: trends in cake sales, consumers' tastes and fashions).

Some good points here, particularly recognising Val might have many other work commitments and that she is probably not a marketing specialist. However, as an answer this is very limited. The candidate should consider issues such as the benefits and costs of quantitative and qualitative research, and appropriate sampling methods (e.g. random?) and sample size (e.g. all customers for the last six months?).

1. TastyCakes is a firm based in the Midlands. It specialises in making wedding cakes. The firm has some local competition. TastyCakes was set up two years ago and has grown gradually over this time. Val Hodson does most of the work herself but employs someone on a part-time basis during busy periods.

The market for wedding cakes is an unusual one in a number of ways: there is no repeat purchasing or brand loyalty and sales are seasonal, peaking during the summer months and falling during winter.

Although Val's cakes are made for weddings, she has received a number of enquiries about making cakes for other special events, such as birthdays and wedding anniversaries. Val would like to expand her business and sees extending her range and types of cakes as a possible development.

(a) What is meant by the following terms?

(i) repeat purchasing **(2)**

(ii) brand loyalty **(2)**

(iii) seasonal **(2)**

(a) (i) Repeat purchasing means buying it again.

(ii) Brand loyalty means staying loyal to the brand you are buying.

(iii) Seasonal is to do with when sales are seasonal.

Val plans to increase her range of cakes to include special occasions other than weddings. She realises that she should carry out market research to assess whether this planned development is possible.

(b) Recommend and justify a market research plan for Val to follow. **(14)**

(b) Val should look at using primary and secondary research. Primary is to do with original research by Val, where she does it herself rather than looking at other people's research. Secondary is when she looks at other people's research.

The benefits of Val doing primary research are that she gets information that is just for her situation and applies just to wedding - and other - cakes. However, she is a sole trader and so she might be short of time to carry out this research. It can also be expensive. If Val does secondary research she should not have the same level of costs, but this type of research is not just for her product or situation and so some of it may not apply.

Val is probably not a marketing specialist so she might struggle to create suitable questionnaires and other items she will need.

Exam practice question

1 Colman's is a leading manufacturer of mustard items and various sauces sold in the UK. It is owned by Unilever. The original brand was founded in Norwich over 180 years ago but, when customers started being offered other forms of mustard and similar items, the company carried out quantitative and qualitative market research. As a result it now offers a wide range of mustards.

(a) What are the benefits that a business such as Colman's might gain from diversifying its product range? **(8)**

(b) To what extent will effective market research guarantee the continuing success of Colman's? **(12)**

9 The marketing mix

The following topics are covered in this chapter:

- The product
- Pricing decisions
- Promotion
- Place

9.1 The product

LEARNING SUMMARY

After studying this section, you should be able to:

- distinguish between the marketing mix and the product mix
- name and describe seven Ps associated with the marketing mix
- give reasons why people buy products
- outline the nature and purpose of product differentiation and branding
- explain how new product development takes place
- name, describe stages of, and assess the value of product life cycle analysis
- describe the nature and purpose of value analysis

Marketing mix and product mix

AQA	**M3**
Edexcel	**M1, M2a**
OCR	**M1. M3**
WJEC	**M2**
CCEA	**M1, M3**

The product mix is itself part of the **marketing mix**.

The four main elements in the marketing mix are:

- **product**
- **price**
- **promotion**
- **place** (distribution strategies).

The mix varies according to influences such as the stage of the product's life, a firm's size and stage of development, and the influence of external factors such as the actions of government and competitors.

Modern analysis suggests that there are at least three more Ps in the mix:

- **People**. People who come into contact with customers influence the level of customer satisfaction and the reputation of the firm and its products.
- **Process**. This is the act of providing a service, including features such as the quality of customer information and length of waiting time.
- **Physical evidence**. This is how a firm helps its customers understand both what they are buying and also the type of business from which they are buying, so features such as the appearance of the reception area are important.

An effective marketing mix has elements that are **integrated** – this leads to a series of decisions and actions that link together efficiently. For example, an innovative new product will be supported by a suitable pricing strategy (such as a skimming strategy) and informative advertising that communicates effectively the innovative nature of the product.

A firm's **product mix** – the full range of products in all markets and segments – consists of different product lines (the group of products aimed at one market segment).

The **mix width** identifies the number of product lines in this product mix. The wider the mix width, the more diversified the firm is and the better chance it has of surviving if a particular market segment collapses. Each product line also has a **mix depth** – the number of different products in a single product line. The deeper the mix depth, the more segments the firm has to operate in to avoid its products competing with each other.

KEY POINT

Firms have to rationalise their products, keeping them compatible if they cannot be positioned in different market segments.

Products

AQA **M3**
Edexcel **M1, M2a**
OCR **M1, M3**
WJEC **M2**
CCEA **M1, M3**

A product may be bought for various reasons, based on the product's attributes. Products may possess **core**, **secondary** and **tertiary** attributes. For example, a car's core attribute may be freedom of movement, with secondary attributes such as economy and reliability, and tertiary attributes of a warranty and the delivery date.

A firm's product can be in the form of **tangible** goods or **intangible** services.

Value analysis

The term value engineering is used when the focus is on manufacturing rather than on marketing.

Firms undertake **value analysis** to see whether their new or existing products are satisfying their consumers, e.g. in terms of style, design and functionality. It is a systematic approach to add value – to the customer – by reducing costs and/or increasing product performance.

Value analysis involves staff studying every feature of a product, to compare the value that the feature adds against its cost. To do this properly usually requires an interdisciplinary approach, with expertise being required from production engineering, marketing and costing staff.

A series of questions can be asked:
- What function does the product have?
- Is the function necessary?
- Can a lower-cost part, that meets quality specifications, be used instead?
- In order to lower its price, can the product be simplified?
- Can the product be re-designed to be made more efficiently or quickly?
- Can features that are valued by the customer be added?

Product differentiation and branding

Product differentiation explores how consumers view products. A highly differentiated product is regarded as being distinct and having no near substitutes. The product may be different (e.g. it is better designed or made), or may be perceived as different due to psychological factors such as advertising or branding.

Product differentiation is helped where a product has a **unique selling point** (USP), a feature which the firm can focus on to differentiate it from competitor products. The USP may be based on an actual difference (e.g. in quality) or on a perceived difference that is enhanced by persuasive advertising.

Branding assures consumers that their next purchase of the branded item will be virtually identical to their last purchase. This consistency creates **brand loyalty**, giving the manufacturer the opportunity to highlight and advertise apparent differences between products.

Specific brand and trade names can be used to describe all products of the same type, e.g. biro, Hoover, tarmac, Jiffy Bag, jeep.

These are some of the effects of branding:

- A respected brand name helps the manufacturer sell new products.
- There is the promise of repeat purchases through brand loyalty.
- Retailers will give display space to the branded product.
- The product image can be reinforced.
- Market segmentation becomes easier.

Branding can be transferred to other products. One form is **product merchandising**, where a successful product – such as a major film or sports event like the Olympics – generates a number of different products, e.g. mugs, caps and T-shirts that feature the brand or logo. A successful brand name can be placed in another market. For example, when Unilever plc bought Colman's mustard, it re-marketed it and then launched other foodstuffs using the well-known Colman's name.

The manufacturer often achieves this by using excess production capacity.

Own-label brands (goods branded with the retailer's name) have increased in popularity. Rather than buying at high prices from a major brand supplier, the retailer buys from another manufacturer after agreeing quality standards, then sells the own-brand goods at competitive prices.

Branding relies on **packaging**. Originally there just for protection, packaging is now a vital feature of the product and is also closely linked with the 'P' of promotion. It carries the brand name or logo, gives product information that must be legally displayed, and offers space that can be used by the manufacturer to persuade the consumer to buy the product.

KEY POINT

Modern packaging offers a communication base, ease of display, impact, and environmental acceptability.

New product development

AQA	**M2**
Edexcel	**M1, M2a**
OCR	**M3**
WJEC	**M2, M4**
CCEA	**M1**

New product development is an activity closely linked to market research.

A product can be classed as 'new' if it is:

- **innovative** – i.e. it is the original model or type, such as the iPod or the Dyson vacuum cleaner (which dispensed with the inner dust bag)
- **imitative** – i.e. it copies the innovative original once it proves successful (different makes of trainers are a good example)
- a **replacement** – i.e. where a new model of an existing product is brought out.

Innovative products are usually created by organisations with an efficient **research and development** function and which have a proactive approach to

It has been estimated that less than 3 percent of all potential new products finally reach the market.

product development – the firm seeks to be leader, attempting to create the market. This strategy carries the highest risk but also has the highest potential rewards, especially where the innovation can be protected by a patent. The alternative approach, where imitative and replacement products are marketed, occurs where firms are reactive and market followers.

KEY POINT

Firms develop new products to maintain a balanced product mix.

Stages in product development

New product development has a number of stages.

1. Assess the demand	• What does market research tell us? • Is the product feasible? • Is there a gap in the market?
2. Obtain ideas	• What can research and development suggest? • Who else can contribute ideas?
3. Evaluate each idea	• What does market research tell us? • Do the ideas fit the corporate plan? • What are the potential 'limiting factors'? – suppliers, demand, market size, break-even point, productive capacity, capital expenditure, etc.
4. Develop one idea	• What resources do we need to develop the product? • What does the prototype look like? • What test marketing can we carry out? • What is the timetable for staff training, financial planning and equipment purchase?
5. Launch the product	• What forms of promotion do we need? • What does the test marketing tell us? • What is our pricing policy?
6. Evaluate success	• What is the consumer reaction?

Supporting product development

Two important aspects of new product development are screening and test marketing.

The first process of screening eliminates many ideas on the grounds of funding or lack of expertise.

Screening takes place at the ideas evaluation stage. It analyses:

- labour availability and cost
- possible market reaction from competitors
- compatibility with…
  - corporate objectives
  - the existing product mix
- likely future market growth
- profit potential
- the anticipated length of the life cycle.

Test marketing relies on the production of prototypes or pilot products. The objective is to simulate as closely as possible the market, the product, and the marketing support that will be provided.

Even if the new product is successful, difficulties remain with its progress.

The difficulties include:

- high capital costs
- increased revenue expenditure through re-training staff, holding additional stocks and running a new advertising campaign, all of which affect the firm's liquidity
- establishing and maintaining new channels of distribution
- the difficulty of creating consumer confidence and loyalty.

The product life cycle

AQA	**M1**	WJEC	**M2**
Edexcel	**M2a**	CCEA	**M1**
OCR	**M3**		

The four stages of the **product life cycle** are:

- introduction
- growth
- maturity
- decline.

A product only has a limited life once it is introduced on the market. It is therefore important for a firm to have a balanced product portfolio (product mix), replacing products in the maturity and decline stages with newer products.

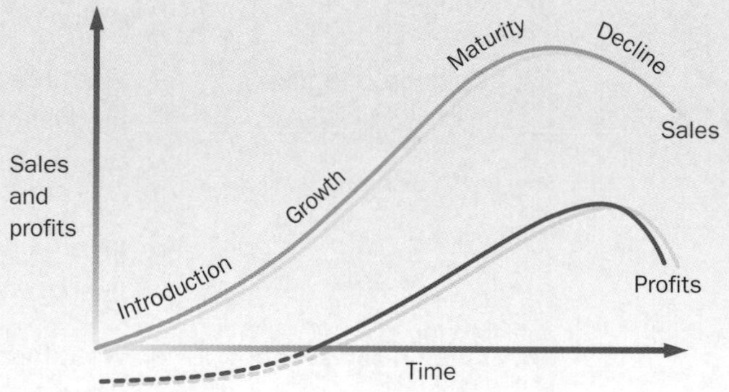

Figure 9.1 Stages of the product life cycle

Some analysts suggest the first stage is Development, before the product is launched, where there are development costs without any sales.

Following planning and development, a product is introduced onto the market.

Characteristics of the **Introduction** stage are:

- low initial sales, due to limited knowledge and no consumer loyalty
- heavy promotion to build brand image and consumer confidence
- losses (low profits at best) due to heavy development and promotion costs
- limited distribution levels, but high stockholding for the manufacturer.

Attempts are made to gain market share (e.g. through penetration pricing), but there remains a high chance of product failure.

The product is changing from a 'star' into a 'cash cow'.

In the **Growth** stage of the product life cycle, as consumer knowledge and loyalty grows, the firm increases sales and starts making profits, possibly helped by economies of scale. Competitors may introduce similar products, or adapt their price and promotion policies.

During the **Maturity** stage, growth slows as the product reaches saturation sales level. Profits are being maximised, but the firm has to fight to defend its market position. Sales are maintained by promotion, customer loyalty (repeat purchases) and product differentiation through initiatives such as developing new packaging.

In the **Decline** stage, total sales fall for the firm (and often the industry). To counter this, the firm may reduce prices, cutting into its profit margin. If other firms abandon their products, production might be maintained in an attempt to gain a larger share of the diminishing market. The firm may also undertake niche marketing in a particular market segment.

KEY POINT

In practice, there are no precise time periods for any stages in the life cycle. Some products, such as those exclusively for Christmas or another festival, have a very short cycle, whereas for others (e.g. the Mini) the life cycle could last for many years.

Extending product life

A firm may try extending an existing product's life by adopting **extension strategies**.

An example of change is Volkswagen's purchase of Skoda, which led to an improved product and image.

Extension strategies involve altering:

- the product – i.e. renewing the image (a 'new improved' model); introducing new models such as a diesel engine version of a car; extending the product into other formats (e.g. ice-cream Mars, originally only a chocolate bar)
- the marketing strategy – i.e. changing the product's image or appeal (e.g. personal computers being used for games/leisure as well as for work).

KEY POINT

By extending product life, a firm hopes to extend the maturity (high-profits) stage.

The usefulness of life cycle analysis

Undertaking product life cycle analysis helps marketers determine other aspects of marketing policy, e.g. how the product is advertised, distributed, priced and developed. However, this analysis can be criticised for overstating the importance of developing new products rather than seeking to extend the lives of existing ones – new product development is risky and expensive.

KEY POINT

The four stages of the product life cycle are not always easily separated, and the life cycle can become a self-fulfilling prophecy.

PROGRESS CHECK

1. Identify three types of 'new' product.
2. What are extension strategies used for?

2 To extend product life by altering the product or the marketing strategy.
1 Innovative; imitative; replacement.

9.2 Pricing decisions

LEARNING SUMMARY

After studying this section, you should be able to:

- describe cost-based and market-based influences on price
- outline the nature of high, low and market-led pricing strategies
- suggest when these strategies may be used by a firm

Influences on price

AQA	**M2**
Edexcel	**M1, M2a**
OCR	**M1, M3**
WJEC	**M2**
CCEA	**M1**

Economists view price as the interaction of supply and demand – economic analysis states that a price should be set where the product's demand equals its supply.

In practice, however, this analysis is influenced by many other factors, such as the following:

A product will not sell if it is not offered for sale at the 'right' price.

- Consumers are unlikely to know the prices of all competing products.
- Consumers may not consider buying certain competing products even though they are less expensive.
- Producers may try to maximise profits and set their prices accordingly, ignoring market demand.

As a result, many marketers regard economic analysis as useful but limited, arguing that the influence of other factors, such as the effectiveness of promotion, is understated.

Many small retailers simply add a fixed percentage mark-up to the cost they have paid for goods bought for re-sale.

Cost-based influences

Production costs are a major influence on product price. **Cost-based pricing** uses production – and other – costs to establish a price for the product.

Cost-plus pricing is one method of cost-based pricing. It is based on absorption costing and takes all costs into account:

1. The product's direct costs are calculated.
2. The product's share of indirect costs (overheads) is added.
3. A percentage (the mark-up) is added for profit to give the selling price. For example, if a product costs £2, a mark-up of 50 percent gives a selling price of £3 (and a profit margin of £1).

Cost-plus pricing has two main drawbacks:

- It is not easy to calculate accurately the exact unit cost of production for a product.
- It ignores competitors' prices and products.

Contribution pricing is an alternative cost-based approach. It uses marginal costing principles and links to break-even analysis, calculating the contribution to total fixed costs made by each product sold. As long as the product's selling price is higher than its variable costs, it is making a contribution towards these fixed costs. The firm uses this information to make pricing decisions such as setting **differential prices** or selling 'loss leaders'.

Rail and airline transport are examples of differential pricing. For example, low-fare, stand-by, off-peak or customer category (e.g. 'students' or 'senior

Break-even analysis and marginal costing techniques are important influences on cost-based pricing.

citizens') pricing is used to fill seats – the marginal cost of these passengers being low – with the contribution helping to cover the fixed costs that must be incurred.

A firm that uses cost-based pricing will ensure that all its costs are met by its selling price. However, if it ignores competitors' prices in the market then it is likely to result in setting an uncompetitive price.

Market-based influences

Market managers concentrate on external market factors, whereas production managers are more influenced by internal production costs.

Market-based pricing occurs when firms set their prices at or near the current market price. The firm can set a competitive price – if there is little product differentiation in the market and therefore a high elasticity of demand, the firm has to charge approximately the same price as its competitors. Where a competitor is the brand leader, the firm may be forced to sell at a lower price to achieve an acceptable sales level. Some firms can set a profit-maximising price by taking the product's elasticity of demand into account.

KEY POINT

Cost-based pricing is influenced by internal factors and market-based pricing by external factors.

Pricing strategies

AQA	**M3**
Edexcel	**M1, M2a**
OCR	**M1, M3**
WJEC	**M2**
CCEA	**M1**

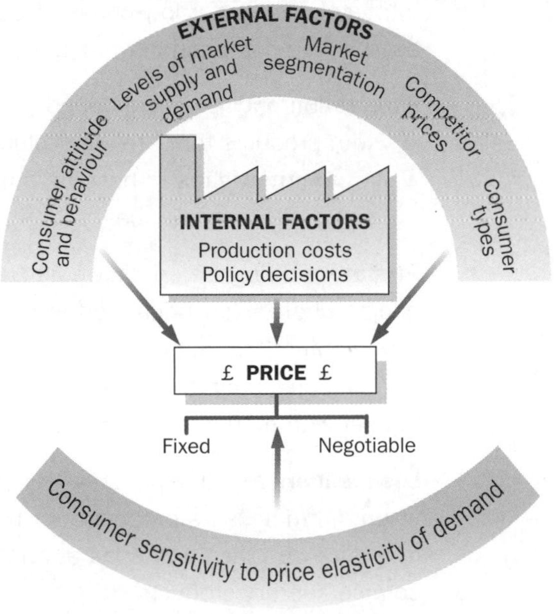

Figure 9.2 Price influences

A firm can price its product:

- near or at an existing market price
- at a price lower than the current market price
- at a high price if its product and market position allows.

The price set is therefore influenced by both the nature of the product and the nature of its market. New products are likely to have different pricing strategies compared with existing products, and the pricing strategy for a luxury product may well differ from that of a basic one. The pricing strategy will also vary depending on whether the product is penetrating an existing market or seeking to establish a new market.

Competition-based pricing strategy

This is also known as parallel pricing.

A **competition-based pricing** strategy occurs when a producer reviews the current market prices and then follows them. This strategy is usually followed because the firm is a market follower rather than a market leader. Competition then occurs not on price but through other factors, such as quality and after-sales service.

Skimming pricing strategy

A **skimming** or '**creaming**' pricing strategy is when a high price is set for a new, innovative product.

The high price maximises profits in the short term and is possible because:

- the product has a scarcity value
- the high price boosts its image and appeal
- the firm has a temporary monopoly position.

Examples of skimming strategies are often found with technologically advanced developments, such as advanced-technology mobile phones, for instance the iPad or iPhone.

Once competitors arrive on the market, often being encouraged by the high price and profit margin, the firm has to lower the price and focus on what becomes more of a mass market.

Penetration pricing strategy

A **penetration pricing** strategy is focused on lower prices and profit margins. The purpose of this strategy is to increase market share. Whilst it can be used with both new and established products, it is more frequently used by new entrants to a market. They offer low prices to establish a target market share or to prevent established competition from competing.

Penetration pricing is often used:

- with products that are high-volume, long-life and price-sensitive
- if the firm wishes to become a market leader, has a cost advantage over its competitors, or can benefit from economies of scale.

EU policy discourages predatory pricing.

Predator pricing – also known as Destroyer pricing – is a form of penetration pricing where a low price – often below the cost of production – is set in order to drive competitors out of the market. This anti-competitive strategy is often used when a conglomerate decides to cross-subsidise its predator pricing in one market with profits from other products and markets.

Loss leaders are associated with penetration pricing. A loss leader occurs when a firm sells its product at or below cost price for a strategic reason (the price can then be raised at a later date). Loss leaders are used with complementary products.

These are some examples of loss leaders in practice:

- Retailers, such as large supermarkets, use loss leaders to attract customers into the store, in the hope they will buy other normal-priced products.
- Mobile phone companies offer a phone at low cost, gaining profits when the consumer signs up to a contract with the company's network.
- Cable and satellite companies offer low-cost (or free) hardware, believing that consumers will then pay for their basic services, and possibly also the premium products, such as sports and film channels.

In 2010, the new coalition government discussed preventing alcohol being sold as a loss leader.

Penetration pricing is a useful strategy if brand loyalty can be established, but psychologically a low price can be associated with low quality in consumers' minds. It is also a high-risk strategy – cutting prices also cuts into profit margins, and competitors may respond by cutting prices, resulting in a price war. Although consumers gain from price wars in the short term, through the lower prices, in the longer term competition may be reduced by firms being forced out of the market, and the remaining firms may then be able to raise their prices.

KEY POINT

The benefits of penetration pricing can be quick growth for the firm, coupled with eliminating competitors from the market and discouraging new firms from entering.

Promotional pricing strategy

Promotional pricing is another low-price strategy. It can be used when entering a new market, but is most closely associated with firms that wish to sell extra volume of a product.

A short-term increase in sales may be required:

- to clear seasonal stock, e.g. Christmas cards, Easter eggs
- to gain space for new stock lines or seasonal fashions.

KEY POINT

Promotional pricing is closely linked to sales, and with sales promotions such as 'buy one, get one free' (BOGOF) offers.

Psychological pricing

Whichever pricing strategy is used, it can be supported by **psychological pricing** techniques.

A price might be set to reflect the product's image and the expectations of its target market. For example, consumers expect to pay more for certain brand names (e.g. Dior, Chanel, Nike, Mercedes) – the high price reinforces the quality image.

Another psychological influence is to set a price below a key figure – e.g. £995 rather than £1000 – so the firm can, for example, promote this product as 'less than £1000'.

KEY POINT

Price represents a profit objective to the seller, and a measure of value to the buyer.

PROGRESS CHECK

1. Give one reason why a firm is able to sell its product at a high price.
2. Name three low-price strategies.

1 **Accept one from:** the firm has a short-term monopoly because its product is unique (e.g. a new technological development); the product has a scarcity value; the high price boosts its image and appeal.

2 **Accept three from:** penetration; loss leader; predator; promotional.

9.3 Promotion

LEARNING SUMMARY

After studying this section, you should be able to:

- distinguish between above-the-line and below-the-line promotion
- explain the difference between informative and persuasive advertising
- give examples of advertising media suitable for different business contexts
- describe the main below-the-line promotional methods
- outline the nature and purpose of the public relations function

The promotion mix

AQA **M2**
Edexcel **M2a**
OCR **M1, M3**
WJEC **M2**
CCEA **M1**

Firms promote their products in order to:

- sell them in either their present market, or a new market or segment
- introduce new products onto the market
- compete with others, to maintain or increase market share
- improve their corporate image, which boosts the whole product range
- counter negative publicity or image problems.

The **promotion mix** consists of 'above-the-line' costs (advertising), and 'below-the-line' costs (personal selling, sales promotion and direct marketing).

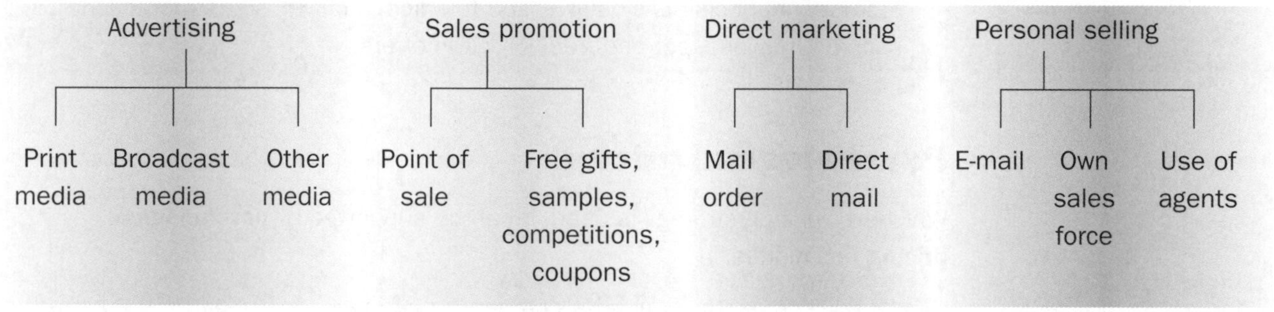

Figure 9.3 The four main methods of promotion

KEY POINT

The mix chosen by a firm depends on the relative cost and effectiveness of each promotional element.

The advertising message

Corporate advertising is also called image advertising.

Advertising is a media-delivered message paid for by a sponsor. Although most advertising focuses on products, firms also undertake **corporate advertising** to promote their image.

An **advertising campaign** puts a firm's advertising strategy into operation. Larger firms can afford to employ specialist advertising agencies – a marketing economy of scale – to create professional advertising campaigns on their behalf.

Most advertising campaigns contain some information, and also an element of persuasion.

Informative advertising is often used by public sector bodies.

Informative advertising provides factual information about the product. The emphasis of the advertising is on providing full details, like technical information.

The objective of **persuasive advertising** is to convince customers that they need the product. It includes persuading them to buy the firm's product rather than a rival one. Persuasive advertising is assisted by the use of branding and other forms of product differentiation – seeking to establish brand image and customer loyalty through repeating its persuasive statements.

Figure 9.4 'Persuasive' and 'informative' advertising

Ethically aware firms adopt advertising campaigns that avoid these criticisms.

Persuasive advertising is often criticised for:

- making outlandish claims – false claims are illegal, e.g. under the Misleading Advertising Directive, and are monitored against the Advertising Standards Authority's code of practice
- manipulating consumers – tactics involving sex or status can be used to make the product more appealing.

The advertising media

Television, radio, cinema and the Internet are the main **broadcast media**. Commercial stations provide mass coverage and are therefore suitable for advertising mass-appeal products. Adverts used in broadcast media have the advantage of sound, colour and movement.

Drawbacks of advertising through broadcast media include:

- the expense (particularly of television advertising)
- the increasing tendency of viewers to channel hop (as the number of available stations increases) and avoid adverts
- the temporary nature of the advert, and the lack of selectivity of this approach.

Print-based media include newspapers – the daily and Sunday 'tabloids' and 'qualities' offer national coverage; regional and local newspapers are widely used by sellers who have a regional or local demand for their products. Other print-based media include 'freesheets', free newspapers such as the *Metro*, and specialist magazines that target specific groups.

Print-based media advertising is more permanent – for example, the advert can be kept for future reference and may also include a reply slip. It also provides more detail than broadcast advertisements and is less expensive than television advertising, though it lacks the impact of sound and movement.

Other media include posters and illuminated signs, which offer a degree of permanence to advertisers, and publish the message to passers-by.

How does a firm choose where to advertise from this variety of media?

The main factors to consider are:

- the **size of the advertising budget** – this is the main limiting factor
- the **target group** – whether national or local, general or special-interest
- the **product** – e.g. advertising industrial goods in trade magazines; using more persuasive techniques for consumer goods
- the **stage in the product life cycle**, e.g. more informative advertising at introduction and growth stages.

Below-the-line promotion

Firms use **sales promotion** – short-term incentives – to encourage new purchasers to try their products, and/or to reinforce existing customers' brand loyalty.

Sales promotion techniques include:

- free samples, to encourage customers to try the product and help establish brand loyalty
- price reductions and premium offers, e.g. the use of free gifts, discount or money-off coupons to encourage customers to repeat purchase
- loyalty cards, to help establish company loyalty (and therefore boost own-brand and overall sales)
- competitions, which act as an inducement to buy the product
- after-sales service, which seeks to persuade customers to buy a particular brand.

KEY POINT

Sales promotion can be used to gain additional market share, or for a more defensive reason (e.g. responding to a competitor's promotion).

POS is popular with firms selling impulse-purchase products, such as sweets.

Point-of-sale (POS) advertising is a form of sales promotion. POS includes any merchandising that **takes place at the point of sale**. It tends to concentrate on packaging and display to provide product recognition.

The benefit to a firm of using **personal selling** is that it can target its message to suit the recipient. This compares favourably with advertising, which is impersonal because it is directed at a mass audience. By individually tailoring its message, the firm has close control over its promotion, e.g. by employing the sales staff or agents. It also receives directly any consumer comments, and its sales staff can handle other matters such as customer queries.

The main disadvantage of personal selling is its high cost. Other drawbacks include the relatively high staff turnover and lack of continuity.

Direct marketing involves a **direct approach to the consumer**.

E-mail is an increasingly popular form of direct mail.

Examples of direct marketing include:

- **mail order**, where customers are encouraged to buy products in a catalogue
- **direct mail** (or 'junk mail', which indicates its very low response rate).

Analysing promotion

AQA	**M2**	WJEC	**M2**
Edexcel	**M2a**	CCEA	**M1**
OCR	**M1, M3**		

Promotion can be analysed using techniques such as **AIDA**.

Using the AIDA technique, promotion must:

- create **Awareness** of the product/brand in the marketplace
- arouse the **Interest** of the consumer
- stimulate **Desire** for the product/brand in the consumer
- provoke **Action** by the consumer.

The **DAGMAR** – Defining Advertising Goals for Measured Advertising Results – model for advertising was developed to set advertising objectives and measure the results. It encourages marketers to focus on the key issues of the target audience and the advertising goals.

A firm can also measure **advertising elasticity**. This is the extent to which changes in advertising spending affect demand. If a small change in advertising spending leads to a large change in demand, the firm has an advertising-elastic product.

KEY POINT

Effective promotion relies on effective communication to tell consumers about products. The communication often consists of both informative and persuasive elements.

Public relations

Although not strictly part of promotion, **public relations** (PR) is often linked to it because it seeks to analyse and improve the relations between a firm, its actual or potential customers, and members of the public.

The PR function uses strategies such as press releases and photo opportunities to publicise good points about a firm's work. It also uses corporate advertising, whereby the firm's name and corporate image is promoted, rather than specific products.

Specific PR tactics include:

- product placement, where products are viewed in settings such as films and television programmes
- small gifts and samples being offered to visitors to a firm's premises
- sponsorship of sports, cultural or other events.

PROGRESS CHECK

1. Give three reasons why firms promote their products.
2. Name three types of 'below-the-line' promotion.

1 **Accept three from:** increase product sales; introduce new products; boost image; compete with others; counter negative publicity.
2 Sales promotion; personal selling; direct marketing.

9.4 Place

LEARNING SUMMARY

After studying this section, you should be able to:

- outline the nature of physical distribution
- explain the four main varieties of distribution channels
- describe services offered by a traditional wholesaler
- outline the nature of e-commerce

Physical distribution

AQA **M2** WJEC **M2**
Edexcel **M2a** CCEA **M1**
OCR **M1, M3**

The role of 'place' in the marketing mix is to ensure that the product arrives at the right place at the right time and in the right condition.

Physical **distribution** involves delivering the correct quantity of goods whilst maintaining the product's quality and security. **Distribution channels** are used for this purpose. All distribution channels offer a level of effectiveness, which must be balanced against their cost.

The choice of channel also depends on the degree of outlet control required:

- Mass-market items such as newspapers are not affected by the outlet's image.
- Technically complex or 'exclusive label' products are distributed with the manufacturer exerting much greater control over the number and quality of the outlets.

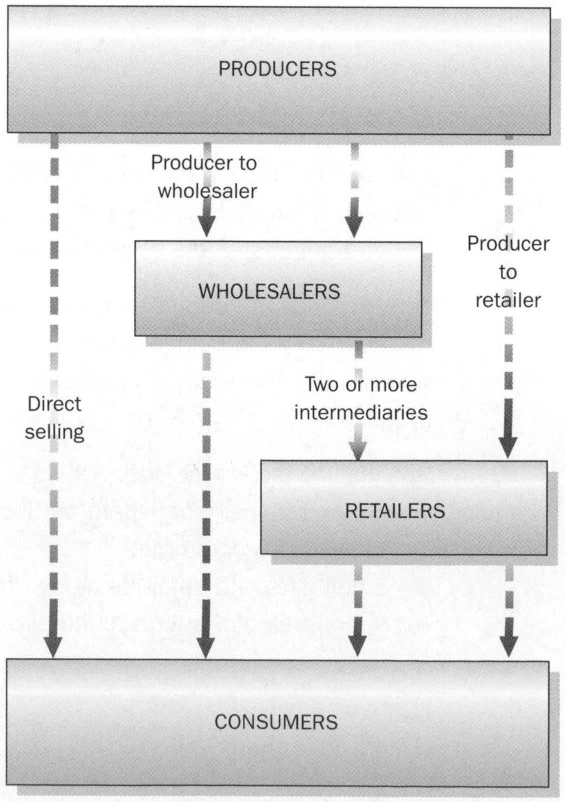

Figure 9.5 Channels of distribution

Many products are **sold direct** from producer to consumer. Examples include 'factory shops' and many industrial goods. Benefits to the seller include greater profit through avoiding intermediaries, and close customer contact.

The **producer–wholesaler** channel is popular with small producer firms that make a limited product range.

However, the producer loses control over the final product outlets and receives lower profit margins when compared with direct selling.

Wholesalers provide several valuable services:

- They bear the risk of not selling the goods – the producer has a guaranteed market.
- They store the goods – the producer's stockholding costs are reduced.
- They advise the producer on market performance.
- They promote the product.

The traditional wholesaler channel is inappropriate for major high-street chains such as Asda and Tesco. They operate their own warehouses, which break bulk for despatch to the outlets. Other forms of **producer–retailer** links include the tied outlet approach, operated by brewers and petrol producers.

The **full chain** is still used, normally where products are sold through smaller retailers.

E-commerce and distribution

In 2009, it was estimated that 86 percent of 16–24 year olds accessed the Internet daily.

Many people in the UK have access to the Internet. Some Internet-based firms, such as eBay and Amazon, have become established household names. Retailers such as Tesco, Argos and Iceland have established websites, and competitors tend to follow suit for defensive reasons.

Other technological developments include digital television and mobile phone shopping and distribution services.

Tesco gains from online shopping

Our online non-food business, Tesco Direct, continues to grow rapidly, increasing sales by more than 50% in the year. ... In the current year we also plan to introduce an online clothing offer – making our fashionable, affordable clothes easier to buy for many more customers.

Tesco Annual Report, 2009

To set up an e-commerce facility, a firm needs to create an e-marketing plan.

This requires the firm to consider:

- how to promote the website and make it functional as well as easy to use
- the extent to which its distribution systems will need modifying
- the influence of data protection and other legislation
- a system for keeping the website up to date
- whether and how to accept online payments.

KEY POINT

Internet- and television-based distribution allows firms closer access to the final market, and greater access through 24-hour trading.

PROGRESS CHECK

1. Name the parties in the full channel of distribution.
2. State two services offered by a wholesaler to a producer.

1 Producer; wholesaler; retailer; consumer.
2 **Accept two from:** breaking bulk; storing the goods; bearing the risk of not selling the goods; advising the producer on market performance; promoting the product.

Sample question and model answer

Detailed and thorough points have been made about both terms.

Again, these points are detailed and accurate.

This is the correct choice of strategy, and it has been clearly justified. Mentioning the lack of suitability of the other strategy supports this answer well.

1. GoGreen is a company that concentrates on making and selling 'environmentally friendly' skin care products for consumers. The directors of GoGreen propose to produce a new range of skin care products under the brand name 'Clean & Green'. These products will compete with other brands already on the market, that are sold in high-street shops such as the Body Shop. The directors would like to establish a high market share for the 'Clean & Green' range.

(a) Explain why the following are important to GoGreen:

(i) branding **(2)**

(i) Branding allows GoGreen to promote the new range by name. Consumers realise that the next item they buy will be the same as the last in terms of quality and use, because they share the brand name.

(ii) product differentiation **(2)**

(ii) Product differentiation allows GoGreen to concentrate its promotion on aspects of the product that are different from competing products - it could have a unique selling point (USP) which the company can highlight as different to its competition.

(b) The Marketing Director of GoGreen has to suggest a suitable range of pricing for the new product range. He is reviewing whether to sell the new range using a skimming or a penetration pricing policy.

(i) Explain the terms:

- skimming **(2)**
- penetration pricing **(2)**

- *A skimming price strategy is high price and sets out to price the product at a figure above that in the market, or is used if the product is unique and exists in the market on its own.*
- *Penetration pricing is a low-price strategy and is often used to launch a new product into an existing market which has competitor products. The low price encourages consumers to try the product, and so brand loyalty may be established.*

(ii) Which pricing strategy should be used in this situation, and why? **(2)**

Penetration pricing is likely to be more appropriate because there is already a market for environmentally friendly products such as the new range. GoGreen will have to establish a market position, and penetration pricing is more suitable for this. A skimming strategy would price the new range higher than its competitors, which is not likely to encourage consumers to buy.

Sample question and model answer (continued)

Effective use of questions to start the answer, and there is an important reference to the 'green' nature of the product.

Very detailed answer, more so than necessary for 2 marks (the second part of the answer is essentially repeated below), but the points are extremely well made.

Good points – perhaps more detail could have been given about the in-store promotion (e.g. reference to display), but this is another strong answer.

(c) The Marketing Director also has to suggest how to promote this new range.

(i) How might advertising be used to market the new range? **(4)**

(i) The Marketing Manager must answer a number of questions, such as: What advertising media are normally used? To which market segment(s) should the adverts be directed? Which media are most suitable for these segments? How does the chosen medium's costs compare to its coverage? How will the advertising link with GoGreen's other forms of promotion? Will the chosen medium require an advertising agency?

The 'green' features of the range will need promoting, which suggests that informative advertising will be important. There is also some evidence that GoGreen is in a competitive market, so it will need to use persuasive advertising to convince people (including competitors' customers) that they should try the new product range.

(ii) Suggest **two** sales promotion methods that could be used to market the new product range. **(2)**

(ii) The offer of free samples would be appropriate so that potential customers can test the product. A linked sales promotion, such as 'buy two items in the range and get a third (lowest-priced) item free', would encourage customers to try (and buy) more than one product in the range and also boost initial sales.

(iii) Select **one** of these methods and show how it could be used to promote the new range. **(4)**

(iii) The sales promotion of 'buy two items in the range and get a third (lowest-priced) item free' would be supported by national advertising if possible, and would feature in an in-store promotion. As a result, customers are likely to buy what they see is good value for money, which might establish their brand loyalty.

Exam practice question

1 Kellogg's is a major supplier and seller of breakfast cereals and other foodstuffs. The company is over 100 years old, and relies for its success on a number of factors, such as a suitable product range. The first UK factory was established in Manchester in the 1930s.

Although the company is well known for the quality of its products and for following its principles of health, balance and nutrition, it faces competition from rival breakfast cereal producers and from the growth in popularity of 'own brand' breakfast cereal products.

Kellogg's therefore needs to continually review its product portfolio in breakfast cereals.

Assume that the company proposes to launch a new breakfast cereal aimed at young children. How can it help to ensure that it gets the following elements of the marketing mix 'right' for this new product?

(20)

Product

Price

Promotion

Place

10 Business organisation and communication

The following topics are covered in this chapter:

- **Internal organisation**
- **Features of organisational structure**
- **The role of communication in business**

10.1 Internal organisation

LEARNING SUMMARY

After studying this section, you should be able to:

- describe line, line and staff, and matrix forms of organisational structure
- differentiate between role and task structures

Types of organisational structure

AQA	**M2, M3**
Edexcel	**M2a**
OCR	**M1, M2, M5, M7**
WJEC	**M2**
CCEA	**M2**

A firm's management carries out a number of functions.

These functions include:

- **planning**, e.g. strategic planning to ensure a firm's future
- **controlling**, e.g. implementing budgetary control
- **co-ordinating**, e.g. making sure there is efficient communication.

Management achieves these by operating within a suitable organisational structure. Nowadays it is recognised that there is no one best structure for all organisations. There are many influences that determine the best structure for an organisation, regardless of size, form of ownership, or sector in which it is based.

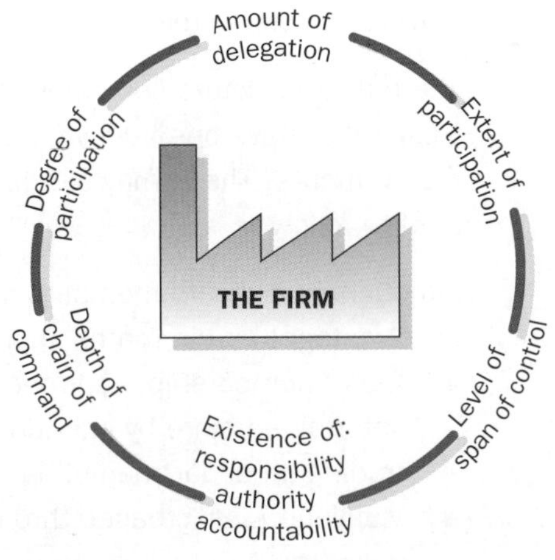

Figure 10.1 Influences on a firm's internal organisation

Line, and line and staff organisational structure

> The best illustrations of functional organisations have often been private sector firms working in the secondary sector of industry.

Most UK organisations were traditionally organised internally on the basis of the different **business functions** such as controlling finance, making items, dealing with employees, selling to customers, and buying stock. The main departments – human resources, accounts, production, purchasing and sales/marketing – reflect these functions. This form of corporate culture is often called **role culture** because individual roles are clearly defined, for example by job descriptions.

The formal, traditional organisational system based on these functions is called **line organisation**. The advantage of this organisational structure is that roles and responsibilities are well-defined, with a clear chain of command.

KEY POINT

A line structure tends to be bureaucratic in nature, with a narrow span of control due to the many layers of hierarchy.

> A good illustration is the frequent use of consultants by larger companies.

As they grow, firms rely more on specialist support functions and personnel. A **line and staff** organisation recognises the importance of these specialists.

Problems can arise with line and staff structures:

- There may be a lack of 'line' understanding of 'staff' procedures and requirements.
- Line managers may feel threatened by the work of the 'staff' specialists.
- Communication slows down due to the increasingly complex structure.

> Organisational charts can date quickly, and do not show informal communication structures.

The traditional **organisational chart** outlines the formal structure shown by line, or line and staff, organisations. It illustrates the degree of **specialisation** in a firm, indicates the layers of **hierarchy**, and defines individual roles. It also provides a summary of a formal structure, which can be used in induction training and which acts as a record of changes and developments.

Matrix organisational structure

> These firms are often working in fast-changing markets, selling products or services with relatively short life cycles (for example, telecommunications).

Today, many organisations have reduced the number of layers in their hierarchy, restructuring to take the emphasis away from functions and towards operations, products or tasks. This matrix structure is associated with firms that have a **task culture**, which is project-oriented and focuses on achieving given tasks or jobs.

The matrix structure combines the use of line departments with **project** (task) **teams** that have been drawn from the various line functions according to task requirements. These may be temporary in nature, or they may have a permanent brief to follow.

> However, overall control becomes more complex, and some team members may face a clash of loyalties between the task and their own department.

Although some team members may face a clash of loyalties, there are a number of advantages of the matrix approach:

- Team membership – and the authority to carry out projects and tasks – is determined more by individual ability than by formal position and rank.
- Traditional departmental barriers are broken down.
- Motivation is increased through varied work (e.g. moving to a new team/task).
- The limitation of only line managers working together is overcome.

KEY POINT

The matrix structure is most effective in firms having wide spans of control and comparatively few hierarchical levels of responsibility.

PROGRESS CHECK

1. Identify two ways in which a company may use an organisational chart.
2. Distinguish between role and task cultures.

1 **Accept two from:** to review existing lines of communication; to illustrate the degree of specialisation in a firm; to indicate layers of hierarchy; to define individual roles; for induction training.
2 Role focuses on person's job role; task focuses on firm's projects.

10.2 Features of organisational structure

LEARNING SUMMARY

After studying this section, you should be able to:

- explain these key organisational terms: delayering, span of control, chain of command
- assess the likely benefits of (a) centralisation and (b) decentralisation
- explain the importance of effective delegation to a business

The five key features

AQA	**M2, M3**
Edexcel	**M2a**
OCR	**M1, M2, M5, M7**
WJEC	**M2**
CCEA	**M2**

Delayering

An organisation may seek to reduce the number of layers in its hierarchy, restructuring through **delayering**, i.e. removing one or more layers of the firm's management hierarchy.

A major side effect may be increased pressure and stress on the staff that are involved.

Delayering may be implemented to:

- increase spans of control (which become wider as a result of the delayering)
- reduce communication problems (and related costs).

How Delta plc delayered

Following his appointment to Delta plc in 1998, Manfred Halper implemented a programme to restructure the plumbing business for growth. The changes he made eliminated an entire layer of management and made the business more market- and consumer- focused, as well as removing unnecessary costs and duplication.

Span of control

Span of control can be defined as the number of subordinates directly under the control of a manager. It is described as **wide** when the manager has many subordinates, and **narrow** when the manager has few subordinates.

Too narrow a span leads to over-supervision, denying the staff the chance to show initiative. Too wide a span means lack of control and the chance of costly mistakes.

The width of an individual's span of control is influenced by three principal factors:

1. The degree of complexity of the work involved – simple tasks that are easily supervised are associated with wide spans, and more complex or advanced work with narrow spans.
2. The skill and ability levels of the staff – well-trained and able employees can be supervised efficiently in larger groups compared with staff that are new or untrained.
3. The manager's own level of ability and training is also an important factor.

By widening the span of control:

- delegation is encouraged (the manager has less time for each subordinate)
- fewer layers of hierarchy are required, thereby improving the speed of communication between the top and bottom of the hierarchy.

By narrowing the span of control:

- there may be less pressure on employees, as a result of better communication
- closer management supervision is possible, which may be important in certain industries (e.g. where safety is at a premium).

KEY POINT

A narrow span of control is most suited to straightforward tasks. A wide span, since it reduces supervision, is more associated with delegation.

Chain of command

The **chain of command** establishes how power and control are passed downwards through an organisation, and how information should flow formally up and down the chain. The chain becomes more complicated as the organisation's size increases – for example, a sole trader may liaise with all employees, whilst large companies have chains of command that go through a number of layers of authority.

Organisational structures can be analysed into **tall** and **flat** forms.

As a general rule, the taller the structure, the larger the firm.

Tall structures indicate long chains of command:

- High-level decisions can take a long time to reach employees at the bottom of the chain, and to be actioned.
- There may be a 'them and us' feeling of remoteness between those at both ends of the chain.
- The 'them and us' feeling is reinforced by the formal communication systems and methods associated with tall structures.
- Spans of control are often narrow.
- Employees are usually highly task specialised.

KEY POINT

Flat structures are increasingly popular nowadays and are associated with smaller organisations and shorter chains of command.

Centralisation

When applied to organisational structures, the **degree of centralisation influences the authority to make decisions**.

Centralisation allows managers to make and communicate quickly decisions that are consistent across the organisation. However, a highly centralised structure denies those lower down the chain of command the power or the authority to make decisions for themselves. As an illustration, many well-known 'fast food' outlets operating as franchises have little, if any, scope regarding display, pricing policy and the style or amount of advertising. The benefit is that customers have a virtual guarantee that every McDonald's or Burger King outlet will be broadly the same. Another typical example of centralised organisations is the 'multiple' retailer, where counter layout, prices, promotions and window displays are determined without the direct involvement of individual store staff.

The term centralisation is also used to identify whether an organisation's services, such as reprographics, are organised on a centralised or decentralised basis.

Sainsbury's gains from centralising its procurement activities

We delivered cost efficiency savings... Improvements to instore productivity from bioptic scanners and self scan. Reorganising the centre as well as our new shared service centre at Manchester. Centralising our procurement activities and reducing waste, packaging, and of course energy use.

Sainsbury's Interim Results Presentation, 2009

Sainsbury's restructuring plans in 2009

In January 2009 we announced plans to restructure our store support centre in London, cutting out duplication of activities and simplifying structures across our Holborn, Manchester and Coventry support teams, aligning them for the future growth of the business. The new structures were in place by the start of the 2009/10 financial year.

Sainsbury's Annual Report, 2009

Decentralised structures are increasingly popular.

They are associated with greater authority at 'unit' (e.g. shop) level and are said to:

- allow a quicker and more effective local response to local needs and conditions
- improve employee motivation through greater involvement in the decision-making process
- lead to more effective **management by objectives** (MBO), because decentralised and personally devised objectives are set
- lead to better **management by exception** by more accurate budgeting, and an improved control system through the use of variances (see page 234).

Delegation

The key to successful delegation is **mutual trust**.

A manager may **delegate** – pass down – certain powers to subordinates. The success of delegation is influenced by the **responsibility**, **authority** and **accountability** of those involved with the tasks.

If employees are to carry out tasks delegated to them, they must accept the responsibility for carrying out the tasks, and therefore for any failure. As a result, the responsibilities must be identified clearly, recorded (e.g. in the job description), and reasonable in nature and scope given the subordinate's training, qualifications and experience.

> A side benefit of delegation is that it results in the junior employee taking on additional responsibilities, therefore being trained for later advancement.

The employee who will carry out the delegated work must be given the **authority** to do so. This authority might have to be communicated to others, such as another manager who is holding information to which the employee would not normally have access.

Delegation, correctly given, results in the subordinate being **accountable** to the manager – and, in turn, the manager to the next person up the chain of command – for the success of the work.

An organisation suffers when delegation has been unsuccessful. This normally occurs where the work delegated is unsuitable (e.g. too complex or specialised), the delegator has difficulty in delegating due to unwillingness to relinquish tasks, or the subordinate lacks adequate training, confidence or motivation.

KEY POINT

Delegation is associated with larger organisations, simply because no one person can effectively control all the functions of such a firm.

PROGRESS CHECK

1. Distinguish between 'span of control' and 'chain of command'.
2. What are the benefits to managers and subordinates of successful delegation?

1 'Span of control' is the number of subordinates under a person's control. 'Chain of command' is the flow of control (down) and information (up and down) through the organisation.
2 Managers have reduced workloads, so can focus on key tasks and make better decisions; subordinates gain experience and are more highly motivated.

10.3 The role of communication in business

LEARNING SUMMARY

After studying this section, you should be able to:

- explain the importance of efficient communication in business
- outline the nature and operation of communication networks and channels
- describe the typical purpose of – and methods used in – business communication
- give examples of recent developments in electronic communications
- explain commonly found barriers to efficient communication

People and communication

AQA	**M3**	WJEC	**M4**
Edexcel	**M2a**	CCEA	**M2**
OCR	**M5**		

An efficient management structure requires efficient business **communication.** Information such as messages, instructions and ideas must be transmitted from one person to another in good time and in such a way that there is full understanding.

The value and importance of effective and efficient communication is universally accepted in business.

Efficient communication leads to:

- clear statements of the organisation's mission, so everyone understands its goals and purpose
- a good reputation, e.g. through effective communication of its corporate social responsibility programme
- motivated employees, who make a more efficient contribution
- increased sales and profits, because the organisation is regarded as efficient, with effective marketing strategies being communicated clearly.

The role of the International Visual Communications Association (IVCA)

The International Visual Communications Association exists to represent its members to Government and other stakeholding bodies and to promote effective business and public service communications of the highest ethical and professional standards.

The Association aims to be a centre of excellence for best communication practice and works with production companies, freelancers, support service providers and clients of the industry to represent their interests and help maximize their competitiveness and professionalism.

Extract from the 'About' page of the IVCA website, 2010

This extract shows effective communication in practice.

The Wrigley Company wins IVCA Clarion awards

The Wrigley Company's educational programme Bin It!, which aims to teach young people about the impact of dropping litter and anti-social behaviour, has won two awards at the 2009 International Visual Communications Association (IVCA) Clarion Awards.

The awards, which were held on 25 September at the BFI Institute in London, saw The Wrigley Company programme named Best Live Event and Best Printed Materials in the Corporate Communications category.

Extract from the Wrigley Company website, 2009

Communication channels and networks

To be efficient, communication should be as brief as possible whilst still providing a clear message.

Communication needs a:

- sender (the **transmitter**)
- **message**
- **medium** through which the communication is sent
- receiver (the **recipient**).

Flatter structures with wider spans of control often give employees more personal autonomy and control.

Business communication transmits information through the **hierarchy/chain of command**. This transmission takes place via communication channels, and formal or informal **communication networks**. The **formal communication channels** are indicated by the firm's formal structure, shown by the vertical chains of command in its organisational chart. The chart shows the formal communication through lines of **authority**, and the relationship between the various business departments or functions. This '**chain**' network is based on the existing chains of command – communications are transmitted from superior to subordinate along the chain. Such a network is associated with **tall structures** and **authoritarian** organisations.

Horizontal communication channels also exist, for example communication taking place at team meetings where the team is drawn from a number of departments. (Horizontal communication occurs between people at the same layer in the organisational chart.) A channel may be either 'open' – to all in the firm, e.g. via a notice board – or 'closed', where the communication is limited to named individuals or roles.

Most managers recognise the value of informal channels because of their typically positive effect on morale and motivation.

Informal communication channels co-exist with formal ones. They can assume great importance in firms with tall structures, and in situations where the formal channels are not working efficiently.

A different communication network is the '**matrix**' (or 'all-channel') network. Here, every member of the matrix group communicates with each other, often without there being a formal leader. Alternatives include the **horizontal** or '**circular**' communication channel, e.g. when team members communicate with each other at team meetings, and the '**wheel**' or 'hub' channel, where there is central control (e.g. a head office).

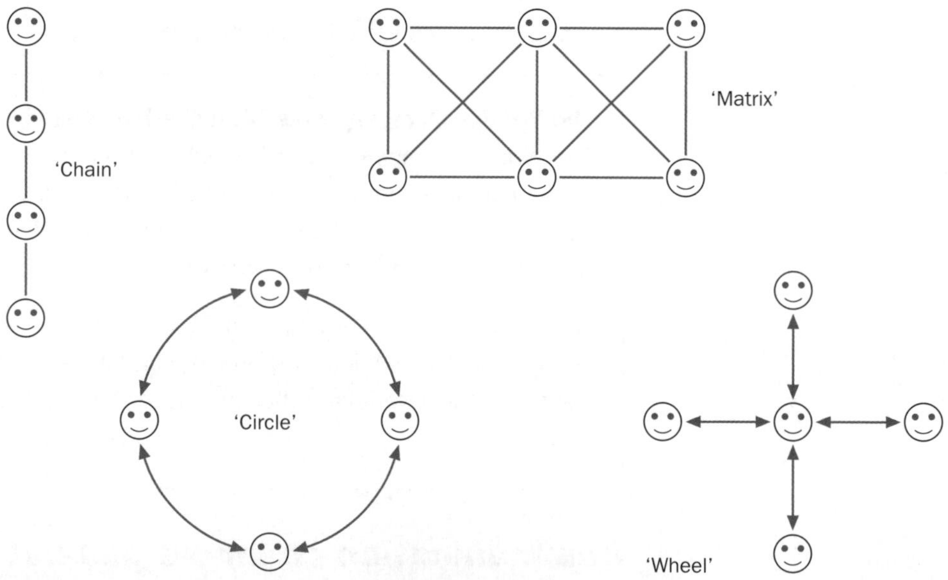

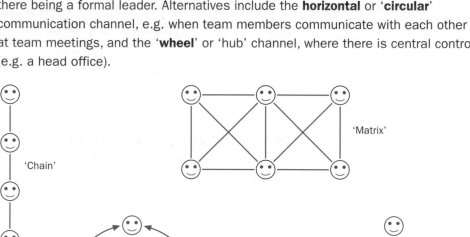

Figure 10.2 Different communication networks

Communication can also be classified as external or internal (or both):

- **External communication** takes place between a member of the organisation and someone from outside, such as a customer or supplier. It tends to be more formal, typically taking place with the main external stakeholders, e.g. suppliers, customers, shareholders, the government and the public.
- **Internal communication** occurs between members of the same organisation. It tends to be less formal because it is contained within the organisation.

Purpose and methods of communication

AQA	**M3**	WJEC	**M4**
Edexcel	**M2a**	CCEA	**M2**
OCR	**M5**		

The purpose of communication

Managers need to make decisions concerning:

- the nature of the communication, e.g. whether it should be formal or informal
- any special skills required to communicate information efficiently, e.g. knowledge of how an e-mail system operates
- the communication methods available, e.g. whether to use oral or written forms of communication.

The purpose of communication varies from situation to situation. Figure 10.3 illustrates some typical reasons why communication takes place.

All types of 'noise' affect the efficiency of communication.

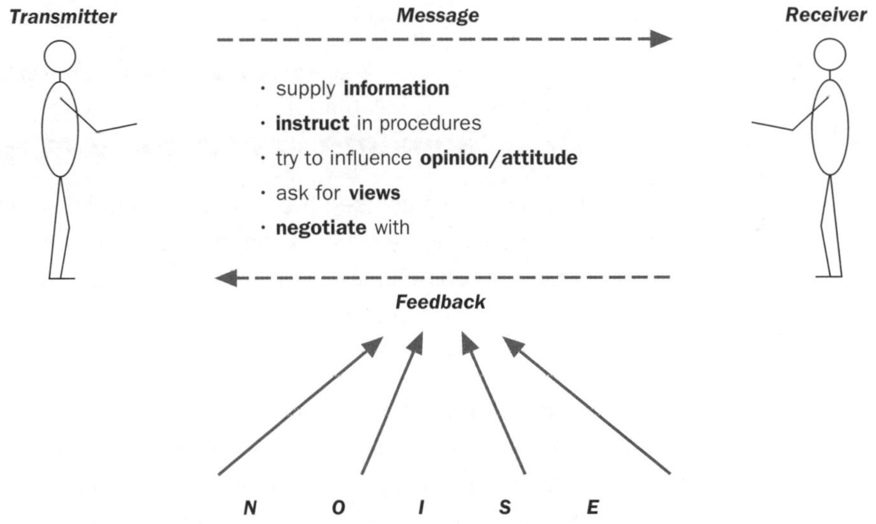

Figure 10.3 Communication

Methods of communication in business

Information communications technology (ICT) is a key transmitting medium for most of these methods.

Business communication methods can be:

- **oral** – with the sender and receiver face to face (e.g. a business meeting or coffee-break discussion) or at a distance (e.g. by telephone)
- **written** – formats include business memos and letters, e-mails and text messaging
- **visual** – e.g. safety posters and signs such as a fire exit, and in the form of 'body language', i.e. **non-verbal communication** (NVC).

The transmitter must choose an appropriate method:

- Oral communication is most valuable for transmitting basic, low-volume information quickly. It has the advantage over written communication of being an immediate two-way process, though given the instantaneous nature of fax and e-mail, this advantage is less important nowadays. Oral communication may be informal (e.g. a telephone call) or formal, such as in a business meeting or an interview.
- Written communication is widely used where high-volume and/or technical information needs transmitting, and has the major advantage that a written record of the communication is available if required. A manager will typically choose a memorandum as an informal form of written communication; popular formal written communication methods include reports, letters and technical manuals.

- Visual communication is appropriate when a point needs making clearly and quickly. Safety – and other key business themes – is often communicated visually to create impact (see Figure 10.4 below). **Numerical information**, such as index numbers, sales statistics and production performance, is often presented effectively and in summary using tables, charts and graphs.

Figure 10.4 **Visual communication in health and safety**

Developments in communication

ICT has revolutionised the way organisations communicate. Electronic forms of communication – such as the Internet, e-mail and mobile phones – are the dominant communication media. In practice, this means that a national or international business can get in touch instantaneously with every factory, outlet and employee.

E-mail in particular has improved the speed and efficiency of business communication. Many organisations have their own in-house 'Intranet' systems that link the different functions and branches – Intranets are secure systems because they do not permit external access.

Other developments used by businesses include:

- **mobile phones** and **text messaging**, which allow employees to contact and stay in touch with other employees
- **video conferencing** and **teleconferencing**, which save time and costs (e.g. travel)
  - video conferencing transmits sound and images through a computer network, allowing national or international contact
  - teleconferencing uses a telephone network to conduct national or international discussion
- **social network** sites – many (typically larger) businesses exist on social network sites
- **podcast** broadcasts that are transmitted via the Internet, broadcasting business information and communications.

KEY POINT

Computers form the backbone of most communication systems. Advantages of their use include improved quality/readability (e.g. laser printers), reduced costs of storing, manipulating and transmitting information, and greater security of stored information.

Communication and motivation

AQA	**M3**	WJEC	**M4**
Edexcel	**M2a**	CCEA	**M2**
OCR	**M5**		

Informal channels assume greater importance when the formal networks are not working efficiently.

There is a close relationship between communication and motivation. An example is in the range of informal networks that co-exist with the formal ones.

Human needs – e.g. for contact, friendship and recognition – help in creating these informal channels.

The main characteristics of an informal network are the **fast transmission** and the **variable accuracy** of the information. The **quality** of the communication will therefore vary, being influenced by the (subjective) judgment of those transmitting the information.

Managers need to recognise the importance of good formal and informal communication in the organisation.

Staff appraisal schemes are often used to communicate employee levels of achievement.

To motivate an employee, managers need to communicate:

- the organisation's mission statement and strategic **objectives**
- the organisation's **performance** in the marketplace
- the **relevance** of the employee's work to the achievement of objectives and market performance
- how **effective** the employee is in relation to this.

By doing so, managers will motivate staff, e.g. in Maslow's terms by improving their self-esteem and achieving levels of self-actualisation.

The influence of size

The larger the firm, the more layers there tend to be in the organisational structure. As a result, communication slows down and becomes over-formalised. In turn, this slows down decision making, and can have a negative effect on staff morale. '**Noise**' also increases, with the message more likely to be distorted as a result of going through more levels (i.e. more people).

The way that many large organisations have to cope with the volume of communication required is to commit it to a written form (including e-mail). As a result, there can be '**communication overload**', with staff having to **prioritise** communications (sometimes without having the information to make this judgment), or even completely ignoring the communication.

KEY POINT

Although ICT is used to overcome the slowness of communication in large companies, it can also create a much greater volume of communication.

Communication barriers

On the next page are examples of how the transmitter, the message, the medium and the recipient can all be barriers to effective communication.

The **transmitter** may:

- use an inappropriate level of language, e.g. jargon or complex technical terms
- select inaccurate language
- use poor sentence structure
- omit important information
- make inappropriate non-verbal signals in supporting the message.

The **message** may:

- be sent using inappropriate methods
- go through an over-long chain of command
- contain a high level of 'redundancy', i.e. the amount of information being transmitted is far more than required.

The **medium** may:

- be unsuitable for the information being transmitted
- be too slow in getting the message to the recipient for action.

The **recipient** may:

- choose to ignore the message
- be in an unsuitable physical or emotional state to receive it
- interpret the message incorrectly, e.g. due to personal bias.

KEY POINT

Most communication suffers from 'noise', which can be either background noise, or some other distraction such as faulty equipment.

Overcoming the barriers

Systems analysis can be used to evaluate the efficiency of the present structure, and **systems design** undertaken to develop improved procedures and routines for the organisation.

Managers must seek to overcome these barriers to communication. The quality of staff training in communication procedures and techniques will need reviewing, communication media need evaluating for clarity and suitability, and the complexity of the organisational structure must be studied.

PROGRESS CHECK

1. Give two examples of **(a)** formal and **(b)** informal communication.
2. Why does the growth in a firm's size often cause communications to deteriorate?

1 **(a)** oral presentation to a group of managers; minutes of a meeting
(b) talk about work at lunch break; informal Quality Circle meeting (**accept any other suitable answers**).
2 Larger size extends the channels of communication and chain networks – there are more layers of hierarchy through which the message must pass.

Sample question and model answer

1. Sheila Long is the recently appointed Managing Director of Barkers Ltd, a dog food manufacturer employing over 100 staff. She is reviewing profitability and turnover and plans to improve the company's financial performance by setting up performance-related pay schemes. Sheila realises the importance of finding out employee views on this, and has asked her management team to make some informal enquiries.

Feedback from the managers suggests that production operatives would support the proposed scheme, believing they could increase their pay. Sales staff, on the other hand, are less supportive, particularly since the dog food market has become even more competitive. There have also been some comments made to managers about the size of both Sheila's salary and those of the other directors.

Sheila has decided to implement the performance-related pay scheme.

(a) What differences exist between formal and informal methods of communication? **(2)**

Formal methods go along the chain of command, informal ones don't.

This is a simple and limited point. More detail should be given about (for instance) vertical flows compared with 'the grapevine'.

(b) Give **two** advantages and **two** disadvantages of using an informal method of communication in this context. **(4)**

Informal communication can expand and further explain a formal communication, which may be necessary in this situation; second, it is inexpensive, normally less so than a formal method. One disadvantage is that, being informal, the information may get changed and so be inaccurate. Also, it can reinforce a feeling amongst staff that management is rather distant (or just incompetent).

This is a good answer, which includes some pertinent points from the question.

(c) Suggest whether or not Sheila should consider changing her management style to one that is more democratic. **(8)**

Many people now recognise that an autocratic approach to leadership can bring as many problems as it solves. It means the manager takes full control of the decision-making process, and this has the weakness that others are not involved. Though decisions are taken quickly, the fact that the manager does not consult with others means the decision is more likely to be a wrong one. Most people enjoy taking on responsibility (e.g. see McGregor) and an autocratic leadership style denies them the chance.

The democratic approach would involve all staff to a greater extent and support the manager's decision making, so I would support a change. Involvement means motivation, and motivation means better quality and quantity of output.

Several implications of autocratic leadership are considered, but there is no recognition that other factors help determine the most appropriate style to use. The answer is not well linked to the question information (e.g. number of employees, type of staff, how recently Sheila was appointed, etc.).

Exam practice question

1 FreshFood plc produces a range of food items sold in supermarkets and cafés throughout the UK. Most of the food items are popular and well-established, and the company has recently introduced its new 'fresh baked just like Mum' range of food items. However, sales of this new product line have been disappointing.

FreshFood plc's Marketing Manager has contacted the company's Operations Manager about the poor customer feedback on the 'fresh baked just like Mum' range. The Operations Manager has not responded to a series of memos sent by the Marketing Manager, but has made a quick telephone call to complain about the work pressures in the various sections of the Operations Management department. This particular department has a multi-site production operation in a number of factories located throughout the UK, with its research and development section located in Head Office.

The Managing Director has asked a firm of management consultants to study the quality of the company's functional co-ordination and other structural issues, and to advise on possible restructuring. The Managing Director's concern is that the span of control exercised in the company appears too narrow.

Here is the current organisational chart of FreshFood plc:

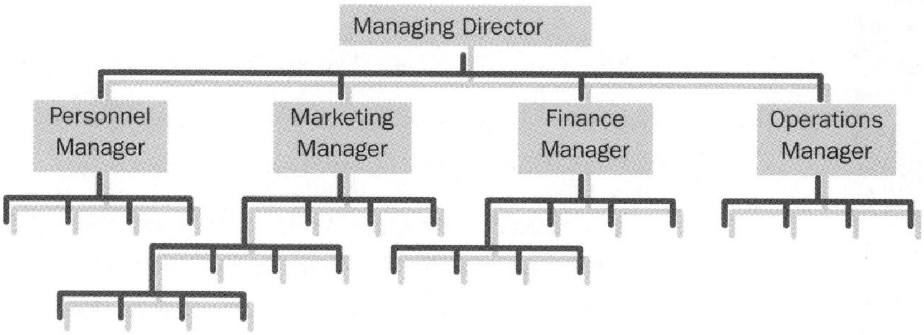

(a) What problems are likely to arise for FreshFood plc from having a narrow span of control? **(8)**

(b) (i) Analyse likely reasons for the conflict between the Marketing Manager and the Operations Manager. **(6)**

(ii) Suggest how these problems might be overcome. **(2)**

(c) What are the alternative structures that a company such as FreshFood plc might adopt? **(8)**

For each of the above responses, continue your answer on separate paper if necessary.

11 People in organisations

The following topics are covered in this chapter:

- **Human resources planning**
- **Recruitment, training and development**

11.1 Human resources planning

LEARNING SUMMARY

After studying this section, you should be able to:

- understand the role of the human resources function
- explain the relevance of workforce planning
- discuss, and give examples of, influences on the workforce plan

The human resources function

AQA	**M1, M3**
Edexcel	**M2a**
OCR	**M1, M2, M5, M7**
WJEC	**M2**
CCEA	**M2**

The role of the **human resources** (**HR**) **function** is to act as the link between the organisation and the people who work in the organisation. The HR function exists in all organisations, either as a specialist department/section or as one of the roles of the owner or manager.

The table below shows the key business areas of HR.

Area	Reasons
Manpower planning	To identify and meet labour shortfalls; to review employees' current skills; to help employees achieve their potential
Recruitment and selection	To ensure organisational objectives are met; to bring in new ideas; to appoint suitably qualified and skilled employees
Training and development	To allow new employees to settle in quickly; to help employees develop and contribute more to the work of the organisation
Appraisal	To encourage employees to achieve their potential; to support employees in their attempts to achieve personal goals
Welfare	To help employees satisfy their personal needs
Consultation and negotiation	To communicate key policies; to motivate employees through involvement; to anticipate and identify employee concerns

HR objectives include:

- assessing business needs in order to match workforce skills against these needs
- working with employees to achieve their potential
- minimising labour costs
- communicating HR-related information efficiently to employees
- maintaining appropriate professional employer–employee relations.

KEY POINT

The HR function exists in all organisations, whether or not a specialist HR department exists.

Workforce planning

AQA	**M1, M3**
Edexcel	**M2a**
OCR	**M1, M2, M5**
WJEC	**M2**
CCEA	**M2**

The importance of workforce planning

One objective for HR is to minimise labour costs. A variety of strategies are available, including having a flexible workforce and using redundancy and redeployment strategies. This is one feature of **workforce planning**.

Workforce planning seeks to ensure that:

- corporate plan workforce requirements are identified and implemented
- workforce levels guarantee that production can take place
- workforce quality leads to improved productivity
- controllable workforce costs meet budget targets.

KEY POINT

The key function of HR is to ensure that there will be the **right number** of employees, of the **right quality**, in the **right place** at the **right time**.

A firm needs an overall workforce (or HR) strategy. To help achieve this, HR needs to work closely with other departments to ensure the firm is employing people with the **right skills** at the **right time**.

The workforce plan therefore depends on **external** and **internal** analysis.

A workforce plan:

- assesses national and local changes in the population, analysed by **numbers**, **ages**, **skills** and **location**
- analyses the current **internal labour supply**
- considers any proposed developments in the company's **organisation**, **location** and **structure**.

This assessment information can be used to evaluate the likely effects on labour turnover, the implications for **recruitment**, expected **training** requirements for existing and anticipated new staff, and the probable effects on **morale** and **labour relations**.

The main difficulty of creating a workforce plan is the problem of **estimating future demand** for labour. Demand will change as a result of the firm changing strategy (e.g. new markets opening up, existing market demand falling), and competitor actions.

Many organisations adopt a '**core and periphery**' approach, employing a core of highly trained full-time staff, which is supplemented by a periphery of part-time – often temporary – employees. This can bring greater staffing flexibility, although part-time staff may lack motivation, and communication becomes more difficult.

KEY POINT

HR emphasises that **people** are an organisation's key resource because of their flexibility, creativity and commitment.

Labour turnover

An important source of information for – and influence on – a workforce plan is the level of a firm's **labour turnover** (LTO). LTO can benefit a firm by introducing new staff with new ideas.

However, high LTO may indicate:

- low morale amongst the employees
- pay levels that are below comparable rates
- high costs of recruitment and training
- lower production.

Retention profiles, showing staff according to the year they joined the organisation, can be constructed and analysed.

$$\text{LTO} = \frac{\text{Number of leavers in the year*}}{\text{Average number employed in the year}} \times 100$$

(*This figure is adjusted to take account of unavoidable reasons for leaving.)

Influences on the plan

Workforce planning requires managers to assess staffing needs for a number of years ahead.

These plans are often based on a **STEP** analysis of the external influences on the organisation.

The 'PESTEL' analysis also includes environmental and legal influences under separate headings.

A STEP analysis looks at:

- **social** influences, e.g. increased numbers of women wanting to return to work
- **technological** influences, e.g. new production processes requiring new skills
- **economic** influences, e.g. free movement of labour in the EU
- **political** influences, e.g. government training schemes.

A firm's workforce strategy is influenced by supply and demand.

If the **labour supply exceeds a firm's demand for labour**:

- there will be voluntary or compulsory redundancy
- there will be redeployment and re-training
- early retirement will be encouraged
- 'natural wastage' will be encouraged.

If a **firm's demand for labour exceeds its supply**, there will be:

- additional advertising
- re-training programmes
- an acknowledgment of labour as a limiting factor in forecasting
- better labour market competitiveness (e.g. through increased pay rates).

Trends in the labour market

Recent trends in the labour market include new working patterns and arrangements, for example the growth in part-time work, and the increased numbers of women in the UK workforce (see Figure 11.1 on the next page).

United Kingdom						
						Millions
	1998			2008		
	Men	Women	All	Men	Women	All
Economically active						
In employment						
Full-time employees	11.0	6.2	17.3	11.7	7.3	19.1
Part-time employees	1.0	4.9	5.8	1.4	5.1	6.4
Self-employed	2.5	0.9	3.4	2.8	1.1	3.8
Others in employment	0.1	0.1	0.3	0.1	0.1	0.2
All in employment	14.6	12.1	26.7	16.0	13.6	29.6
Unemployed	1.1	0.7	1.8	1.0	0.7	1.7
All economically active	15.6	12.9	28.5	16.9	14.3	31.2
Economically inactive	6.3	10.9	17.2	6.9	10.9	17.8
of which, working age	2.9	4.8	7.7	3.2	4.7	7.9

Source: ONS

Figure 11.1 Economic activity in the UK, 1998 and 2008

There are three main **demographic** changes:

1. **The effects of migration** – the UK has a history of both net immigration and net emigration, although the effect on **skill levels** is probably more important than the total numbers involved. The continuing removal of barriers to the free movement of labour in the EU is a major influence on migration levels. Internally, the **geographical distribution** of the workforce also affects firms' workforce planning. Recent trends include organisations moving to south-east England from other regions, and a general move by firms from city centres to save costs (further encouraged by developments in the infrastructure and in technology, enabling employees to work off-site).
2. **An ageing workforce** – effects include the likelihood that more time will be lost to sickness with an older workforce and that additional or more frequent training and re-skilling may be necessary. However, older workers bring greater experience and a wider knowledge base.

Age	2004	2005	2006	2007	2008
50–54	78.8	79.4	79.9	80.2	80.1
55–59	67.7	68.6	69.0	69.0	70.3
60–64	41.5	41.7	43.1	44.6	45.9
65 and over	6.0	6.3	6.7	6.8	7.4
All aged 50 and over	37.1	37.5	38.1	38.2	38.7

Figure 11.2 UK employment rates by percentage of people aged 50 and over

3. **New working patterns** – the traditional view of employment as a full-time permanent contract with a single employer is now outdated. Increasing

numbers of people are being employed under new and more flexible working arrangements:

- **Part-time work** has grown in importance throughout the economy. Employers gain from increased flexibility, but legislation means they now have to provide the same conditions of employment for part-time workers, which can increase their costs.
- **Flexitime** has increased. Employee morale improves by being able to adapt work to fit personal needs, but employers have to ensure that a 'core' of staff will be available during key periods.
- **Job sharing** – where two or more people share a full-time position – has grown in popularity. The employer faces additional administrative costs, which may be offset by increased motivation of the job-sharing employees.
- **Fixed-term employment contracts** are often agreed. The employer has greater control over labour costs, and the employee may be motivated by the 'carrot' of a renewed contract.

United Kingdom			
	Percentages		
	Men	Women	All employees
Full-time employees			
Flexible working hours	10.4	14.7	12.0
Annualised working hours	4.5	4.9	4.6
Four and a half day week	1.2	0.8	1.1
Term-time working	1.3	6.2	3.2
Nine day fortnight	0.5	0.4	0.4
Any flexible working pattern	18.3	27.7	21.9
Part-time employees			
Flexible working hours	7.7	10.0	9.5
Annualised working hours	3.1	4.6	4.3
Term-time working	4.1	11.5	9.9
Job sharing	1.2	3.1	2.7
Any flexible working pattern	18.1	30.1	27.6

Source: ONS

Figure 11.3 Flexible working patterns in the UK, 2008

Effect on the workforce plan

For the employee, part-time and flexible work may suit family needs, but can make it difficult to plan ahead financially.

These demographic changes means that there is a more **flexible and cheaper labour force**. As mentioned above, an ageing workforce may result in greater absenteeism (through illness), be less flexible and need re-training to update skills. Many businesses adopt '**family-friendly**' or '**work–life balance**' policies, such as job sharing and shift-swap (e.g. at Asda), so that in their workforce plan they can accommodate people with young families. Measures to improve work–life balance are seen as important, and can improve attendance and productivity.

KEY POINT

Changing working patterns can make communication more difficult for both parties, e.g. with part-time employees, and full-time staff working from home.

PROGRESS CHECK

1. Why do organisations undertake workforce planning?
2. How will an organisation use STEP analysis to assess its labour force strategy?

1 To counter loss of staff; to meet production and other plans; to respond to the changing competitive environment.
2 To assess social trends (e.g. part-time working); technological developments (e.g. new work skills needed); changes in the economy (e.g. pay levels); political influences (e.g. minimum pay legislation).

11.2 Recruitment, training and development

LEARNING SUMMARY

After studying this section, you should be able to:
- explain the benefits of efficient recruitment, selection and training for a business
- describe why appraisals are undertaken

Recruitment and selection

AQA	M2	WJEC	M2
Edexcel	M2a	CCEA	M2
OCR	M1, M5		

The HR function specialises in **recruitment** and **selection**. Recruitment is the process that starts when a business needs a new employee. It continues until the most suitable person is selected and appointed.

The usual stages involved in recruitment are:
- writing a **job description** and a **person specification**
- **advertising** the vacancy
- **shortlisting** applicants
- **interviewing** applicants
- **appointing** the successful applicant.

Job descriptions and personal specifications are prepared when recruiting staff.

The **job description** contains:
- the title and location of the post
- a summary of the job tasks
- an outline of the work environment
- employment conditions.

The **person specification** contains:
- the experience and qualifications required
- any physical characteristics required
- the personality factors required
- any special aptitudes required.

Semi-skilled workers are likely to be recruited using local papers and job centres, whereas senior executives are more likely to be recruited nationally (or internationally) through 'headhunting' and national press advertising.

External recruitment sources include advertising (local papers, national press or specialist publications), job centres, careers offices, employment agencies or executive search agencies ('headhunters').

An alternative is to recruit **internally**, e.g. by promotion. The employee is known to the firm and will be familiar with work routines, staff morale and motivation improves, and it is less expensive. However, internal recruitment limits the firm's choice, and will not bring new ideas in from outside.

Interviews are the most popular selection method. They may be formal or informal, and conducted on a one-to-one or group basis.

An interview has the advantage of being a two-way process, but is not a reliable form of selection because it is often subjective. There is no clear correlation between the ability to interview well and to do the job well.

The **interviewer** can assess:

- oral communication skills
- physical appearance
- personal attributes.

The **interviewee** can assess:

- physical working conditions
- future prospects
- the working atmosphere.

These types of tests are sometimes classified as psychometric testing.

Other selection procedures include:

- **aptitude tests and simulations**, which are used to test the candidate's skills and ability to carry out the duties of the post
- **achievement testing**, to see if the candidate has the relevant skills
- **personality tests**, to measure the candidate's personality 'type'
- **intelligence tests**, to check the candidate's reasoning and mental abilities.

KEY POINT

The choice of selection procedure depends on its **suitability** for the post under consideration, its **cost**, its **coverage**, and the **time** available.

Training and development

AQA	**M1**	WJEC	**M2**
Edexcel	**M2a**	CCEA	**M2**
OCR	**M1, M5**		

Training Needs Analysis (TNA)

TNA is nowadays often called Training and Learning Needs Analysis (TLNA).

Training, learning and development are key factors in efficient organisational performance. Training Needs Analysis – **TNA** – involves gathering information to discover skill gaps (and other gaps) in the existing workforce. It is a form of 'health check' on the organisation. It is developed from the organisation's strategy, with the purpose of constructing a plan that ensures employee capabilities are appropriate to meet the organisation's aims.

TNA involves:

- gathering information about current employees in terms of their:
  - knowledge and understanding
  - skills and capabilities
  - attitudes and motivation
- gathering information about the organisation's demand for these employee qualities and attributes
- analysing the likely implications that come from changing the capabilities of the employees.

Types of training

The following extract shows how Marks & Spencer views training.

> **Training and development**
> Providing meaningful development opportunities is critical to our talent strategy. We want to identify and nurture our future leaders, as well as provide engaging and relevant training to employees across M&S.
>
> **Our development programmes include:**
> **Lead to Succeed** This year over 100 of our most senior employees have completed our flagship leadership programme, 'Lead to Succeed'. This programme is built around our brand values – Quality, Value, Service, Innovation and Trust – and aims to identify and develop our pipeline of talent for the future.
>
> **Managing for Success and Leading with Impact** Last year we launched the first phase of this training programme for the 2000 line managers across M&S.
>
> **Your M&S Career Path** Employees across the UK and Republic of Ireland benefit from your M&S Career Path training and learning programmes. Section and Store managers receive tailored workshops and all newly hired customer assistants complete a thorough 26 week induction.
>
> *M&S online Annual Report, 2010*

Induction training introduces a new employee to the firm, and the firm to the new employee. Effective induction will make the employee comfortable – and therefore **motivated and productive** – as quickly as possible.

Internal – or **on-the-job** – training is where employees learn as they work. Training is usually limited to particular skills or procedures, and uses work manuals. Internal training is easy to organise, it can be adapted to the trainee's needs, and is relatively inexpensive and job-specific. It can, however, disrupt work – the trainer may not possess adequate training skills and/or may be a poor communicator, so bad work practices will continue, and new approaches and methods are not introduced into the firm.

External – or **off-the-job** – training occurs where employees attend off-site training institutions (e.g. a local college).

Advantages to the firm are that:

- specialist trainers are used
- training can be intensive
- general theories and ideas are introduced
- training occurs away from job distractions.

However, this training can be relatively expensive, it is isolated from work practicalities, and the trainee is away from the workplace and is not productive.

> **KEY POINT**
>
> The costs of **not** training include demotivated staff, poor production and productivity levels, increased accidents and absenteeism, dissatisified customers, and loss of market share.

The **management by objectives** approach helps appraise performance, with employee achievement being measured against stated objectives. Performance appraisal is normally supported by an appraisal interview.

Appraisal

By appraising staff, managers seek to improve **present performance** levels by identifying individual strengths and weaknesses, and **future performance** by identifying individual potential for development.

STAFF APPRAISAL SCHEME

Name of appraisee: . . . .   Name of appraiser: . . . .

PRIORITY KEY PERFORMANCE AREAS

PERFORMANCE OBJECTIVES   TARGETS AGREED   METHOD OF MEASUREMENT

Agreed: . . . . Appraiser   Agreed: . . . . Appraisee

Date: . . . .   Date: . . . .

Figure 11.4 Document from a company staff appraisal scheme

PROGRESS CHECK

1 How does the HR department help a firm achieve labour targets?

1 Workforce planning; recruiting staff; appraising staff.

Measuring human resource competitiveness

AQA **M2** WJEC **M2**
Edexcel **M2a** CCEA **M1**
OCR **M5**

The two commonly used national measures of the UK's **labour productivity** are **output per worker** and **output per hour worked**. Productivity across the whole economy can be measured.

		Output per worker in the UK	
		(% change on previous year)	**(% change on previous quarter)**
2008	Q1	0.9	0.2
	Q2	0.3	–0.2
	Q3	–0.4	–0.5
	Q4	–2.0	–1.5
2009	Q1	–4.2	–2.0
	Q2	–3.6	0.4
	Q3	–3.3	–0.2
	Q4	–1.4	0.5

Figure 11.5 Labour productivity in the UK

One way of avoiding recruiting additional staff is to get more from the existing workforce. Although the HR function acknowledges that, to the organisation, people are **an asset rather than a cost** to be controlled, management are concerned with improving the workforce's **cost-effectiveness**, which they do by measuring its productivity.

Other influences on competitiveness include product design and quality, and the efficiency of other functional areas (especially marketing).

'Productivity' can be defined as measuring outputs in relation to inputs. It is an important determinant of a firm's national and international competitiveness. The more productive the firm is, the lower its unit costs and the more price-competitive it will be.

Labour productivity measures **employee efficiency**, and is calculated as follows:

$$\frac{\textbf{output per period}}{\textbf{number of employees}}$$

The level of this efficiency depends on individual employees, but is also influenced by the following:

- The level of employee **motivation** – e.g. acknowledging the importance of motivators as well as hygiene factors will improve motivation (see page 197 for more details about hygiene factors); the more efficient the organisation's communication system, the more motivated and productive the staff will be.
- The amount and quality of staff **training** – many firms acknowledge the value of investing in staff training, e.g the increase in product quality and reduction of the percentage of rejects.
- The **equipment** being used – investing in more modern machinery can improve output and thereby increase productivity; it may also be possible to use existing equipment more efficiently.
- The firm's **culture** – e.g. adopting the **Kaizen** approach to continuous improvement is associated with increases in productivity.

The short-term emphasis may be to increase production rather than productivity (which is a longer-term goal).

There are three related indicators of a firm's productivity:

1. **Labour turnover** – LTO will alter according to how staff react to any changed production methods and new equipment introduced to improve productivity.
2. **Health and safety** – changes in this performance indicator may reflect how staff have accepted and reacted to the new work practices.
3. **Absenteeism** – staff may miss work due to non-avoidable factors such as illness; others miss work because of avoidable factors, e.g. because there is a lack of Herzberg's hygiene factors present.

The costs of high LTO, a poor health and safety record, and high levels of absenteeism include having to employ staff for extra hours (often on overtime rates) to make up production, and being forced to prioritise work whenever there is not enough available labour.

Problems of improving productivity

There can also be a reluctance to accept all forms of change, particularly changes to working practices.

Managers may face difficulties increasing productivity as a result of **shortage of resources** (mainly shortage of funds). They may also experience **problems in persuading employees**. Even though productivity improvements are often linked with pay, many staff fear that an increase in productivity will lead to a loss of jobs. However, if managers fail to increase productivity they may find that the firm becomes uncompetitive, with the need for major job losses and restructuring.

KEY POINT

The faster productivity grows, the less need there will be to appoint new staff, thus saving substantial costs.

PROGRESS CHECK

1. Why do companies undertake HR planning?
2. How is labour productivity calculated?

1 To ensure the right people with the right skills are employed at the right time.
2 Output per period divided by number of employees.

Sample question and model answer

1. BizzeeBee Ltd is a newly formed company from a former partnership. Its two owner-directors used to handle all recruitment, selection and training matters themselves, but now wish to appoint a Human Resources (HR) Officer to take responsibility for these matters. The owner-directors have written a job description and a person specification for the post of HR Officer.

(a) Distinguish between a job description and a person specification. Use examples likely to be found in these documents for a position such as HR Officer. **(4)**

The job description relates to the duties of the job. The person specification relates to the attributes the person needs to carry out the job.

Quite good descriptions, but examples are needed, e.g. pay £20 000 per annum for job description; ability to communicate effectively with other members of staff for person specification.

(b) How might the owner-directors recruit for this position? **(4)**

I would suggest a local newspaper, because a suitable person is likely to be living in the locality. TV advertising is too expensive and national, so is a national paper.

Well selected (local focus) choice, though other examples such as job centre could be given.

(c) What tasks should the owner-directors carry out when planning the interview for this position? **(4)**

They should plan questions in advance, using suitable question styles that elicit answers, so I would suggest open rather than closed questions. If they are both there, they need to plan who asks what. The room needs arranging appropriately, and staff must be told not to interrupt. The shortlisted candidates will need informing of the time and place of the interview.

This is a suitable list of the planning requirements necessary.

(d) Identify four areas of legislation that will influence the recruitment and selection process. **(4)**

Race relations; disability discrimination; sex discrimination; age discrimination.

These are four relevant items of legislation.

Exam practice questions

1 According to a number of reports in recent years, the United Kingdom is in the midst of a 'workstyle revolution', with the traditional 'nine to five' working week gradually disappearing and being replaced by flexible working. As a result of these changes, many businesses report increased employee performance and satisfaction.

Suggest why flexible working may prove beneficial for:

(a) the employer **(4)**

(b) the employee **(4)**

2 Read the extract below and answer the questions that follow.

Report forecasts the continuing decline of full-time work

As EU and national government policies continue to create more flexible work opportunities for people, forecasts suggest that the UK's labour market will continue to move away from traditional full-time employment. One result of this, according to a recent report, is increased feelings of job insecurity amongst the working population. This feeling of insecurity has not been helped by the recent economic downturn in the economy. The report also highlights the fact that, in an ever-changing global economy, many employees lack appropriate skills for the future workplace.

(a) What are the likely disadvantages for businesses if their workforce suffers from 'increased feelings of job insecurity'? **(6)**

(b) How might businesses react if their 'employees lack appropriate skills for the future workplace'? **(6)**

12 Employer–employee relations

The following topics are covered in this chapter:

- Motivation
- Trade unions

12.1 Motivation

LEARNING SUMMARY

After studying this section, you should be able to:

- apply key motivation theories to the work of an organisation
- suggest how an organisation can improve its motivation in practice

Motivation theories

AQA	M2	WJEC	M2
Edexcel	M2a	CCEA	M2
OCR	M5, M7		

When an employee is given a task to carry out, and it is carried out badly, this may be due to a lack of motivation rather than a lack of ability.

The work of the classical theorists is regarded as being limited, and has been modified by other theorists.

Theorists differ on what makes a job 'satisfying'.

Examples include:

- pay levels
- working hours
- work environment
- fringe benefits
- nature of work tasks
- management styles
- degree of job security
- promotion prospects
- organisational culture.

Classical theory

The classical theorists studied organisational behaviour by examining the **nature of the work done**. **F W Taylor** used scientific management principles to separate jobs into their elements – this aspect of his work led to the development of work study and method study principles. Taylor believed that **high pay** acted as the prime motivator, largely ignoring morale and other influences.

Human relations and content theories

The human relations and content theorists concentrate on people's **needs**, and not exclusively on the job being done. They define the organisation in terms of its **social environment**, and measure both individual needs and how groups work together.

Elton Mayo undertook research into groups at the Hawthorne works of the Western Electric Company (1927 to 1932). He kept changing working conditions, discovering that output increased even when conditions worsened.

These were his conclusions about the employees being observed:

- They were a tightly-knit group who enjoyed the attention being paid to them.
- This attention increased their self-esteem, and, as a result, increased their output.

Abraham Maslow formulated his '**hierarchy of needs**' in the 1940s.

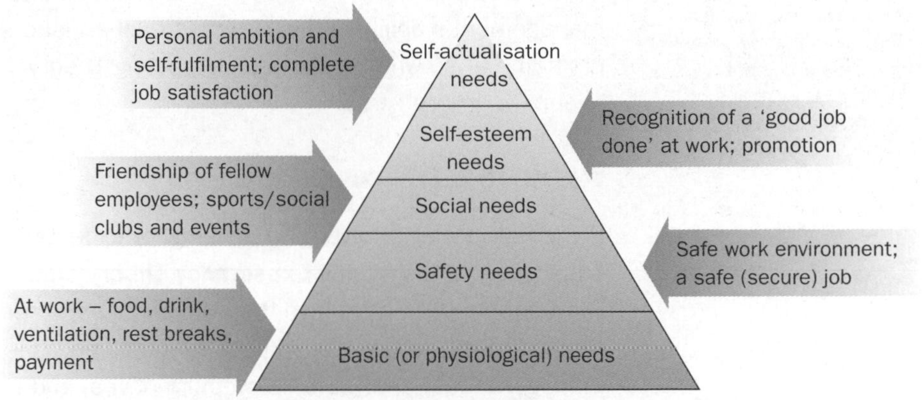

Figure 12.1 Maslow's hierarchy of needs

Maslow's ideas illustrate the importance of work to individuals, and help in explaining some of the social costs of high unemployment levels.

At any one time, one group of needs is dominant, and the needs in this group must be met before the individual can proceed to the next group. In a work context, employees must be provided with the opportunity to fulfil these needs.

Frederick Herzberg analysed needs as **motivators** (which broadly relate to work content and to Maslow's higher-order needs) and **hygiene factors** (which relate to the working environment and to Maslow's lower-order needs). He suggests that, while hygiene factors should be present (motivation falls if they are neglected), they do not by themselves motivate employees.

Motivators are:

- achievement
- recognition
- responsibility
- promotion
- the work itself.

Hygiene factors are:

- company policies
- status
- supervision
- security
- working conditions
- money.

KEY POINT

Herzberg's theory suggests that managers must provide motivators in the form of satisfying jobs, e.g. by using **job enrichment**, but must also ensure that negative hygiene factors do not detract from work being done.

Douglas McGregor analysed two opposing attitudes concerning the formal organisation of workers. **Theory X** management – his negative attitude – assumes that people dislike and will avoid work, and must be controlled and directed to get sufficient effort towards achieving organisational objectives. **Theory Y** management – the positive attitude – assumes that employees can exercise their own control and direction, and can learn to seek and accept responsibility.

Theory X links with the work of earlier classical theorists such as Taylor, emphasising money as the main motivating factor. Theory Y recognises (like Herzberg) the importance of Maslow's higher-order needs in motivating employees.

The Japanese approaches to management have been called '**Theory Z**', which recognises the Japanese emphasis on human relations at work and on employment for life.

Supporters of Theory X argue an **authoritarian** form of organisational structure. Supporters of Theory Y argue that the main limiting factors in a firm are management's ability and willingness to channel employee potential. Specific problems arise when employees expecting Theory Y management are subject to Theory X, or vice versa.

Process theories

Process theories analyse the thinking, or expectations, behind decisions made by employees. **V H Vroom's Expectancy Theory** argues that motivation depends on two factors – how attractive the outcome is, and the degree of expectation that the action will produce this hoped-for outcome. This theory suggests that managers must analyse employees' motives, and ensure they have realistic goals to achieve.

Motivation in practice

AQA	**M2**	WJEC	**M2**
Edexcel	**M2a**	CCEA	**M2**
OCR	**M5, M7**		

Employees with similar abilities, skills and training will carry out their tasks at different levels of efficiency depending on their level of motivation.

Motivating the workforce

The 'hard' model of human resources management concentrates more on assessing the quantity of staff needed by an organisation. The 'soft' model emphasises the **quality** of employees through a motivational, humanistic approach to labour relations, e.g. by encouraging **employee involvement**.

Managers may try to motivate staff using individual or group-based approaches:

- **Job rotation** provides staff with a range of different work activities. It is easy to plan, although staff will require additional training to carry out unfamiliar tasks. Job rotation works most efficiently when the tasks being rotated require similar skills, and are at similar levels of difficulty.
- **Job enrichment** incorporates job rotation, but also provides the opportunity for employees to undertake **additional work with additional responsibility**. As a result, it is more time-consuming and costly to implement than job rotation, but provides greater levels of motivation through greater involvement.
- Encouraging **team work** brings the benefits to individuals associated with working in groups. Managers also gain from greater employee flexibility, e.g. the ability and willingness of group members to cover for absent staff.

Maslow's social needs illustrate the value of group-based approaches.

Management by objectives

Managers can use **management by objectives** (**MBO**) as a **motivational** tool. MBO is based on objectives being agreed between a manager and subordinates.

Management by objectives must be distinguished from management by exception.

Targets are set for staff at all levels to achieve – these targets are '**personalised**' because the subordinates have been involved in setting them and, as a result, employees are encouraged to take responsibility for their actions. MBO **co-ordinates** effort through encouraging staff to work towards agreed common goals. The set targets provide an element of **control**, allowing performance to be judged against target.

The weaknesses of MBO as a motivational approach are that it can be **time-consuming** and it encourages **easily achieved targets** to be set.

Management and leadership styles

A **democratic** manager – associated with McGregor's Theory Y – will guide and advise, but will also involve the group in decision making. With **autocratic** management (linked to Theory X), the manager might allow group involvement, but decision making remains at the top of the organisation. A ***laissez-faire*** ('let it be') manager chooses not to interfere in the work of the group – this approach can be successful if there are cohesive groups prepared to work in achieving common objectives.

The 'best' management/leadership style is determined by, for example:

- the nature of management training
- preferences of individual managers
- the size and complexity of the organisation
- manager awareness and knowledge of the different styles
- the organisational culture
- the stage of the organisation's evolution.

The top five companies to work for in 2010, according to *The Sunday Times*, are listed below.

Rank	Company name	Type
1	P3	Charity
2	Luminus	Community housing
3	Beaverbrooks the Jewellers	Jewellery retailer
4	Office Angels	Recruitment consultancy
5	Napp Pharmaceutical Holdings	Pharmaceuticals

Overcoming poor motivation

Poor motivation causes employee dissatisfaction and **alienation**, leading to high labour turnover, increased absenteeism and sickness, poor time keeping, and more disputes in a firm.

These problems are not easily overcome, so firms try to avoid them occurring in the first place through strategies such as:

- changing **leadership styles** – e.g. by moving towards a more democratic style
- establishing **team work** – to develop a sense of common purpose
- reviewing **pay levels** – also, perhaps, offering incentives or fringe benefits
- ensuring greater **employee involvement** – e.g. through quality circles
- **job enrichment** – giving employees the chance to use their full abilities.

Remuneration

AQA	**M2**	WJEC	**M2**
Edexcel	**M2a**	CCEA	**M2**
OCR	**M5**		

Payment systems may be **incentive based** (e.g. a piece rate per item produced), or **time based**, such as an annual salary, or may combine the two (e.g. overtime at an increased hourly rate).

Fringe benefits may also be awarded – examples include company cars, subsidised meals and travel, and private health schemes. Time-based and incentive-based schemes are nowadays often supported by schemes that are **participation based**.

Other participation-based schemes, e.g. bonus and suggestion schemes, also illustrate 'reward management' practice.

Performance-related pay (PRP) schemes reward staff according to the quality of their work – individual targets are set, and staff who exceed these targets receive a higher-than-average payment, e.g. earning more commission through making more sales. The PRP approach is increasingly criticised on the grounds that it can be **divisive**, e.g. when it focuses on the individual rather than the group, or when there is a belief that some employees receive PRP not on merit but due to favouritism.

These kinds of schemes enhance motivation by giving staff a greater stake in the firm's success.

The use of **profit-sharing** and **share ownership** schemes motivate employees by making them (feel) part of the firm's success. Such schemes now exist in most of the UK's public limited companies. Share ownership schemes may be in a 'save as you earn' (SAYE) form, whereby employees can save with an option to use these savings to buy shares at a reduced price, or in a 'share option' format – managers are given the option of buying shares at favourable rates.

Share-based remuneration schemes

Through share ownership and share incentive schemes, over 170,000 of our people have a personal stake in Tesco. Staff were awarded shares worth a record £91 million last May under our Shares in Success scheme. 52,000 staff were able to benefit when Save As You Earn schemes matured in February, giving them access to shares worth £126 million.

Tesco Annual Report, 2009

M&S continues to offer a competitive reward package, with a generous retirement plan, Sharesave options and bonus scheme. It's important to recognise and reward hard work and excellent customer service, even in a difficult trading environment. This year, our customer assistants were awarded a 'Sharing in Success' bonus, receiving between £200 and £500 each.

Marks and Spencer Annual Report, 2010

We conduct a review of salaries every year. Managers are eligible for variable, performance-related bonuses, and the long-term share incentives for our most senior managers are linked to BT's total shareholder return and cash generation performance measured over a period of three years.

BT Group plc Annual Report & Form 20–F, 2010

KEY POINT

Additional forms of remuneration can motivate staff, although – since no one employee can have a significant effect on profit performance – they may not always have a substantial incentive effect.

As a result of the **Minimum Wage Act** 1998, from April 1999 the UK has had a **national minimum wage** in line with many other economically advanced economies. The argument advanced for the minimum wage was to provide a reasonable return for all employees, which would give additional motivation, as well as lift some of them out of the 'poverty trap'. The argument against this was that employers' wage costs would rise and therefore increase prices and affect competitiveness.

The social purpose of the minimum wage is therefore to make all employers pay wages that give employees a basic standard of living. In October 2010, the rate was £5.93 per hour for workers aged 21 and over (£4.82 for those aged 18–20 and £3.64 for those aged 16 and 17). As mentioned above, for the employer wage costs may rise and therefore affect competitiveness, though employees on the minimum wage are likely to be more motivated and therefore more productive.

KEY POINT

Employment statistics and other evidence indicate that the UK economy has not been adversely affected by the introduction of the minimum wage.

Employee participation and industrial democracy at work

The main ways that employees participate directly in decision making at work are through **quality circles, works councils** and being appointed as **worker directors**. There is also increasing participation through creating **employee shareholders** and introducing **profit-sharing schemes**.

Although the value of involving employees in discussions and decision making is recognised by many theorists, problems can also arise from employee participation:

- There can be a **slowing** of decision making.
- **Costs** increase (e.g. because of attendance at meetings rather than active involvement in production).
- Managers may show **resentment** of employee involvement.

PROGRESS CHECK

1. How should analysing Herzberg's theory influence the work of a firm?
2. In what practical ways can a firm improve motivation levels?

1 It should ensure that positive hygiene factors (e.g. work conditions) and motivators (e.g. recognition) are present for employees.
2 By reviewing pay levels, level of involvement, management style, feeling of job security, degree of recognition by others.

12.2 Trade unions

LEARNING SUMMARY

After studying this section, you should be able to:

- describe the types, functions and aims of trade unions
- explain the typical benefits of union membership
- explain the various forms of industrial action
- outline the role of ACAS in settling industrial action

Types and functions of trade unions

AQA **M3**
OCR **M5, M7**
WJEC **M4**

Unlike a company's own staff association, a trade union is an **independent** organisation.

Why do people join unions?

The reasons that are normally given, in order of importance, are:

- to protect **jobs**
- to improve **working conditions**
- to improve **pay**
- to have **more say** over management's long-term plans.

The table shows the four main types of trade union and their features.

Type	Nature	Features
Craft	Originally set up to control entrants to particular skilled occupations.	Often very small, and one company may find a number of them representing its workforce, making negotiations difficult.
Industrial	Contains most of the workers in an industry.	Managers tend to find negotiations are more straightforward through dealing with only one union.
General	Often very large, may contain high proportions of semi-skilled and unskilled workers from different industries.	The large size of the union and the wide range of interests it represents can create difficulties for the union.
White-collar	Contains clerical and professional staff.	Often 'industrial', containing members from a single white-collar occupation.

Trade unions are normally structured as shown in Figure 12.2.

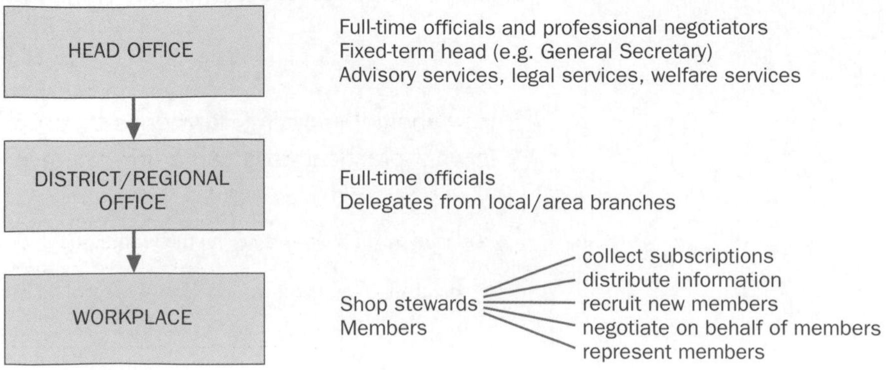

Figure 12.2 Trade union structure

The majority of union members (4.1 million in 2009) work in the public sector.

The main trend for unions in recent years has been for **union membership to fall**, both in total (from about 13 million in 1979 to below 7 million in 2009), and as a percentage of the UK's employees (27.4 percent in 2009). Reasons for this include increased numbers of temporary or part-time jobs (these employees are less likely to join unions), and fewer manufacturing-based jobs, where union membership was traditionally very high.

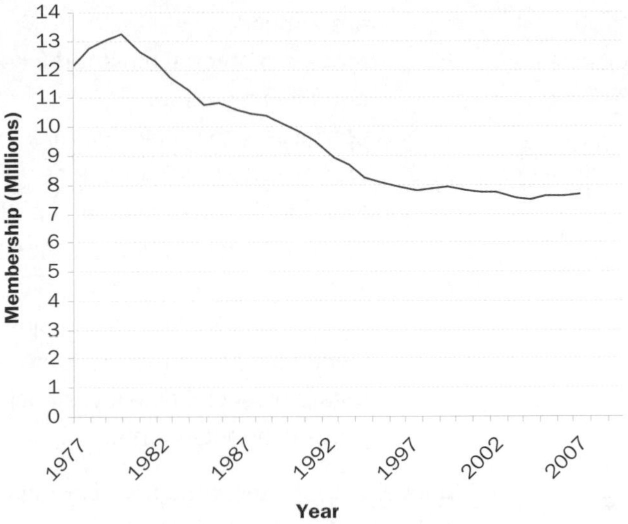

Figure 12.3 Fall in union membership

In 2008, Unite and the United Steelworkers Union (USA) signed an agreement to create the first 'global union'.

Other important recent trends have been for:

- unions to **merge and grow in size** – most of the total union membership belongs to a few large unions, such as Unite (nearly 2 million members in 2010) and UNISON, the public sector union (1.3 million members in 2010)
- unions to negotiate **single-union agreements**, which from the management's view can help negotiation and may rule out strike action.

Union membership varies throughout the UK and from sector to sector.

Nation	Percentage of employees in a union, 2009
England	26.1
Wales	31.8
Scotland	35.4
Northern Ireland	39.9

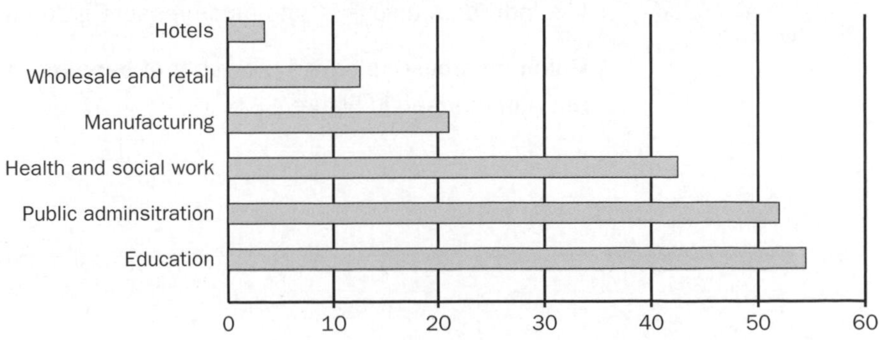

Figure 12.4 How union membership varies

Union activity

A trade union undertakes a range of activities:

- It **advises, represents and protects** members:
  - it advises on procedures following industrial accidents, represents employees at industrial tribunals, and gives general legal advice
  - it ensures members receive sick pay and other benefits to which they are entitled
  - it helps protect against redundancy, unfair dismissal, disciplinary action and discrimination.
- It **negotiates** with employers for:
  - improved pay and conditions
  - greater job satisfaction and better job security
  - improved pension and retirement arrangements.
- It **seeks to influence others**:
  - as a pressure group influencing employers and governments on legislation and other matters
  - regarding social objectives such as full employment and better social security arrangements.

Unions win over £300 million each year as compensation for members who suffer injuries or discrimination at work.

Many members see **collective bargaining** as the most important function of their union.

The two main methods of collective bargaining are:

- **integrative** bargaining, where both sides seek to negotiate a pay and productivity deal
- **distributive** bargaining, where each side negotiates from its exclusive standpoint.

In 2010, a third of UK employees said their pay and conditions were influenced by a collective agreement – this ranged from below 20 percent for employees in the private sector to two-thirds of public sector employees.

KEY POINT

The main aim of a trade union is to improve the working life of its members.

The employer equivalent of the TUC is the **Confederation of British Industry** (CBI), which represents a cross-section of companies in the UK economy.

Since unions have similar goals and mutual concerns, it is in their collective interest to come together and agree common policies and approaches. The **Trades Union Congress** (TUC) acts as a central body and the collective voice of its affiliated unions. It promotes the general aims of the union movement and – like individual unions – acts as a pressure group to influence government policy.

Union membership brings a number of **benefits** to its members. These benefits are summarised in Figure 12.5.

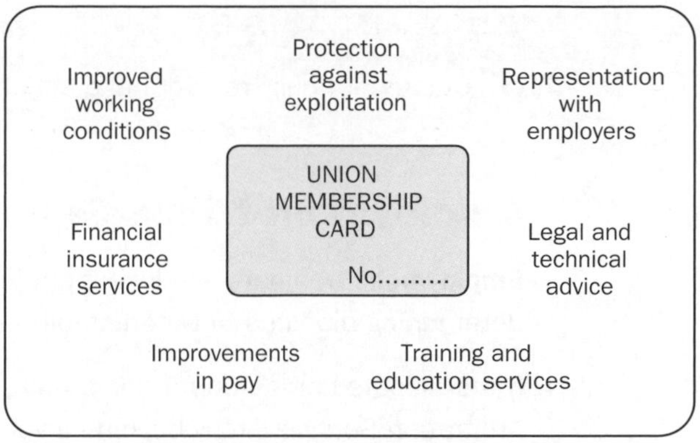

Figure 12.5 Benefits of union membership

Industrial disputes

AQA	**M3**
OCR	**M5, M7**
WJEC	**M4**

Total working days lost through labour disputes (000)	
2009	455
2008	759
2007	1 041
2006	755

Figure 12.6 The effect of labour disputes

A union may take different forms of industrial action:

- With **overtime bans**, the union instructs its members not to work overtime – this leads to falling output and puts pressure on the employer to agree to the union's demands.
- In a **work-to-rule**, employees follow the 'rule book' very closely, which can slow down or even halt production.
- A **go-slow** occurs when members carry out their work more slowly than normal – this also reduces output.
- Employees may resort to **sit-ins**, refusing to leave the premises and occupying them in an attempt to make sure that goods neither enter nor leave the firm. Most sit-ins take place when there is a threat to close the business.

Finally, union members may go on strike and **withdraw their labour**. The losses to the economy as a whole include unemployed factors of production, lost output, less consumer choice, reduced tax revenue, and the possibility of increased imports and greater overseas involvement in the UK economy.

For the striker

· loss of income · potential loss of job	**BUT**	· possible long-term improvement in pay and conditions

For the employer

· loss of – output – sales – cashflow – reputation – customers – worker goodwill	**BUT**	· reduction in – wages – stock levels · winning results in a position of greater power

KEY POINT

Unions normally regard strike action as a 'last resort' activity.

Employment tribunals and ACAS

Employment tribunals – independent judicial bodies – have the role of determining disputes between employers and employees over employment rights.

If the dispute carries on for some time, **ACAS** – the Advisory, Conciliation and Arbitration Service – may become involved. ACAS was set up in 1975 to improve industrial relations.

ACAS is independent from both employers and unions, and offers a range of services:

- **Conciliation** – an ACAS official discusses the dispute with both parties to find areas of common ground, which might form the basis for further negotiations.
- **Arbitration** – if both sides agree, their dispute 'goes to arbitration'. ACAS provides an independent third party to listen to the points made, and offers a settlement (the employer and the union, by going to arbitration, have agreed to accept whatever settlement is offered). If 'pendulum' arbitration is used, the arbitrator makes a straight choice between the two sides (this discourages either party from taking an unrealistic bargaining position).
- **Mediation** – the ACAS official suggests a solution to the dispute, which is then considered by the parties.

Other ACAS services include publishing guidelines and codes of practice on industrial relations.

Our vision

Acas's vision is to be Britain's champion for successful workplaces and a motivated workforce.

This vision is underpinned by six pledges:

- We are a fair, unbiased and professional public service
- Our priority is to meet customers' needs
- We are committed to, and promote, equality and diversity
- We are proud of our staff, respect their views and invest in helping them meet their potential
- At all times we are accountable for our performance
- We are one organisation, no matter where we are based or what job we do

ACAS website, 2010

PROGRESS CHECK

1. State the main aim of a trade union.
2. Name four forms of industrial action other than strike action.

1 To improve the working lives of its members.
2 Overtime ban; work-to-rule; go-slow; sit-in.

Sample questions and model answers

Only two marks are available, so the examiner expects a succinct definition.

The question does not state how many 'reasons' – two may be sufficient if you clearly relate them to environmental issues and to the firm's situation.

The examiner will expect you not only to identify a relevant stakeholder, but also to explain why your amendment is appropriate.

Avoid merely reciting theorists – you must apply 'theory' to the situation.

1. Northern Nosh plc is a large company with interests in food processing and the retail trade. Its directors are devising a new mission statement based on a draft submitted by the company's managing director. In its current mission statement, the company seeks 'honourably to serve the needs of the community by providing products and services of superior quality at a fair price to all customers'. The draft of the new mission statement includes references to environmental concerns and to stakeholders other than customers.

(a) Explain what is meant by a mission statement. **(2)**

A mission statement summarises an organisation's key values and priorities.

(b) Suggest reasons why the directors might be considering a reference to environmental concerns in its revised mission statement **(5)**

The present mission statement seems narrow in context and scope. Since Northern Nosh has interests in food processing, it should acknowledge the concerns of customers and specific pressure groups (e.g. Friends of the Earth) regarding safe and environmentally friendly food production. The company's staff may well share these concerns, and so the new mission statement could improve morale and motivation. There are defensive reasons - for example, to respond to competitors, and/or to avoid bad publicity, and a resultant fall-off in sales and profits, arising from environmental exploitation.

(c) Suggest and justify amendments to the mission statement that might refer to a stakeholder other than a customer. **(9)**

The question indicates that Northern Nosh has interests in 'the retail trade'. It is therefore appropriate to extend the mission statement to include the fact, e.g. by recognising the importance of good relationships with local residents, and of working in partnership with local communities. The suggested amendment is that the company seeks 'to work with its local communities in supporting local needs, through conducting business ethically, and in giving proper regard for health, safety and the environment which is consistent with the commitment to contribute to sustainable development'.

(d) Suggest problems of motivation which might arise for assembly line workers employed in the food processing division of this firm. Evaluate methods of maintaining and improving motivation. **(10)**

Assembly line workers are likely to carry out repetitive, boring tasks - this is a common criticism of the flow-line method of production, where the level of capital investment can determine what is done and how frequently it is done.

The workers may be put on a new incentive scheme, such as 'piece-rate', but many motivation theorists argue that money is not necessarily the prime motivator. The company might consider implementing schemes such as job rotation - where the employees move between different jobs over a period of time - or job enlargement, where additional tasks and responsibilities are given, although this can be difficult to apply in certain mass-production situations. Improved working conditions - Herzberg's 'hygiene factors' - such as better ventilation, or additional 'perks' such as subsidised meals, may also help improve motivation. Another alternative is a more flexible approach to work, e.g. by implementing some form of 'flexitime' attendance. Again, this can be difficult to achieve given that the method of production is continuous and therefore requires certain and regular staff numbers.

Sample questions and model answers (continued)

This is a good analysis of employing part-time staff, but is not a balanced answer. It should outline the features of employing full-time staff, and reach some conclusion. Advantages of employing full-time staff include greater continuity and known stability, future planning is helped by knowing skill levels, productivity increases with greater commitment and loyalty, and there are lower personnel-based costs and more efficient channels of communication. A good conclusion is that the company should employ an appropriate 'mix' of full-time and part-time employees, to suit its short-term and long-term goals.

A good answer, though it is worth mentioning that there is greater consistency for both parties with a single negotiating and organising voice.

A good effort to a difficult question. When you mention theorists by name, always try to refer to their theories. We could add to these references as follows: [1] Maslow's feelings of worth, and Herzberg's motivators (e.g. recognition and responsibility) and hygiene factor of security; [2] Mayo, interest in employees stimulates production; [3] Maslow, esteem and self-actualisation; [4] McGregor, Theory Y workers exercise their own control and direction.

2. Read the following newspaper report on the achievement of a local firm.

Local firm receives award

Salopian Ltd has won this year's '*Wrekin Read*' Best Employer award. The company employs 185 full-time and 70 part-time staff, and – despite facing problems in filling its order books – it has managed to retain its 'no redundancy' policy.

The Human Resources Director at Salopian is Natalie Osborne. Born in the Wrekin area, Natalie joined Salopian two years ago. Soon afterwards, she introduced a staff appraisal scheme for all employees (including managers), and has implemented a policy of promoting from within. The company has an excellent safety record. It offers profit-related bonuses and a non-contributory pension scheme to all staff, and has recently implemented a Single Union agreement in the expectation that this will lead to even more flexible working practices.

Natalie is particularly proud of innovations she has introduced to improve quality. All employees attend weekly quality circle meetings, discussing issues such as the working environment. Evidence of success here is in the company's growing productivity.

(a) Explain the possible benefits to Salopian of employing both full-time and part-time staff. **(6)**

I would recommend Salopian employs more part-time staff. By doing so, Salopian may be able to save money because the wage bill will be lower. This is because the company can monitor hours worked and therefore control labour costs. Although it can be difficult to communicate with - and monitor the work quality of - part-timers, Salopian will have a more flexible workforce able to respond more quickly to changing market conditions. Salopian can also vary the skill levels employed more easily.

(b) Examine the benefits to staff of having a Single Union agreement. **(6)**

The advantages to employees of a single union policy are that negotiations become more efficient, and that demarcation disputes shouldn't arise. The disadvantages are that there is a lack of recognition for members of other unions, and the possibility that the local branch will become subject to control by one group of employees who have their own interests.

(c) Evaluate the extent to which working practices at Salopian reflect the ideas of motivational theorists. **(8)**

What we know from the article is that the company has a no redundancy policy, which will improve morale and motivation (Maslow and Herzberg [1]). It also has annual appraisal schemes (Mayo [2]). A policy like internal promotion would be supported by Maslow [3], and it is an example of Herzberg's motivators. There is evidence of flexible work practices (McGregor [4]), and the profit-related bonuses and non-contributory pension scheme are examples of satisfying Maslow's lower-order basic needs. Finally, the excellent safety record illustrates how the company takes account of Maslow's safety needs and Herzberg's hygiene factors of working conditions.

Exam practice question

1 The text below gives some information about an employee participative scheme.

> **Employee share schemes**
> Through share ownership and share incentive schemes, over 170,000 of our people have a personal stake in Tesco. Staff were awarded shares worth a record £91 million last May under our Shares in Success scheme. 52,000 staff were able to benefit when Save As You Earn schemes matured in February, giving them access to shares worth £126 million.
>
> *Tesco Annual Report and Review, 2009*

Critically appraise the value of employee participative schemes to companies such as Tesco. **(12)**

13 Accounting for finance

The following topics are covered in this chapter:

- **Sources of finance**
- **The nature and purpose of financial accounting**
- **Financial accounting**
- **Interpreting financial statements**

13.1 Sources of finance

LEARNING SUMMARY

After studying this section, you should be able to:

- differentiate between the main providers of finance for the private and public sectors
- outline the key factors involved in choosing a relevant source of finance
- describe appropriate short-term, medium-term and long-term sources of internal finance
- suggest a relevant source of finance for a given situation

Factors influencing finance decisions

AQA	**M3**	WJEC	**M1**
Edexcel	**M1**	CCEA	**M1**
OCR	**M1, M4**		

Public sector organisations may also generate some finance from trading or other commercial activities.

The source of finance used by an organisation largely depends on the sector in which the organisation operates.

Public sector organisations rely to a much greater extent on government funding. Public corporations are funded mainly by tax revenues and through borrowing from the Treasury. Local authorities may also be financed by borrowing, and through raising rates, i.e. income from business and commercial residents in their area.

Private sector firms rely on other private sector businesses such as banks, and also receive regular finance through their normal trading activities. The government is another important provider of financial support, particularly to small and/or new businesses through grants.

The key questions that entrepreneurs in the private sector need to answer are:

- **how much** finance is needed
- whether the finance can be obtained **internally**
- whether the finance should be **borrowed temporarily**, with a view to paying it back, or obtained as **permanent capital** (e.g. share capital)
- (if borrowed) the **length of any loan**, e.g. short (up to one year), medium (1–5 years) or long term.

The amount and nature of this finance varies from firm to firm, and is influenced by a firm's **size**, its form of **ownership**, the type of **technology** currently being used within the firm, the relationship between **capital and labour**, the length of **credit** periods (taken and allowed), and the age of the firm's **assets**.

Internal sources

AQA **M3** WJEC **M1**
Edexcel **M1** CCEA **M1**
OCR **M1, M4**

The finance available is determined by the **ownership** and **size** of the firm.

Retained profits

Private sector firms can preserve cash through retaining **profits**, e.g. where a limited company decides to move profit to reserves rather than distributing it as cash (share dividends). This is the main internal source of funds for many firms, although the source depends on the level of profits.

Control of working capital and cash flow

Extending the average credit a firm takes from suppliers, and/or reducing the average credit period it allows its customers, will improve a firm's cash flow; ratios to calculate debtor and creditor days are relevant here. Other controls include reducing stock levels and postponing the payment of **expense creditors** (e.g. the electricity bill) to preserve cash.

A firm's operating cycle describes the link between cash movements and working capital. It provides a clear indication to the accountant of how the firm's production cycle – and credit periods allowed and taken – affect cash flow.

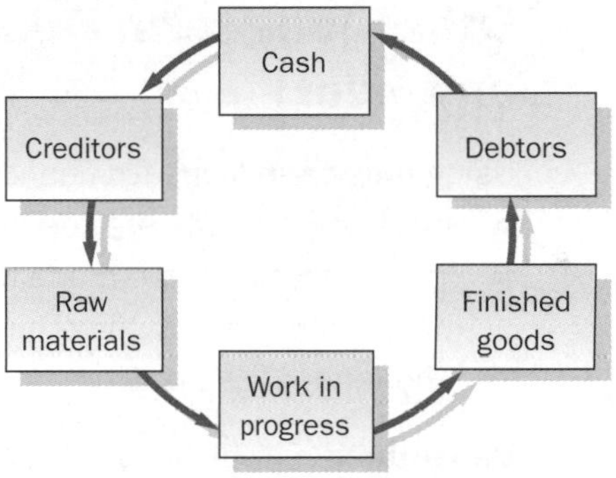

Figure 13.1 The operating cycle

Sale of assets

A firm may have surplus assets, e.g. during an economic recession or internal rationalisation. These assets can be sold to raise finance. The firm may also sell an asset to a buyer, then lease it back over a period of time. This is known as **sale and leaseback** – funds are generated for the firm, and it still has use of the asset.

External sources

AQA **M3** WJEC **M1**
Edexcel **M1** CCEA **M1**
OCR **M1, M4**

Family and friends

Associated with the sole trader and partnership forms of business organisation, family and friends can provide low-cost finance, usually with little – if any – security required. The amount of finance available in this form is often quite small.

Share issues

A limited company normally obtains most of its permanent capital by issuing ordinary and/or preference shares. Its **authorised capital** (the maximum that can be issued) is contained in its **memorandum of association**.

Ordinary shares (**equity**) receive a variable dividend, which relies on surplus profits after all other payments – they may receive high dividends in times of high profits, and no dividend when profits are low.

Preference shares have a fixed dividend and do not carry a vote, so – unlike ordinary shares – their issue does not affect the control of a company.

	£m
Authorised ordinary shares of 25p each	800
Allotted, called up and fully paid ordinary shares of 25p each:	
at start of year	396.6
shares issued on exercise of share options	0.5
shares purchased in buy-back	(2.7)
At end of year	394.4

Extract from Marks & Spencer plc 2009 Annual Report (Notes to the financial statements)

Figure 13.2 Marks & Spencer share capital, 2009

The figure in brackets indicates a negative amount.

Other long-term finance (normally five years and over)

Unlike dividends, however, the interest payments must always be met. Failure to do so may lead to closure of the firm.

Using **long-term loans** for finance brings certain benefits:

- Interest payments may be eroded by inflation.
- These payments are made out of gross profit (untaxed income), whereas dividend payments come out of (taxed) net profit.
- The lender has no direct say in the running of the firm.

The term 'debenture' refers to the issued document outlining the nature of the loan.

Debentures may be secured against specific assets, or assets in general – the lender recovers the asset if the borrower fails to make interest payments.

Medium-term finance (between one and five years)

Bank – and other – loans are fixed sums agreed between the borrower and lender, for a fixed term. Unlike overdrafts, a special account is opened, and interest is charged on the full balance. Security is required by the lender.

With **leasing**, the firm obtains equipment without having to buy (own) it:

- A large capital outlay is therefore avoided by the lessee (hirer).
- Payments are regular, known in advance, and made out of taxable income.
- Income generated from using the asset can contribute towards payment.
- No specific security is normally required.
- Over time, the asset can be upgraded or the agreement ended.

But the lessee continues to pay for an item that will never be owned.

Hire purchase (HP) and credit sale agreements allow the buyer to acquire the asset immediately, and pay for it over time. The asset is owned – on the first payment with a credit sale, on the final payment with HP – and the cost is spread.

However, the amount paid on credit will far exceed the original purchase price.

Short-term sources of finance (less than one year)

Overdrafts are agreed with a bank, letting a firm overdraw on its account up to an agreed maximum, with a charge based on the amount overdrawn.

Although usually less expensive and more flexible than loans, an overdraft facility can easily be withdrawn by the lender.

Factoring occurs when a firm sells trade debts at below face value to a factoring agent in return for immediate cash. The firm loses some of the value of the debt, offset by the quick receipt of cash that can be used immediately.

PROGRESS CHECK

1. State the difference between leasing and credit sale.
2. Give three differences between shares and debentures.

1 Leasing: the asset is never owned; credit sale: owned after first payment.
2 Shares – dividends, debentures – interest; shares – owner(s); debentures – lender(s); shares – dividends paid from net profit; debentures – interest from gross profit.

13.2 The nature and purpose of financial accounting

LEARNING SUMMARY

After studying this section, you should be able to:

- explain the roles of financial accounting and management accounting
- identify the main users and sources of financial information

The roles of the accounting function

AQA	**M3**	WJEC	**M2**
Edexcel	**M1**	CCEA	**M2**
OCR	**M2, M4**		

Entrepreneurs set **financial objectives**.

Typical financial objectives include:

- ensuring **adequate cash flow** – to provide sufficient liquidity for the business
- **minimising costs** – to control selling prices and therefore remain competitive, and to preserve or increase profit margins
- receiving an acceptable **return on capital employed** (ROCE) and **return on shareholders' investment** – to make investing in the business worthwhile, when balanced against both the risk of losing the investment and the opportunity cost of investing elsewhere.

Managers require **information** in order to make sound financial judgments. Management accounting contributes some of this information. It draws upon financial accounts (e.g. the final accounts and their ratios), and uses its own techniques and budgeting, costing and investment appraisal.

Financial accounting involves:

- collecting and recording information
- analysing this information
- presenting it to management
- evaluating different sources of finance.

Management accounting involves:

- setting and controlling budgets
- forecasting and controlling cash flow
- classifying and calculating costs
- making investment decisions.

Users of financial information

Figure 13.3, on the next page, shows that users of financial information may be **internal** or **external** to the firm.

These are typical internal and external stakeholders.

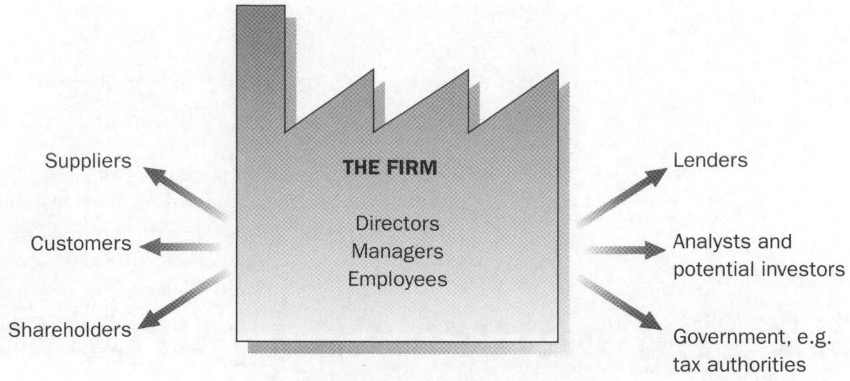

Figure 13.3 Internal and external users of accounting information

KEY POINT

Financial information deals with **external influences** on a firm – notably debtors, creditors, lenders and shareholders. Management accounting supplies an **internal analysis** of a firm's operations.

PROGRESS CHECK

1 Name two internal, and two external, groups that are users of a company's financial information.

1 **Internal**: directors and employees; **external**: lenders and shareholders (**accept any other suitable answers**).

13.3 Financial accounting

LEARNING SUMMARY

After studying this section, you should be able to:

- describe the different types of account
- state the difference between capital expenditure and revenue expenditure
- explain the causes, and calculate the amount, of depreciation

Types of accounts

AQA	**M1**	WJEC	**M2**
Edexcel	**M1**	CCEA	**M2**
OCR	**M2, M4**		

Asset accounts record details of the **items owned** by a firm. **Fixed assets** are long-lasting assets such as premises and machinery, which are used indirectly to make profit and which depreciate. **Current assets** – e.g. stocks, debtors and cash – fluctuate regularly and are used directly to make profit.

Capital (and profit) is a liability because of the business entity concept, which requires that the financial affairs of the owner(s) are kept separate from those of the business. The capital and profit are **owed** (a liability) to the owner(s).

Liability accounts record details of **amounts that are owed** by a firm. The **capital** account shows the value invested by the owner(s) – it is a liability because it is owed by the business to the owner or owners. **Long-term liabilities** are debts such as debentures that are not due to be repaid for at least one financial year. **Reserves** are also long-term liabilities of limited companies. **Current liabilities** are repayable within one year, and fluctuate regularly in value (e.g. bank overdraft, creditors – suppliers of goods on credit).

KEY POINT

The terms 'fixed assets' and 'long-term liabilities' are gradually being replaced by 'non-current assets' and 'non-current liabilities' respectively.

Expense accounts record costs (expenses) incurred by a firm. Examples include rent, salaries and wages, advertising, insurance, and the cost of stationery.

Income accounts – also known as 'revenue' accounts – record the results of a firm's trading. The sales account is the main income account.

KEY POINT

Assets and liabilities are shown in a firm's balance sheet. Income (revenue) and expenses are shown in a firm's profit and loss account.

Financial statements (final accounts)

AQA **M1, M3**
Edexcel **M1**
OCR **M2, M4**
WJEC **M2, M3, M4**
CCEA **M2**

The term 'final accounts' refers to a firm's trading and profit and loss account and its balance sheet. These final accounts have important differences.

Strictly speaking, the balance sheet is not an account, just a financial statement.

	Trading and profit and loss account	**Balance sheet**
Purpose	To act as an income statement and to calculate net profit	To summarise the firm's financial position
Information base	Expense and revenue accounts (revenue expenditure)	Asset and liability accounts (capital expenditure)
Heading	'For the period ending ...' (profit is made over a period of time)	'As at ...' (the financial position at a given point in time)

Figure 13.4 Final accounts

The trading account

Firms making the goods they sell will construct **manufacturing accounts** to record costs of manufacture. These are either **prime costs** (direct production costs) or **factory overheads**.

The purpose of the trading account is to calculate **gross profit**, by deducting a firm's cost of sales from its sales income. Its basic construction is shown in Figure 13.5.

N. Merchant Trading account for year ending 31 December

	£ (000)	£ (000)
Sales		400
Less cost of sales:		
Opening stock	55	
Purchases	290	
	345	
Closing stock	(45)	
		300
Gross profit		**100**

Figure 13.5 Trading account

The profit and loss account (income statement)

The purpose of the profit and loss account is to calculate **net profit**, which is the excess of a firm's gross profit (plus any other revenues, such as rent receivable from sub-letting premises) over its expenses. Figure 13.6 illustrates a typical profit and loss account.

N. Merchant Profit and loss account for year ending 31 December

	£ (000)	£ (000)
Gross profit		100
Less expenses:		
Administration	32	
Selling and distribution	16	
Financial	12	
		60
Net profit		**40**

Figure 13.6 Profit and loss account

Appropriation is not necessary for sole proprietors, who own all profits made, but will be necessary for partnership and limited company profits.

The profit may have to be **appropriated** (shared out).

Partnership appropriation of profits may be influenced by:

- the amount of capital invested by each partner
- the amount of work each partner does in the partnership.

A limited company's net profit presents the directors with the same decision that people have to make regarding their own income – how much to **spend** and how much to **save**. The 'spending' element consists of compulsory spending on corporation tax, and voluntary spending through distributing share dividends. The higher the dividend, the more content shareholders will be – but more cash must be paid out, which puts pressure on a company's cash resources. The 'saving' element occurs where the directors decide to hold back some of the net profit (and by doing so, preserve cash) in the form of **reserves**.

The balance sheet

The purpose of the balance sheet is to show a firm's financial position at a stated point in time. It lists assets and liabilities under their group headings.

Modern balance sheet layouts show a firm's **net current assets**, often called '**working capital**'. Working capital is the difference between current assets and current liabilities, and is one of the most important figures for a business because it indicates **liquidity**, the ability of the business to repay its debts as these debts become due for payment.

KEY POINT

Working capital = **Current assets** minus **Current liabilities**

Current assets cash and 'near cash' (e.g. amounts owed by debtors that will shortly be paid)

Current liabilities short-term debts owed, which will soon have to be paid by a firm

N. Merchant Balance sheet as at 31 December	£ (000) Cost	£ (000) Depreciation	£ (000) Net
Fixed assets			
Land and buildings	100	–	100
Plant and equipment	24	6	18
Vehicles	5	3	2
	129	9	120
Current assets			
Stocks		45	
Debtor		25	
Bank and cash		20	
		90	
Current liabilities			
Creditors	20		
Accrued expenses	10		
		30	
Net current assets			60
Net assets			180
Capital			
Opening balance			140
Net profit for year			40
			180

Figure 13.7 Balance sheet

KEY POINT

The term 'financial statements' is widely used instead of 'final accounts', and 'income statement' instead of 'profit and loss account'.

Capital and revenue expenditure in financial statements

Asset and expense accounts record the purchases a business makes. These purchases can be classified under two headings (capital expenditure and revenue expenditure), as shown below.

Capital expenditure
Occurs when new assets are bought or existing assets are improved

e.g. buy a new delivery van

Shown in the **balance sheet**

Revenue expenditure
Occurs when everyday running expenses are being paid

e.g. pay business rent and rates

Shown in the **income statement**

This is an important distinction in financial statements for the following reasons.

If revenue expenditure is wrongly shown as capital expenditure:

- expenses are understated
- net profit is overstated.

If capital expenditure is wrongly shown as revenue expenditure:

- expenses are overstated
- net profit is understated.

The key concepts influencing how a firm classifies its expenditure are accruals, consistency and materiality.

Depreciation in financial statements

Depreciation is an example of a **provision**. This is created when a firm has expenses, but the exact amount of the expenses is not known with any certainty.

Fixed assets **depreciate** (fall in value) each year. An estimated annual charge – the depreciation provision – is made against profits so that each year's profit bears its share of the total cost of depreciation. If this was not done, one year's profit – the profit for the year in which the fixed asset was sold – would bear the full cost, and comparisons between it and other years' profits would be unfair. The annual depreciation provision is charged against (gross) profit, and total depreciation is deducted from the fixed asset value in the balance sheet.

Depreciation of fixed assets can be caused by:

- wear and tear – everyday use (e.g. a vehicle) will gradually wear out that asset
- obsolescence – the asset (e.g. a computer) becomes out of date
- depletion – the fixed asset is used up, e.g. extraction of minerals from a mine.

There are two popular methods used to calculate depreciation.

The first is the **straight line (equal instalment) method**:

$$\frac{\textbf{original cost – residual (resale value)}}{\textbf{estimated life}}$$

This allocates the estimated depreciation cost equally to each year of the fixed asset's life. For example, a vehicle costing £16 000 with an estimated life of five years and resale value of £6 000 has an annual depreciation of £2 000 (£16 000 – £6 000 = £10 000, divided by 5).

The second method is the **reducing (diminishing) balance method**:

a fixed percentage is applied each year to the written-down value of the fixed asset

Depreciation illustrates the **accrual** (or 'matching') concept, where income and expenses are matched against the period to which they refer.

This method allocates greater amounts for depreciation to the earlier years of the fixed asset (which often more realistically reflects the true value of the asset).

If the above vehicle was depreciated by this method, using a 25 percent figure:
Year 1 = £4 000 depreciation, leaving £12 000 net book value (NBV)
Year 2 = £3 000 depreciation, leaving £9 000 NBV
Year 3 = £2 250 depreciation, leaving £6 750 NBV (etc.)

Depreciation is a non-cash expense, which is taken into consideration when a firm's cash flow (its third major financial statement) is calculated.

The **consistency** concept ensures that the same calculation method (straight line, reducing balance and revaluation are the most popular ones) will normally be used for similar assets. The **accruals** concept, where costs are matched to the period to which they refer, means that each year's profit will be charged with its own share of the total depreciation. A firm can change its depreciation policy and method of calculation, but only for good reason.

The purpose of applying depreciation is therefore to adjust annual profits, to avoid charging the full amount of depreciation in a single year (which would distort that year's profits). This leads to a **fairer comparison** between the profit figures for the years over which the asset is owned.

Depreciation is **subjective** – the accountant has to decide which method of calculation to use. If selecting the straight line method, decisions must be made concerning two of the three figures involved in the calculation (the estimated life of the asset, and its expected resale value); if the reducing balance method is used, the percentage written down each year must be decided.

A provision is defined as 'a liability of uncertain amount' – the exact figure at the time is not known with certainty.

Since depreciation is a **provision**, an adjustment will be made when the asset is disposed of. A firm will make either a loss or a profit on sale, which is recorded in the profit and loss account. Over the full life of the asset, the total depreciation charged will be the same **regardless** of method selected and amounts charged, because of this final adjustment. For this reason, total profits over the asset's life will also be the same, even though the individual figures will vary.

Accounting concepts

Accounting concepts operate as basic 'rules' that accountants are required to take into account when constructing financial accounts and statements.

There are traditionally four main concepts:

1. **Accruals** – financial accounts are prepared not on a cash basis, but on an **earnings** (accruals) basis. Sales and purchases are recognised in the period in which they are made, and not merely when the cash is received or paid. Therefore, a company with a financial year running January–December and making a credit sale in December 2010, but not receiving the cash until January 2011, will show the sale as increasing its 2010 profits.
2. **Prudence** – where alternative procedures or valuations are possible, the one selected should give the **most cautious** presentation of the firm's financial state. Losses therefore tend to be anticipated, but profits are never anticipated (this is why, for example, closing stock is valued at cost price rather than selling price – to value using the latter figure assumes the stock will be sold and a profit made).
3. **Going concern** – the assumption is that the firm will continue for the foreseeable future. This means that its assets will normally be valued at their (historical) cost rather than at their break-up or resale value.
4. **Consistency** – similar items should be given similar accounting treatment. If, therefore, it is the firm's policy to use the straight line depreciation method for existing vehicles, any new vehicle bought will be subject to the same treatment.

There are some **other relevant accounting concepts**:

The accountant's view here differs from the legal one with regard to sole traders and partnerships.

- The **entity** concept – accountants treat every business as an entity which is separate to, and distinct from, its owners.
- The **money measurement** concept – accounts only record and analyse those items that have a monetary value (thus, for example, the quality of management and other employees is not directly considered by accountants).
- The **duality** concept – every transaction has two effects (this forms the basis of **double-entry bookkeeping**).
- The **historical cost** concept – items are normally stated in accounts at their historical cost, i.e. the cost that was paid for them (revaluation can take place, e.g. property is often shown at a higher value than its original cost).
- The **materiality** concept – only items that are sufficiently material (important) will affect the 'true and fair view' that must be given by accounts.

A good example is where small, long-lasting items such as waste-paper bins (technically fixed assets) are treated as revenue, rather than capital, expenditure.

These concepts provide a degree of **objectivity** in financial accounting – using historical cost for all items is a good example of this. The materiality concept illustrates where financial accounts may still be **subjective** – what is 'material' in one firm may not be regarded as material by the accountant in another firm.

KEY POINT

Financial accounting applies rules in an attempt to make it more objective, though a degree of subjectivity still exists.

Examples of financial statements

'Consolidated' refers to combining the financial statements of different companies in a group.

Here is an example of the main financial statements of a company.

Consolidated statement of comprehensive income (52 weeks ended 31 January 2010)

	2010 £m	2009 £m
Turnover	15 410	14 528
Cost of sales	(14 348)	(13 615)
Gross profit	1 062	913
Other operating income	65	37
Administrative expenses	(224)	(281)
Profits arising on property transactions	4	2
Operating profit	907	671
Finance costs	(60)	(60)
Finance income	11	44
Profit before taxation	858	655
Taxation	(260)	(195)
Profit for the period attributable to the owners	598	460
Other comprehensive (expense)/income:		
Actuarial loss arising in the pension scheme	(71)	(101)
Foreign exchange movements	(1)	6
Cash flow hedging movement	(11)	6
Tax in relation to components of other comprehensive (expense)/income	22	31
Other comprehensive expense for the period, net of tax	(61)	(58)
Total comprehensive income for the period attributable to the owners of the Company	537	402
Earnings per share (pence)		
– basic	22.80	17.39
– diluted	22.37	17.16

Adapted from Morrisons 2010 Annual Report

Figure 13.8 Summarised income statement

Reading the account indicates that:

- 'profit' is not a single figure, but is measured in different ways
- the main costs, such as finance, are stated in total (and detailed elsewhere, e.g. in accompanying notes)
- earnings per share are shown at the end of the account.

Consolidated balance sheet (31 January 2010)	2010 £m	2009 £m
Assets		
Non-current assets		
Property, plant and equipment	7 180	6 587
Lease prepayments	257	250
Investment property	229	242
Other financial assets	–	81
	7 666	7 160
Current assets		
Stocks	577	494
Debtors	201	245
Other financial assets	71	–
Cash and cash equivalents	245	327
	1 094	1 066
Liabilities		
Current liabilities		
Creditors	(1 845)	(1 915)
Other financial liabilities	(213)	(1)
Current tax liabilities	(94)	(108)
	(2 152)	(2 024)
Non-current liabilities		
Other financial liabilities	(1 027)	(1 049)
Deferred tax liabilities	(515)	(472)
Net pension liabilities	(17)	(49)
Provisions	(100)	(112)
	(1 659)	(1 682)
Net assets	**4 949**	**4 520**
Shareholders' equity		
Called-up share capital	265	263
Share premium	92	60
Capital redemption reserve	6	6
Merger reserve	2 578	2 578
Retained earnings and hedging reserve	2 008	1 613
Total equity attributable to the owners of the Company	**4 949**	**4 520**

Adapted from Morrisons 2010 Annual Report

Figure 13.9 Summarised consolidated balance sheet

Studying this statement shows that:

- assets and liabilities are classified – note the use of the modern terms 'non-current assets' and 'non-current liabilities' – and the main types are listed
- net current assets are not displayed in this format
- the net assets total equals the total equity total.

Consolidated cash flow statement (52 weeks ended 31 January 2010)

	2010 £m	2009 £m
Cash flows from operating activities		
Cash generated from operations	1 004	964
Interest paid	(60)	(70)
Taxation paid	(209)	(104)
Net cash inflow from operating activities	735	790
Cash flows from investing activities		
Interest received	8	29
Proceeds from sale of property, plant and equipment	7	22
Purchase of property, plant and equipment and investment property	(906)	(678)
Net cash outflow from investing activities	(891)	(627)
Cash flows from financing activities		
Proceeds from issue of ordinary shares	34	3
Shares repurchased for cancellation	–	(146)
Finance lease principal payments	–	(2)
New borrowings	200	250
Repayment of borrowings	(1)	(2)
Decrease in long-term cash on deposit	–	74
Dividends paid to equity shareholders	(159)	(131)
Net cash inflow from financing activities	74	46
Net (decrease)/increase in cash and cash equivalents	**(82)**	**209**
Cash and cash equivalents at start of period	327	118
Cash and cash equivalents at end of period	**245**	**327**

Adapted from Morrisons 2010 Annual Report

Figure 13.10 Summarised consolidated cash flow statement

This statement details the cash movements that have taken place during the year. Each movement category is summarised, with a further summary of annual cash movements at the end.

The five-year summary

The five-year summary is another feature of modern financial statements.

These summaries vary in detail and layout. Here is an extract from a recent five-year summary, which is presented in the form of key performance indicators.

	2009	**2008**	**2007**	**2006**	**2005**
Gross profit margin (%)	37.2	38.6	38.9	38.3	34.7
Net (operating) profit margin (%)	9.6	13.4	12.2	10.9	8.0
Basic earnings per share (pence)	32.3	49.2	39.1	31.3	17.6
Return on equity (%)	25.2	45.6	46.3	50.0	35.1

Figure 13.11 Part of Marks & Spencer's five-year summary

PROGRESS CHECK

1. What is the purpose of **(a)** an income statement **(b)** a balance sheet?
2. A business buys a fixed asset for £400 000. How much will this asset be depreciated by in year 2, using:
   (a) the straight line method (it has a useful life of four years and a residual value of £80 000)?
   (b) the reducing balance method (an annual rate of 20 percent is to be applied)?

1 **(a)** Statement of financial performance (revenue, expenses, profit)
(b) statement of the financial position (assets, liabilities and capital) at a point in time.
2 **(a)** $\frac{£400\,000 - 80\,000 = £320\,000}{4} = £80\,000$
(b) Year 1 = 20% of £400 000 = £80 000; year 2 = 20% of £320 000 = £64 000.

13.4 Interpreting financial statements

LEARNING SUMMARY

After studying this section, you should be able to:
- explain the difference between profitability, liquidity, efficiency and debt/gearing
- calculate relevant ratios
- reach appropriate conclusions on the basis of your calculations
- describe the limitations of interpreting financial information

Accounting ratios

AQA	**M2, M3**
Edexcel	**M2a, M4a**
OCR	**M7**
WJEC	**M3**
CCEA	**M3**

Financial statements must be created for external purposes, e.g. for tax calculations, legal requirements or shareholders. One result of creating these statements is to allow **analysis** to take place.

Accounting ratios are important indicators in the benchmarking process.

This analysis can have an:
- **internal** focus, e.g. when a firm compares its present financial performance with past ones
- **external** focus, e.g. when a firm assesses its **competitiveness** by comparing its results with those of other firms in the same industry.

Interested stakeholder groups

The table on the next page shows the main interested stakeholder groups, the type of interest, and the main reason(s) for this interest.

Group	Interest	Main reasons for interest
Managers	Liquidity Profitability Asset efficiency Investment	Re-election of directors; share dividend levels; financial reward; survival of the firm
Employees	Liquidity Profitability	Job prospects; pay claims; reward (e.g. if in profit-sharing scheme)
Lenders	Liquidity	Assess the firm's ability to meet their debts
Investors	Liquidity Profitability Asset efficiency Investment	Dividends and share values (short term) Share values; security of investment (long term)
Government	Liquidity Profitability	Income from taxation; meeting economic objectives (e.g. full employment)

Profitability and liquidity

AQA **M2, M3** WJEC **M3**
Edexcel **M2** CCEA **M3**
OCR **M4, M7**

Profitability

Profitability measures a firm's **total profit against the resources used** in making that profit. On its own, profit is a relatively meaningless figure – it needs comparing against figures such as **turnover** and **capital employed**.

There are **three profitability ratios**.

1. The first is **return on capital employed**:

$$\textbf{Return on capital employed (ROCE)} = \frac{\textbf{Net profit}}{\textbf{Capital employed}} \times \textbf{100}$$

ROCE shows the profitability of the investment by calculating its percentage return. The return shown can then be compared with the expected return from other investments. The normal figure used by companies is profit on ordinary activities before taxation rather than after tax (the tax charge may vary from year to year, so using profit after tax would not lead to comparing like with like). If **PBIT** – profit before interest and tax – is used, the profit figure is compared with **capital employed,** i.e. share capital plus long-term loan capital.

Capital employed = net assets, so the figure of capital employed used in the calculation equates to net assets (assets less liabilities).

ROCE can be sub-divided:

$$\textbf{ROCE} = \textbf{Profit margin} \times \textbf{Asset turnover}$$

$$\frac{\textbf{PBIT}}{\textbf{Capital employed}} = \frac{\textbf{PBIT}}{\textbf{Sales}} \times \frac{\textbf{Sales}}{\textbf{Net assets}}$$

The **profit margin** ratio (see the next page) shows whether a company is making a low or a high profit margin on its sales; the **asset turnover** ratio measures how efficiently a company's net assets are being used to generate its sales.

2. The second profitability ratio is **gross profit margin**:

$$\textbf{Gross profit margin (GP ratio, or GP \%)} = \frac{\textbf{Gross profit}}{\textbf{Turnover}} \times 100$$

This indicates the percentage of **turnover** – net sales (sales less VAT and any returns) – represented by gross profit. If the gross profit margin is 30 percent, this means that the firm's cost of sales are 70 percent of its turnover (because turnover = cost of sales + gross profit).

3. The third profitability ratio is **net profit margin**:

$$\textbf{Net profit margin (NP ratio, or NP \%)} = \frac{\textbf{Net profit}}{\textbf{Turnover}} \times 100$$

This shows the percentage of turnover represented by net profit, i.e. how many pence out of every £1 sold is net profit. The NP margin will fall if the GP margin has fallen and rise if the GP percentage has increased – but it is also affected when a firm's other expenses as a percentage of turnover have changed.

Liquidity

Liquidity is **the amount of cash a firm can get quickly in order to settle its immediate debts**. Although a firm can survive in the short term without profit, it cannot survive for long without sufficient liquidity.

Liquidity funds consist of:

- cash in hand and at the bank
- short-term investments and deposits
- trade debtors.

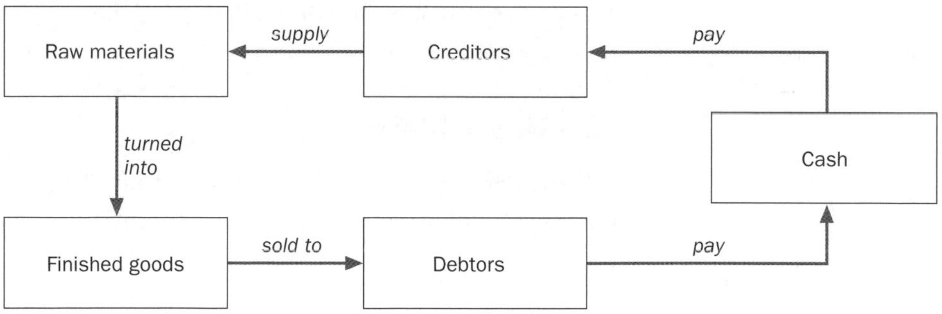

Figure 13.12 The cash (or 'operating') cycle

An efficient **credit control** system is particularly important in ensuring that cash flows into the firm remain constant and efficient.

Examining the cash cycle shows the following:

- The timing of cash flows will not necessarily coincide with sales and purchases (cost of sales) – allowing and taking credit will cause this difference.
- Delays also occur with cash receipts, through allowing credit or increasing the credit period, and by holding additional stock.
- Cash payments may be delayed through taking credit.

Liquidity ratios help establish whether a firm is **overtrading**, expanding without sufficient long-term capital. This puts pressure on its **working capital**, the **excess of current assets over current liabilities**.

There are four liquidity ratios.

1. The first is the **working capital ratio**:

Working capital (current) ratio = Current assets (CA) : Current liabilities (CL)

> A firm may also have too high a level of working capital, indicating that liquid assets are not being used productively (e.g. they are tied up in surplus stocks).

If current liabilities exceed current assets, a firm may have difficulty in meeting its debts. Extra short-term borrowing, to pay off creditors, costs the firm money (interest). If a firm sells assets to help meet its debts, it risks loss of production and future expansion.

2. The second liquidity ratio is the **liquid ratio**:

Liquid ratio ('acid test' or 'quick assets') = CA minus stock : CL

Using this ratio lets us see whether a firm can meet short-term debts without having to sell stock, which is regarded as the least liquid current asset (and the prudence concept encourages accountants to assume a firm will not automatically sell – **realise** – its stock).

3. The third liquidity ratio is the **debtors' collection period**:

> We have to be careful to ensure the debtors and creditors figures we use are representative (i.e. typical) totals.

$$\textbf{Debtors' collection period ('debtor days')} = \frac{\textbf{Debtors}}{\textbf{Sales}} \times \textbf{365}$$

This liquidity (or efficiency) ratio shows the time, measured in average days, that it takes debtors to pay a firm.

4. The final liquidity ratio is the **creditors' collection period**:

$$\textbf{Creditors' collection period ('creditor days')} = \frac{\textbf{Creditors}}{\textbf{Purchases}} \times \textbf{365}$$

This ratio calculates the average length of credit the firm receives from its suppliers.

'Window dressing'

'**Window dressing**' is the term used to describe techniques for **improving a company's balance sheet position**, in particular its apparent liquidity.

Examples include:

- paying additional money into the bank account just before the year end, in order to boost the cash balance (the amount is then withdrawn later)
- using inter-group transfers – one cash-rich company in a group forwards a cheque to another group company with an overdraft, then cancels the cheque after the year end (this hides the other company's overdraft, which would otherwise have to be shown in the group accounts)
- undertaking sale and leaseback just before the year end.

> Financial regulations help prevent companies from using window dressing.

KEY POINT

Liquidity, associated with cash flow, measures a firm's ability to survive in the short run. **Profitability** is a better indicator of its ability to survive in the long run.

Other ratios

AQA	M3	WJEC	M3
Edexcel	M4a	CCEA	M3
OCR	M7		

Asset efficiency

Firms need to use their assets as efficiently as possible. The efficiency of both current and fixed assets can be measured.

There are two main **asset efficiency ratios**.

1. The first is **rate of stock turnover**:

$$\textbf{Rate of stock turnover ('stockturn')} = \frac{\textbf{Cost of sales}}{\textbf{Average stock}} \quad \textbf{(stated as '... times per period')}$$

Stock must be valued at the **lower of cost or net realisable value** (another example of the Prudence concept in operation).

The purpose is to calculate how frequently a firm sells its stock – if stock turnover is slowing, a firm is holding more stock than before, it may be facing problems selling its products, or it may have bought additional stock to take advantage of discounts offered.

An alternative calculation to display 'stock days' is $\frac{\textbf{Average stock}}{\textbf{Cost of sales}} \times \textbf{365}$

This is a useful analysis when used in conjunction with debtor days and creditor days in showing cash flow timings.

2. The second asset efficiency ratio is **asset turnover**:

$$\textbf{Asset turnover} = \frac{\textbf{Sales}}{\textbf{Net assets}}$$

This 'secondary ratio' from ROCE (see page 224) assesses the value of sales generated by the net assets representing the capital being employed in a firm. It illustrates how efficiently a firm is using its assets to generate turnover.

Debt and gearing

The **debt** ratios show **how much a company owes in relation to its size**. This analysis indicates whether lenders are likely to loan additional funds given the level of a company's debt.

Gearing analyses the **different types of payments made to capital**. Companies with more than 50 percent prior charge capital are called 'high geared'– those with less than 50 percent are 'low geared' (see gearing ratio on the next page).

Higher gearing is often found in large companies and varies between countries (e.g. Japanese firms have tended to be more highly geared than UK ones).

Gearing is important when additional capital is required. If a company is already highly geared, it may find it difficult to take out further loans. Also, the more highly geared the company, the greater the risk that the shareholders will not receive a dividend distribution. A highly geared company having external loans may find that, because it must pay a large amount of interest annually, the lenders force it to sell assets to generate payments. If their loans are secured on assets, they may remove the assets if interest payments are not met.

KEY POINT

The advantages of high gearing are similar to those associated with loan, rather than share, capital.

There are four main **debt and gearing ratios**.

1. The first of these is the **debt ratio**:

Debt ratio = Ratio of total debts : Total assets

Fifty percent is often regarded as the generally accepted maximum figure – again, an important consideration is whether this figure is rising or falling.

2. The second is the **gearing ratio**:

$$\text{Gearing} = \frac{\textbf{Prior charge capital}}{\textbf{Total long-term capital}} \text{ (long-term loans + preference shares)}$$

3. The third ratio is the **debt/equity ratio**:

$$\text{Debt/equity ratio} = \frac{\textbf{Prior charge capital}}{\textbf{Ordinary share capital + reserves}}$$

This gives similar information to the gearing ratio.

4. The final ratio is **interest cover**:

$$\text{Interest cover} = \frac{\textbf{PBIT}}{\textbf{Interest charges}}$$

An interest cover of at least 3 is normally expected, and a figure below 2 is regarded as low.

The interest cover ratio shows if the company is making sufficient profits (before interest and tax) in order to pay interest costs easily.

KEY POINT

A company's gearing should be assessed from the differing viewpoints of the directors, the investors (shareholders), and the actual and potential lenders.

Investment

Actual and potential shareholders are interested in assessing the value of an investment in (ordinary) shares of a company. Since the value of a **listed company** is its market value, some of these ratios take account of the share price as well as the information in the published accounts.

Shareholders are normally interested in two aspects of their investment.

These are:

- the **share price** – any increase here provides **capital** growth
- the **dividend received** – this forms the **income** element.

As a result, companies can often be under pressure to adopt policies that will ensure **adequate short-term profits** (e.g. to finance dividend distribution) – this may conflict with their **plans for long-term growth**.

There are four main **investment ratios**.

1. The first is **earnings per share**:

$$\textbf{Earnings per share (EPS)} = \frac{\textbf{Profit available for ordinary shareholders}}{\textbf{Number of ordinary shares}}$$

This represents the return on each ordinary share, and is nowadays stated in the published accounts.

2. The second investment ratio is **dividend cover**:

$$\textbf{Dividend cover} = \frac{\textbf{EPS}}{\textbf{Net dividend per ordinary share}}$$

Dividend per share will be stated in pence per share.

The dividend cover shows the proportion of profit available for ordinary shareholders that has been distributed, and the proportion that has been retained to help fund future growth. For example, a cover of two times indicates that half the available profits have been distributed and half retained.

3. The third investment ratio is **price/earnings (P/E) ratio**:

Price/earnings (P/E) ratio = The current share price : The EPS

The higher the P/E ratio, the greater the confidence shareholders have in the company. It is particularly important to compare this ratio to those of other companies in the same industry.

4. The final investment ratio is the **dividend yield**:

In practice, the previous year's share dividend can be used to calculate this ratio.

$$\textbf{Dividend yield} = \frac{\textbf{Share dividend for the year}}{\textbf{Current market value of the share (ex dividend)}}$$

This indicates the return the shareholder is expecting on the share.

Limitations of interpreting financial information

AQA	**M3**	WJEC	**M3**
Edexcel	**M4a**	CCEA	**M1**
OCR	**M7**		

Although ratios can show key trends, ratio analysis on its own is not a sufficiently detailed guide to a firm's performance.

For companies, additional information comes from:

- analysing the chairman's and directors' reports
- reviewing the age and type of assets
- assessing the company's markets.

Even this analysis will not provide the full picture, however. One key reason for this is that financial accounting information is **historic** in nature, looking back rather than forwards. As a result, accurate projections may not be made easily from the analysis. Also, financial accounting (through applying the money measurement concept) concentrates only on those items to which a monetary value can be made. This is again an incomplete analysis, ignoring factors such as the likely obsolescence of a company's main product, and the strength of its market share and competition.

KEY POINT

Financial statements are analysed using ratios, the results of which can be used for inter-firm comparisons and to identify trends.

PROGRESS CHECK

1. Merchant Ltd buys raw materials on five weeks' credit, issues them after a week's storage and takes another three weeks to turn them into finished products. These products are stored for another week, then sold to debtors who pay in a further four weeks. What is the length of the cash cycle?
2. During a year, a business bought stock costing £40 000. Stock at the start of the year was £5 000 and at the end of the year was £11 000. What was the stockturn?
3. Outline the nature and purpose of the three main financial statements.

1 1 week storage + 3 weeks' production + 1 week storage + 4 weeks to pay = 9 weeks; deduct 5 weeks' credit from suppliers = 4 weeks.
2 5 times $\frac{£40\,000}{£8\,000}$ (average stock).
3 Profit and loss account: contains revenues and expenses, shows profit; balance sheet: summarises a firm's financial position; cash flow statement: analyses cash movements.

Sample question and model answer

1. Below is an extract from the most recent financial statements of Cortland plc. Some ratios have not yet been calculated.

	£million		£million
Sales revenue	1.40	Non-current assets	2.5
Cost of sales	0.58	Current assets	0.7
Gross profit		Less current liabilities	0.3
Less expenses	0.65	Net assets	
Net profit		Non-current liabilities	1.6
		Shareholders' funds	1.3
		Capital employed	

(a) Showing your workings in full, calculate the:

(i) gross profit margin **(2)**

An excellent answer – the only minor point is that workings for the net profit margin are not shown.

(i) The gross profit must be £820 000, so the GP margin is 58.6% (£820 000 as % of £1 400 000).

(ii) net profit margin **(2)**

(ii) Net profit is £170 000 (£820 000 less £650 000) so the margin is 12%.

(iii) return on capital employed. **(2)**

(iii) Net assets (2.5 + 0.7 – 0.3) = capital employed (1.6 + 1.3) = £2 900 000, so ROCE = £170 000 as a percentage of £2 900 000 = 5.9%.

(b) Calculate and comment on the firm's:

(i) current ratio **(4)**

Correct, and workings shown clearly. The 'rule of thumb' figure may not be relevant for this firm/industry and this could be stated.

(i) Current ratio = 2.3 : 1 (0.7 : 0.3), which is above the 'rule of thumb' figure of 2 : 1. The company is in a strong position to meet short-term debts as they fall due.

(ii) gearing ratio. **(4)**

Correct, with a relevant comment in support – a good answer throughout.

(ii) Gearing is 0.55 (55%) calculated by 1.6 compared to 2.9 (1.6 + 1.3). The company is therefore highly geared. Interest payments are probably not excessive at this figure (although it depends in practice on the type of industry).

Exam practice question

1 Homespun plc is a major manufacturer of home furniture and is quoted on the London Stock Exchange. Homespun plc's authorised share capital is £10 million and it has a capital employed total of £15 million.

The company's long-term capital is as follows.

It has:

- issued £10 million share capital in the form of ordinary shares
- issued debentures to the value of £2 million
- a ten-year loan from the bank to the value of £1 million.

The home furniture market is increasingly competitive and so the directors of Homespun plc realise that the company has to modernise many of its manufacturing and other processes if it is going to compete effectively with its rivals. The company requires £2 million to upgrade its plant and machinery.

(a) (i) What is meant by the term 'gearing'? **(2)**

____

____

(ii) Using the above information, calculate the gearing of Homespun plc in relation to its capital employed. **(2)**

____

____

(b) You have a substantial shareholding as an investor in Homespun plc.
What is your view, as an investor, concerning the level of the company's gearing? **(4)**

____

____

____

____

(c) The directors have now decided to issue £2 million debentures in order to finance the purchase of the plant and machinery required.

Assess this decision. **(8)**

____

____

____

____

____

____

14 Budgeting and forecasting

The following topics are covered in this chapter:

- **Budgeting and standard costing**
- **Cash flow forecasting**
- **Break-even analysis**

14.1 Budgeting and standard costing

LEARNING SUMMARY

After studying this section, you should be able to:

- describe the nature and purpose of the main business budgets
- explain variance analysis and how it leads to management by exception
- outline why budgets are flexed in practice
- describe the nature and purpose of standard costing

Setting budgets

AQA	**M1, M2**
Edexcel	**M2a**
OCR	**M2, M4, M7**
WJEC	**M2**
CCEA	**M2**

A **budget** is **a plan expressed in money**, which relates to a **defined time period**.

Budgets allow a firm's activities to be:

- **co-ordinated** – through the master budget, which brings together the different functions of the firm, ensuring managers plan and work together
- **controlled** – by comparing actual performance with budgeted performance, the level of individual and departmental spending is reviewed, and individual managers take responsibility for meeting targets
- **communicated** – by involving all staff in creating budgets, allowing delegation to take place, and motivating staff to achieve budgeted performance.

Budgets are not easy to set in practice. One problem is incomplete or inaccurate data, e.g. in estimating future sales volumes and prices. Also, budgets can be seen as a financial 'straightjacket' – the temptation is to set too easy a target to achieve.

A **zero base budget** may be set – the budget is set at zero, requiring the manager to justify all expenditure. An alternative zero budget approach is where a manager uses last year's cost figures, having to present a case for an increase (e.g. due to inflation). Zero budgeting makes managers **set priorities** – the zero budget constraint makes them eliminate those activities with the lowest priority.

In smaller businesses, budget creation is often quick and informal.

Budgeting is a formal process. **Budget committees** oversee the creation of budgets and co-ordinate the completed budgets, and a **budget manual** gives a written record of procedures and individual responsibilities.

Budgeting is subject to the **principal budget factor** – this is the item that limits a firm's activities. The most common principal budget factor is the level of demand for products – other examples include the availability of raw materials or skilled labour, and machine capacity.

The main budgets

Budgets can be prepared for each major function or activity of a firm. Figure 14.1 summarises the main budgets, in their normal order of creation.

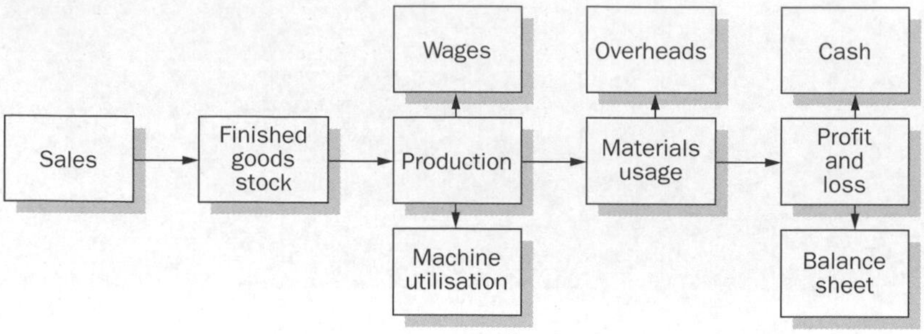

Figure 14.1 The main budgets

A **budgeted profit and loss account** – and, at a later stage, a **budgeted balance sheet** – will be prepared from a range of functional budgets, including the following:

- A **sales budget** – sales units and value are calculated on the basis of past sales, current market research, and an estimate of the competition.
- A **production budget** – based on the sales budget, it includes budgeted changes in stock. Budgeted production is analysed into resource requirements for materials, labour and machine operating hours.
- A **cash budget** – this summarises anticipated cash inflows and outflows. Inflows are based on the sales budget, and other receipts are also included. Budgeted cash outflows for labour, materials and other costs are identified from other budgets. Capital expenditure is also included.

Budgetary control

AQA **M2**
Edexcel **M2a**
OCR **M2, M4, M7**
WJEC **M4**
CCEA **M2**

Budgeting helps **control** the finance available to a business. **Budgetary control** produces **variances** that allow managers to **compare the expected (budgeted) performance of their department with its actual performance**. Control therefore takes place through **management by exception**, a technique that focuses management's attention on the difference between budgeted and actual amounts.

Management by exception is based on this comparison of expected against actual.

The difference between budgeted and actual performance (the variance) can be either:

- **favourable** – e.g. where actual sales exceed budgeted, or where a particular cost comes in below budget
- **adverse** (unfavourable) – e.g. actual sales have not reached budgeted targets, or an actual cost is above its budgeted level.

For example, here is a cost and income summary for a firm.

	Budget (£)	Actual (£)
Sales income	250 000	260 000
Labour costs	80 000	85 000
Materials costs	40 000	38 000
Overheads	10 000	11 000
Profit (sales less costs)	120 000	126 000

The actual profit is £6 000 higher than the budgeted profit. The variances making up this difference are:

sales **£10 000 favourable (actual revenue higher than budget)**
labour **£5 000 adverse (actual cost higher than budget)**
material **£2 000 favourable (lower actual cost)**
overheads **£1 000 adverse (higher actual cost)**

(£12 000 total favourable less £6 000 total adverse = £6 000 overall favourable.)

These individual variances can be analysed into **sub-variances**. For example, a favourable sales variance might consist of a favourable **volume** variance – more are sold than had been planned – and an adverse **price** variance (the actual selling price is below the budgeted level, which may be the reason for the favourable volume variance).

Efficient variance analysis requires accurate calculation and interpretation.

Some variances are due to factors **controllable** by an individual manager. In this example, the manager may have authorised the lower selling price in the hope that, by selling more, the product's price elasticity would increase total revenue. Managers can only be held accountable for controllable variances. Other variances may not be under a manager's control, in which case the manager is not held responsible. For example, an adverse wages variance may result from an unexpected national pay rise, outside the control of anyone in the firm.

Flexing the budget

Budgets and variances must be adjusted for changes in volume. Comparing production budget figures based on an expected output of, say, 3 000 units with the actual costs based on an actual output of 3 500 units is not comparing like with like. The budget figures have to be **flexed** – scaled – accordingly, and these amended budget figures can then be compared accurately with the actual ones.

Cost and profit centres are created to support budgetary control. A **cost centre** is a location such as a production line, an item of equipment (e.g. a photocopier) or even a person, acting as a collecting point for costs. These costs can then be analysed. A **profit centre** is similar in that it collects costs, but also collects income associated with those costs. A profit figure can then be calculated and used in budgetary control and decision making generally.

KEY POINT

Budgeting creates financial plans – budgetary control assesses the success of this planning.

Standard costing

OCR **M4**

A 'standard cost' is a cost estimated by managers from information on expected prices and efficiency levels of production. Like budgets, standard costs provide **targets** for managers against which their individual performances can be appraised. It is linked with budgetary control – for example, it is easy to establish sales and production budgets once standard costs have been set.

Setting standard costs is a more detailed and thorough process than establishing budgets, though budgeting estimates the costs of all business areas (standard costing concentrates on products and services).

These are the main variance groups in standard costing:

- **Sales variances**
  - the sales **price** variance measures the difference between the standard and actual selling prices
  - the sales **volume** variance measures the effect on profit of the difference between the actual and expected numbers sold.
- **Production cost variances** – total cost variances are calculated for **direct labour**, **direct materials** and **production overheads**, each being subdivided to show 'price' and 'quantity' sub-variances.

Direct labour A **rate** variance based on the difference between actual and standard pay; an **efficiency** variance based on whether output is above or below standard	*(standard – actual rate) × actual hours worked* *(standard – actual hours) × standard hourly rate*
Direct materials A **price** variance based on the difference between actual and standard unit prices; a **usage** variance based on the difference between actual and standard quantities	*(standard – actual price) × actual quantity* *(standard – actual quantity) × standard price*
Production overheads Variances based on differences between expected and actual volumes of use, efficiency and expenditure	*Fixed overhead total variance, subdivided into* ***expenditure*** *(budgeted – actual expenditure) and* ***volume*** *([budgeted – actual volume] × unit absorption rate)*

KEY POINT

Management accounting draws on financial accounting information, but also involves detailed internal analyses through setting budgets and standard costs.

PROGRESS CHECK

1. What is the difference between budgeting and budgetary control?
2. What is 'management by exception'?

1 Budgeting is the act of setting budgets; budgetary control compares actual and budgeted figures to aid decision making.
2 Controlling by calculating and analysing the reasons for budgetary variances.

14.2 Cash flow forecasting

LEARNING SUMMARY

After studying this section, you should be able to:

- construct a cash flow forecast
- understand how a cash flow forecast should be interpreted

Constructing the forecast

AQA	**M1, M2**
Edexcel	**M2a**
OCR	**M1, M2, M4**
WJEC	**M2**
CCEA	**M2**

Cash flow is sometimes confused with profit – the assumption is that, if a firm makes £1 million profit after tax, it has also increased its cash and bank balance by £1 million. Large profits can be made, and yet the cash and bank balances may at the same time have fallen.

Reasons include that:

- cash is used to buy fixed assets (this has no great effect on the profit figure)
- sales are made on credit (no immediate cash, but profit increases)
- suppliers are paid quickly (cash falls, with no effect on profit).

Credit control is an important function for any business trying to control its cash flow.

The profit figure is a key element in calculating **profitability**, whereas a firm's cash flow is used to check the **liquidity** position. Profit is often seen as being more important to the **long-term** survival of a firm, and cash flow as the key factor in **short-term** survival.

Cash flow forecasts are therefore used. We can use the following figures to illustrate how a cash flow forecast is prepared.

Balance sheet extracts (end of 2010): cash £60 000; debtors £150 000; creditors £160 000; tax owing £300 000. The debtors will pay in January; the creditors will be paid January (50%) and February (50%); tax will be paid in March.

Year 2011 forecast:	Jan	Feb	Mar	Apr	May	Jun
Sales £ (000)	120	600	600	400	120	120
Materials £ (000)	80	80	90	90	90	90

Other information for the first 6 months of 2011:

- Sales are on one month's credit, materials on two months' credit.
- Monthly overheads are £45 000, payable in the same month.
- Wages are paid in cash each month: total monthly wage bill is £90 000.
- New shares will be issued in February: £50 000.

1. Total receipts are calculated – debtors pay one month after the sales so, for example, December's sales figure equals January's cash received figure.
2. Total payments are calculated – half of December's creditors are paid in January and half in February, and the materials figures appear as cash payments two months later; the other payments occur in the same month.
3. The net receipt/payment of cash is calculated for each month.

	Jan	Feb	Mar	Apr	May	Jun
Receipts (£000):						
from debtors	150	120	600	600	400	120
from new share issue		50				
Total receipts	150	170	600	600	400	120
Payments (£000):						
to creditors/for materials	80	80	80	80	90	90
for overheads	45	45	45	45	45	45
for wages	90	90	90	90	90	90
for tax			300			
Total payments	215	215	515	215	225	225
Net monthly receipts/payments	(65)	(45)	85	385	175	(105)
Opening cash balance (£000)	60	(5)	(50)	35	420	595
Closing cash balance (£000)	(5)	(50)	35	420	595	490

4. The closing cash balance is calculated from how the month's opening cash balance is affected by the net receipts/payments. Brackets are used to indicate a negative balance.

In this example, the firm would have to make sure it had overdraft facilities for January and February, or another way of covering the shortfalls of cash. Also, there is a large surplus of cash later in the period, which will need investing or otherwise using efficiently on behalf of the firm.

The example can also be used to illustrate the problems of cash flow forecasting. Any forecast is likely to prove inaccurate – for example, actual sales will differ from forecast sales. The firm's directors will therefore need to **monitor the accuracy** of the cash flow forecast, and take appropriate action.

Interpreting the forecast

If the forecast indicates that cash flow must be improved, the directors have a number of options.

They can:

- calculate and review the **cash cycle** – e.g. calculate 'debtor days' and 'creditor days' ratios to assess credit periods taken and allowed
- examine other methods of **controlling working capital** (e.g. reduce stock levels, factor debtors, use sale/leaseback)
- **lower sales prices** (if demand is elastic) to generate higher cash inflows
- arrange **overdraft** facilities or a **short-term loan**.

KEY POINT

It is just as important to identify and act upon large cash surpluses as it is with large cash deficits, ensuring surplus cash is used efficiently.

PROGRESS CHECK

1. How does cash flow forecasting aid the survival of a business?

1 By indicating likely future liquidity problems, enabling the business to plan for these.

14.3 Break-even analysis

LEARNING SUMMARY

After studying this section, you should be able to:

- explain the difference between fixed and variable costs
- calculate the break-even point from given information
- interpret a break-even chart
- outline the limitations of break-even analysis in practice

Breaking even

AQA	**M1**
Edexcel	**M1**
OCR	**M2, M4, M6**
WJEC	**M2**
CCEA	**M2**

Classifying costs as fixed or variable is required for break-even analysis.

This classification of costs as fixed or variable is based on the way costs behave when output changes:

- **Fixed costs remain constant as output changes**. Two examples often given are factory rent and business rates, although in practice rent may be a **stepped cost** – as output increases, a firm may need extra space and therefore at some stage may have to pay additional rent on an extra building (so the cost increases unevenly, by a 'step').
- **Variable costs change in proportion to changes in output**. A popular illustration is direct materials – doubling production output typically doubles the cost of materials used. In practice, there may not be a perfect match between increase in output and increase in the variable cost, because economies of scale lower unit prices (e.g. bulk buying of materials) as output increases.
- **Semi-variable costs** are found in practice. Commonly used illustrations are power and (landline) telephones, which often include a fixed element (a standing charge, e.g. for line rental) and a variable element based on the number of units used.

This classification is also used for marginal costing calculations and for contribution pricing, and provides valuable information for analysing production performance.

Calculating the break-even point

The **break-even point** can be calculated mathematically and can be displayed as a diagram.

The calculation used for the break-even point is based on the concept of **contribution**. Every product made has a variable cost – it also has a (higher) selling price. The difference between these two figures is known as the 'contribution' made by the individual product. This contribution is made towards a firm's fixed costs. When enough of these individual contributions have been made, a firm's total costs will be covered and it is at break-even point, making neither a profit nor a loss.

KEY POINT

Contribution = Selling price – Variable cost

$$\text{Break-even point} = \frac{\text{Fixed costs}}{\text{Unit contribution}}$$

If, therefore, a firm has fixed costs totalling £6 000, variable costs of £1 per unit and a unit selling price of £2.50:

- unit contribution is £2.50 – £1.00 = £1.50
- break-even point is £6 000 / £1.50 = 4 000 units

It is easy to calculate profit or loss once the break-even point is known.

Profit = contribution × number of units **above** break-even

Loss = contribution × number of units **below** break-even

The firm must make and sell 4 000 units to break-even – every unit sold above this figure increases net profit by £1.50, and every unit that the firm fails to make and sell below 4 000 produces a loss of £1.50.

At an output of 4 000 units:

- **total revenue = 4 000 × £2.50 = £10 000**
- **total costs = 4 000 × £1 = £4 000 variable + £6 000 fixed = £10 000**

If the firm currently makes and sells 6 000 units, its **margin of safety** – the number of units by which production and sales can fall before it starts to make a loss – is 2 000 units.

The profit at this level of production and sales is as follows:

			£
Total revenue	**= 6 000 × £2.50**	**=**	**15 000**
Total costs	**= fixed**	**=**	**(6 000)**
	+ variable (6 000 × £1)	**=**	**(6 000)**
Profit		**=**	**3 000**

Since contribution above 4 000 break-even units = profit:

profit = 2000 x £1.50 = £3000, agreeing with the full calculation shown.

Graphical display

Graphical display is shown in Figure 14.2. The sales revenue line is plotted and the total cost line is represented by the fixed costs line (parallel to the horizontal axis) plus the variable costs line. The information used above in calculating the break-even point is also used here.

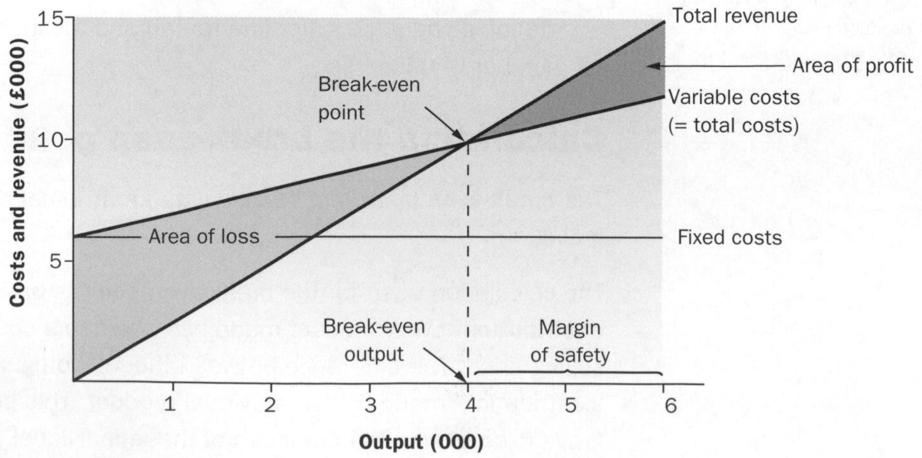

Figure 14.2 Break-even chart

Limitations of break-even analysis

Break-even analysis remains helpful to management in planning production and selling levels.

These are the limitations of break-even analysis:

- The chart only applies to a single product, or to a fixed 'mix' of products.
- Not all costs can be easily and accurately classified as fixed or variable (e.g. those semi-variable costs with a standing charge).
- Sales prices are assumed constant at all activity levels – this may be unrealistic.
- Production and sales are assumed to be the same figure.
- Fixed costs change over time and can change with volume (e.g. stepped costs – see page 239).
- Unit variable costs may change with output, due to economies or diseconomies of scale.

PROGRESS CHECK

1. Distinguish between direct and indirect costs, and give an example of each.
2. Calculate the break-even point for a firm with fixed costs of £110 000, unit variable costs of £3.45 and a selling price of £8.95.

1 Direct costs: directly linked to product, e.g. materials and manufacture;
indirect costs: not directly linked to product, e.g. general factory cleaning materials.

2 Contribution = £8.95 − £3.45 = £5.50

Break-even point = $\frac{£110\ 000}{£5.50}$ = 20 000 units

$\frac{\text{Break-even cost}}{\text{Revenue figure}}$ = 20 000 × £8.95 = £179 000

Sample questions and model answers

1. The accountant of a manufacturing firm has produced this information:

Balance sheet (extract) as at 31 December 2010	**£000**	**£000**
Fixed assets	1 500	
Depreciation	300	1 200
Current assets:		
Stocks	300	
Debtors	150	
Cash	100	550
Current liabilities:		
Creditors	150	
Corporation tax	300	(450)
Net current assets		100

The sales forecast for the first six months of 2011 (£000) is:

	Jan	**Feb**	**Mar**	**Apr**	**May**	**Jun**
Sales (£000)	120	600	600	120	120	120

These sales will be on one month's credit. The year-end debtors will have paid by the end of January. Raw materials will be bought (£90 000 per month) on two months' credit (year-end creditors will pay by the end of February). Other figures are £30 000 for operating expenses and £90 000 for wages, both paid in the month in which they are incurred. The tax owing will be paid in March.

(a) Prepare a monthly cash flow forecast for the first six months of 2011. **(6)**

This is well laid out, and accurate. Using this format, the net cash flow can clearly be seen.

(a)

	Jan £000	Feb £000	Mar £000	Apr £000	May £000	Jun £000
Receipts from debtors	150	120	600	600	120	120
Payments:						
to creditors	75	75	90	90	90	90
for expenses	30	30	30	30	30	30
for wages	90	90	90	90	90	90
for tax			300			
Net cash inflow/(outflow)	(45)	(75)	90	390	(90)	(90)
Cash at start	100	55	(20)	70	460	370
Cash at close	55	(20)	70	460	370	280

(b) Comment on the results of your calculations. **(4)**

An accurate assessment, but comments regarding (a) the large cash surpluses in the last three months, and (b) the gradually reducing total balance, should have been made.

(b) *The company has plenty of cash available, except at the end of February, when it will need to sort out an overdraft with its bank.*

Sample questions and model answers (continued)

(c) How will depreciation affect your forecast? **(2)**

(c) *Depreciation isn't paid out in cash, so it won't show in the workings.*

A reasonable comment, though the phrase 'non-cash expense' would help make the explanation clearer.

2. Bentley Ltd produces kitchen scales that are sold to retailers for £10 each. Its expected output is 80 000 scales per annum, which is 80 percent of full capacity. Fixed costs have been calculated at £1.50 (based on full capacity), wage costs £1 per item, materials £4 per item and other variable costs £1 per item.

(a) Calculate the break-even level of output and the margin of safety. **(2)**

(a) *Contribution is £10 selling price less £6 variable costs = £4 per unit.*

$$\text{Break-even point} = \frac{\text{£150 000 fixed costs}}{\text{£4 contribution}} = 37\,500 \text{ units}$$

Margin of safety = 100 000 - 37 500 = 62 500 units

The answer is laid out clearly, though all calculations (e.g. how the variable cost total is arrived at, and the fixed cost calculation) should still be shown. The 'proof' of the break-even calculation should be calculated.
It is:

total revenue 37 500 × £10 = £375 000
total cost: variable 37 500 × £6= 225 000
Fixed = £150 000
Total = £375 000

42 500 is a more accurate statement of the margin of safety (it is better to use the actual output of 80 000 rather than the maximum of 100 000).

The firm has received an offer from a major high-street chain to buy 20 000 scales at £6.50 each. These scales would feature a different plastic casing, and a machine costing £10 000 would need to be bought to make this casing.

(b) Should the company accept this offer? Evaluate both the numerical and non-numerical factors that should be taken into account. **(8)**

(b) *Contribution for the new order = 50p per unit, £6.50 selling price less £6.00 variable costs. If the firm can sell 20 000, it will receive £10 000, but has had to pay out £10 000. It therefore makes neither a profit nor a loss, and breaks even on this order. I do not think it is a good idea because no profit is made.*

Accurate calculations again, though workings for total revenue (20 000 x 50p) should still be displayed.

The analysis is lacking in detail, however. The candidate should consider points such as the following:

- **All the spare capacity is now being used.**
- **Can the new machine be re-used?**
- **Where will the £10 000 required come from?**
- **Is there a prospect of future orders?**
- **Will the firm gain from publicity (is it an 'own label' order)?**

Exam practice questions

1 Leigh and Steve are in business together, operating as a partnership and producing cuddly toys. They have been successful over the last five years, making large profits. They have decided to try and increase their output by obtaining new premises and machinery. They also plan to employ additional staff.

How could budgeting help Leigh and Steve? **(18)**

2 FastWare Ltd makes sports clothing. One product line is a women's running shoe range which the company sells to retailers at £20 each. The figures below show the relevant costs for the shoes.

Overhead costs	£300 000
Labour cost per unit	£2
Material cost per unit	£8
Other variable costs per unit	£2

Showing your working in full, calculate:

(a) the contribution of each shoe sold **(2)**

(b) the break-even level of output in respect of quantity and revenue **(4)**

(c) the margin of safety at the proposed level of output **(2)**

(d) the standard cost of each shoe at the proposed level of output. **(4)**

For each of the above responses, continue your answer on separate paper if necessary.

15 Financial decision-making

The following topics are covered in this chapter:

- Investment decisions
- Cost analysis and decision making
- Marginal costing and decision making

15.1 Investment decisions

LEARNING SUMMARY

After studying this section, you should be able to:

- explain the difference between the payback, average rate of return, and discounted cash flow methods of investment appraisal
- apply each method to given data and reach appropriate conclusions

Capital investment decisions

AQA	**M3**	WJEC	**M4**
Edexcel	**M4a**	CCEA	**M3**
OCR	**M2, M4**		

Because of the major capital outlay involved, managers try to calculate **expected profitability** and **expected cash flows** for a proposed investment.

The three methods of investment appraisal that managers use are:

- the payback period method
- the accounting rate of return method
- the discounted cash flow method.

Payback period method

These calculations also help decisions to be made between alternative capital projects.

The **payback** period method of investment appraisal calculates how long it takes a project to repay its original investment. The method therefore concentrates on **cash flow**, highlighting projects that recover quickly their initial investment. Here is an example of how it works.

A company is considering two different capital investment projects. Both are expected to operate for four years. Only one of the projects can be financed.

Profit/(loss):	Project A: £22 000	Project B: £22 000
year 1	2 000	2 500
year 2	4 000	1 500
year 3	7 000	3 000
year 4	(3 000)	5 000
Expected scrap value	2 000	2 000
Annual depreciation	5 000	5 000

The payback periods are calculated by adding annual depreciation back to the cash flows – depreciation is a **non-cash expense** that reduces profit, and so the profit figures given understate the cash inflows by the amount of the depreciation. Cash flow in year 4 is also increased by the scrap values for each project.

Year	Project A		Project B	
	Annual cash flow (£)	Cumulative cash flow (£)	Annual cash flow (£)	Cumulative cash flow (£)
0	(22 000)	(22 000)	(22 000)	(22 000)
1	7 000	(15 000)	7 500	(14 500)
2	9 000	(6 000)	6 500	(8 000)
3	12 000	6 000	8 000	—
4	4 000	10 000	12 000	12 000

Although the payback method is widely used in practice, it is often as a supplement to the other, more sophisticated, appraisal methods.

The payback period for project A is two and a half years. At the start of year 3, outflows exceed inflows by £6 000. Net inflows for year 3 are £12 000 (£1 000 per month) – it therefore recoups its original investment after six months of year 3. Project B's payback period is three years. The manager would therefore select project A on the basis of this method, even though project B generates a greater total cash inflow by the end of its life.

These are some of the benefits of the payback period method:

- It is easy to calculate and understand.
- Its use emphasises **liquidity**, because calculations are based solely on cash flow.
- It also helps managers to **reduce risk** by selecting the project that recovers its outlay most quickly.
- Early cash flows can be predicted more accurately than later ones, and are less affected by inflation.

The main drawback of this method is that it completely **ignores profit and profitability**. It also takes no account of interest rates.

Accounting rate of return method

This method is also known by the name **'return on investment'**.

The **accounting rate of return** (**ARR**) method of investment appraisal calculates the expected profits from the investment, expressing them as a percentage of the capital invested. The higher the rate of return, the 'better' (i.e. the more profitable) the project is. The ARR is therefore **based on anticipated profits rather than on cash flow.**

$$\textbf{ARR} = \frac{\textbf{Expected average profits}}{\textbf{Original investment}} \times 100$$

Using the figures in the table on page 245, project A generates total profits of £10 000 and project B total profits of £12 000.

Project A (£)	Project B (£)
$\frac{2\,500}{22\,000}$	$\frac{3\,000}{22\,000}$
ARR = 11.4%	ARR = 13.6%

Project B would therefore be selected using ARR.

The benefits of the ARR method are that:

- it is easy to use and simple to understand
- it measures and highlights the **profitability** of each project.

Its disadvantages are that **it ignores the timing of a project's contributions**. High profits in the early years – which can be estimated more accurately, and which help minimise the project's risk – are treated in the same way as profits occurring later. It also concentrates on profits rather than cash flows, **ignoring the time value of money** (profits in the later years being eroded by the effects of inflation).

DCF assumes that a firm prefers to use cash in year 1 rather than in year 2, because **the earlier the cash is received, the sooner it can be reinvested.**

Discounted cash flow method

The principle of **discounted cash flow** (**DCF**) is based on using discounted arithmetic to get a **present value for future cash inflows and outflows**.

This method is sometimes divided into two elements, which complement each other:

1. The **net present value (NPV)** takes account of all relevant cash flows from the project through its life, discounting them to their 'present value'.
2. The **internal rate of return (IRR)** method compares the rate of return expected from the project with that identified by the company as being the cost of its capital – projects having an IRR that exceeds the cost of capital are worth considering.

As an example, a company receiving £100 at the start of a year might be able to invest it at 10 percent *per annum* – by the end of the year this investment will be worth £110. Given the choice of £100 now or a higher sum in a year's time, the managers will choose the higher sum only if it exceeds £110. The principle works in reverse – the managers know that a project generating £110 in a year's time is worth the same as one generating £100 immediately, the project with the future value being discounted to its present value (by using a set of discounting tables).

The NPV method calculates the **present value of the project's future cash flows**. Each year's cash flow is discounted to a present value, which shows how much the managers would have to invest now at a given rate of interest to earn these future cash benefits. The present value of the total cash outflows is compared to that of the total cash inflows to calculate the **net present value** of the project.

The project with the highest positive NPV will be chosen:

- **If the NPV is positive** – cash benefits exceed cash costs – this means that the project will earn a return in excess of its cost of capital (the rate of interest/discounting used in the calculations).
- **If the NPV is negative**, this means the cost of investing in the project exceeds the present value of future receipts, and so it is not worth investing in it.

If the company planning to invest in either project A or B has a cost of capital equal to 12 percent, the future cash flows can be discounted to their present values using discounting tables.

The present value of £1 when discounted at 12 percent is as follows:

Thus, £1 in a year's time is the same as 89.3p invested now at 12 percent for one year; £1 in two years' time is the same as 79.7p invested at 12 percent over 2 years, etc.

Year	Present value (PV) factor 12%
0	1.000
1	0.893
2	0.797
3	0.712
4	0.636

	Project A			Project B		
Year	**Cash flow**	**PV factor**	**PV**	**Cash flow**	**PV factor**	**PV**
0	(22 000)	1.000	(22 000)	(22 000)	1.000	(22 000)
1	7 000	0.893	6 251	7 500	0.893	6 698
2	9 000	0.797	7 173	6 500	0.797	5 180
3	12 000	0.712	8 544	8 000	0.712	5 696
4	4 000	0.636	2 544	12 000	0.636	7 632
		NPV =	**2 512**		**NPV =**	**3 206**

If the cost of capital is 12 percent, both projects are worth undertaking if possible, because the average annual returns on capital are above the 12 percent figure.

Project B has the higher expected NPV and would therefore be selected.

The IRR method involves comparing the actual rates of return (in this illustration, both rates exceed 12 percent since both show positive NPVs when discounted at 12 percent) with the company's cost of capital.

The use of DCF takes account of all cash flows, and it acknowledges the time value of money. The main problem is in **establishing a suitable discount rate** to use, because this rate (and the firm's cost of capital) is likely to vary over the life of the project.

KEY POINT

Organisations undertake investment appraisal to evaluate the likely success and value of capital investments, which tie up the firm's finance for a long period, normally for a number of years.

PROGRESS CHECK

1. Which appraisal method concentrates on **(a)** liquidity **(b)** profitability?
2. Why are profit figures adjusted for depreciation when calculating payback?

1 **(a)** payback **(b)** ARR.
2 Depreciation is a non-cash expense that has reduced profit; to get the cash flow equivalent, depreciation must be added back to the profit figure.

15.2 Cost analysis and decision making

LEARNING SUMMARY

After studying this section, you should be able to:

- explain the difference between direct and indirect costs
- classify and analyse a range of costs
- explain the role of absorption costing

Cost classification and analysis

AQA **M3**
OCR **M2, M4, M6**
WJEC **M4**

Classifying costs allows analysis to take place. For example, break-even analysis classifies costs as fixed or variable. Classifying costs as direct or indirect is necessary for **absorption costing**, which is a costing method that 'absorbs' overheads into product costs – for example, a factory rent (a factory overhead) must be absorbed into the cost of products made in the factory. Costs are also analysed for product pricing, stock valuation, and comparing the relative profitability of product lines.

Direct materials + Direct labour + Direct expenses = Prime cost

Indirect labour + Indirect material + Indirect expenses = Overheads

Direct and indirect costs

Direct costs are linked with particular product lines – they are therefore costs that can be identified **precisely** with a product or process.

Indirect costs are shared between product lines, because they do not relate to one product in particular. In practice, these costs must be apportioned to the different products.

For example, a car manufacturer has:

- sheet steel and engine parts as direct materials
- assembly-line employees as direct labour
- the cost of transporting product-specific items (such as engine parts) as direct expenses.

Indirect costs for this manufacturer include supervisory wages and business rates.

These costs appear in the firm's **manufacturing account**.

KEY POINT

Indirect costs (overheads) that occur in offices are:

- administration costs, e.g. office staff salaries
- selling/distribution costs, e.g advertising costs.

Administration and selling costs are shown in the profit and loss account.

Allocation, apportionment and absorption

Overheads are **allocated** when the cost is incurred wholly by a **single department** or **cost centre**. The overhead can then be charged exclusively to that cost centre. Overheads have to be **apportioned** when the cost is incurred by **more than one** cost centre. A good example is factory rent, with the total cost having to be shared between all relevant cost centres in the factory.

Companies not in traditional manufacturing may use **activity-based costing** (ABC) – it uses 'cost drivers' based on its major non-manufacturing activities (e.g. ordering, despatch) to absorb overheads.

The **basis of apportionment** will vary according to the nature of the overhead.

Here is an example.

Overhead	Possible basis of apportionment
Rent and rates	Floor area
Equipment depreciation	Volume or floor area
Lighting and heating	Cost or book value of equipment
Maintenance staff	Hours clocked for each department
Stores staff	Value of material requisitions
Administrative support, e.g. personnel and canteen costs	Number of employees

In absorption costing, all overheads (indirect costs) must be **absorbed**, i.e. **recovered**, by the products, otherwise there will be no source of income to pay for these overheads. For example, if a product's share of total overheads comes to £300 000, this amount needs to be recovered throughout the period when the product is sold.

Absorption methods include:

- **direct labour hours** – e.g. in a garage, if the budgeted number of direct labour hours is 100 000, each hour spent working on a car will be charged with an extra £3 (i.e. $\frac{£300\ 000}{100\ 000}$), so by the end of the period the £300 000 costs will be recovered
- **machine hour rate** – e.g. where machinery is heavily used, budgeted machine hours being 50 000 in the period, each hour that a machine is used will be charged at £6 ($\frac{£300\ 000}{50\ 000}$).

Examples of process costing industries include chemicals, distillation (e.g. petrol) and food.

Costing methods

There are two main categories of costing methods:

1. **Specific order** costing is where costs are charged directly to cost units, e.g. job, batch and contract costing.
2. **Continuous operation** costing is where costs have to be apportioned to cost units, e.g. service and process costing.

The different costing methods are used in the following contexts:

- **Job** costing is used when work is undertaken to a **customer's specific requirements** – all costs are charged to the job. **Contract** costing is similar, though the contract (e.g. for construction of a ship) tends to be for a longer duration.
- **Batch** costing is used when a **quantity of identical articles** (such as similar houses on an estate) are manufactured.
- **Service** (or **function**) costing is concerned with establishing the costs of services rendered, and controlling these costs (e.g. within a hospital).
- The **process** costing method is used when products are made **in a single process**.

KEY POINT

The costing method chosen must suit the manufacturing method.

PROGRESS CHECK

1. What is the difference between apportionment and absorption?

1 Apportionment: sharing the cost between more than one cost centre; absorption: recovering overhead costs.

15.3 Marginal costing and decision making

LEARNING SUMMARY

After studying this section, you should be able to:

- calculate contribution, break-even and margin of safety
- apply marginal costing principles to decision making

Contribution and marginal costing

Edexcel **M4a**
OCR **M2, M4, M6**
WJEC **M4**

Break-even analysis shows that the difference between unit selling price and unit variable cost is the **contribution** made by the individual product towards a firm's fixed costs. When enough individual contributions have been made, a firm's total costs will be covered and it is at break-even point, making neither a profit nor a loss.

Contribution analysis therefore divides costs into their fixed and variable elements. Traditional **absorption costing** takes all costs into account when making decisions. A **marginal costing** approach can be used in decision making, based on the argument that **factors having no bearing on a decision are ignored**.

In this context, we ignore fixed costs on the argument that:

- they have to be paid regardless of income
- the apportionment of these fixed costs between different product lines is often arbitrary.

Examples of where a marginal costing approach is often used to make decisions include special orders, whether to discontinue a product, and 'make or buy' decisions.

Special orders

Here is a question where marginal costing and product contribution can be used to make a decision.

A single-product manufacturer has this cost structure – materials £25, direct labour £28, and variable overheads £12 per unit; fixed overheads total £420 000. Its product price is £120, annual output (80 percent of capacity) being 20 000.

A DIY store has enquired whether it can buy an extra 4 000 units per annum, to sell as 'own label' items. It will pay £85 for each unit. The manufacturer will have to incur £10 000 set-up costs.

Is the offer worth accepting?

The present contribution is £55 per product, selling price £120 less £65 variable costs (i.e. £25 + £28 + £12). Break-even point is $\frac{£420\,000}{£55}$ = 7 636 sales, the margin of safety is 12 364 (20 000 – 7 636) and the forecast profit is £680 000 (12 364 × £55).

Rounding of figures may mean slight differences in totals obtained.

Note how these calculations can be checked:
- Break-even revenue is £120 × 7 636 = £916 320.
- Break-even costs total the same, i.e. £420 000 + £496 340 (7 636 × £65) (the £20 difference is due to rounding).
- Profit at 20 000 output = revenue £2 400 000 (£120 × 20 000) less cost £1 720 000 (£420 000 fixed + £1 300 000 variable, i.e. 20 000 × £65) = £680 000.

The key question is: Should the new order be taken on?

Numerically, the calculations for this order show:
- unit contribution £20 (£85 – £65)
- total contribution £80 000 (4 000 x £20)
- total profit £70 000 (£80 000 – £10 000 set-up costs).

The main marginal costing principle here is that, **because all fixed costs are already covered** (by the normal production and sales exceeding the break-even point), **the contribution made by this special order is all profit.**

Extra contribution equals extra profit, once the break-even point has been reached.

Non-financial factors are also important in making such decisions, as shown in these examples:
- Is the special order the most profitable way of utilising spare capacity, or will long-term plans for using this capacity be affected?
- Will the lower selling price influence other customers?

Discontinuing products

Another area of decision making involves whether to discontinue an apparently unprofitable product or line. Here is an example.

A company makes three products: A, B and C. Costs are split one-third fixed and two-thirds variable. Figures are:

	A	**B**	**C**	**Total**
Sales (£000)	32	50	45	127
Total costs (£000)	36	39	33	108
Profit/(loss)	(4)	11	12	19

Should product A be dropped?

Being indirect in nature, fixed costs may be shared arbitrarily between products.

Apparently, the overall profit of £19 000 masks a loss of £4 000 for product A. Since fixed costs are apportioned without certainty, we can remove them from the calculations and display the information as a marginal costing statement, as shown below:

	A	**B**	**C**	**Total**
Sales	32	50	45	127
Variable costs	24	26	22	72
Contribution	8	24	23	55
Less fixed costs				36
Profit				19

Total profit remains the same, but by calculating individual product contributions we can see that **each product makes a contribution towards total fixed costs.** On this argument, therefore, product A should be retained.

KEY POINT

Marginal costing approaches take account of contribution made towards total fixed costs, and avoid the arbitrary apportionment of fixed (indirect) costs to individual products.

PROGRESS CHECK

1. How is break-even calculated?
2. What is the relationship between fixed costs, contribution and profit?
3. How does a marginal costing statement differ from a traditional cost statement?

1 Total fixed costs are divided by unit contribution.
2 Once total contribution covers fixed costs, further contribution = profit.
3 Costs are separated into fixed and variable, and contribution is calculated, from which the fixed costs are deducted.

Sample question and model answer

1. The directors of a company are wondering whether to invest £180 000 in a project that would make additional profits before depreciation as follows:

Year 1	£100 000
Year 2	£80 000
Year 3	£60 000

The company's cost of capital is 10 percent and the present value (PV) table is as follows:

Year	PV
1	0.909
2	0.826
3	0.731

(a) Using the above information, assess whether the investment is likely to benefit the company financially. **(6)**

An excellent answer – accurate calculations supported by a suitable conclusion based on the results.

My calculations are as follows:

Year	Cash flow	PV factor	PV
0	(180 000)	1.000	(180 000)
1	100 000	0.909	90 900
2	80 000	0.826	66 080
3	60 000	0.731	45 060
		NPV	22 040

This suggests the company will benefit from the investment because there is a positive net present value figure of £22 040.

(b) Compare the discounted cash flow method with one other method the directors could use to assess whether this project is worthwhile financially. **(8)**

A thorough and accurate set of statements about DCF.

The discounted cash flow (DCF) method assesses capital investment projects by discounting future cash returns to present values in order to decide whether or not a project is worthwhile. This means that it takes into account the time value of money, because £1 000 now is likely to be worth more than £1 000 in the future (the company could invest the money now and therefore earn interest). The DCF method uses cash figures before depreciation in its calculations.

Again, good points made and a clear comparison with DCF.

An alternative method to use would be the Accounting Rate of Return (ARR) method. Unlike DCF, the ARR method is based on accounting results (profits) rather than cash flows. It has the benefit that a target can be set against which the return is measured, and it also uses readily available accounting information. However, it fails to take into account the timing of the cash flows involved.

Exam practice question

1 FastWare Ltd makes sports clothing. One product line is a women's running shoe range which the company sells to retailers at £20 each. The company's projected output is 80 000 units a year, although it has the capacity to make 100 000. The figures below show the relevant costs for the shoes.

Overhead costs	£300 000
Labour cost per unit	£2
Material cost per unit	£8
Other variable costs per unit	£2

The company has been approached by a high street retail chain with an order for 20 000 pairs of shoes at £13 each. The shoes would be produced under an own brand label and would require the purchase of a new machine costing £20 000.

Assessing the numerical and non-numerical factors together, what advice would you give to FastWare Ltd in terms of accepting or rejecting the order? **(20)**

16 Locating and developing operations

The following topics are covered in this chapter:

- **Locating operations**
- **Developing operations**

16.1 Locating operations

LEARNING SUMMARY

After studying this section, you should be able to:

- list and describe the main factors that determine where entrepreneurs locate their business operations
- analyse how these factors are used in deciding where a business is to be located

The importance of location

AQA	**M1, M3**	WJEC	**M1**
Edexcel	**M3**	CCEA	**M4**
OCR	**M6, M7**		

An organisation combines the various factors of production as efficiently as possible, to produce its goods and services and sell them at a profit. The lower it can keep its unit costs, the greater its potential profit. The eventual choice of location is based on a **compromise** between various influences.

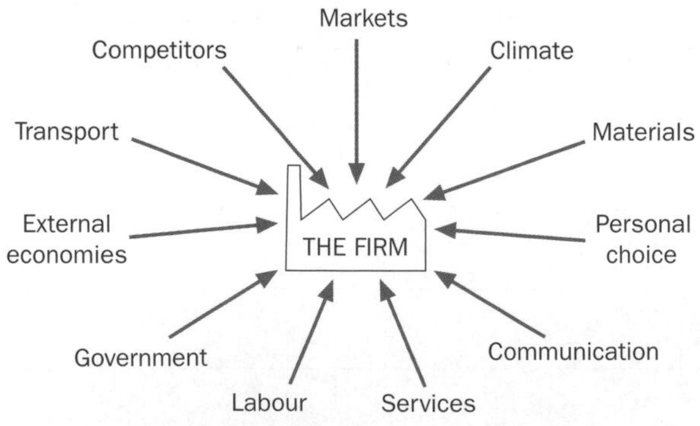

Figure 16.1 Influences on location

The main factors that determine where entrepreneurs locate their business operations are:

- historical and natural influences
- transport and communications
- labour
- materials and markets
- government
- personal and social influences
- external economies.

Each of these factors is discussed in turn below.

Historical and natural influences – a significant historical influence on location was the availability of **power**. For example, water power, coupled with a suitable climate, encouraged the location of the old staple industries of cotton and wool weaving in the north of England.

The **agricultural industry** has always been influenced by the suitability of local climactic and soil conditions. Other physical advantages, such as good natural harbours near to areas of high population, influenced industries such as shipbuilding to locate in – and contribute to the growth of – cities like Belfast and Sunderland. The topography and situation of the land can also influence location. For example, a chemical factory complex may need a large flat area of land near the coast.

Cities like Birmingham and Manchester publicise the fact that their airports are becoming more important internationally.

Transport and communications – location near to an efficient transport network has become an increasingly important influence. Many firms now examine closely the **road and air links**, for both their raw materials and their finished products. Good transport systems are also required for a firm's labour.

Although the UK has national postal and telecommunications services, some 'high-tech' firms choose to locate in areas that offer more **advanced technological support** (e.g. where there are advanced cable technology systems available).

A firm has to examine the availability of suitable **quality** (skills) as well as suitable **quantity** of staff.

Labour – the availability of a sufficiently large and well-trained labour force is an influence, although the move by some firms towards a more capital-intensive production, coupled with a greater willingness by staff to commute, can reduce the importance of this influence. When relocating, a firm may offer a range of financial inducements to encourage its workforce to move with it, due to the geographical immobility of labour – the alternative is to meet increased training costs. The availability of suitably skilled **managers** is a related influence.

The **cost** of labour, as well as its availability, varies from area to area. If a firm is labour intensive, it might be tempted to move to an area of the country with relatively low wage costs.

Materials and markets – firms involved in 'weight-gaining' production, where the end product is heavier or bulkier than the inputs (for instance, the brewing industry), have traditionally located close to their markets. Those firms using 'weight-reducing' production processes, e.g. sugar refining, sawmills, and having bulky raw materials (and therefore high transport costs) have tended to locate near to the supply of these materials.

Many industries located where there was a concentrated supply of their raw materials nearby. Examples include the china industry in and around Stoke-on-Trent, and Sheffield's steel industry. Now that these firms have to import their raw materials from abroad, newer firms in the industry may choose to locate elsewhere, although the existence of **external economies** and '**industrial inertia**' still encourage them to locate in the traditional area. Many extractive industries have no choice, having to be located by their materials (e.g. coal mines).

The **cost of land** has become an increasingly important influence in making the location decision.

Some firms are heavily influenced by the **population distribution** of their final consumers. For instance, many firms supplying mass consumer goods locate production close to densely populated areas such as south-eastern England, though other influences (e.g. high property prices) may discourage this. Firms whose markets come to them, such as retail shops, have little choice but to be geographically dispersed. A related factor is the **image created for customers** by the location (e.g. the 'Harley street specialist', and Bond and Regent Streets as London shopping areas).

Government – the UK and the EU, through their development of regional policies, have become increasingly important influences on location.

> We aim to help every region in England to increase sustainable regional economic development and narrow the gap in growth rates between regions.
>
> *Extract from 'What we do' page, BIS website, 2010*

The EU allows individual governments to support economically disadvantaged regions by providing **regional aid**. The UK has established **Assisted Areas**, locations where regional aid is allowed.

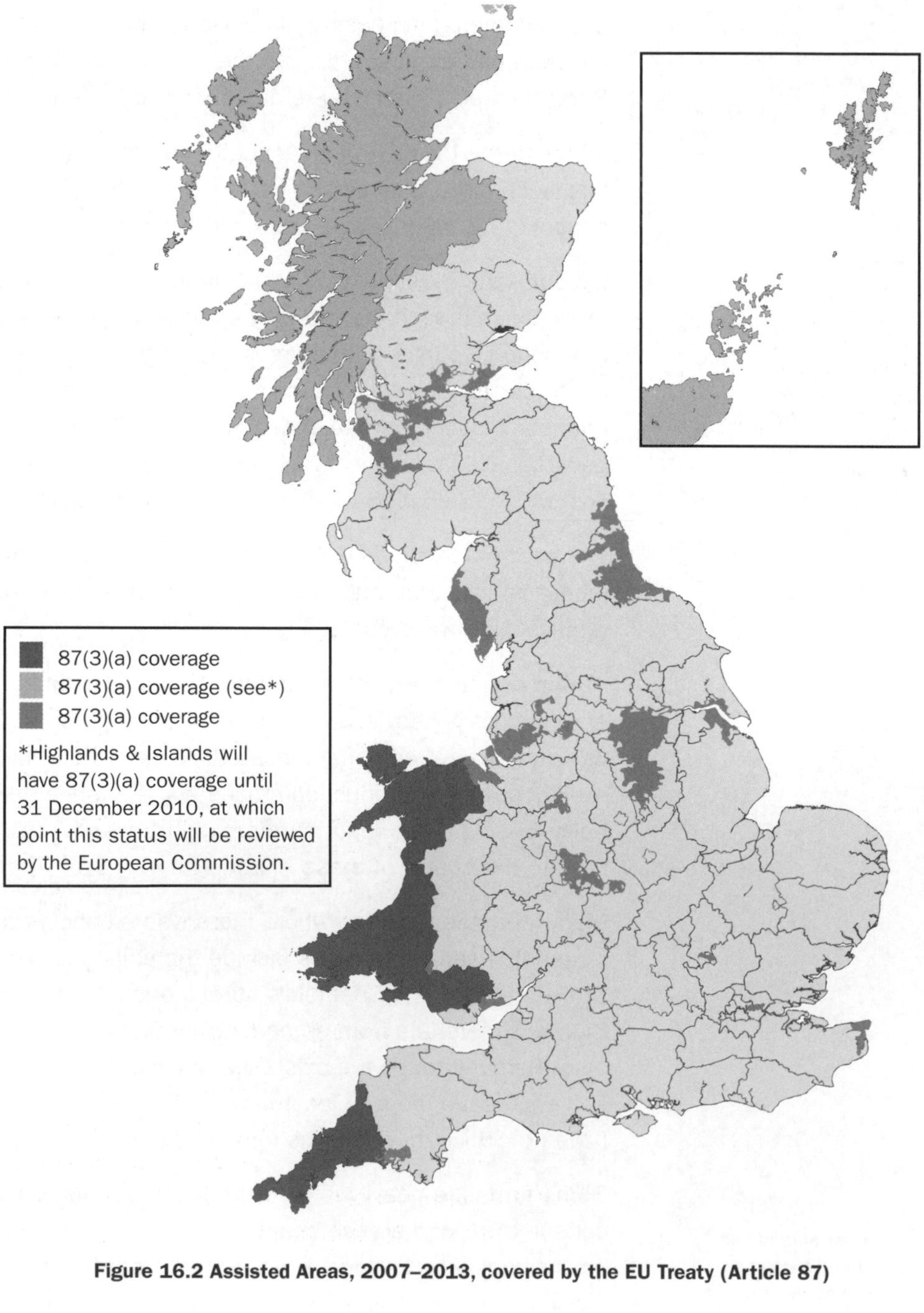
87(3)(a) coverage
87(3)(a) coverage (see*)
87(3)(a) coverage
*Highlands & Islands will have 87(3)(a) coverage until 31 December 2010, at which point this status will be reviewed by the European Commission.

Figure 16.2 Assisted Areas, 2007–2013, covered by the EU Treaty (Article 87)

In the UK, the main forms of aid are through discretionary grant schemes.

Here are two examples from 2010:

- **Grants for Business Investment (GBI)** helped fund new investment projects, leading to long-term improvements in productivity, skills and employment.
- **Regional Selective Assistance** in Scotland and Wales sought to encourage new investment projects, strengthen existing employment and support new job creation.

There is geographical immobility of entrepreneurship as well as of labour.

Personal and social influences – the personal preferences of the entrepreneur are important. Some entrepreneurs have ties to particular areas of the country, and may be unwilling to move elsewhere.

A firm's location can be influenced by **pressure groups**. Concern over factors such as the protection of natural habitats is an increasingly important influence, sometimes linked to a 'NIMBY' ('Not In My Back Yard') attitude to the location of those firms based in less attractive industries, such as waste disposal and nuclear power.

External economies – the existence of external economies of scale and concentration encourages firms to base their production in certain areas. For example, the UK car industry developed mainly in the Midlands, which led to a supply of skilled labour and component manufacturers in the area.

Locating internationally

AQA	**M1, M3**	WJEC	**M1**
Edexcel	**M3**	CCEA	**M4**
OCR	**M6, M7**		

Many of the above influences apply when an international decision is being made. Additional reasons for international location include the existence of **global markets**, locating to **control costs** (e.g. through a country having a favourable tax regime for business profits), and locating to **avoid trade barriers**.

The existence of the EU's Single Market with its Common External Tariff is a factor encouraging non-EU businesses to locate within the EU.

Other specific factors to consider when deciding where to locate internationally include:

- the **exchange rate** – a history of highly fluctuating exchange rates will discourage an entrepreneur from locating in the country concerned
- **language and culture** – different cultural work habits and language communication problems may also discourage entrepreneurs
- **relative inflation** – an entrepreneur may be put off from locating in a country that traditionally suffers from high inflation levels
- the **political climate** – countries with politically unstable regimes often find it difficult to encourage inward investment as a result of international location.

Making the decisions

Whether an entrepreneur decides to locate within the UK or internationally, the use of decision-making techniques provides additional information when making the decision. For example, **investment appraisal** techniques and the use of **break-even analysis** can give additional financial-based information to support any qualitative judgments made.

KEY POINT

Location decisions are influenced by both qualitative (e.g. the entrepreneur's preferences) and quantitative (financial costs and revenues) factors.

PROGRESS CHECK

1. State three influences on the location of a firm.
2. Identify one location factor that specifically influences whether to locate internationally.

1 Three from: government assistance; infrastructure; availability of suitable labour; transport and communications; historical and natural influences; materials and markets; personal and social; external economies.
2 Relatively high inflation compared with other countries/possible locations (**accept any other suitable answers**).

16.2 Developing operations

LEARNING SUMMARY

After studying this section, you should be able to:

- distinguish between different forms of research and development
- explain the importance of research and development to organisations

The nature of research and development

AQA	**M2**	WJEC	**M2**
Edexcel	**M2a**	CCEA	**M1**
OCR	**M2, M6**		

Research explores the possibility of making new products and using new processes.

Development turns this research into the new product or process.

Research and development (**R&D**) can be analysed into:

- **pure** research – original research to gain new knowledge or understanding, i.e. there is no obvious immediate commercial application
- **applied** research – also original research, but which has a practical application or aim in mind
- **development expenditure** – to produce new or substantially improved products or systems before starting commercial production.

Applied research often focuses on improving an existing product or system.

Since large companies spend significant amounts on these activities, R&D is often a major cost. Accountants either write off the R&D expenditure as an **expense**, or carry it forward as an **asset** and include it in the company's balance sheet. Some development costs may be treated as capital expenditure and are offset against future revenues associated with the project, enabling its cost to be spread over a number of accounting periods.

The research and development procedure

R&D is often associated with **new product development**. The typical R&D procedure is shown on the next page.

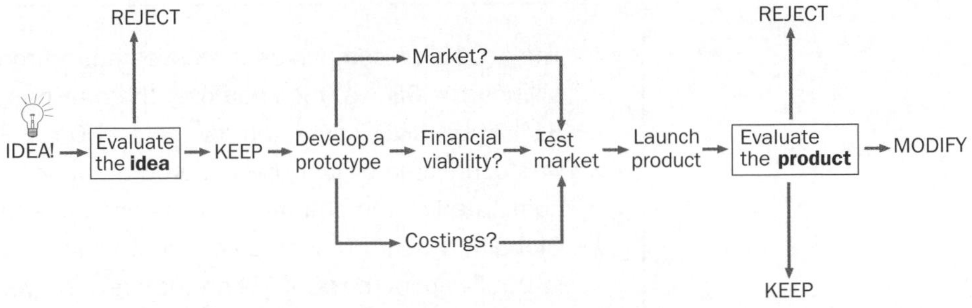

Figure 16.3 The R&D procedure

KEY POINT

The R&D procedure may be halted at any time, because failure does not occur only at the start or end of this procedure.

The importance of research and development

AQA **M2** WJEC **M2**
Edexcel **M2a** CCEA **M1**
OCR **M2, M6**

In 2010, the Grant for Research and Development helped individuals and SMEs in England (the other home countries ran equivalent schemes).

The UK government encourages business innovation and R&D projects. It offers information and advice, and some businesses may be eligible to apply for financial support in the form of an R&D grant. These grants cover research and development of new technologies and innovative products or processes.

In 2008, the UK's gross domestic expenditure on R&D was £25.6 billion, about 1.8 percent of gross domestic product (GDP) (see Figure 16.4 below).

Gross domestic expenditure on R&D, 2002–2008

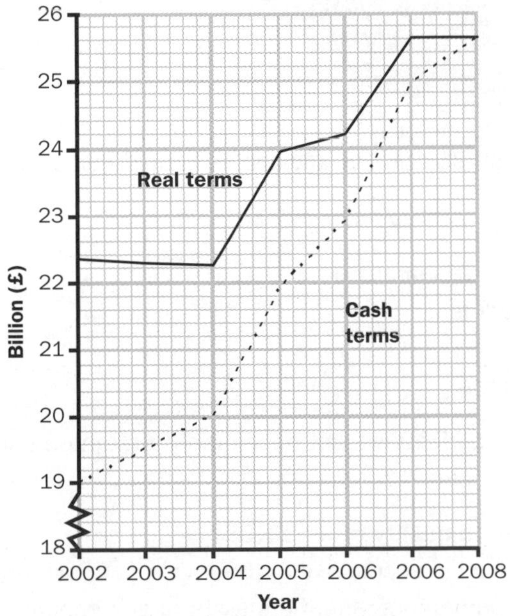

Sector carrying out the R&D work, 2008

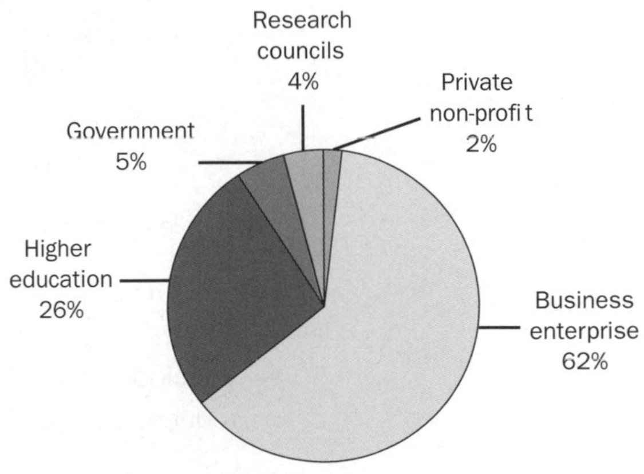

Source: ONS

Figure 16.4 R&D in the UK, 2002–2008

The UK government is keen to ensure that businesses invest sufficiently in R&D to ensure an international **competitive advantage**. The Department for Business Innovation & Skills monitors R&D investment and issues an annual **R&D Scoreboard**.

- The 1,000 UK companies that invested the most in R&D spent £26.6 billion in 2008 – a 9.2% rise over the previous year.
- 81% of UK R&D, carried out by the 1,000 top R&D investing companies, was conducted by just one hundred of these companies, and is dominated by the pharmaceuticals and biotechnology sector.
- Globally, the 1,000 companies most active in R&D invested £396 billion in 2008, an increase of 7% on the previous year. The 46 UK companies in this group increased their R&D spend at a faster rate (11.1%).
- 80% of investment in R&D by the global 1,000 companies occurs in five countries: the US, Japan, Germany, France and the UK.

Extract from the 2009 R&D Scoreboard (Department for Business Innovation & Skills)

Pharmaceuticals and biotechnology is the biggest UK sector by spend (37 percent), with aerospace and defence, software, and automobiles and parts each having a 6 percent share.

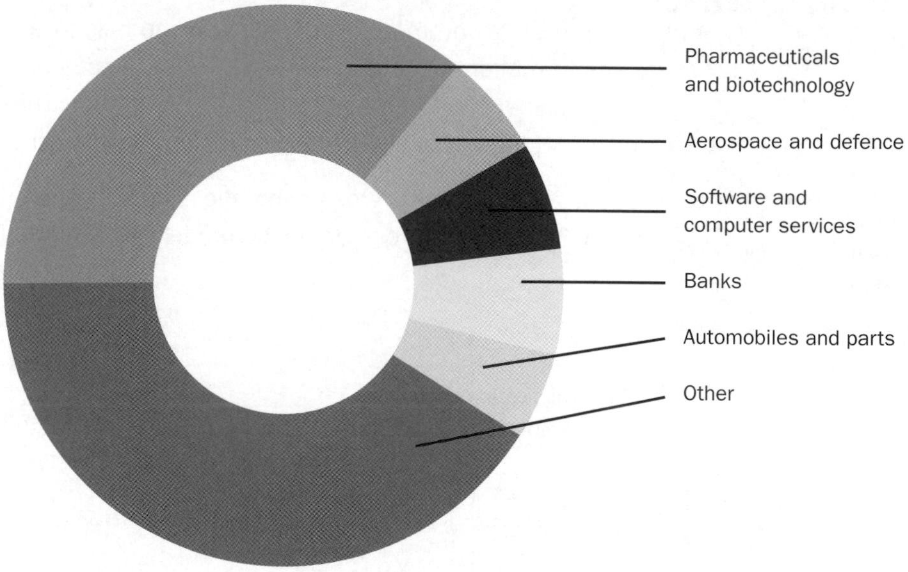

Figure 16.5 Distribution of UK 100 R&D expenditure (2008, %)

Does investment in R&D guarantee success?

A lack of R&D investment may lead to:

- slower product development
- a lack of innovation
- reduced competitiveness.

However, greater spending on R&D will not necessarily guarantee success.

This is because:

- it does not guarantee the **quality** of the R&D
- other factors are involved in success, e.g. the level of competition, exchange rate fluctuations for competitors, and the effects of government legislation.

An example of research and development

The A380 illustrates the economy of increased dimensions.

The growth in air travel in recent years encouraged investment in R&D. Airbus designed its new A380 'jumbo' at a substantial development cost, estimated to be in the region of £10 billion. Although only two metres longer than the best-selling Boeing 747, the Airbus saves on fuel costs and does not require a longer runway. The A380 is the largest jet airliner ever built and the world's first 'double-decker' passenger aircraft. It entered service in 2007 with Singapore Airlines.

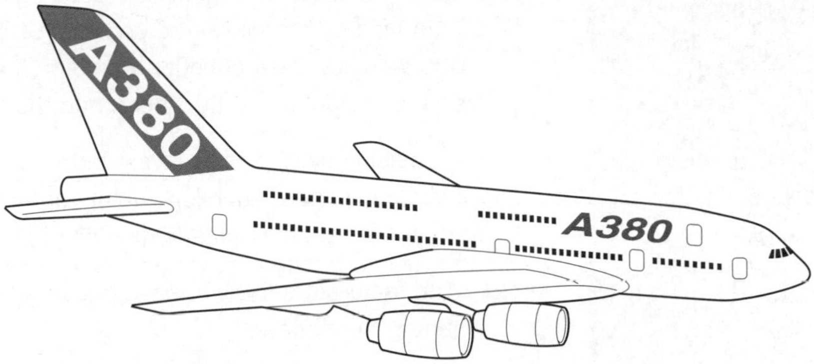

	Airbus A380	Boeing 747
Seating capacity	555 (up to 830)	up to 400
Length	72.9 metres	71 metres
Height	24.1 metres	19.4 metres
Range	8 000 miles	8 000 miles

Figure 16.6 The Airbus A380

Protecting the results of research and development

R&D may result in a profitable new product or system, i.e. some form of **invention** that will give the company a competitive advantage.

To defend its invention, the organisation may:

- establish a **patent** (the sole right to use the invention)
- register the **design**
- register a **trade mark** – the feature that distinguishes the firm or its products from its competitors.

KEY POINT

If R&D is ignored, the firm risks losing future sales by over concentrating on present sales.

PROGRESS CHECK

1. Why is the level of R&D expenditure of interest to **(a)** an individual firm and **(b)** the government?

1 **(a)** It indicates the financial investment in the firm's future **(b)** for comparison against international R&D investment rates.

Sample question and model answer

1. Read this article and answer the questions that follow.

Nissan in the north-east

In the 1990s a new industry – vehicles – grew up in the north-east of England, centred on Nissan's purpose-built production plant in Sunderland. Nissan invested some £700 million, and employed about 5 000 workers. Its production was aimed at both the UK and export markets, including the EU, Japan and the Far East.

The decision by Nissan to invest led to a development in the region of vehicle component suppliers. Joint ventures were also set up to produce components such as plastic mouldings, tyres and car seats.

(a) What factors are likely to have encouraged Nissan to establish its plant in Sunderland? **(6)**

(a) It is likely that Nissan was offered some financial incentive by the British Government to locate in the north-east. This is because the area has suffered from a lack of investment, and there was high unemployment there. It doesn't mean, however, that the workers in the region have the relevant skills for Nissan, so it may need to do a lot of training. Since Nissan is an exporter, it would have wanted to make sure it could export its vehicles easily, so transport lines and general communication lines needed to be good. This also applies when importing its raw materials. Finally, Nissan would have considered where its suppliers are based, perhaps being influenced by the UK's history of making vehicles and building the components to go in them.

Valid points are made, but the decline in the traditional industries (e.g. mining and shipbuilding) could also be mentioned as supporting evidence. Also, the fact that Nissan produced vehicles in the UK meant that, as a member of the EU, the Common External Tariff would be avoided when exporting to other EU countries.

(b) Nissan decided to produce in the UK for export, rather than establishing plants in several other countries where it planned to sell its vehicles. Examine the benefits and drawbacks of this approach. **(8)**

(b) Nissan gains from economies of scale. A single plant is capable of greater mass production, so unit costs could well be lower than if it had several factories making the same vehicles. These economies would include technical economies, such as using specialist equipment like welding equipment or computerised robots doing some assembly tasks. Also, financial economies, marketing economies and purchasing economies are likely to exist.

The answer ignores the drawbacks and also would be strengthened by providing more illustrations, e.g. borrowing at lower cost (financial), centralised marketing function is less costly than one at each plant (marketing), and bulk-buying (purchasing).

(c) What factors would influence Nissan's decision to 'buy-in' components rather than to make them itself? **(6)**

(c) By making the components itself, Nissan has greater control. It can also reduce costs, because the suppliers have the expertise and can make the components efficiently, store them for Nissan, and deliver them when needed. There are likely to be hundreds of different components in a vehicle, so it would be very complicated for Nissan to co-ordinate all this production. The problem it may have faced involves ensuring the quality of what the suppliers are making. Also, failure by one supplier could halt production.

The answer could refer to the strengths and weaknesses of the 'just-in-time' approach, and also to Nissan avoiding some other (e.g. R&D) costs, which could be borne by the component suppliers.

Exam practice question

1 **(a)** Outline three factors that an entrepreneur should consider when deciding where to locate a business. **(6)**

(b) Which of these factors will be important for a multinational vehicle producer? Give reasons for your answer. **(8)**

17 Organising production

The following topics are covered in this chapter:

- **Organising production**
- **Lean production**
- **Critical path analysis**

17.1 Organising production

LEARNING SUMMARY

After studying this section, you should be able to:

- compare the characteristics of job, batch and flow production
- assess the relevance of these production methods to business

Methods of organising production

AQA	**M2**
Edexcel	**M2a**
OCR	**M2, M6**
WJEC	**M1, M2**
CCEA	**M1**

Job production

Production of goods and services is either **intermittent** or **continuous** in nature.

Job production involves the output of a **single product** to **individual specifications**. Examples include the construction of a single machine tool, a ship, the Millennium Dome and the Severn Bridge. Firms using job production have to estimate accurately the 'three Cs' – **costs**, **cash flows** and **completion date**.

This can prove difficult. For example, in 1993 Eurotunnel had to find an extra £0.8 billion to fund the **cost** of the Channel Tunnel, and postponing the Tunnel's opening (**completion**) put an extra pressure on the company's **cash flow**.

Characteristics of job production are:

a high-priced product

made with

equipment flexible enough to meet individual job demands

used by

highly skilled and versatile labour

supervised by

centralised management

who use

techniques to plan and monitor the production process

Some jobs – such as the construction of bridges and tunnels – are very large scale and may result in the lead manufacturer **contracting out** certain tasks and activities to other firms known as **sub-contractors**.

Any firm using job production faces certain challenges:

- Employees have to be flexible and versatile because different jobs may require different skills.
- Equipment used must also be versatile.
- Economies of scale are not achievable.

Job production is therefore costly for the customer because of the highly-skilled employees, the nature of the machinery and equipment, and the lack of economies of scale. This makes job production appropriate for 'one-off' jobs and where there is not a large demand for the item.

Examples include producing batches of bread and cakes, and making a number of furniture items to the same design.

Batch production

In **batch production**, a quantity of a product is made without using a continuous production process. The characteristics are similar to job production, although unit costs are normally lower since fixed costs are spread over the number of items in the batch. The production area is often organised by grouping together similar machines and processes, such as welding and assembly.

An **economic batch quantity** (**EBQ**) can be calculated by using the same formula as economic order quantity (EOQ):

$$\mathbf{EBQ} = \sqrt{\frac{\mathbf{2bd}}{\mathbf{h}}}$$

where: b = batch setting-up costs
d = demand
h = holding costs

These are the key decisions required in batch production:

- How many items are to be made in a batch?
- In which order are the batches to be made?

Flow production

Examples include cars, TVs, washing machines and other 'white goods'.

Also known as **mass production**, **flow production** involves the output of **identical**, **standardised products** using continuous production with highly specialised inputs, each being employed continually on the same operation. Flow production relies on the support of an advanced marketing function and is associated with products having high and long-term levels of demand.

The characteristics of flow production are:

- a lower-priced product (compared with those made using job production)
- a greater proportion of semi-skilled or unskilled labour
- high capital investment costs, offset by economies of scale
- specialised plant and equipment having relatively little flexibility
- a production layout that minimises the movement of parts and sub-assemblies
- highly automated production and assembly lines
- costs being subject to standard costing and budgetary control procedures.

KEY POINT

Flow production is based on specialisation and the division of labour principle, creating surpluses that can be traded.

Compared with job production, flow production is usually more cost-effective, but this **extra productivity** means a **loss of flexibility** (of both capital and labour). Firms using mass production techniques may find it difficult to respond to changing market – and therefore production – requirements.

The drawbacks of flow production therefore include low morale arising from worker boredom, lack of flexibility of labour and machinery, and major production stoppages due to equipment failure. This has led to the Japanese-influenced development of **lean production** to eliminate wastage of materials and time, and to develop a more flexible approach.

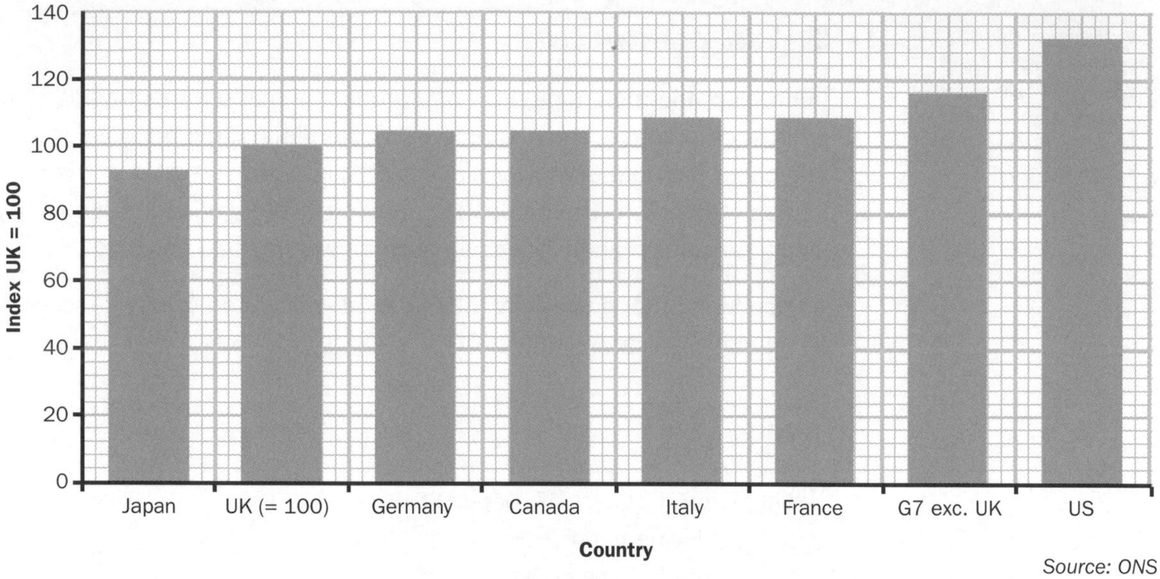

Source: ONS

Figure 17.1 International comparisons of productivity, 2008

Automation and flexible specialisation

Automation and robotics allow repetitive and dangerous jobs to be undertaken.

In flow production, the production process is divided into its separate parts, which lends itself to **automation**. Developments in computer-based technology have encouraged firms to use automation and **robotics** (using robots).

Businesses often retain those employees who are highly skilled.

Using automation improves productivity because it means that:

- equipment and machinery can operate on a '24/7' basis without breaks
- robots can undertake different tasks by being re-programmed
- **capital is substituted for labour**, leading to cost savings.

However, a substantial capital investment is needed to set up an automated production line, and industrial relations problems can be created (for example, it is likely that redundancies will occur).

A **flexible specialisation** approach argues that, since the tastes and demands of today's customers change regularly, production must be able to respond quickly and flexibly to these changes. Traditional flow-line production, with its emphasis on making a single product continuously, is not well equipped to meet this because its machines are too specialised and labour is insufficiently skilled.

Firms wishing to adopt this manufacturing approach face similar costs to when they automate. Capital investment is needed in flexible (e.g. re-programmable) machinery and equipment, and the need to develop a multi-skilled and versatile workforce means extra and improved training for existing employees (which may mean extra wage costs), as well as a review of the firm's recruitment policies of new staff.

Time-based management

Managers are encouraged to consider managing time in the same way that they manage a firm's human and physical resources.

Encouraging managers to concentrate on time-based management should lead to shortened production times (e.g. machinery set-up times), which in turn:

- reduces stockholding costs – lower stocks are held because the firm can be more responsive to market changes by having shorter production runs
- improves customer satisfaction because the firm can meet orders more quickly.

KEY POINT

The types of production system chosen normally depend on the scale of production being used, and will influence the physical layout of the production area.

PROGRESS CHECK

1 State the likely traditional production methods for the following: **(a)** six identical houses being built on a new estate **(b)** an extension to an existing house on the estate **(c)** the cars owned by the householders.

1 **(a)** batch production **(b)** job production **(c)** flow production

17.2 Lean production

LEARNING SUMMARY

After studying this section, you should be able to:

- outline the meaning of 'lean production'
- describe different ways in which lean production can be achieved
- assess the value of lean production to business

The 'lean production' approach

AQA	**M2**
Edexcel	**M2a**
OCR	**M2, M6**
WJEC	**M1, M2**
CCEA	**M1**

The **lean production** approach seeks to improve the use of a firm's productive resources in order to:

- reduce wastage, stockholding and other costs
- improve labour productivity levels
- increase capacity utilisation
- improve quality
- heighten employee morale through involvement and input.

By achieving lean production, a firm will be in a better position to respond to changes in its market. Key elements in a lean production approach include **cell production**, **continuous improvement** and **just-in-time** approaches.

KEY POINT

Products made using mass and lean production techniques are widely found in international trade. Governments will want to ensure that their industries are competitive internationally.

Cell production

A development from mass production, **cell production** is a manufacturing approach that divides a continuous production line into 'cells'– self-contained units producing an identifiable section of the finished item. In this way, staff in the cell are made to feel more involved in the firm's production.

Continuous improvement

Kaizen is a Japanese term describing the philosophy that investing in employees' views and ideas can often be more productive than investing in new equipment. The principle behind Kaizen is that there is always room for improving the quality of the work and product, or an opportunity to lower costs.

The Kaizen philosophy stresses that an employee has two jobs – carrying out the job, and also looking for ways to improve it.

Widely introduced in UK firms in the 1990s, Kaizen groups are set up throughout a firm, e.g. a shop-floor production cell may operate as a Kaizen team. These groups meet regularly to discuss production and other problems, and to offer solutions.

For Kaizen to be implemented successfully:

- employees must be willing and motivated to make contributions
- employees must be able to work in teams (such as a production cell)
- a firm's organisational culture must support its implementation.

The Kaizen philosophy is not limited to production – it is based on many small improvements being identified and implemented throughout a firm, by staff in all functions.

Quality circles may be established. This is another way of empowering employees who meet regularly with supervisors and managers to discuss (as equals) what is happening at work.

Just-in-time

The role of the **purchasing** function is to obtain the right items for the right price, to be delivered at the right time to the right place. An efficient purchasing function needs to work effectively with the suppliers of their stock.

Factors a customer needs to take into account when selecting suppliers include:

- prices offered
- payment terms
- quality of the supplied item(s)
- reliability of delivery.

The **just-in-time** (**JIT**) approach is based on the wish to reduce stockholding costs by – if possible – operating with a zero buffer stock. To do this, a firm must establish close working relationships with the suppliers, because frequent deliveries of satisfactory quality stocks are needed for JIT to function efficiently. JIT requires arranging for stock to arrive just when it is needed. As a result, there is no need to hold buffer stocks, so holding costs are cut because the firm has just enough stock for its immediate needs. The result should be lower rental cost, lower insurance, less wastage and theft.

Advantages of JIT	Disadvantages of JIT
• Holding and storage costs are cut • Fewer problems of wastage and rotation • Liquidity improves • Quicker response to market change	• Order processing costs increase • Total reliance on the supplier • Delivery problem stops production

The kanban system involves employees to a greater extent in the production process.

One feature of JIT is the **kanban** order card system. An example is where components are stored in two bins. When one is emptied, it – with its kanban card – is taken to where the component is made. The component is manufactured 'just-in-time' for when it is needed in production (as the other bin becomes empty).

KEY POINT

Successful lean production results in producing more (and making it more efficiently) by using less (i.e. fewer resources).

PROGRESS CHECK

1. How does a 'continuous improvement' approach operate?
2. Identify why 'just-in-time' production is becoming increasingly popular.

1 Teams review problems and suggest improvements, and managers adopt and review solutions with the teams.
2 Lower stockholding and other costs, less wastage, and quicker response times to market changes.

17.3 Critical path analysis

LEARNING SUMMARY

After studying this section, you should be able to:

- explain the nature and relevance to business of critical path analysis
- calculate the critical path from given information

The nature of critical path analysis

AQA	M3	WJEC	M4
Edexcel	M4a		
OCR	M6		

Critical path analysis (**CPA**), also known as **network analysis**, is used to identify the best way of scheduling a complex series of related tasks, to minimise the time taken in their completion. It is widely used in industries such as construction, to schedule the different phases of planning and building. Most new and complex projects that take some time to complete can apply CPA techniques.

CPA allows planners to:

- forecast completion time for a project
- identify
  - **EST** (earliest start time)
  - **EFT** (earliest finish time)
  - **LST** (latest start time)
  - **LFT** (latest finish time)
- highlight all stages where timing is critical – the **critical path**
- monitor progress and delays throughout a project's life
- establish in advance the precise resources required
- identify ways to overcome resourcing and/or timing problems.

The CPA plan will only be as good as the staff's commitment to it.

Stages in the construction of the network

There are six stages in the construction of the network:

1. **Subdivide the project** into its different activities. Each activity uses some resources, and takes some time to complete.
2. **Decide on the order of completion**. Some activities obviously precede others, e.g. building materials must obviously be bought before they can be used – although judgements often have to be made (for example, whether to plumb and fit a kitchen in a building before plumbing and fitting the bathroom). An activity may well depend on several preceding ones. For example, 'install heating units' depends on activities such as 'wire room', 'install floor', 'plaster room' and so on.
3. **Construct the network model** and record the activity times.
4. **Analyse the network**. This establishes the total time for the project, and the critical path through it. This is the path where any delay to the activities also delays the whole project – there is no slack time. The total slack time, or '**float**', represents the time the non-critical activities can over-run before they start delaying the project.
5. **Draw up a timetable** to schedule resources.
6. **Monitor progress** of the project by using the network.

KEY POINT

Because the CPA network of tasks is normally created by computer, the effect of changing variables such as the order in which the tasks are carried out can be evaluated.

CPA – an illustration

The directors of a company wish to buy and assemble temporary additional office space. The activities are as follows.

	Length (days)	Preceding activities
A Obtain permission	3	—
B Buy material for base	4	A
C Obtain assembly	6	A
D Lay base	3	B
E Assemble office frame	5	C
F Attach frame to base	2	D, E
G Paint frame	2	C

Each activity is identified by a node represented by a circle (see Figure 17.2). Nodes are numbered for identification, and represent the start and finish of an activity. They record the EST and LFT for each activity.

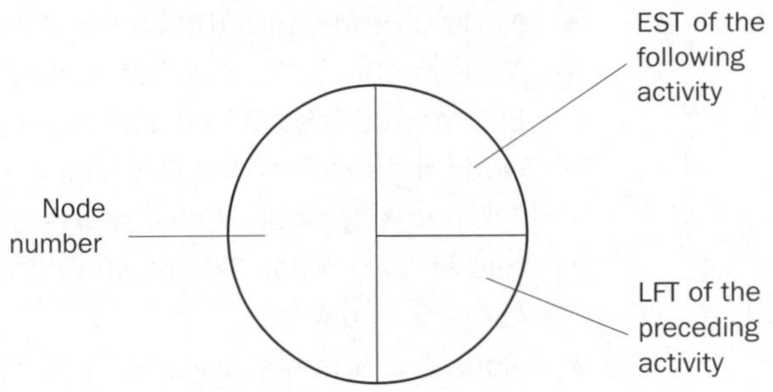

Figure 17.2 Structure of the node

Nodes are joined by arrows representing the flow of activities – the length of each arrow is not significant. Figure 17.3 shows the network model for the above activities. (In practice, the details by each arrow of the activity's name and length are usually omitted, but we show them here for reference.)

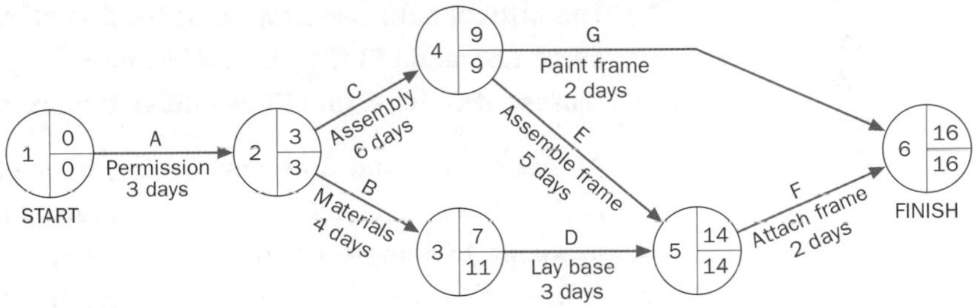

Figure 17.3 The network diagram

The EST represents the earliest date at which an activity can commence:

- Node 1 shows the start of activity A, which is day 0.
- Node 2 represents the start time for B and C. These must follow A, which takes three days to complete, so node 2 has an EST of day 3.
- Node 3 shows the start of activity D, which must follow B. B takes four days to complete, so node 3 has an EST of day 7.
- Node 4 represents the start of E and G, which follow the end of C. C takes six days, so E and G cannot start before day 9.
- Node 5 shows the start of F, which follows the end of both D and E. The earliest D can end is after ten days (EST day 7 plus three days to complete), and the earliest E can finish is day 14 (EST day 9 + five days). Activity F cannot start before both D and E are finished, so its EST is day 14.
- Node 6 ends with the finish of activities F (EST day 14 + two days) and G (EST day 9 + two days), so the whole project must take a minimum of 16 days.

The LFT represents the latest date by which an activity must be completed to avoid delaying the whole project.

Each activity's LFT is calculated by *working backwards* from the completion date:

- Node 6 represents the end of the project, so its LFT must be 16 days.
- Node 5 shows the start of activity F, which takes two days to complete. The LFT for activities D and E shown by this node is therefore (16 – 2 =) day 14.
- Node 4 starts activity G, which takes two days. The LFT is not (16 – 2) day 14, because node 4 also starts activity E. This activity takes five days and has an LFT of day 14 shown in node 5. The LFT for node 4 must be (14 – 5 =) day 9.
- Node 3 starts activity D, with an LFT of 14 shown in node 5. D takes 3 days to complete, so the LFT for activity B which precedes it is (14 – 3 =) day 11.
- Node 2 represents the LFT for activity A. Although activity B could start on day 7 (it takes 4 days and its LFT is day 11), activity C's LFT is day 9 (node 4) and it takes six days to complete. The LFT for activity A is day 3 (9 – 6).
- Node 1 represents the start of the project and has an LFT of day 0. The LFT at the start must be the same as the EST.

The critical path can now be seen. It is shown by those nodes with the same EST and LFT, i.e. 1, 2, 4, 5 and 6. Any delay in the activities they represent (A, C, E and F) will delay the project as a whole.

Activities B, D and G are non-critical because they can over-run without the project being delayed – they have 'floats' that indicate the spare time available to complete them:

- Activity B could be delayed without affecting the project. Its EST is day 3, but it could start later to meet its LFT of day 11. It has a float, which is calculated by deducting its earliest start time from its latest start time (LST – EST). The LST in turn is calculated by taking an activity's duration from its LFT. For activity B, the LST is day 7 (11 – 4); the EST is day 3; its float is four days. Eight days could therefore be taken to complete B without the project being delayed.
- Activity D also has a float of four days. Its LST is day 11 and its EST is day 7.
- Activity G has a float of five days. Its LST is day 14 and its EST is day 9.

By using CPA and establishing the critical path, managers make their planning more efficient. For example, CPA allows them to time the placing of orders, and to identify those events in a project that can be carried out simultaneously.

The **Gantt chart** is an alternative form of display – it is usually drawn as a horizontal bar chart that shows each activity as a bar against time.

As with critical path analysis, a Gantt chart indicates:

- what should have been achieved at any point in time
- what remedial action is necessary to bring a project back on time.

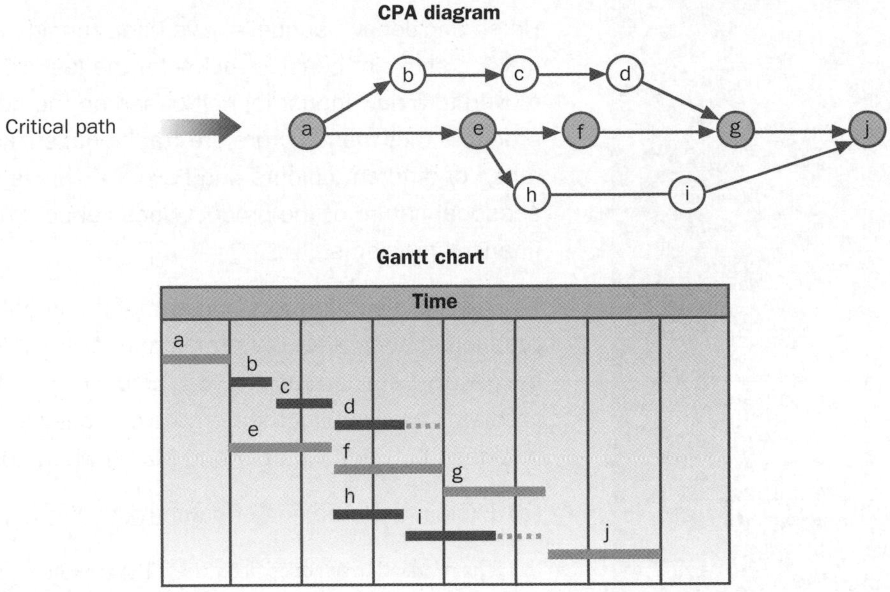

Figure 17.4 CPA diagram and Gantt chart

KEY POINT

CPA is used as a **control technique** – in particular, it controls time and working capital.

PROGRESS CHECK

1 What is the purpose of critical path analysis?

1 To show the optimum way to schedule a range of related tasks; to minimise time taken.

Sample question and model answer

1. Helen and Jenny Saunders have been running a small family company – making sticks of seaside rock – for the last 10 years. They have recently moved to a new industrial unit based on the south coast of England. The products they manufacture are traditional sticks of seaside rock in a range of different colours and flavours. This is quite profitable, although the seasonal nature of the product does cause a number of production and financial problems.

The high demand in the summer months is not a problem because they begin production soon after Christmas, steadily building up stocks. This is necessary because rock is best produced in small batches. The real problems are keeping their employees busy and ensuring funds come into the business between October and March when not much rock is sold.

(a) Explain the meaning of batch production. **(4)**

(a) *The production of goods in batches. The economic batch quantity can be calculated using a formula containing set-up costs, demand and holding costs.*

The term has not been defined, although there is some relevant knowledge about how the batch level can be calculated. The point should be made that a limited number of products are made in one go.

(b) Helen has suggested that the company produces a range of Christmas rock novelties. Discuss the implications of this proposal for the production function. **(12)**

The batch production method currently being used can also be used for the production of Christmas rock novelties. They will probably be able to use the same machinery, although the employees may need extra training to teach them to make the new products. This training may be on-the-job or off-the-job. The company will probably not be able to afford to provide much training, so they will have to do it themselves.

The main problem with batch production is that time is lost having to change the equipment to produce different products. If they are now making different rock novelties, they may find that their costs go up because they spend so much time re-setting the equipment.

The answer has two faults – the details about training are not relevant to the question, and there is poor use of the case study information. The candidate could mention that this would help fill the gap in the production run and provide extra finance. However, they will need to check demand and calculate if the extra revenue will cover the extra costs, and review whether new machinery or additional training is needed.

Exam practice questions

1 Newton Ltd supplies components used in car and van manufacture. The company's largest customer has just decided to implement a 'just-in-time' stock control policy.

(a) What is meant by 'just-in-time' in this context? **(4)**

(b) Examine the implications of this approach for both Newton Ltd and its customer. **(8)**

2 Carnival Ltd needs to plan the time required to manufacture its product, which goes through nine processes. Each process takes the following number of hours to complete:

Process	Time (hours)
A	6
B	4
C	15
D	10
E	8
F	6
G	3
H	9
I	4

(a) Complete the network to show the EST and LFT for each activity, and the critical path. **(6)**

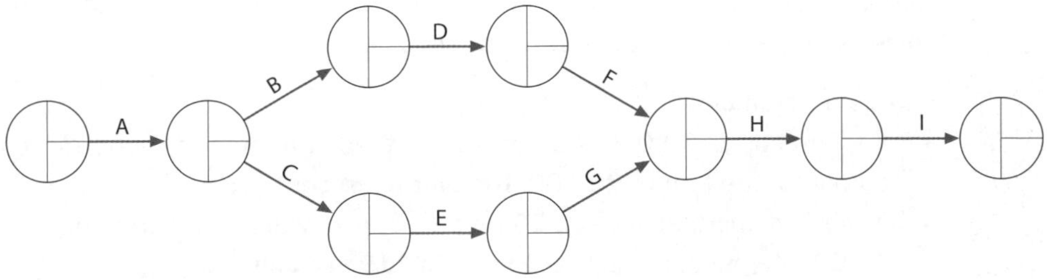

(b) Outline the advantages of using CPA. **(4)**

18 Ensuring operational efficiency

The following topics are covered in this chapter:

- Capacity utilisation
- Controlling stock
- Quality management
- Technology in production

18.1 Capacity utilisation

LEARNING SUMMARY

After studying this section you should be able to:

- calculate a firm's capacity utilisation
- explain the relevance of high and low utilisation to business

Calculating capacity utilisation

AQA	**M2**
Edexcel	**M2a**
OCR	**M2, M6, M7**
WJEC	**M2, M4**
CCEA	**M1, M4**

Capacity utilisation measures actual output as a percentage of maximum output. A firm's productive capacity is based on its **resources** – in particular, its premises, capital equipment and labour. When all are working at maximum output, the firm is operating at **full capacity** (it has 100 percent capacity utilisation).

The formula for calculating capacity utilisation is:

$$\frac{\text{Present output}}{\text{Maximum output capacity}} \times 100$$

The importance of capacity utilisation

Why is capacity utilisation important? A firm incurs fixed costs, and these do not change in the short term as output changes. **If a firm can spread these fixed costs over greater output, unit costs will fall.**

Here is an example:

- If a firm has £100 000 fixed costs and these are spread over a maximum output for the firm of 20 000, **the unit fixed cost is £5**.
- If the firm operates at, say, 50 percent capacity utilisation (an output of 10 000 items), the fixed cost **rises to £10 per unit**.

The higher the capacity utilisation, therefore, the lower unit costs should be – not just because unit fixed costs fall, but also because of economies of scale, which **reduce unit variable costs** (e.g. through bulk buying raw materials).

Working at or near full capacity can also create pressures for a firm.

There can be:

- pressure on **machinery** – e.g. maintenance is difficult because the machines are always needed for production
- pressure on **employees** – e.g. absenteeism due to increased stress caused by high workloads.

By operating at or near full capacity, a firm also finds it hard to cope with any additional work. It can achieve additional capacity, for instance by employing part-time staff (a strategy often used by particular industries, e.g. seasonal-based ones) and/or using extra capital resources (e.g. hire of machines or premises). **Work study** – the analysis of a specific job in an effort to find the most efficient method in terms of time and effort – is another way to make production more efficient.

Sub-contracting is another option, where a firm employs another business to complete part of the work. This gives some flexibility in meeting changing demand and market conditions.

Figure 18.1 illustrates **low capacity utilisation**. It was acknowledged in 2010 by the Chief Executive of Ford's European operations that the European auto industry had in the region of 35 percent over capacity.

Figure 18.1 Over capacity in Europe's car industry (excluding the UK), 2006

This low utilisation brings problems, such as either absorbing higher unit fixed costs through accepting lower profit margins, passing them on as higher selling prices, or – particularly in the car industry – offering a range of incentives (e.g. three years' free servicing) that again cut into profit margins. Whilst a firm can increase utilisation by taking measures to **boost product demand** where it has fallen temporarily, e.g. by advertising campaigns and special offers, it can also increase utilisation by **reducing excess capacity** if demand has fallen permanently. Strategies here include not replacing leavers ('natural wastage'), cutting shifts, moving to cheaper premises, or cutting fixed costs in other ways.

Reducing capacity is often called rationalisation – where major restructuring occurs with job losses, the terms downsizing or right-sizing may be used.

KEY POINT

As capacity utilisation increases, unit fixed costs fall. As capacity utilisation falls, unit fixed costs rise.

PROGRESS CHECK

1. Outline why a firm seeks to maximise its capacity utilisation.

1 So that its (fixed) costs are spread over high output to lower the unit fixed cost, and to use resources to their maximum efficiency.

18.2 Controlling stock

LEARNING SUMMARY

After studying this section, you should be able to:

- describe the main stock-related costs faced by a firm
- explain how a firm can optimise its stock control

Controlling operations

AQA **M2**
Edexcel **M2a**
OCR **M3, M6, M7**
WJEC **M2**
CCEA **M4**

Firms must hold sufficient stocks of items for a number of reasons.

Item	Reason	Costs of zero stock
Raw materials and work in progress	To meet production requirements	Idle time (worker and machine); knock-on effect of delayed production
Finished goods	To meet customer demand	Loss of goodwill and orders; financial penalties for missing deadlines
Consumables, spares, equipment	To support sales and production	Idle time (worker and machine); delayed production

Efficient stock control is based on establishing the most appropriate – or the **optimum** – stock level.

If stocks are too high, unnecessary **holding costs** will be incurred – these include operation costs for storage and stores, interest charges on the capital tied up in the stocks, insurance costs, and any costs of deterioration, obsolescence or theft. Costs of having zero stock are outlined above – these costs also apply to a firm holding too little stock. A firm faces the **opportunity cost** of being without stock, i.e. the opportunity of being able to meet an order and, possibly, losing the customer to a competitor.

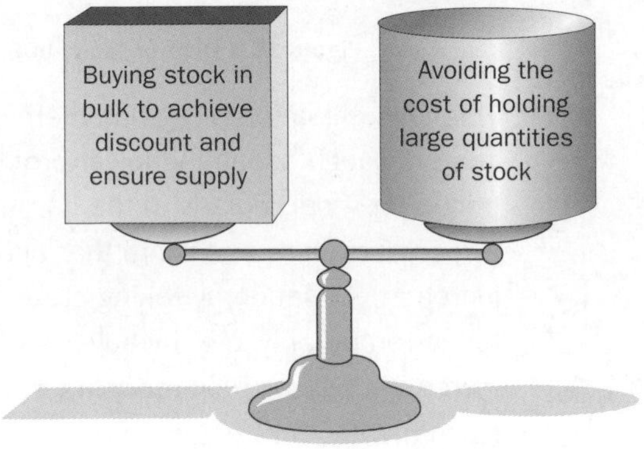

Figure 18.2 The purchasing balancing act

Firms need to **manage** their stock efficiently. The oldest stock will normally be used first (stock **rotation**), and stock **wastage** must be minimised.

Stock control calculations

There are four critical control levels used in keeping optimum stock.

1. **Reorder quantity (Economic Order Quantity or EOQ)**

$$\textbf{EOQ} = \sqrt{\frac{\mathbf{2od}}{\mathbf{h}}}$$

where o = ordering cost of item
d = (annual) demand for item
h = holding cost of 1 item per annum

If, therefore, the annual demand for an item is 5 000 units, its ordering cost is £80, and the annual unit holding cost is £5:

$$\text{EOQ} = \sqrt{\frac{2\,(80)\,(5\,000)}{5}} = 400 \text{ units}$$

This EOQ calculation is based on a number of assumptions, i.e. that:

- there is a constant demand for the stock item
- there is a constant lead time (time between placing an order and receiving it)
- stock-outs are not acceptable
- costs of making an order are constant, regardless of order size
- costs of holding stock vary proportionately with the amount of stock held.

Maximum lead time = ordering time + delivery time + inspection/ storage time.

2. **Reorder level**
This level triggers a reordering stock, and is calculated by:
Reorder level = Rate of usage × Maximum lead time

To illustrate calculating reorder level and minimum stock, assume maximum stock is 10 000, weekly usage between 2 200 and 1 800, and delivery time between 4 and 8 weeks. Re-order level is 17 600 (2 200 × 8) and minimum stock is 17 600 – (2 000 × 6) = 5 600 units.

3. **Minimum stock**
This is the **buffer** stock level, and is calculated by:
Minimum stock = Reorder level – (Average usage × Average lead time)

4. **Maximum stock**
This is a warning that the stock level is at a maximum:
Maximum stock = Reorder level + Reorder quantity – (Minimum usage x Minimum lead time)

Stock control **charts** may be constructed to show these elements visually.

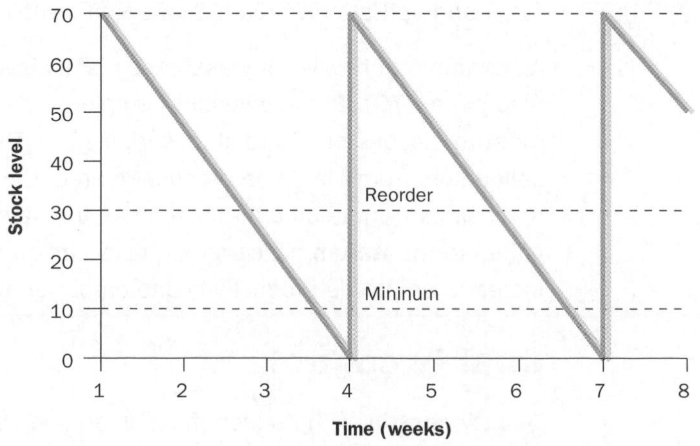

Figure 18.3 Stock control chart

Waste management is a feature of controlling stock. Entrepreneurs are increasingly aware of the significance of waste management in terms of controlling costs and meeting 'green' objectives. Efficient stock control leads to less waste and therefore more effective waste management.

PROGRESS CHECK

1. Why does a retailer such as Tesco need efficient stock control?
2. What costs are associated with a firm's stocks?

1 To minimise stockholding costs; ensure stock is available for customers as and when required.
2 Purchasing cost; opportunity cost; holding costs (wastage, obsolescence, insurance, etc.).

18.3 Quality management

LEARNING SUMMARY

After studying this section, you should be able to:

- explain why quality control is important in business
- explain how quality initiatives (such as Total Quality Management) influence the work of a firm

Developing quality

AQA	**M2**	WJEC	**M2**
Edexcel	**M2a**	CCEA	**M1**
OCR	**M3**		

The 'quality' of an organisation's products or operations varies according to the circumstances. For example, customers buying a luxury cruise are likely to expect better quality customer service than customers on a cross-channel ferry, though both expect quality in terms of issues such as safety. Businesses will adopt a '**quality culture**' appropriate to the level of good or service, and seek to give customers the quality they want. This quality culture is based on the principle that it is better to get things right from the start than to face costs and delays as a result of selling poor quality items.

Many businesses no longer pay piece work rates, because when employees are paid by pieces made they can be more concerned with quantity than quality.

Many businesses believe they can improve quality without increasing production costs, by involving the workers in **quality assurance** (**QA**). QA seeks to ensure that customer satisfaction is achieved by agreeing and implementing quality standards throughout the organisation, achieving this through quality management. Modern QA techniques rely upon employees taking responsibility for ensuring that only products of a sufficiently high standard are produced.

An example of how quality assurance is achieved is through **quality circles** (see also page 270). These consist of employee groups with a common interest, who meet to discuss quality-related work issues. The groups consist mainly of colleagues from the same production area, though they may also include specialists from related areas such as the sales and quality departments. Closely linked to the **Kaizen** philosophy, quality circles can improve product quality, and increase employee productivity and employee morale through involvement.

Quality control

Quality control, with its identification and scrapping of unsuitable output, is an important feature of production control. Traditionally carried out by quality control inspectors, a recent trend has been for employees to adopt a **self-checking**

Flow and batch production methods help manufacturers carry out quality control checks.

Quality control charts plot the percentage of defective items made over time, highlighting variations so action can be taken.

approach – this is an example of the **people-centred management** philosophy that quality is the responsibility of all employees.

The purpose of quality control is to ensure that standards are being maintained, at the very least, especially where traditional flow-line production is used.

Quality control is achieved by concentrating on:

- **preventing** problems from arising in the first place
- **detecting** quality problems before the goods reach the customer
- **correcting** problems and procedures
- **improving** quality to meet improved customer expectations.

A quality control system is based on **inspection** and testing products as they are made. A sample is normally taken, and if one from the sample proves faulty the whole batch could be scrapped. This is costly for the firm, and – because quality control relies on a sample – there is no guarantee that sampling will identify all faults. This is because faulty products that do not form part of the sample will not be identified.

Specific costs associated with quality control include the costs of:

- materials scrapped
- labour time wasted
- inspection and measurement
- rectifying poor workmanship
- lost customers due to defective products
- training employees to monitor output quality.

KEY POINT

Arguably the most important cost of quality is the loss of customer goodwill.

Quality initiatives

AQA **M2** WJEC **M2**
Edexcel **M2a** CCEA **M1**
OCR **M3**

These two examples illustrate how organisations are showing an increasing awareness of the importance of quality at all stages of their operations.

> We grew because we managed our costs prudently, listened and responded to our customers' changing needs and stayed true to our core values of Quality, Value, Service, Innovation and Trust, reminding our customers of what makes M&S different. This year we have worked hard to further improve our quality and our customers have told us they have noticed this improvement.
>
> *Extract from Chairman's overview, Marks & Spencer Annual report, 2010*

> **A continuous improvement culture**
>
> At the very core of how we operate in GKN is a culture of continuous improvement, which is reinforced through the application of Lean Enterprise techniques in our business and production processes worldwide. All sites are required to develop an annual continuous improvement plan, aligned to their business objectives, which engages every employee in driving the flow of value through the business.
>
> *Extract from GKN plc Annual Report, 2009*

Different organisations implement different quality initiatives.

ISO 9000

The general name **ISO 9000** is given to a set of standards that have been developed to provide a framework around which an organisation implements its quality management system.

The main sections of ISO 9001:2000 (the requirement standard) include:

- Quality Management System
- Management Responsibility
- Resource Management
- Product Realisation
- Measurement Analysis and Improvement.

A possible criticism of ISO 9000 is that a firm could set up and 'achieve' low quality standards.

Firms are required to document their procedures in a quality manual, and to evaluate their quality management systems.

Total Quality Management

Associated with quality circles and emphasising the importance of after-sales service, TQM emphasises the 'get it right first time' philosophy.

Total Quality Management (or **TQM**) seeks to establish a 'quality culture' that assures the quality of work of all staff at all stages of production and sale, by changing the philosophy of a business so that all employees – not only production workers – become responsible for maintaining the quality of their own work. The TQM approach establishes a framework within the business that allows quality to be achieved. It means that quality is assured at all stages, and not just checked through inspection and testing.

An example of the TQM approach is the idea of 'zero defects', which encourages employees to develop a commitment to accurate work. There may also be financial rewards for achieving zero defects.

A business that adopts the TQM philosophy is likely to:

- create a new culture that will help it survive and become more competitive
- reduce the level of waste of materials and other resources
- improve employee co-operation through establishing employee teams.

KEY POINT

Firms nowadays adopt a quality culture based on the belief that it is better to get the job done correctly in the first place than to incur the costs and delays associated with failure.

PROGRESS CHECK

1. What does a quality control system concentrate on?
2. State a difference between ISO 9000 and TQM.

1 Prevention, detection, correction, improvement.
2 ISO 9000: systems and procedures based; TQM focuses on the 'get it right first time' approach.

18.4 Technology in production

LEARNING SUMMARY

After studying this section, you should be able to:

- outline the importance of technology in the production process
- explain the ways in which technology makes production more efficient

Technology in production

AQA	**M2**	WJEC	**M2**
Edexcel	**M2a**	CCEA	**M4**
OCR	**M7**		

The role of the production function is to turn input into output as efficiently as possible – this is a measure of a firm's **productivity**.

Labour productivity is the most common measure – falling productivity makes a firm, industry or country uncompetitive, whereas rising productivity improves competitiveness. One problem with rising labour productivity is that it may lead to job losses, since fewer employees are now needed to produce the same output.

It is also important for a firm's **capital** to be productive. Computer technology has encouraged manufacturers to change the way they produce goods and has led to increased efficiency in production. These changes increase productivity as a result of improving efficiency or by reducing the number of employees required in the production process.

Many firms benefit from using new technologies in the production process:

- **Computer-aided design** (**CAD**) packages generate efficient product designs that can be altered immediately, e.g. using light pens or touch-sensitive screens. 3D designs can be produced and studied without the need to redraw the design each time a change is made.
- **Computer-aided manufacture** (**CAM**) uses and links robotics and other forms of automation, using the designs produced by CAD to program Computer Numerically Controlled – CNC – manufacturing machinery.
- **Computer-integrated manufacture** (**CIM**) takes this further by getting computers to control most – or all – of the production process. Robots carry out the manufacturing, being faster, providing greater consistency of output and integrating all aspects of production, e.g. linking production control with stock ordering.

When capital is substituted for labour, whilst a firm's productivity and efficiency may improve, there is a corresponding social cost of increased unemployment.

KEY POINT

CAD, CAM and CIM allow design and manufacture to progress efficiently, and provide valuable data that is used to make production more efficient.

PROGRESS CHECK

1 How can technological developments improve productive efficiency?

1 CAD improves design efficiency, CAM improves manufacturing efficiency, CIM integrates all aspects of production efficiently.

Sample questions and model answers

The examiner expects a definition plus a brief expansion, but make sure you place JIT in the context of mass production.

The question states that only a brief answer is required, and this answer is suitable in both detail and length.

A strong answer. Recognition that this is a small company is a good use of context.

Another strong answer, concentrating on two alternatives and presenting arguments for and against.

1. (a) What is meant by 'just-in-time' production? **(3)**

(a) 'Just-in-time' is associated with mass (or 'flow') production and is where stockholding is reduced to amounts required to just meet production demand. Tight delivery schedules are set, which may involve delivering the stock only hours or even minutes before it is needed.

(b) Outline briefly the benefit to be gained by firms from using this approach. **(5)**

(b) A company should find that its cash flows are improved because less stock is held, and wastage, obsolescence and the other stockholding costs are reduced. The customer gains from lower prices since the company can be more price competitive; the company's sales and market share should therefore increase.

2. Hollingworth Fabrics Ltd is a fast-growing family business that makes toys from pieces of material that are stitched together by hand into animal shapes. The Operations Director has just heard that an order placed by a large toy store has been returned owing to faulty stitching. She is concerned because this is the third order returned in a month, by different customers. The Director feels that it may be time to replace the traditional method of quality control at the end of the production line.

(a) Explain two likely costs of poor quality control for Hollingworth Fabrics Ltd. **(6)**

One cost of poor quality control is the effect on the company's reputation. Any adverse publicity that may occur will be particularly bad for a small company such as Hollingworth Fabrics Ltd, as they will rely on 'word of mouth' to gain orders. If a potential customer finds out about these returned products, they may be reluctant to order from this company themselves.

A second cost will be that of re-working the returned products to bring them up to a saleable standard. Not only will profits decrease, there is the possible knock-on effect of delaying other orders. Because the toys are handmade, employees will have to spend a lot of time concentrating on the returned products rather than producing new ones.

(b) Assess possible quality control methods that the Operations Director could implement. **(8)**

One possible system could be to introduce random checks at all stages of production. However, the fact that the present quality control system is not working may suggest this system will not work. An alternative is to introduce a system of Quality Assurance, maybe as part of a TQM strategy. It may be that the material received from the supplier is in a poor state - if quality control takes place at the end of the line, this fault will not be noticed until all the work has been done.

If each employee is given responsibility for quality, this will not only increase the amount of quality checking taking place, but also make employees feel more involved in the company and therefore will increase their motivation and sense of commitment.

Exam practice question

1 'An organisation in the 21st century cannot hope to succeed without effective use of ICT.'

Discuss this statement. **(8)**

Exam practice answers

Chapter 1 The business environment

(a) The 'number of employees' is only one of several indicators that can be used to measure a firm's size. The 'number of employees' may give a misleading indication of size for the following reasons:
- Some industries (e.g. chemicals) are capital-intensive and others (e.g. tourism) are labour-intensive – firms that are the same size when measured by, say, capital employed or turnover, can have greatly differing employee levels.
- Within a single industry, the level of technology varies – a firm replacing labour with capital might be growing and yet have a falling number of employees.
- 'Employees' needs defining because one firm might include only productive and direct support (office) employees, whereas another could count part-time staff, cleaners, etc. (there can be a lack of consistency in whom to include).
- Some industries (e.g. agriculture, tourism) face large seasonal fluctuations in their workforce – when does the count take place?

(b) The small-firm sector remains important because it:
- contributes to the UK's balance of payments through exporting
- often provides service support to larger firms
- can adapt and respond quickly to changing conditions
- fills gaps in the economy where larger firms may not operate (e.g. meeting local demand)
- may act as a 'seed-bed' of ideas and developments.

Chapter 2 Size and growth

(a) Demon Drinks plc: technical – use of technologically advanced machinery to make the drinks reduces costs per drink; LeisurePleasure: purchasing – centralised purchasing of commodities (e.g. soap and towels) used in all leisure centres allows bulk-buying discounts.

(b) Reduced costs for transport and communications (more efficient, single location); reduced production costs likely (more modern machinery); temporary increase in staff costs (e.g. redundancy payments, training or re-training to use the new machines).

(c) External growth rather than internal, known as Conglomerate (or lateral), because the two businesses operate in different markets – drinks and leisure activities – and not in the same industry.

Chapter 3 Business goals and strategy

(a) Their skills may be in high demand and in short supply – as a result, the price of their labour will be high. They provide leadership for a company, e.g. representing it in its relationships with the outside world at meetings with the media and shareholders – they also represent it internally when liaising with unions or employees. They provide motivation for internal (e.g. employee) and external (e.g. shareholder) groups, through effective leadership, establishment and communication of the company's policy. They set the company's strategic plan, and help translate it into achievable objectives.

(b) A democratic management style normally creates motivated employees, and encourages them to work harder. There is likely to be good communication, and the directors will be in a position to explain their high incomes – with a democratic role, they would probably be expected to justify these incomes. The democratic style normally means that employees are aware of the organisation's objectives – these objectives should support the sort of pay discrepancies that occur when directors receive high pay. Some employees may find the existence of highly paid directors de-motivating, and this could influence their work and be communicated through the hierarchy/chain of command.

Chapter 4 International business

(a) A fall in the value of sterling means that imports become more expensive and exports less expensive. RedShed Ltd faces extra costs for its raw materials – if it decides to pass on these costs it will increase the price of the buildings. However, it might be able to do this since the product's export price becomes more competitive due to the fall in sterling.

(b) Protectionism could mean the UK's balance of payments improves by discouraging imports and encouraging the sale of home-produced goods. It also helps safeguard home industries and therefore employment (the UK has relatively high wage levels and other production costs and finds it difficult to compete with low-cost economies), and newer industries are also protected. Protectionism helps avoid unfair competitive practices such as dumping. However, free trade is discouraged, so UK consumers will be restricted in the choice of products, and may face higher prices because of less competition. The owner is likely to be wrong because RedShed exports its finished products, and the importing countries may retaliate by adopting their own protectionist measures, thereby reducing RedShed's sales.

Chapter 5 External influences (1)

The British government will wish to see jobs remain through companies such as Ford and Vauxhall staying in the UK, and new jobs created by other firms setting up manufacturing plants in the UK. These companies do not only provide direct employment; they purchase items they require – for manufacture, food and drink for employees, etc. – from component and other firms, and so support employment elsewhere. A fall in employment, e.g. through Ford or Vauxhall moving production overseas, increases demand on the 'public purse' (unemployment and other benefits being paid). At the same time, the government's tax income – from corporation (profits) tax, and income tax from employees – would fall. If the companies move production overseas, this will also adversely affect the UK's balance of payments position, through both increasing imports and losing exports.

Chapter 6 External influences (2)

(a) **Finance**: investment in 'environmentally friendly' equipment; possible cash flow problems.
Human resources: employee training; greater employee awareness; increased public relations responsibility. **Marketing**: influencing advertising/selling policy; the need to create consumer awareness of changes; alterations in packaging policy. **Operations management (production)**: lower economies of scale; products less standardised in nature; increased production costs; more expensive quality control; manufacturing with new materials; discontinuing some processes and ingredients adds to research and development costs.

(b) Social costs: costs borne by the community through the actions of the firm; increased pollution through burning. **Financial costs:** capital expenditure (purchase of machinery); revenue expenditure (depreciation of machinery, wages to operate it, maintenance, etc.). **Opportunity cost**: the cost of the alternatives required to land fill; and the cost to the firm of buying the machinery (this capital expenditure is not available for different uses).

Chapter 7 Markets and marketing

(a) (i) The company is analysing the existing products in the market and placing its product on the basis of at least two key characteristics, such as price and image.

(ii) The consumers at whom the company is aiming its product or service.

(iii) The company examines its overall market to study the types of consumers who are buying its products, and then breaks it up (segments it) into different parts on this basis.

(b) (i) Such a strategy involves developing new products for new markets.

(ii) By developing a differentiated marketing strategy, TJE Ltd will get involved in other markets/segments. Benefits of differentiation include reducing risk by diversifying into new products and new markets/different market segments. There will be a cost consideration, because market research will be required. Linked to this is whether TJE Ltd is already producing a range of products that will appeal to different segments. If not, it will need to commit resources, e.g. to new product development. New products and new segments will require the company to consider its pricing strategy, to see what extent its current pricing strategy is suitable for the new segments and products. TJE Ltd also needs to examine its existing 'place' strategy, e.g. different channels of distribution may be required. There is also the effect on other business functions (e.g. new staff needed, new production processes, new suppliers, the need to seek advice from government, e.g. on exporting).

Chapter 8 Market research and analysis

(a) Diversifying should help Colman's sell more products and therefore increase profits. It enables Colman's to target its marketing at different groups. Risk is spread because of the wider product portfolio. Niche markets may be developed.

(b) Benefits: market research should help identify trends and other market movements, to which Colman's can respond. Marketing decisions are based on information, some of which is likely to be quantitative and can therefore be analysed statistically. Resources can therefore be assigned to relevant business areas. There is less chance of failure of new products, which are costly and risky to launch.

Limitations: many new products still fail, and any new Colman's product is therefore not guaranteed to succeed. The primary research may be limited or inaccurate, e.g. because of too small a sample size or an inappropriate sampling method. Secondary research used may be inappropriate or out of date. Economic conditions in the market will change, over which Colman's has no control.

Conclusion: although market research will help Colman's in many ways, it cannot guarantee success.

Chapter 9 The marketing mix

Product: this becomes 'right' through, for example, ensuring it is functional (meets customer requirements); using consumer tasting panels at the market research stage; creating an innovative rather than an imitative product; ensuring hygiene/food safety during the production process; differentiating, e.g. through packaging, ensuring appearance meets consumer expectations; using the company's good brand name.

Price: this becomes 'right' by, for example, reviewing customer expectations; checking against rival and own-product range prices; comparing proposed price against costs to ensure profit; deciding whether to penetrate or (if 'unique') cream/skim the market; adopting psychological pricing strategy, e.g. sell at £1.95 rather than £2.

Promotion: this becomes 'right' through, for example, suitable advertising media (e.g. target children's TV programmes); balancing informative (e.g. healthy ingredients) and persuasive elements in the message; sales promotion, e.g. product tasting in selected stores, free small pack with an established Kellogg's cereal product for children, ensuring point-of-sale or other displays are created.

Place: this becomes 'right' by, for example, negotiating with major retailers about how it is to be distributed; ensuring efficient distribution from the factory; ensuring it is displayed in the stores.

Chapter 10 Business organisation and communication

(a) There is a relatively narrow span of control of four subordinates at each level of the hierarchy. As a result, there are up to five levels in parts of the hierarchy, representing only 32 employees or employee groups below the Managing Director. This suggests that there may be over-long lines of formal communication through the chain of command, leading to potential problems created by the 'distance' between top and bottom in the hierarchy. A narrow span of control is also sometimes associated with bureaucratic procedures, autocratic and impersonal management, and poor levels of morale.

There is a discrepancy between Marketing and other departments. There are additional levels in Marketing, which is surprising given the nature of the business. A food processing manufacturer is likely to use flow-line production. Given this, and the fact that the company is located on five sites, with a plant manager for each site, the Operations Department would normally have at least as long a hierarchy as Marketing, so the existing structure should be reviewed.

(b) (i) There could be several reasons for the conflict between the managers. For example, a personality clash may exist (solutions include team-based training or a re-allocation of duties); there seems to be lack of personal contact, given the use of memos rather than face-to-face discussions (solutions include reviewing formal communication systems, e.g. number of – and attendance at – meetings). Another reason may be that, due to poor formal or informal communications, the Managing Director is not aware of this problem (solution again may be to review communication); if he/she is aware, this indicates poor leadership

Exam practice answers

(solution is for Board to review appointments and leadership). Another reason may be that the firm is overstretched, because it is based on a number of sites.

(ii) Management will have to review its location and its internal structure (e.g. consider removing Research and Development from under the control of Operations).

(c) Re-organisation could take place as follows: The firm may become task-based, and therefore operate using a matrix-based structure rather than its present, traditional, role-based one. It could base its organisation on its products or it may base the restructuring on geographical area, since it operates on more than one site. Whatever restructuring format is adopted is likely to increase the importance of the Operations element, given the nature of the firm (see Part **(a)** of this question).

Chapter 11 People in organisations

1. (a) For employers, there will be enhanced performance at work by staff; as a result, costs should fall/output should rise. Staff are also likely to be more loyal, thereby reducing labour turnover and associated costs.

(b) For employees, it should be easier to accommodate work and domestic/leisure time, thereby improving motivation and commitment, and possibly leading to higher pay (e.g. through greater efficiency).

2. (a) This may lead to poor morale and motivation, reducing productivity. Reduced quality output will damage sales and profits. Increased labour turnover is likely, increasing future recruitment and training costs.

(b) Better workforce planning increases the flexibility of the workforce. This will improve the firm's ability to forecast the supply of – and demand for – labour. Recruitment methods may need changing to identify potential workers with more appropriate/flexible skills. More training is necessary to increase employee skill levels and prepare them for change.

Chapter 12 Employer–employee relations

Shareholder and profit-sharing schemes bring with them the feeling of greater involvement – owning a share of the firm's success and having a direct benefit (profit) from direct involvement (work). However, like all financial rewards, these schemes are of limited motivational value only, since theorists such as Maslow and Herzberg have identified the importance of non-financial factors in motivating staff. Large companies such as Tesco acknowledge this, using other motivational approaches such as job enrichment.

Chapter 13 Accounting for finance

(a) (i) Gearing refers to the relationship between 'prior charge' capital (the 'fixed-interest' capital such as debentures and other long-term loans, and preference shares) and equity (ordinary shares). A highly-geared company is one having over 50 percent prior charge capital.

(ii) $\frac{3\ 000\ 000}{15\ 000\ 000} \times 100 = 20\%$

(b) I would be happy with the level of gearing. Homespun plc is a low-geared company and therefore loses comparatively small amounts of its income in the form of interest payments. This means there will be more net profit available for the ordinary shareholders. Also, the company is a relatively low-risk business in which to invest, because it has to meet relatively small interest payments, and so there is less chance that it will face financial difficulty through not being able to pay interest.

(c) By finding an additional £2 million loan finance, Homespun plc's gearing ratio will change: £5 million as a percentage of £17 million (29.4 percent). The ratio still shows it as a 'low-geared' business, and so the risk factor hasn't increased substantially, although this ratio should be benchmarked against the industry average. If the alternative is to issue ordinary shares, as things stand the company cannot make an additional issue (Issued Capital = Authorised Capital) – it would need to increase the amount of its authorised capital. Issuing additional ordinary shares risks losing an element of control, since the ordinary shareholders can vote – debenture holders, as lenders, don't have such a direct control in the company's affairs. Another benefit to the company is that debenture interest is paid out of untaxed (gross) profit, whereas ordinary share dividends have to be paid from taxed net profit. The drawbacks of issuing debentures are that the company's commitment to paying interest is increased substantially – interest payments would, apparently, almost double. The company would need to check its interest cover ratio to establish by how many times its operating profit (profit before interest and tax) 'covered' its interest payments. There is a requirement to repay debenture capital in the future – this is not so with ordinary shares – and therefore the company will need to take this into account.

Chapter 14 Budgeting and forecasting

1. The act of going through the budgeting process will encourage Leigh and Steve to co-ordinate the various business activities, and will provide the main element of financial control they will need, especially considering their plans to expand. Since budgeting provides a financial plan of the business's future, it could help Leigh and Steve by indicating the capital cost of the proposed new premises and machinery, and the cost of wages/salaries for the new staff. 'Rent or buy' decisions will have to be made regarding the premises and machinery, i.e. whether capital or revenue expenditure is involved. The budget (e.g. a cash flow forecast) will provide a clear indication of the cash flows involved, when financing is required, and the level of that finance. This in turn will suggest an appropriate source for the finance.

2. (a) £8: workings £20 – (£2 + £8 + £2)

(b) Quantity of 37 500: workings £300 000 / £8. Sales revenue of £750 000 (37 500 × £20).

(c) 42 500 (80 000 – 37 500) is the margin of safety.

(d) Unit variable cost is £12; unit fixed cost is £300 000 / 80 000 = £3.75; so unit standard cost = £12 + £3.75 = £15.75.

Chapter 15 Financial decision-making

Numerical factors: FastWare has the 20 000 spare capacity required; there is a contribution of £1 per pair of shoes (£13 less £12 unit costs), which will cover the cost of the machine. It will therefore break even with the order.

Non-numerical factors: there is a benefit from using the spare capacity (e.g. fixed costs are spread over more output); it may lead to additional work for the firm; the firm may be able to make effective future use of the new machine. However, the 'own label' product will compete with Fastware's own product – other customers may find out and expect lower prices.

Chapter 16 Locating and developing operations

(a) Availability and cost of resources – e.g. whether suitable land is available, whether there is suitably skilled labour (and costs); suitability of the infrastructure (e.g. transport/accessibility, also broadband access); whether government incentives are available (e.g. Assisted Areas and grants).

(b) At least two of the three are relevant – a vehicle manufacturer needs sufficient land for the factory/offices, and requires a pool of labour with appropriate skills (e.g. welding, engine assembly, testing); accessibility is important due to the need to transport the vehicles to their final destinations (nationally and possibly internationally) and the need to access appropriate ICT facilities; government assistance may not be relevant, though it would be welcome in terms of (e.g.) financial benefits.

Chapter 17 Organising production

1. (a) Just-in-time' (JIT) suggests that the customer is reducing stockholding to amounts required to meet demand, possibly even operating with a zero buffer stock.

(b) Newton Ltd could improve cash flow and reduce costs from waste, obsolete stock and storage space, because the customer requires regular, smaller amounts of stock. Closer links with the customer are likely; the efficiency of Newton Ltd's stock recording systems will need reviewing. Newton Ltd must ensure the customer's demands can be met and whether it can meet any short-term requests for stock from the customer. The customer also gains from lower costs (and lower costs possibly being passed on by Newton Ltd), but faces a greater chance of Newton Ltd or another supplier not being able to meet orders on time, especially unexpected ones.

2 (a)

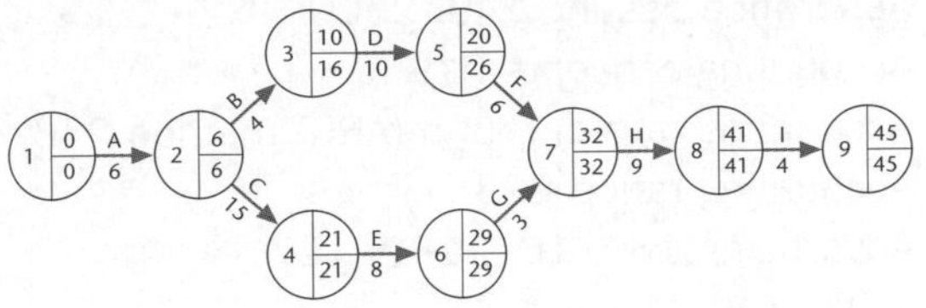

Activity	Duration	EST	LFT
A	6	0	6
B	4	6	16
C	15	6	21
D	10	10	26
E	8	21	29
F	6	20	32
G	3	29	32
H	9	32	41
I	4	41	45

The critical path is where EST = LFT, i.e. nodes 1, 2, 4, 6, 7, 8, 9.

(b) The 'critical time', i.e. where there is no slack production time, is now known. Any time lost in any of these processes will affect the overall time spent in production. This allows the firm to prioritise and to ensure the processes run smoothly. Efficiency is therefore improved.

Chapter 18 Ensuring operational efficiency

ICT's importance is recognised, e.g. in making communication more efficient and in providing tools (e.g. spreadsheets) to assist decision making. For example, ICT brings almost instantaneous information into the business, and the speed and power of computer-based applications software means it can be used to quickly translate data into meaningful information. As a result, a firm may gain a competitive advantage.

ICT has a role to play in all functional areas, e.g. marketing (databases for market research), finance (analysis of variances), purchasing (calculation of EOQ), and production (scheduling of production runs).

Two limitations need considering: **(a)** it is only a support tool, and cannot by itself make decisions and solve problems; and **(b)** how efficient the firm's ICT system is depends on factors such as correct selection of hardware/software, efficient installation, suitable technical support, and adequate staff training in its use.

Index

Index

Acknowledgements

Page 20 Text reproduced with kind permission of DOGS TRUST, the UK's biggest dog welfare charity, www.dogstrust.org.uk, 020 7837 0006, 17 Wakley Street, London, EC1V 7RQ

Pages 22, 64, 71, 87, 88, 186, 187, 268 Reproduced from the Office of National Statistics (www.ons.gov.uk). Crown Copyright material is reproduced with the permission of the Office of Public Sector Information (OPSI). Reproduced under the terms of the Click-Use Licence C2010002191

Page 30 Text reproduced with kind permission from Card Connection, a trading division of UK Greeting Limited

Page 31 Text reproduced with kind permission from John Lewis Partnership

Pages 33, 103, 126 Text from WM Morrison Supermarket PLC

Pages 39, 65, 126, 138, 165, 209 Thanks to Tesco Stores Limited for permission to reproduce this text

Pages 50, 111 Text from the Body Shop website

Pages 64, 173 Text from Sainsbury's Supermarkets Ltd

Page 77, 93, 95, 106 Source or tables adapted from Eurostat © European Communities, 1995–2010

Pages 87, 190, 200, 212, 283 Text reproduced with kind permission from Marks and Spencer

Page 98 Text from bis.gov.uk. Crown Copyright material is reproduced with the permission of the Office of Public Sector Information (OPSI). Reproduced under the terms of the Click-Use Licence C2010002191

Page 108 Text reproduced from the Office of Fair Trading, www.oft.gov.uk

Page 124 Text reproduced with permission from Asda

Page 126 Text from BSkyB

Page 175 Text copyright at Wrigley Company Limited. Used with permission

Page 175 Text from IVCA

Page 206 Text from ACAS website